China's
Domestic
Private
Firms

China's Domestic Private Firms

Multidisciplinary Perspectives on Management and Performance

Anne S. Tsui, Yanjie Bian, and Leonard Cheng

EDITORS

M.E.Sharpe
Armonk, New York
London, England

An East Gate Book

Library of Congress Cataloging-in-Publication Data

China's domestic private firms : multidisciplinary perspectives on management and
performance / edited by Anne S. Tsui, Yanjie Bian, and Leonard Cheng.
  p. cm.
 Includes bibliographical references and index.
 ISBN 13 978-0-7656-1382-0 (cloth : alk. paper)
 ISBN 10 0-7656-1382-4 (cloth : alk. paper)
  1. Small business—China. 2. Small business—Management—China. 3. China—
Economic conditions. I. Tsui, Anne S. II. Bian, Yanjie, 1955– III. Cheng,
Leonard K. (Leonard Kwok-Hon)

HD2346.C6C4835 2006
338.6'10951—dc22   2006005558

Printed in the United States of America

The paper used in this publication meets the minimum requirements of
American National Standard for Information Sciences
Permanence of Paper for Printed Library Materials,
ANSI Z 39.48-1984.

∞

IBT (c)   10   9   8   7   6   5   4   3   2   1

CONTENTS

PREFACE AND ACKNOWLEDGMENTS

One of the most important outcomes of market-oriented reforms in China over the past twenty-five years is the emergence of a significant domestic private business sector. It now accounts for more than a third of the gross domestic product and its growth is continuing in leaps and bounds. It is by far the most important source of income and employment growth for China. By all measures, the private sector is an undisputedly important part of China's economic future, especially in light of the continuing privatization of the state assets in many industries and sectors. The increasing significance of privately owned firms cannot be underscored enough in a land of over 1.3 billion people and millions of firms, the majority of which are in the private sector. It should be obvious that, with this magnitude of workers and firms, developing a systematic knowledge base on the growth and development of China's domestic private firms is of utmost importance to both social scientists and management scholars.

To date, scientific studies of China's organizations have concentrated mainly on state-owned enterprises and foreign-funded firms. The lack of research on the emerging private sector is not surprising because this sector has a short history of less than twenty years. Furthermore, until recently, government policies have not provided a secure or favorable environment for these firms. As the firms struggled for survival, many vanished as quickly as they appeared, implying that they were not easy subjects to study or targets to follow. However, the situation has improved substantially in recent years and all indications are pointing toward a more favorable and hospitable environment for these firms. Recent government policies have shown a recognition of the importance of the private sector to China's continuing economic development and prosperity. This is an ideal time to embark on systematic research programs to track the birth, growth, transformation, and development of the private firms over time, along with contemporaneous analyses of their management patterns, interaction with their environments, and performance. This book represents a modest contribution to an enormous need, along with an ambitious goal to stimulate rigorous and systematic research.

This book's distinguishing characteristic is the multidisciplinary approach to analyzing China's domestic private firms. It contains three comprehensive literature reviews of published work to date on these firms in the disciplines of economics, sociology, and management. This is an excellent resource for any student or researcher interested in studying Chinese organizations. It contains nine chapters that report the findings of research projects conducted immediately before this book's publication. These new and timely studies offer fresh insights on the development and performance of a variety of Chinese domestic private firms. Also included are original chapters written by several distinguished scholars and China experts. In sum, this book fills a void in the literature on Chinese management and organizations, offers fresh knowledge on a sector that is of great importance but not well understood, and may open many exciting new directions for future research.

This is the third edited book supported by the High Impact Area research grant for "China

Business and Management" from the Hong Kong University of Science and Technology (HKUST). The first book, *Management and Organizations in the Chinese Context*, was published in 2000 by Palgrave Macmillan (edited by J.T. Li, Anne S. Tsui, and Elizabeth Weldon) and its primary focus was foreign firms in China and employee behavior in the overseas and Chinese firms. The second book, *The Management of Enterprises in the People's Republic of China,* was published in 2002 by Kluwer Academic Press (edited by Anne S. Tsui and Chung-Ming Lau) with an emphasis on state-owned enterprises. It reported the results of ten empirical studies at both the firm and individual levels, again funded by the HKUST High Impact Area grant. We are pleased to now offer this third book, *China's Domestic Private Firms: Multidisciplinary Perspectives on Management and Performance,* with an exclusive focus on firms in China's rapidly growing domestic private sector. In addition to the three edited books, the High Impact Area grant has also supported the publication of a special issue of the journal *Organization Science,* "Corporate Transformation in the People's Republic of China" (vol. 15, no. 2 [March/April 2004]). Collectively, all the authors of these three edited books and the *Organization Science* special issue have contributed significantly to an increasing body of knowledge on an emerging field of research: management and organizations in China.

In addition to generous financial resources provided by HKUST, this book could not have been produced without the intellectual contribution of the thirty-two authors, who devoted much time to the research and writing of their chapters. We salute their dedication and admire their excellent scholarship. We offer special thanks to Winee Wu for providing administrative and editorial support throughout the project, including organizing a workshop in December 2003, which brought together all the authors of the book to share their progress and offer suggestions to each other's work. The book was greatly improved in both content and style by the professional editing of Persephone Doliner. Lastly, we dedicate this book to our families, who have had to endure our "absences" over many weekends and evenings, when we hid in our offices, totally engrossed in the interesting writings of the contributing authors.

Anne S. Tsui
Yanjie Bian
Leonard Cheng

LIST OF ABBREVIATIONS

CAS	Chinese Academy of Sciences
CCP	Chinese Communist Party
CEO	Chief Executive Officer
CPPCC	Chinese People's Political Consultative Conference
EBRD	European Bank for Reconstruction and Development
EFA	Exploratory Factor Analysis
EU	European Union
FDI	Foreign Direct Investment
GDP	Gross Domestic Product
HKUST	Hong Kong University of Science and Technology
HP	Hewlett Packard
HR	Human Resources
HRM	Human Resource Management
IACMR	International Academy of Chinese Management Research
IBM	International Business Machines Corporation
ICT	Institute of Computing Technology
IPO	Initial Public Offering
ISP	Internet Service Provider
IT	Information Technology
JSC	Joint-Stock Cooperative
MBA	Master of Business Administration
MNC	Multinational Corporation
MOR	Management and Organization Review
NATO	North Atlantic Treaty Organization
NBS	National Bureau of Statistics
NPC	National People's Congress
NSE	Nonstate Enterprises
OLS	Ordinary Least Squares
PC	Personal Computer
PL	Paternalistic Leadership
PLS	Paternalistic Leadership Scale
PRC	People's Republic of China
R&D	Research and Development
RBV	Resource-based view
RMB	Renminbi
RMRB	Renmin Ribao (*People's Daily*)
SOE	State-Owned Enterprises

TVE	Township-and-Village Enterprises
UNCTAD	United Nations Conference on Trade and Development
USSR	Union of Soviet Socialist Republics
VC	Venture Capital
VRIN	Valuable, rare, inimitable, nonsubstitutable
WTO	World Trade Organization

China's Domestic Private Firms

EXPLAINING THE GROWTH AND DEVELOPMENT OF THE CHINESE DOMESTIC PRIVATE SECTOR

ANNE S. TSUI, YANJIE BIAN, AND LEONARD CHENG

China has captured the imagination of people with an interest in world affairs. Virtually every day there are stories about China in newspapers such as the *Wall Street Journal,* the *New York Times,* the *International Herald Tribune,* and the *Financial Times.* China also commands frequent appearances in journals like *Time, BusinessWeek,* and the *Economist.* There is no disputing the cliché that "China is hot these days." The facts seem to warrant this popular attention. China now leads the world in foreign direct investment (FDI). In 2003, its inward FDI of US$53.5 billion topped figures for both France (US$47 billion) and the United States (US$29.8), the second and third largest recipients of FDI during the same period (UNCTAD, 2004, Annex table B.1).[1] In 2002, China's total merchandise trade (exports plus imports) stood at US$620.7 billion and ranked fourth in the world, if the European Union (EU) was treated as a single entity. In 2004, China's total merchandise trade shot up to US$1 trillion, making it the third largest trader in the world, after only the EU and the United States.

Chinese exports are no longer limited to garments, textiles, toys, and plastics. They now may also be information and telecommunication products and consumer electronics, some of which are beginning to compete head-on with the world's leading brands. Between 1978 and 2004 the Chinese economy grew at an average of 9.4 percent per year (Wong 2004). While Japan and the four "Asian tigers" (Taiwan, Korea, Singapore, and Hong Kong) have experienced comparable growth rates, such growth for China was particularly impressive and particularly important in the history of the world economy, given China's diversity and size.

Even more amazing is that China's rise as a major economic power in the world has been accomplished in less than twenty-five years. It began in 1979, when China embarked on economic reform and opened its doors to international trade and foreign investments. The phenomenal growth of the Chinese economy is not only a force for the world's business and political leaders to reckon with, but also an intellectual puzzle for economists, sociologists, political scientists, and management scholars.

Scholarly debates abound as to what has accounted for this phenomenal growth and how long it can be sustained. To most economists, there is not much difference between China's experience and those of the East Asian economies, except for the fact that China has had to face an additional hurdle: the hurdle of switching from central planning to a market economy and of creating the new institutions required for a market economy to work. Furthermore, both policymakers and economic analysts agree that the annual growth rate will slow down, perhaps to 7 percent in the next decade, and to even lower rates in the subsequent decades. That is to say, one would be truly naïve to think that the Chinese economy will continue to grow at its past high rates forever, given that Japan and the Asian tigers slowed down after the early phase of learning and imitation was exhausted. Others are even more pessimistic, predicting that the growth is itself a bubble waiting to burst in the near future. Chang (2001) is one member of a cottage industry predicting China's collapse. A recent book by Huang (2003) argues that the vast amount of FDI into China is detrimental to that nation because it favors foreign firms over domestic firms and makes China less competitive in the global market in the long term.

Despite controversy about the future, there seems to be a broad consensus that China's economic success in the past twenty-five years has been less a result of reviving state-owned enterprises (SOEs) than a consequence of creating an increasingly market-oriented environment in which non-state-owned firms have been able to survive and flourish. The private sector, also known as the nonstate sector, takes many forms, as we shall see below—but collectively it has become China's most important engine of growth. As a result of the nonstate sector's rapid growth, SOEs' share of industrial output fell from almost 100 percent at the start of the economic reform in 1978 to 54.6 percent in 1990 and to less than 33 percent in 2003 (see chapter 8 in this volume, Table 8.1). The share of GDP contributed by state-owned firms fell to less than 50 percent in 1990 and to 33.3 percent in 2000 (Wu 2005, Table 2).

Without a doubt, the foreign-invested firms and domestic private firms are major contributors to China's economic growth. But, the importance of the private sector to China is not limited to the economic sphere alone, as it may also be a key driver of China's political and social processes. China's development path reflects complex interactions between entrepreneurs, whose primary objective is to create wealth, and local government officials, whose objectives include both wealth creation and social order. This interaction embodies the friction between an authoritarian political regime and an increasingly competitive market economy. In this book, we aim to contribute to the discourse on what may account for China's success in economic growth by analyzing the growth, development, current position, and future prospects of firms in its emerging *domestic* private sector.

Each of the core disciplines of economics, sociology, and management can contribute to the understanding of different aspects of the intellectual puzzle mentioned above. These are the three social science disciplines in which most research on China's private-sector firms has been conducted, and, with support from the Hong Kong University of Science and Technology (HKUST) provided through its High Impact Area, an initiative for China's business and management, we have sought to achieve an interdisciplinary perspective by juxtaposing contributions of scholars from these core disciplines. This book is organized into three sections, each containing four to six chapters. The first section consists of six chapters presenting the sociological perspective (chapters 2–7). The second section, with four chapters (chapters 8–11), represents the economic perspective. The third section presents the management perspective, in five chapters (chapters 12–16). Each section starts with a chapter that reviews the literature on the private sector in the relevant discipline, continues with two to four empirical studies, and then concludes with a chapter that offers original ideas that go well beyond commentary on the previous chapters by suggesting new perspectives and avenues for future research. The final chapter (chapter 17), by Andrew Walder, provides a global perspective by comparing the different development paths of the private sector in different regions of the world and offering a unique account for the path taken by China.

In this introduction, we first attempt to define the term "domestic private sector," drawing on "work in progress," because the sector is continuously evolving and its boundary is rapidly changing. As we shall see, the domestic private sector comprises traditional private firms, household businesses (small family businesses), village-and-township enterprises, and privatized state-owned firms and their spin-offs. Following the delineation of the private sector, we summarize the findings of the three reviews of the sociological, economic, and management literatures contained herein. We then present some highlights of the nine empirical chapters. These are original works that study different business and management issues faced by firms in the amorphous Chinese private sector. Finally, synthesizing the research directions suggested by the authors of the final chapters of each of the three sections in this book (Tom Gold, Yijiang Wang, and Claudia B. Schoonhoven) and the insights of Andrew Walder in the final chapter, we highlight some key research directions that would be useful in advancing knowledge about these firms as well as contributing to global management knowledge about firms in different economic, political, and social-cultural contexts.

DEFINING CHINA'S DOMESTIC PRIVATE SECTOR

What is China's domestic private sector? To offer a clear definition of this term as it exists in China today is a daunting task. As will be seen in some of the chapters in this book, some private firms hide their real status by "attaching" ("hanging" or *gua*) themselves to state-owned firms in order to avoid discrimination or to gain privileges. Others register as township or village enterprises to gain protection or seek support from local governments. The above are examples of private firms masquerading as nonprivate firms by wearing "red hats"—that is, by donning the garb of politically correct status. Since the reverse is unlikely to be true—except as an intermediate step of converting state-owned assets into privately controlled and eventually privately owned firms—the actual number of private firms may far exceed the official figures. For the purpose of this book, we define the domestic private sector in China as including all firms that are not exclusively owned by the state (i.e., the central government in Beijing and its ministries): (a) urban and rural township-and-village enterprises (TVEs); (b) urban and rural small-scale household enterprises or family businesses (*getihu,* with fewer than eight employees); (c) privately owned firms (*siren qiye,* with eight or more employees); (d) spin-offs of state-owned enterprises; and (e) publicly listed joint stock companies (including formerly state-owned enterprises).

This definition excludes firms that are wholly owned by investors from Hong Kong, Macau, and Taiwan, and joint ventures formed by these investors with their Chinese partners. The joint ventures may take the form of joint exploration and development, contractual joint ventures, and equity joint ventures. Also excluded are firms classified as "foreign-invested or managed" in the form of international joint ventures or wholly foreign-owned subsidiaries of multinational corporations.

In general, the domestic private sector in China is made up of several subsectors. Some authors (e.g., Li, chapter 8 in this volume) refer to all of these as the "nonstate sector." The focus of this book is on the true domestic private firms—that is, firms with primary state ownership and with foreign investments are excluded from this analysis. It is a sector that is evolving, dynamic, minimally researched (relative to the state-owned and foreign-invested firms), and most deserving of systematic scholarly attention.

Another complication in defining the private sector is that a firm in one sector may become a firm in another sector. For instance, when the political environment was unfavorable to privately owned firms, some of them sought political protection by becoming collectively owned enterprises; later, when conditions became favorable to the formation and operation of new forms of firms, some transformed back into private enterprises, such as joint stock companies or firms owned by employees or employee associations. Another example is provided by individual (family) businesses that grow in size and are reclassified as private enterprises. The fluidity of firm status and ownership category not only makes it hard to correctly identify private firms, but also creates difficulty in tracking their development over time and comparing them with other types of firms in the same period.

The discrepancy between the official and real identities of firms creates a serious problem for correctly measuring the size of the private sector, whether in terms of employment or output. Researchers have little choice but to rely on figures provided in recent issues of the *Almanac of China's Economy* (State Council Development Research Council 2002, 2003) and other, related, sources. In 2002, it was estimated that there were about 300,000 urban collectives and 1.88 million rural TVEs, employing 11 million and 133 million workers, respectively; the employment figures for 2003 were 10 million and 136 million, respectively. In 2003, there were 3 million private firms and 23.5 million small individual and family businesses, employing 43 million people and 46 million people (owners plus employees), respectively. In 2003, there were also 300,000 foreign-invested enterprises, employing a total of 8.6 million workers. That is to say, in 2003 the above private subsectors together employed 243.6 million people, representing 32.7 percent of China's total employment.[2] In 2003, the state sector; the collective sector; and the sector of private enterprises, individual businesses, and foreign-invested enterprises each contributed about one-third to China's GDP.[3] Even though findings about the split between the collective subsector and the rest of the nonstate sector vary, the total share of the broadly defined private sector remains more or less the same: it accounts for two-thirds of China's GDP.[4]

To put the above numbers in perspective, it should be remembered that, less than twenty-five years ago, the only recognized firms in China were state-owned and -managed firms, which contributed virtually all of China's GDP outside of agriculture and employed the entire Chinese urban workforce. Today, nonstate firms can be found in all industries except those that are still monopolized or dominated by the state, such as airlines, banking, insurance, telecommunications, oil and gas, power generation, and some others. In some of the latter industries, entry by domestic private firms is not allowed, even though restricted entry by foreign-invested firms is permitted. Only recently, domestic private firms' entry into some of these protected industries became allowed: airlines, railways, and even defense are examples. In general, with minor exceptions, domestic private firms tend to be small in scale and to flourish in markets not dominated by big state-owned enterprises or foreign multinationals. They are found in many labor-intensive industries.

An understanding of what constitutes a domestic private firm would be enhanced by tracing the origin and evolution over time of these firms. The first private firms to appear were the small individual and family businesses *(getihu)* that were restored in rural China in the late 1970s (Lin 1990, Zhang 1999). In the early 1980s, their urban counterparts arose to supplement the SOEs in the commercial and service industries (Gold 1990, Shi 1993, Young 1989). These individual or family businesses were limited to employing no more than seven workers. In 1988, the right of a private business to hire eight or more workers was formally approved, setting the legal foundation for the rise of the domestic private sector. The development of the private sector accelerated after Deng Xiaoping's 1992 South China tour. The 15th Congress of the Chinese Communist Party in 1997 further reduced legal and economic barriers to private ownership (Lau 1998). In 2001, for the first time since the founding of the Communist regime, private business owners were allowed to join the Chinese Communist Party, offering a significant signal that private ownership of economic assets was socially and legally accepted.

By definition, private ownership should mean independence from undue government interference in a firm's internal management and activities, except for legal regulations that advance fair competition (e.g., antitrust laws) or that protect workers from exploitation by employers (e.g., labor laws). Interestingly, the history of the private sector is replete with evidence of the continuing involvement of public officials in the internal affairs of private firms, sometimes even to the extent of effective control. Bian and Zhang (chapter 2 of this book) use an "entrepreneur-bureaucracy connection perspective" to explain the importance of local and state official involvement for the private entrepreneur. Citing the work of Bruun (1993, 1995), Oi (1992, 1998, 1999), and Wank (1995, 1996, 1999), they point out how local government involvement and connections to government officials were crucial to the development of the private firms. This symbiotic relationship offers mutual benefits to both bureaucrats and entrepreneurs. The study by Chen, Fan, and Wong (chapter 9 in this volume) offers the latest evidence of government involvement in private Chinese firms. These authors observe that current and past government officials, by serving as members of corporate boards, have been involved in the decision making of publicly listed companies that were previously SOEs. Such involvement has had both benefits and costs. These government connections might give a firm some competitive advantage in local markets or improve its access to funds, but they might also mean an extra burden in the form of contribution to local development, employment, and public finance. Given the power and proclivity for intervention of a Communist state, private firms in China must maintain a delicate balance between distance and closeness in their relationships with the government. In this sense, the domestic private firms operate in a quasi-free-market environment that is more politically charged than that found in the developed market economies with democratic political systems.

China was formally admitted to the World Trade Organization (WTO) in December 2001. This new status has meant both challenges and opportunities for all kinds of firms in China, not only those in the private sector. Are the private firms better prepared to compete in the increasingly competitive arena than are other firms? They have the right "business DNA." Even though they were born without government support and special privileges, their business DNA allows them to survive under harsh institutional and market conditions. Their local knowledge gives them an advantage in the domestic markets over foreign firms. However, most private firms do not have the scale or scope to compete against the large multinationals, and more of these powerful foreign firms will enter the Chinese market as China's WTO agreements are implemented in sequence.

The lack of firm size and product variety will not be so detrimental if the domestic private firms are able to tap financial and human capital to build up organizational capital that addresses their shortcomings. However, given the meteoric rise and fall of many star private businesses and a general perception that they lack trustworthiness, the challenge of growing major companies from China's domestic private sector appears to be enormous. How the private firms will fare in the post-WTO era depends on whether there are favorable institutional changes (such as the establishment of social norms with regard to personal and corporate integrity and creditworthiness) that enable the transformation of some successful market opportunists into major modern corporations whose organizational capital enables them to survive and prosper for the long term under rapidly changing conditions.

It is widely recognized that human capital (the knowledge, know-how, and skills embodied in humans) and intellectual property rights are the twin sources of the profits and incomes of the developed economies, and that major modern corporations are the key repositories and guardians of patents, brand names, and other forms of intellectual property rights. Thus, success in transforming small private firms into sizable modern corporations will be crucial to China's economic well-being, especially so because the prognosis for turning SOEs that lack the right business DNA into efficient modern companies is not promising.

THE THREE REVIEWS ON THE CURRENT STATUS OF RESEARCH

The three review chapters in this book provide an extensive account of the relatively limited literature on China's private firms. In chapter 2, Yanjie Bian and Zhanxin Zhang make reference to 107 English- and Chinese-language publications in sociology journals and books. In his survey of the economics literature in chapter 8, David Li identifies a total of 46 papers and books that are related to the private sector in China. In chapter 12, Jiatao Li and Ji Yu Yang identify 92 papers from 24 management and business journals. The overlap among these three bibliographies is minimal. The sociology and management reviews share only six cited publications. There is one publication in common for the sociology reference list and the economics reference list. The economics reference list and the management list have no overlap. In total, the three reviews cite 248 unique publications that focus on the private sector in China, of which 12 are Chinese-language publications. Together, these three reviews offer a rather comprehensive account of the research questions and findings to date on the Chinese private business sector.

According to Yanjie Bian and Zhanxin Zhang (chapter 2), sociologists were among the first to study the rise of a domestic private economic sector from a social science perspective. On the surface, it seems odd that sociologists should be interested in what appears to be an economic phenomenon. Yet, as Tom Gold states, "The emergence of private business, however tentative, was more of a sociological than an economic phenomenon" (chapter 7, p. 120) . We would add that this emergence is clearly also a political phenomenon. It was a major political decision by the central government to allow private business to emerge and grow, a decision that has had important implications for both the social and the economic development of China. The management aspects of the waxing of private business have been less salient than its political, economic, and social aspects, especially in the beginning, when firms were concerned primarily with survival.

The sociology literature has touched on issues of the formal and informal statuses of private businesses—the class position and composition, as well as the political attitudes of, private entrepreneurs, and the networks of social relationships that seem to be central to the emergence, growth, and operation of individual and family businesses and private firms. Because of their theoretical interest in societal transformation, sociologists have tried to explain the nature and implications of a private economy for an emerging socioeconomic order in postreform Chinese society.

Bian and Zhang identify three such explanations in the sociology literature they review. The first is the "market transition" explanation (Nee 1989, 1996), which bridges two great historical events in transitional China: the revival of markets and the emergence of the private economy. This explanation has followed the logic of the "convergence school" in economic research in accounting for China's transition, attributing the advance of the private economy to the growth of markets. It points to an emerging socioeconomic order of market capitalism in which the redistributive state plays a limited role in the economy.

The second explanation is the "entrepreneur-bureaucracy connection" idea (Bruun 1993, 1995; Oi 1998; Wank 1995, 1999), according to which the emerging private economy was born out of and continues to live on business-official ties. Central to this explanation is a judgment that the exchange between the state and the market is fundamental to the operation of the emerging market economy, a phenomenon not unique to China but common to all market economies. This explanation implies the persistence of the party-state and political power in the market economy and society.

The third explanation is to look at the "social roots" of the private economy (Gold 1990, Whyte 1995), namely, Chinese family life. This explanation is a good fit to the economies of Hong Kong, Taiwan, and Singapore, where Chinese family tradition is strong. Within China, the empirical evidence is that private economic activities tend to receive more social support and to grow in a village community with a high concentration of family surnames. The socioeconomic order implied by this explanation is one in which the private economy is deeply embedded in the networks of ongoing social and kinship relationships.

The three sociological explanations reviewed by Bian and Zhang can be considered complementary to each other as they address theoretically different but empirically related aspects of China's domestic private sector. The market transition explanation focuses on the revival of markets and emergence of a domestic private sector, two phenomena that were either passively allowed or positively promoted by the state. The entrepreneur-bureaucracy connection explanation examines the transactions between the state and its agents (and there is even a principal-agency problem between the central government and various levels of local governments that has been identified explicitly in the economics literature). This explanation addresses the conditions under which the domestic private sector was allowed to grow and the extent to which the market was allowed to play its role in allocating resources. The social roots explanation points to the particular dominant organizational form and source of dynamism observed in China's domestic private sector in terms of family tradition.

David Li's survey (chapter 8 in this volume) of the economics literature on China's nonstate enterprises (NSEs) suggests that the steady emergence of China's nonstate sector in the early 1980s was like a reversal of the gradual disappearance of China's private sector from 1949 (when the Communist Party came to power) to the early sixties.[5] He identifies the reform of the appointment of government officials and fiscal decentralization as two important changes in government policy and attitude toward the NSEs. These two new policies were key implementations of the strategy of economic reform. Despite these positive developments, the NSEs continued to suffer discrimination in market access to certain industries, bank loans, and property rights protection. In response to this harsh environment, the NSEs adopted organizational arrangements that helped them operate more successfully than they would have been able to without these organizational innovations. In particular, they sought protection from local governments. The collective enterprises' ambiguous property rights enabled local governments, local communities, and the owners and founders of these firms to benefit jointly from the firms' prosperity. The symbiotic relationships between entrepreneurs and government bureaucrats observed in the sociology literature might have been either imposed by the bureaucrats or initiated by the entrepreneurs.

Nevertheless, the collective enterprises were not an efficient organizational form, and they created many distortions in competing against the truly private and foreign-invested firms. Managerial incentives alone could not substitute for ownership reform forever, and privatization of collective enterprises logically became a direction of further economic reform. Regions with private firms were shown to grow faster, suggesting that privatization of collective and state-owned enterprises might be the key to sustainable economic growth (Han and Pannell 1999).

Li goes on to raise the questions of whether nonstate firms behave like labor-managed firms, and whether education and occupational attainment on the one hand, and political background on the other, have been rewarded in the form of higher wages and salaries differently in collective enterprises and private enterprises. Li's findings are that village cadres,[6] formerly the most important source of collective enterprise managers, became the most important source of private entrepreneurs. The main source of the initial investments of private enterprises was found to be family and social connections. Bian and Zhang report similar findings in their review and analysis of the sociological literature.

Surveying twenty-four leading scholarly and area study journals from 1986 to 2003 for articles that address management and organization issues in China's emerging private-sector firms,

Jiatao Li and Jing Yu Yang (chapter 12 in this volume) found ninety-two articles and categorized them along three dimensions: subject of study (macro or firm level versus micro or individual level), research methods (quantitative, qualitative, or conceptual), and substantive topics (institutional context/environment, firm strategy/structure, and psychological/individual). Proportionally, many more studies have focused on context (sixteen) and firm (sixty-two) than on individual workers (fourteen). A majority of the institutional context studies described the changing institutional environment in China and how it affected the growth and development of private firms. The firm-level studies focused on the strategy and structure of the firms and the relationship between strategy, structure, and performance. Most of the individual-level studies analyzed managerial behavior and values.

On the basis of their review, Li and Yang identified different strategies pursued by private firms in three different stages of market transition: (a) the beginning stage; (b) the early stage, and (c) the later stages. They do not provide a precise time period for each stage, but the demarcation corresponds roughly to the periods of development identified in the Bian and Zhang review. The dividing line between the first and second stages of market transition was 1988, the year the private sector received formal recognition by the government; whereas 2001, the year entrepreneurs gained the right to join the Chinese Communist Party (CCP), marked the dividing line between the second and third stages of market transition. Within the second stage, the 15th Congress of the CCP in 1997 reduced many remaining legal and economic barriers to private firms, but the right to CCP membership in 2001 lifted the status of successful entrepreneurs to a new height, and could arguably be considered as signaling China's entry into the later stage of market transition.

Li and Yang found that, in the beginning stage, private firms pursued a relationship- or network-based corporate strategy, because the roles and functions of China's market at that time were suppressed or modified by personal relationships and networks. At this stage, both horizontal and vertical relationships were important. These observations prompted the use of the term "network capitalism" to capture the structure of interfirm relationships in the emerging market economy in China (Boisot and Child 1996). In the early stage of market transition, the influence of personal relationships began to recede, so private firms could pursue strategies based on price and volume, relatively free of noneconomic considerations.

However, until institutional rules and regulations for a genuine market economy were adopted in recent years, firms were motivated by shorter-term considerations and adopted cost- and price-based strategies of competition, suggesting that they were mainly market opportunists. In recent years, imbued with the belief that the market economy is here to stay and that China will increasingly become a genuine market economy, private firms have started to plan for the longer term by pursuing a capability-based strategy that focuses on the quality, variety, and technology of their goods and services. In short, the firms' resources, capabilities, and innovations have now become the basis of their competitive strategies. The story of Lenovo, by White and Xie (chapter 15 in this volume), is an excellent example of a firm making strategic changes as it has evolved from a distribution and service firm to a manufacturer, and most recently to a technological innovator.

What have we learned from the three literature reviews about the growth and development of the private-sector firms to date? Apparently, the market transition explanation in the sociology literature is not so different from that of the economics or the management literature, as they all note the increasing role played by markets in allocating resources in China. From a logical point of view, the emergence of a private sector seems to be inevitable if China is to succeed in building a real market economy, as private firms are the basic building materials of any market economy.

But from a political point of view, the road that led to this outcome was by no means guaranteed, given the government bureaucrats' natural instinct for defending their self-interest. The focus on the entrepreneur-bureaucracy connection in sociology is not too dissimilar from the economics literature's emphasis on the TVEs as an organizational innovation capable of turning conflicts grounded in self-interest into win-win solutions, at least as both have moved forward to make a larger pie for many to share.

But both economics and sociology can benefit from a political perspective that explains why the Chinese Communist leaders decided to launch economic reforms and to open to the outside world while simultaneously maintaining political control. Taking the political context primarily as an exogenous variable, the management literature has focused instead on the implications of the political environment for private firm growth and development, particularly in terms of how firms structure their internal organization and deal with the market on the outside. Firms were largely reactive and defensive as a way to deal with environmental uncertainties and fluidity, but some firms responded with innovative ideas, such as the ambiguous ownership of TVEs. The term "network capitalism" (Boisot and Child 1996) reveals its connection to the market transition theses in both sociology and economics. The management literature, then, focuses primarily on the adaptive actions of firms within the changing social-political-economic context and their implications for firm growth and development—rather than trying to account for changes in the institutional context as private firms emerge and develop.

There are also disciplinary differences in the interpretation of China's experience with the TVEs. The sociologists, citing the achievements of these enterprises and pointing to the principal-agent problems suffered by modern corporations in the West, conclude that the economists were wrong in emphasizing the wholesomeness of property rights. Economists tend to see the TVEs as an innovative organizational form only in the short run, and as one that has its own drawbacks and distortions. Therefore, they emphasize the importance of undertaking the logical next step of ownership reform as China's market economy matures and as foreign firms play an increasingly more important role. To them, the agency problem will be solved by requiring better and more transparent corporate governance, not by blurring property or ownership rights. Management scholars, acknowledging the importance of property rights in a broad sense, focus more on how firms with different types of ownership (i.e., different property rights structures) adjust their competitive behavior when facing different external environments, and on the implications of these competitive approaches for firms' economic performance.

The economics literature's empirical findings about private entrepreneurs and the main source of initial investment of private enterprises are similar to the findings in the sociology literature. Both show the importance of family and social connections. The management literature's findings—private firms' greater emphasis on relationships and connections in the earlier periods of China's economic reform, and the change in competitive strategies from the earlier to the later period (from relations-based to cost-based and then to quality- and innovations-based strategies)—are congruent with the economics approach as well. According to this approach, both the organization of private firms and their choice of competitive strategies depend on their operating environment, which has been progressively more market oriented and less preferential to any particular group of firms.

In summary, the three core disciplines of sociology, economics, and management either focus on different aspects of Chinese private firms or approach the same aspect of private firms from different perspectives. By including all three disciplines in this book, we have provided a more comprehensive and deeper understanding of the growth and development of China's domestic private firms.

Figure 1.1   **A Schematic of Relationships Studied in the Nine Empirical Chapters**

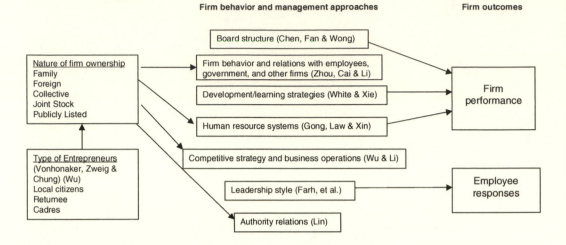

THE NINE NEW EMPIRICAL STUDIES IN THIS BOOK

This book reports nine original and most current empirical studies on private-sector firms. Seven of them focus on the firm as the unit of analysis, and two of them focus on individuals, both within and across firms. The larger number of firm-level studies is not surprising, since sociological and economic analyses generally focus on firms and the larger units built upon them, such as industries and sectors. Of the three management studies within these nine empirical studies, two focus on firms and one on the individuals within firms. The topics are wide ranging, but most of them concern the influence of private ownership on business activities and firm outcomes. We use a schematic to organize the key aspects of the nine chapters for a comprehensive and integrative view of the contributions of these studies. Using firm ownership regime as the major independent variable, these studies analyze the sources of entrepreneurs (Vanhonacker, Zweig, and Chung; Wu); firms' competitive strategies and business operations (Wu and Li) and their evolution across periods (White and Xie); board structure (Chen, Fan, and Wong); firm behavior and interfirm relationships (Zhou, Cai, and Li); human resource management systems (Gong, Law, and Xin); leadership style (Farh, Cheng, Chou, and Chu); and authority relations (Lin). Three studies also relate firm behavior and management approaches to firm performance (Chen et al., Gong et al., White), and one analyzes employee reactions to a paternalistic leadership style on the part of family business owners (Farh et al.). Table 1.1 summarizes the samples, years in which data were collected, research questions addressed, and key findings. Below, we give brief highlights of each of the nine empirical studies, beginning with the four sociological studies, continuing with the two economic studies, and finishing with the three management studies.

Four Sociological Studies

The domestic private economy in reform-era China began with family businesses, or *getihu,* a term officially defined (see chapter 2) as a unit owned by an individual or household conducting economic activities by hiring no more than eight employees. In the 1980s, when private enterprises had no legitimacy and their survival was threatened, family businesses were central to the life and death

Table 1.1

Summaries of the Nine Empirical Studies in this Volume

Authors	Data: Year and sample	Research questions and findings
Lin (chapter 5)	• 1998 survey of 1,350 employees in 206 firms in 12 provincial entities	What are the types of authority relations in private firms? Are there alternatives to the sweatshop?
	• 2003 interview of 58 employees in 17 firms in Beijing, Zhejiang, Shaanxi, Gansu, and Guangdong	• On the basis of interviews, author proposes four types of authority relations based on the breadth of incentive/motivation systems and extent of legal-rational regulation.
		• The four types are rationalist, postrationalist, human relations, and protocapitalist approach (the sweatshop) with narrow incentives and low level of regulations. • The survey data showed diversity in labor practices in private firms.
Wu (chapter 3)	• 1996 national survey of 6,090 households (3,003 rural and 3,087 urban)	What determines the entry and performance of family businesses?
		• Education and cadre status facilitated entry in rural cities but deterred entry in urban cities.
		• As reform progressed, cadre families had increasing business opportunities in both rural and urban settings.
Zhou, Cai, and Li (chapter 6)	• 2000–2002 interviews of 621 firms in Beijing and Guangzhou.	What is the relationship between firm ownership and firm behavior?
		• Firms with different property rights regimes were found to exhibit different patterns of resource dependence, interaction with other firms, relationship with political authority, and employment relationships within the firm.
Vanhonacker, Zweig, and Chung (chapter 4)	• 2004 interviews of 200 entrepreneurs (100 returnees and 100 local)	How do social capital and transnational capital contribute to the success of local and returnee entrepreneurs?
		• Locals and returnees equally value their ties with local governments.
		• Returnees benefit from their transnational capital—the knowledge, skill, experience, and vision associated with their overseas learning and living experiences.

(continued)

Table 1.1 *(continued)*

Authors	Data: Year and sample	Research questions and findings
Chen, Fan, and Wong (chapter 9)	• 1993–2000 archival data (from IPO prospectuses) of 632 companies listed on the Shanghai and Shenzhen stock exchanges	How do politician directors affect the board structure and business operations of firms? • Political connections of board members lower boards' professionalism and increase their geographical concentration, subsidies, and employment. • Political connections of board members lower earnings and returns on assets.
Wu and Li (chapter 10)	• 1999–2001 data on 130,000 firms from the database of the National Statistical Bureau	How does the ownership structure of a firm affect its competitive strategy and business operations? • Firms under different ownership indeed behave differently, but some results were contrary to expectations. • The degree of market mix of private firms and state-owned firms also plays an important role in determining the behavior of the firm.
Farh, Cheng, Chou, and Chu (chapter 13)	• 2003 survey of 292 employees in 52 firms in a variety of industries in Soochow	How do employees react to a paternalistic leadership style? • Authoritarianism is negatively and benevolence positively related to employee compliance, satisfaction with supervision, and organizational commitment • These effects are mediated by subordinates' fear of the supervisor or by subordinate gratitude and repayment, and identification with supervisor. • Subordinate resource dependence and traditional orientation interact with paternalistic leadership dimensions in affecting several subordinate outcomes.
Gong, Law, and Xin (chapter 14)	• 2003 survey of 117 firms (28 state-owned, 32 private, 20 Sino-foreign joint ventures, and 17 wholly foreign-owned firms). • Three middle managers and one human resource manager from each firm.	What is the utilization pattern of commitment-focused HR systems in firms with different ownership structures, and how does it relate to firm performance? • Use of commitment-focused HRM in domestic private firms is higher than that in state-owned firms, but not significantly different from that in the wholly foreign-owned firms and international joint ventures.

(continued)

Table 1.1 *(continued)*

Authors	Data: Year and sample	Research questions and findings
		• Commitment-focused HRM is positively related to overall firm performance, in all types of firms.
White and Xie (chapter 15)	• 2001–2004 interviews and archival records of Lenovo	How did Lenovo achieve strategic fit in a dynamic environment?
		• Lenovo simultaneously allocated resources to both exploitation activities that successively deepened its existing resources and capabilities, and exploration activities through which it developed new ones.
		• Through this process, Lenovo has introduced beneficial changes and maintained the fit among its strategic goals, internal resources and capabilities, and complex external environment.

of privatization in China. In chapter 3, Xiaogang Wu asks the question of who entered family businesses in urban and rural areas, and pays specific attention to the effects of human (education) and political (cadre status) capital. Drawing on a 1996 national survey of households that collected retrospective data about family businesses, Wu found that in the initial stages of reform a higher level of education and cadre status deterred urban households' entry into family businesses but promoted rural households' entry. However, as the reforms progressed further and deeper, urban households with these advantages increasingly became owners and operators of family businesses. The fact that China's transition trajectory has afforded increasing entrepreneurial opportunities to the better educated and politically advantaged implies an emerging socioeconomic order that recognizes both the forces of change and continuation from the socialist-redistributive past.

As the private sector increasingly gained its legitimacy, it attracted not only local residents but also Chinese individuals who returned with overseas experiences to operate their businesses in twenty-first-century China. To what extent is the transnational capital of overseas education, experience, and connections valuable for operating in China's emerging market economy? What is the relative advantage of transnational capital compared to that offered by the social capital networks of social and business relations that are known to be so important for conducting private businesses in China? In chapter 4, Vanhonacker, Zweig, and Chung examine these questions by comparing "local" and "returnee" entrepreneurs. They found from their survey that locals and returnees almost equally valued their ties with local governments in conducting their businesses, a finding that confirms the sheer importance of social networks and local social capital in China's business setting. But they also found that returnees, rather than locals, valued and benefited from the knowledge, skills, experience, and wider perspective that were gained from their overseas learning and living, a finding that the authors interpreted to have increasing importance for a post-WTO Chinese economy.

How is the growing private workforce governed by profit-driven entrepreneurs? The "sweatshop model" of coercive and abusive labor control implies that private-sector workers will be treated badly under any type of entrepreneurial capitalism. However, is this model a predominant mode of internal organization among China's private enterprises in localities with different paces of market reform and privatization? In chapter 5, Yi-min Lin raises this question and presents a theoretical analysis supported with empirical data. His survey of 1,350 private-firm employees from five provinces with varying degrees of marketization and privatization shows that the sweatshop model indeed characterized labor–capital relations in many private firms. However, his respondents revealed that other types of authority relations that ran against the sweatshop model existed as well. More specifically, Lin also found in the surveyed firms a series of labor control measures, including work-related hazards, insufficiency of protection, arbitrary pay cuts, assaults on workers, and institutional arrangements for dealing with personal and family problems. Lin concluded that the large variation in labor control points to the need for further research on where different patterns are likely to be found using data of more extensive coverage and better quality.

To be sure, China's private economies grew in an institutional context in which public, semipublic, and private forms of ownership coexisted. Do private firms perform differently from public and semipublic firms in such an institutional context? In chapter 6, Zhou, Cai, and Li examine the association between property rights regimes and firm behavior. Their survey reveals some identifiable behavioral patterns across property rights regimes, but these patterns are by no means as distinctive, consistent, or systematic as economic or sociological theory would predict. More specifically, firms of different ownership types may have different degrees of dependence on government, market, and networks as the predominant channel through which to mobilize factor resources, and these channels exist under all property rights regimes. The authors argue that the elusiveness of the link between property rights regimes and firm behavior is due to the blurred boundaries between these property rights regimes, which are increasingly overlapping and intertwining in a process of reconfiguration. These observations raise significant challenges to theories of property rights and to explanations based on such theories.

Two Economic Studies

Using a data set about the size and composition of the boards of directors of over 600 listed Chinese companies, Chen, Fan, and Wong (chapter 9) test a number of hypotheses about the impact of politician directors on board composition, operating efficiency, and overall firm performance. The starting point of this study is that while decentralization of decision-making power from the central government and its agencies to incorporated companies, together with market-based competition, have brought significant economic benefits, partial privatization of Chinese state-owned firms has limited these benefits because current and past government officials are still involved in corporate decision making by virtue of their board membership. The close relationship between local government officials and the partially privatized formerly state-owned enterprises may mean that the companies use their connections to restrict entrants and to protect local markets, or even to obtain government subsidies. On the other hand, it may also mean incurring an extra burden in the form of contributions to local development, employment, and public finance. The authors find that the political connections of board members lowered boards' professionalism but increased their geographical concentration, and these political connections also increased both firm subsidies and employment but lowered firm earnings and returns on assets.

In chapter 10, Wu and Li pose the following question: In a market where firms with different ownerships coexist, how does the ownership structure of a firm affect its competitive strategy and business operations? This connection is largely ignored in the economics literature despite researchers' substantial attempts to understand the connection between ownership and economic performance, which is usually measured by productivity increases or profitability. Wu and Li base a number of testable hypotheses on three major observations about the differences between firms with different degrees of state ownership. First, state-owned firms may pursue objectives other than profitability, such as social welfare or "value-added." Second, state-owned firms tend to suffer from a serious agency problem, because the state is an absentee owner, allowing management to pursue its own objectives, such as empire building. Third, state-owned firms enjoy privileges and advantages that are not available to privately owned firms, such as loans from state-owned banks. China's market-oriented economic reform has succeeded in reducing the differences between private firms and nonprivate firms (including state-owned firms and collective enterprises), but significant differences between them still persist to this day.

Using a huge data set involving more than 130,000 firms over the three-year period 1999–2001, Wu and Li found empirical support for some, but not all, of their hypotheses. They explore reasons behind the rejections and set out directions for further research. Given the richness of the data set, these authors can obtain more information about the behavioral differences between private and state-owned firms. These and other empirical findings will be useful in developing theories about Chinese firms in transition.

Three Management Studies

Paternalistic leadership is an indigenous Chinese leadership style that is rooted in China's patriarchal tradition. In chapter 13, Farh, Cheng, Chou, and Chu hypothesize that the three dimensions of paternalistic leadership (authoritarian, benevolent, and moral) are related to a variety of employee responses. Further, they hypothesize that employees' orientation toward tradition will moderate these responses. Using survey data from 292 employees in 52 businesses owned by families and joint ventures, they found authoritarianism to be negatively associated but benevolence and morality to be positively associated with subordinate outcomes such as compliance, satisfaction with supervision, and commitment to one's organization. These effects depend on the extent to which employees are "traditional" and the extent to which they are dependent on their supervisor for resources. A major implication of this study is that the traditional image of a benevolent dictator in a Chinese-owned company is still present in China, though most employees do not seem to appreciate this style of leadership—especially those with less traditional values, such as the younger generation of workers in contemporary China (Egri and Ralston 2004).

In chapter 14, Gong, Law, and Xin examine the adoption of a commitment-focused human resource management (HRM) system and its relationship to firm performance in domestic private firms, Sino-foreign joint ventures, state-owned firms, and wholly foreign-owned firms. Commitment was measured by a firm's use of elaborate hiring processes, extensive training, job security, and employee participation in decision making and profit sharing. These authors found that the rate of adoption of commitment-focused HRM in domestic private firms was significantly higher than that in state-owned firms, but not statistically different from that in the wholly foreign-owned firms and international joint ventures. The adoption of commitment-focused HRM, as reported by a firm's human resource executives, was positively related to overall firm performance as rated by a sample of the firms' middle managers. The positive relationship between commitment-focused HRM and firm performance was similar in all the types of firms. The implication of this study is that the adoption of a high-commitment HRM system by private domestic firms could be a competitive advantage, especially in light of the increasingly competitive terrain created by China's entry to the WTO.

In chapter 15, White and Xie analyze the process by which Lenovo, a private spin-off from a state-owned research institute, has grown and succeeded in the hostile and volatile environment of the computer industry. They analyze the firm's growth and development process by using a framework that integrates March's (1991) exploration-exploitation perspective on organizational learning with Zajac, Kraatz, and Bresser's (2000) conceptualization of dynamic strategic fit. Over the years, Lenovo has simultaneously allocated resources to both exploitation activities, which successively deepened its existing resources and capabilities, and exploration activities by which it developed new resources and capabilities. Through this ongoing process, Lenovo has been able to introduce beneficial changes and maintain the fit among its strategic goals, internal resources and capabilities, and the complex external environment. This study attests to the importance of both types of learning for firms seeking growth.

In summary, these nine empirical studies reveal new insights on the growth, development, management, and performance of domestic private firms in China. From the respective chapters by Wu, Li, and Vanhonacker et al., we know that entrepreneurs have come from a variety of sources and include private citizens; returnees from overseas; and prior government officials, cadres, and politicians. Each entrepreneurial origin brings different advantages for private firms. However, it is also clear that government connections are a necessity for access to key resources and thus a fact of life for the survival of private businesses. This mandate accounts for the need for network- or relationship-based business strategies and interfirm relationships in the early stages of privatization. As the business environment becomes more favorable for private firms, and legal regulations become more rationalized and transparent, firms will be able to practice professional management, including more systematic ways of hiring, retaining, and rewarding employees. It also has been revealed that employees in the Chinese private firms do not react favorably to the authoritarian leadership style that is quite typical of the owners of small family businesses. The sweatshop image of the private firms may be disappearing gradually, but new forms of management have yet to be developed, tested, and evaluated. The results of these nine empirical studies reinforce our initial impression that the Chinese private sector is still a "work in progress," an evolving entity. However, the evidence is encouraging as to its evolving into the "later stage of market transition" described by Li and Yang (chapter 12 in this volume). As China completes its market transition and establishes itself as a fair and mature participant in the WTO, private firms will account for an increasingly larger share of the nation's GDP; however, as pointed out above, the quality of their contribution to China's economic success will depend on successful transformation of some small private firms into sizable modern companies.

CHALLENGES IN STUDYING CHINESE PRIVATE-SECTOR FIRMS

One of the frequent complaints about conducting scholarly research in China is the lack of high-quality data, especially data on the financial performance of firms. Despite these difficulties, studies have relied on two kinds of firm-level data; namely, those collected by China's statistical agencies and those collected by academic and nonacademic researchers. An example of the former is the data used by Wu and Li (chapter 10). The data were collected by the China Statistical Bureau in its surveys of industrial firms with annual sales above certain thresholds (e.g., exceeding RMB 200,000, or US$25,000). They contain firm-level data on sales, selling expenses, output measured in current and constant prices, the value of new products produced, inventories, debts, assets, ownership structure, year of founding, employees, and more. The quality of these data is unknown, but if one assumes that the motivation to report poor data would not vary too much across firms, these random errors become a constant.

The data collected by researchers themselves usually go beyond those collected by statistical agencies. Researchers have often collected data in collaboration with China's academic institutions and research organizations. Information is difficult to obtain and is usually the result of great individual or group effort and substantial expenditure. The study by Gong, Law, and Xin (chapter 14 in this volume) provides an example of such efforts. The respondents were participants in an executive MBA course taught by one of the authors of the study. The author would provide some feedback to the participants on the issue being analyzed in the context of the course, an action that encouraged candid and careful responses when they completed the survey. Such efforts by necessity produce smaller and perhaps nonrepresentative samples, compromising a study's potential generalizability. Wu's study of family businesses (chapter 3) was based on a national survey of families using a stratified sampling technique. Because this study did not require the family firms to report their financial performance, the respondents were cooperative, and a relatively large sample with some generalizability resulted.

However, collecting firm- and individual-level data is rather labor intensive. The study by Farh and colleagues in this book (chapter 13) reveals another kind of difficulty of social science research in China in general, and of management research in particular. The questions asked are about the leaders of companies and employee attitudes toward their companies. Many managers find it threatening to know how employees feel about their leadership and about the company. Only enlightened managers may be willing to undertake such an assessment, again restricting the generalizability of findings.

It is not difficult to understand the reluctance of private firms to become the objects of interviews and careful studies. One reason may be that some actions that they had to take during their firms' growth stage may have been in the "grey areas," including, for example, "creative accounting" in reporting their sales or financial performance. It is not uncommon to discover substantial discrepancies between the financial data firms provide to researchers and figures posted on their Web sites or contained in their top executives' public statements. The sales figures in public statements may be either larger or smaller than what they give to researchers. Which set of figures is truer, and what the motivation for differential reporting is are interesting questions for study.

Another reason for discrepancies is the desire of some entrepreneurs to avoid envy and attention. They may therefore prefer to keep a low profile or to underreport their earnings. Many firms that appeared on a list of China's richest individuals put out by *Forbes* later got into trouble with the government and regulatory agencies; these incidents suggest that keeping a low profile is a safer posture. It is no surprise that the new rich in China are reluctant to respond to requests for information, because being identified as one of the richest people in China can be a deadly kiss. A good example is Yang Bin, a developer of the "Dutch Village" in Northern China and designated chief executive of a special economic zone to be created in North Korea near its border with China. He was listed by *Forbes* as the second-richest man in China in 2001, and found guilty of illegal use of arable land, contract fraud, and bribery in July 2003.[7] Another example is Zhou Zhenyi, a Shanghai property tycoon who was rumored to have mingled with female movie stars until he was jailed in Shanghai.[8] Further, companies that are preparing for public listing have every reason not to make public their financial or operational data, since IPOs may make it necessary to "cook the books."

Data are generally easier to obtain from publicly listed companies than from other types of firms because of the former's information disclosure requirements. Even then, it may be difficult to ascertain the quality of the data contained in the annual reports of China's publicly listed companies because irregular accounting and reporting are quite common.

In summary, both the literature reviews and the studies in this book converge on the observation that studies of China's private-sector firms have been primarily at the firm level and that few have been individual-level analyses of the nature of work and employee reactions within these firms. We have offered a few possible reasons for the lack of within-firm studies, including the harsh reality that many of these private firms are at the stage of struggling for survival. Few entrepreneurs at this stage have enough appreciation for social science research to invite or welcome outsiders to observe and analyze their internal processes and employment conditions. Yet, with the dynamic changes in both the external and internal environments of China, the private sector provides an ideal "research laboratory" (Shenkar and von Glinow 1994, 56) for social scientists. It is a setting in which the results of both natural evolution and deliberate interventions at the societal, industry, firm, group, and individual levels can be observed. We would like to urge researchers in all disciplines to grasp this golden opportunity to engage in more field experimentation and action research as well as in longitudinal process research (Poole, Van de Ven, Dooley, and Holmes 2000) to track the challenges of private firms as they embark on or continue their growth and development journeys. We elaborate on the directions for future research in the final section below.

THE ROAD FORWARD

In addition to a critical analysis of the empirical studies, Tom Gold, Yijiang Wang, and Claudia B. Schoonhoven (respectively the authors of the last chapters in each of the three sections in this book) offer original perspectives on future research implications of the Chinese private-sector firms. In the final chapter, Andrew Walder takes the issue to the global level and compares China's privatization path to those in several other developing economies in the world. In the closing section of this introductory chapter, we will not repeat the eloquent expositions of these scholars, but highlight a few areas that offer management, sociology, and economics scholars unique opportunities for further research by building on and extending the ideas proposed by these authors.

Clearly, the Chinese economy is still in flux, and its legal, political, and social-cultural institutions are still evolving. In other words, the organizational field for all firms in China, private or otherwise, is dynamic. The subject of our studies, therefore, is a "moving target." Also, the institutional environments of Chinese firms differ in both degree and kind from those under which Western firms operate, and from which much of the current stock of knowledge about firms was developed. These two conditions—static differences and dynamic changes—create both challenges and opportunities for researchers in terms of both theory and empirical methods.

Tracking the changes in the environment and documenting their effect on the firms or the firms' responses to these changes will continue to be an important agenda for future research. Wang (chapter 11) points out the need to further study the relationship between firms and the environment, especially the role of the government in firms' governance and the political actions firms take to either proactively or reactively manage their relationships with government bodies and officials. Walder (chapter 17), by explaining the complicated paths that many Chinese firms have taken toward privatization, highlights their intricate relationships with government and government officials. He contends that knowing the history of a firm and its outside network ties are crucial to understanding the firm's chance of future success. Gold (chapter 7) refers to government ties as an entrepreneur's political capital and distinguishes them from economic and social capital. These three forms of capital are not exchangeable, and they are all important for entrepreneurs. We would add another form, human capital. A relevant example here is the specialized education, knowledge, and overseas experiences brought to China by the "returnee entrepreneurs" (Vanhonacker et al., chapter 4 in this volume). How do these four forms of capital develop, in what order, and how do they contribute to entrepreneurial success within the political, economic, and sociological fields of China? This question would make an interesting and valuable research topic.

As the environment changes, attention to the corresponding changes at the firm level is needed. Here, Li (chapter 8 in this volume) ponders about the future development of the nonstate enterprises, questioning if they will become more like overseas Chinese family-owned firms or U.S. publicly listed firms. We wonder if the nonstate enterprises will become more like Chinese state-owned firms, given their increasing legitimacy in the political arena (through their owners' entry into party membership and service as officers in political organs), as well as their tighter connection to the government through its partial ownership and involvement in their governance. It is clear that theorizing about the development of the private sector in China must take into account the role of the government as an important actor in the organizational fields.

Interestingly, Walder (chapter 17) argues for the need to study the state-sector firms, indicating that the further expansion of China's private sector will involve the transformation of the "remaining bastion of large-scale state corporations" (p. 324). Research on corporate governance and ownership reform in the state sector will contribute to understanding the puzzle of the future development of the Chinese private sector. Li (chapter 8) also points to the changing objectives of the state-owned enterprises, relative to the nonstate firms. The surprising behaviors of the state firms found in the study by Wu and Li (chapter 10) further support the view that the state firms are evolving. In turn, this suggests that future research should examine firm behavior as a function not only of type of firm ownership but also as a function of *degree* of firm ownership. Schoonhoven (chapter 16) calls for such examination when she discusses quantifying the concept of ownership by specifying the proportions of ownership held by different investors. The categorical variable has dominated the literature, but the fuzzy boundaries of firm ownership in relation to the state require a more precise conceptualization and measurement of the ownership concept among Chinese firms.

Does the future development of the private-sector firms include globalization or expansion beyond Chinese borders? Can they compete in the global market as freely and effectively as can the state or foreign-invested firms, or will they continue to be second-class citizens with limited state protection and few of the endowments enjoyed by the other types of firms? Will returnee entrepreneurs serve as a bridge toward globalization? Gold (chapter 7) suggests that one can compare the current entrepreneurs of mainland China to those of Taiwan, Hong Kong, and Southeast Asia. The mainland entrepreneurs can be further compared to private entrepreneurs in formerly socialist settings such as Russia, Vietnam, and Eastern Europe. Such comparative research offers "rich potential for examining the relation between culture and institutions" (p. 122). Schoonhoven (chapter 16) also suggests the need for comparative studies to test the assumption of economic rationality, albeit bounded, that has dominated Western theories of organizations. There is a need for more inductive, grounded research to generate new insight and develop new theories of management that may not emerge through applying or extending existing constructs and models (Tsui 2004). Given the paradigm shaped by the common North American training of most scholars studying Chinese firms, we are not surprised that much of the current work, including the empirical studies in this volume, reflects the use of a Western lens.

Thus far, we have focused primarily on studying the private-sector firms going forward. Further examination of their past paths will also add to general knowledge of the evolution of these firms. To this end, Schoonhoven (chapter 16) argues for the importance of "comprehensive and longitudinal data about the overall distribution of China's private firms over time, by industry (size, number of firms, employment, and industry-level performance statistics), and individual firms within industry (age as date of founding, size, ownership distribution, and various financial indicators of performance)" (p. 301). Such data are available for the large state firms, though the quality may vary with different sources. Corresponding data for the private-sector firms are important for meaningful research.

Last, but not least, there is a need for more studies to analyze management process and approaches within firms. Do family and privately owned firms pursue different competitive strategies than the publicly listed, state-controlled, and foreign-invested firms? Do their social networks differ from those of the other firms? What about leadership style, employment relationships, and human resource management systems? Wang (chapter 11) includes leadership and development of a sustainable firm culture and structure in his long research agenda. Chen, Fan, and Wong (chapter 9) suggest that researchers need to know more about the personnel, governance, and organizational features of China's listed companies.

In conclusion, we note that the private sector in China is a force that must be reckoned with. As Walder concludes,

> The final stages of this [Chinese privatization] process will have ramifications far beyond the fields of management, sociology, and economics. It will determine whether large Chinese corporations—when they emerge as private or quasi-private entities—will become a significant force in the international economy. It will determine who owns these assets, what a new propertied elite will look like, and thereby remake the upper reaches of the Chinese social structure. It is hard to imagine a process that will be more decisive in determining China's economic and political future, and its future role in the world. (chapter 17, p. 325)

As organizational scholars, we have a rare opportunity to study organizational birth, growth, and death in real time. Economists can study which government and economic policies stimulate the birth and survival of new firms. Sociologists can analyze the implications of these firms' histories for social processes, and management scholars can examine how internal management and external relations contribute to firm performance and employee outcomes. Such knowledge will contribute to the further practical development of these firms and to the accumulation of global management knowledge. We hope this book makes a modest contribution to both of these two goals.

NOTES

1. Tax havens such as Bermuda, the Cayman Islands, and Luxembourg are ignored in this ranking.

2. According to a survey reported in the *Hong Kong Economic Journal* for February 14, 2005, by the first half of 2004, there were 3.34 million (up from 3 million in 2003) private firms in China, which employed a total of more than 47 million (up from 43 million in 2003) people.

3. According to the *Almanac of China's Economy 2003* (834) and a government white paper cited by the Web site www.china.org.cn/e-white/20040426/4.htm, in 2003 rural township-and-village enterprises accounted for 31.4 percent of China's GDP.

4. According to Wu (2005, Table 2), in 2001 the GDP share of the collective sector was 14.6 percent, whereas that of the private sector was 47.5 percent, implying that the share of the collective sector would be much smaller than one-third by 2003, whereas the share of the private sector would be much larger than one-third by 2003. The different findings of Wu from the *Almanac of China's Economy 2003* and the government white paper could be the result of his broader definition of the private sector, which was taken to include rural and urban enterprises that were nonstate and noncollective economic entities.

5. Li uses the term "nonstate" sector rather than the terms "private" or "domestic private" sector, but the latter are the predominant usage in the other chapters in this volume. Li's term represents a shared economic viewpoint on the ambiguity of ownership form in China's private sector.

6. This term refers to personnel who hold a position of authority in government offices. In broader connections, cadres also include managers, professionals, and technical staff working in state-owned firms and nonprofit organizations. The authors collected in this volume adopt the first, narrower definition of the term.

7. The story was reported in *People's Daily,* http://english1.people.com.cn/200307/14/eng20030714_120183.shtml.

8. The story was reported in *Ming Pao* (a Chinese newspaper in Hong Kong) on August 3, 2005.

REFERENCES

Boisot, M., and J. Child. (1996). From fiefs to clans and network capitalism: Explaining China's emerging economic order. *Administrative Science Quarterly,* 41, 600–24.

Bruun, O. (1993). Business and bureaucracy in a Chinese city: An ethnography of private business households. *Contemporary China, Chinese Research Monograph,* 43. Berkeley: Institute of East Asian Studies, University of California.

———. (1995). Political hierarchy and private entrepreneurship in a Chinese neighborhood. In A. G. Walder (Ed.), *The waning of the communist state: Economic origins of political decline in China and Hungary,* pp. 184–212. Berkeley: University of California Press.

Chang, G. (2001). *The coming collapse of China.* New York: Random House.

Egri, C. and D. Ralston. (2004). Generation cohorts and personal values: A comparison of China and the United States. *Organization Science,* 15(2), 210–20.

Gold, T. B. (1990). Urban private business and social change. In D. Davis and E. F. Vogel (Eds.), *Chinese society on the eve of Tiananmen.* Cambridge, MA: Harvard University Press, pp. 157–78.

Han, S., and C. Pannell. (1999). The geography of privatization in China, 1978–1996. *Economic Geography,* 75, 272–96

Huang, Y. (2003). *Selling China: Foreign direct investment during the reform era.* New York: Cambridge University Press.

Lau, R.W.K. (1998). The 15th congress of the Chinese Communist Party: Milestone in China's privatization. Unpublished text, Division of Social Studies, City University of Hong Kong.

Lin, Q. S. (1990). Private enterprises: Their emergence, rapid growth, and problems. In A. B. Willian and Q. S. Lin (Eds.). *China's rural industry: Structure, development, and reform,* pp. 172–88. Oxford: World Bank, Oxford University Press.

Nee, V. (1989). Theory of market transition: From redistribution to market in state socialism. *American Sociological Review,* 54, 663–81.

———. (1996). The emergence of a market society: Changing mechanisms of stratification in China. *American Journal of Sociology,* 101: 908–49.

Oi, J. C. (1992). Fiscal reform and the economic foundations of local state corporatism in China. *World Politics,* 45, 99–126.

———. (1998). The evolution of local state corporatism. In A. G. Walder (Ed.), *Zouping in transition: The process of reform in rural north China,* pp. 35–61. Cambridge, MA: Harvard University Press.

———. (1999). *Rural China takes off: Incentives for industrialization.* Berkeley and Los Angeles: University of California Press.

Poole, M.; A. Van; de Ven; K. Dooley; and M. Holmes. (2000). *Organizational change and innovation processes: Theory and methods for research.* Oxford: Oxford University Press.

Shenkar, O., and M. A. von Glinow. (1994). Paradoxes of organizational theory and research: Using the case of China to illustrate national contingency. *Management Science,* 40, 56–71.

Shi, X. M. (1993). *The breakthrough of the system* (in Chinese). Beijing: Zhongguo shehui kexue chubanshe.

State Council Development Research Council. (2002). *Almanac of China's Economy.* Beijing: Almanac of China's Economy Press.

———. (2003). *Almanac of China's Economy.* Beijing: Almanac of China's Economy Press.

Tsui, A. S. (2004). Contributing to global management knowledge: A case for high quality indigenous research. *Asia Pacific Journal of Management,* 21, 491–513.

United Nations Council on Trade and Development (UNCTAD). (2004). *World Investment Report 2004.*

Wank, D. L. (1995). Bureaucratic patronage and private business: Changing networks of Power in urban China. In A. G. Walder (Ed.), *The waning of the Communist state: Economic origins of political decline in China and Hungary,* pp. 153–83. Berkeley: University of California Press.

————. (1996). The institutional process of market clientelism: Guanxi and private business in a south China city. *China Quarterly,* 29, 820–38.

————. (1999). *Commodifying Communism: Business, trust and politics in a Chinese city.* Cambridge: Cambridge University Press.

Whyte, M. K. (1995). The social roots of China's economic development. *China Quarterly,* 144, 999–1019.

Wong, J. (2004). China's dynamic economic growth: Implications for East Asia. Paper presented at the International Symposium "Perspective of the Chinese Economy: Challenges and Opportunities." China Center for Economic Research, Peking University, Beijing, September 16–17.

Wu, J. (2005). Market socialism and Chinese economic reform. Paper presented at the International Economic Association Round Table on Market and Socialism in the Light of the Experiences of China and Vietnam, Hong Kong University of Science and Technology, Hong Kong, January 14–15.

Young, S. (1989). Policy, practice and the private sector in China. *Australian Journal of Chinese Affairs,* 21, 57–80.

Zajac, E.; M. Kraatz; and R. Bresser. (2000). Modeling the dynamics of strategic fit : A normative approach to strategic change. *Strategic Management Journal,* 21, 429–53.

Zhang, Houyi. (1999). The rising of another bloc—the restoration and growth of the private economy in the reforming and open-door time (in Chinese). In H. Zhang and L. Ming (Eds.), *Report on the development of Chinese private enterprises* (in Chinese), pp. 3–59. Beijing: Shehui kexue wenxian chubanshe.

2

EXPLAINING CHINA'S EMERGING PRIVATE ECONOMY

SOCIOLOGICAL PERSPECTIVES

YANJIE BIAN AND ZHANXIN ZHANG

The Chinese private economy gained legitimacy after Deng Xiaoping's south China tour in 1992. Deng's calls for bolder reform measures boosted both the growth of the private economy and the restructuring of state-owned enterprises (SOEs) (Gregory, Tenev, and Wagle 2000, 10). An important milestone was the 15th Congress of the Chinese Communist Party (CCP) in 1997, which formed resolutions to privatize small and medium-size SOEs and to further reduce legal and economic barriers to private ownership (Lau 1998). In his speech of July 1, 2001, CCP Secretary General Jiang Zemin vowed—for the first time in the CCP's history—to permit private business owners to join the Party.[1] This statement represented a fundamental shift away from the Communist ideology that denounced class exploitation based on the private ownership of economic assets. This ideological shift was formalized in a resolution passed at the Third Plenary of the 16th CCP Congress, held in November 2003; the main agenda of the plenary session was in fact to institutionalize China's market economy in the post-WTO era.[2]

Despite the popular view that China differs from Russia and the Eastern European countries in not having mass privatization (Jefferson and Rawski 1994, Oi 1992, Walder 1995), sociologists now feel that China's private economy and its impacts on the emerging socioeconomic order are significant enough to warrant attention. To prepare this review essay, we collected more than 100 sociologically relevant publications (in English or Chinese). In the next section, we begin with an overview of the development of the Chinese private economy. We then go on to present three sociological perspectives that account for the emergence of the private sector and shed light on its implications for the socioeconomic order. Finally, we offer an assessment of the rising property class of entrepreneurs—the result of an increasingly expanded private economy.

THE CHINESE PRIVATE ECONOMY: AN OVERVIEW

The Formal Status of the Private Economy

The officially recognized Chinese domestic private sector is composed of individual/household *(geti)* businesses and private enterprises *(siying qiye)* that operate in the nonagricultural economy

25

(Gregory et al. 2000, Young 1998). According to the official definition (Zhang 1999), an entity is an individual/household business if it employs no more than seven laborers; one that hires eight or more workers must be registered as a private enterprise. Karl Marx's *Das Kapital* is the source of this distinction: in Marx's formulation, when a business owner hires fewer than eight workers, the surplus values exploited are not his or her main source of income (Q. Li 1993, 313–14). This definition of an entity was a successful device for making room for private economies to grow in what was still an antiprivatization political-economic culture in the early 1980s (Wu 2003, 169).[3] Currently, individual/household businesses are predominantly run by either single persons or family units, but those that are recognized as private enterprises vary tremendously in size and capital investment. According to official statistics, as of 2002 China has 2,435,000 private enterprises and 23,770,000 individual/household businesses.[4]

Household businesses were restored in rural China in the late 1970s (Q.S. Lin 1990; Zhang 1999, 19–22), and their urban counterparts emerged subsequently to "supplement" SOE operations in commercial and service industries in the early 1980s (Gold 1990, Shi 1993, Young 1989). In both rural and urban areas, fast-growing individual/household businesses began to hire more than seven laborers, raising a loud alarm among the authorities (Young 1992, 65–67). From 1981 to 1986, the upper limit on the number of employees that individual/household businesses would be allowed became a hot policy debate (Zhang 1999, 30–38); in reality, the employment restriction was softened in the name of "experiments" in most reformed areas, including Guangdong and Zhejiang (Young 1995, 105–111). A 1988 state document, "Tentative Stipulations on Private Enterprises," finally approved the rights of private enterprises to hire eight or more workers. This approval was the legal foundation for the rise of the domestic private sector.

The real advancement of the Chinese private economy took place in the 1990s. Although the initial boom of this sector occurred in the 1980s, private businesses were an anomaly then, vulnerable to ideological attacks and economic constraints (Hershkovitz 1985; Wu 2003, 168–74). Consequently, in spite of their accumulating wealth from their business gains, private entrepreneurs did not have any sense of security (Young 1992). Immediately following the 1989 Tiananmen Square protest movements, the private economy was stymied (Kraus 1991, 2) until Deng Xiaoping's 1992 south China tour, which gave new life to development. Since 1993, the growth of the private sector has accelerated: Its share of total industrial output increased markedly from 1992 to 1997, and in 1998 the private sector's share of gross domestic product (GDP) was approximately 33 percent, near the 37 percent share of the state sector (Gregory et al. 2000, 18). In manufacturing, the SOEs' contributions to total industrial output values decreased from 80 percent prior to 1980 to 36 percent in 2002.[5] The private sector hired 33 percent of the urban labor force in 1997, 49 percent in 1998, 54 percent in 1999, and 67 percent in 2002 (Wu 2003, 181). While such impacts varied across regions, there is no doubt that private businesses became an integral part of the Chinese economy in the opening years of the twenty-first century.

The Informal Status of Private Businesses

Official statistics underreport the size, output, and other evaluations of the private sector primarily because many private entities are unregistered. The "informal status of domestic private enterprises" (Gregory et al. 2000, 20–21) is a salient issue. One organizational form of private business is the "red hat" or "fake collective" firm: a firm that is registered as a collective but is in fact owned and operated through private investments and control. For example, in Wenzhou—the city that has been the vanguard of the private economy in China—during the 1980s, private enterprises were registered and treated as collective enterprises by the local government (Liu 1992, 302–3). Another organizational form is a private firm registered as a subsidiary or supplemental unit of an SOE. In one tactic of private entrepreneurs known in Wenzhou (and elsewhere) as *guahu,* or "hanger-on," a private business uses the name of the publicly owned entity to which it was previously connected (Dai 1998, 49–51). A private enterprise can even be "adopted" by a government agency as its supervising body *(zhuguan danwei)* and thus obtain the status of a public enterprise (Lin and Zhang 1999, 214). In these ways, a considerable proportion of private enterprises have been hidden under other forms of ownership (Jia and Wang 1989, 90). Zhang (1999, 15) estimated that in 1995 the number of "forged collective enterprises" nationwide was two times the number of firms registered as private enterprises.

Hiding private ownership in a disguised property arrangement, private entrepreneurs can gain the benefits of avoiding ideological discrimination and enjoying the favorable economic and financial privileges afforded state and collective enterprises. Local governments and officials— the most significant of the players connected one way or another with private enterprises—are inherently interested in having these businesses under their jurisdiction so that they can both reap financial benefits and avoid the political risks of private ownership (Zhang 1999, 51–53). Some private enterprises have disguised themselves as foreign-invested firms by funneling funds to Hong Kong and then back to the mainland for investment (Sabin 1994, 957).

A New Source: Privatization of Public Enterprises

Most recently, privatizing SOEs has become a driving force of the private sector's expansion. In the early 1980s, leasing or contracting SOEs or urban collectives to managers was experimented with, and this experimentation often led to partial privatization from inside the state sector (Young 1995, 98–100), in which Communist cadres and managers became entrepreneurs (Wang 1994, 166–67). In the 1990s, various programs for privatizing small, medium, and even large SOEs were tried (Cao, Qian, and Weingast 1998, 107–15). Township-and-village enterprises (TVEs), registered as rural collective enterprises, also saw mass privatization (Byrd 1990, 209–12; Ho 1994, 174–200), especially in the Pearl River and Yangzi Deltas (Kung 1999; Peng 2001, 1366; Wu 1998) and in southern Jiangsu, where TVEs had been coordinated by local governments under the model of what scholars called "local state corporatism" (Oi 1992, 1998, 1999). Often, these privatization efforts transformed SOEs and TVEs into shareholding companies without direct proprietorship.

This wave of privatization did not arise suddenly but as the result of the past transformation of SOEs. In urban China, one transformation is the devolution of executive control rights to SOE managers, a process that Lin (2001) labeled "corporatization." Other authors have deemed corporatization to be informal privatization in which SOEs mimic the operations of private firms under hard budget constraints (Morita and Zaiki 1998, 101; Nee and Su 1996, 1998). This reform measure provided a needed condition for privatizing SOEs (Swartz 1998). As of 2002, 50 percent of China's 159,000 SOEs had been transformed into shareholding companies.[6] In rural China, local cadres have long had "gray ownership" of TVEs under their jurisdiction (Wu 1998, 165–68), and when the political situation relaxed in the first years of the twenty-first century, they converted their de facto property rights into formally recognized legal rights, completing the privatization of the TVEs (Lin 2001). Thus, the present restructuring of SOEs and TVEs is the continuation of informal privatization already in place for a long time. It is in this setting that we review contending sociological perspectives on China's private economy before its most recent drastic surge.

CONTENDING SOCIOLOGICAL PERSPECTIVES ON CHINA'S PRIVATE ECONOMY

In the research literature we found three perspectives that aimed at explaining the primary cause and dynamics of China's private sector: the market transition perspective, the entrepreneur-bureaucracy connection perspective, and the social roots perspective. Each gives special emphasis to a distinct reason for the emergence and development of the Chinese private economy, and each also has implications for the emerging socioeconomic order.

The Market Transition Perspective

The market transition perspective has been forcefully argued by Victor Nee (1989, 1991,1992, 1996a, 1996b, 2000; Nee and Cao 1999, 2002; Nee and Matthews 1996; Nee and Su 1996, 1998). Following Szelényi (1978), Nee views state redistributive and market economies as two fundamentally different socioeconomic systems, and he argues that reforming state socialism should be characterized as a transition whereby market mechanisms replace redistributive mechanisms. According to Nee, during the transition, markets—rather than the party-state apparatus—increasingly generate power, opportunity, and incentives, and in so doing determine the character of the emerging socioeconomic order. Under this order, state bureaucrats give way to entrepreneurs and professionals who have the human capital and economic capacities to capitalize on market exchanges. State managers, before anyone else, have been charged with the historical task of "informal privatization" in public enterprises.

Nee does not neglect the role of the state in building market institutions in the reform of state socialism (Nee 1996b, 2000). The crucial point of the market transition perspective, however, is that the market has its own motives for growth; direct producers, or private entrepreneurs, inherently will have both the incentive and the capital capacities to expand market exchanges, which inevitably undermine the state redistributive economy. Consequently, the growth of markets will increasingly decrease political elites' control over opportunity and privileges and increase the credibility of human capital and entrepreneurship (Nee 1989, 1996a). These changes dilute the vertical ties of patron-client relationships that characterize the macro structure and management of state socialism and stimulate the horizontal ties of voluntary market exchanges (Nee 1992, 1996a). A tipping point that signals the revolutionary change of mode of economic coordination from redistribution to market is the private sector becoming the main source of output volume and growth; it is at that point that one can confidently claim a transition is completed and thus forcefully test hypotheses derived from the market transition perspective (Nee and Cao 2002).

The market transition perspective offers every hope to ambitious and proactive private and quasi-private entrepreneurs with the desire to be the agents of change. The emerging socioeconomic order will be one that basically follows in the footsteps of all Western capitalist societies. Cultural legacies are not regarded as having a first-order impact on China's transformation (Nee and Cao 2002). Historical and local factors may matter and can complicate the transitional process, but their influences are contingent and temporary (Nee and Cao 1999). A market-dominated Chinese economy and society will eventually converge on the general model of modern capitalism without too many "Chinese characteristics."

The Entrepreneur-Bureaucracy Connection Perspective

The entrepreneur-bureaucracy connection perspective denies the claim that the rise of the private economy and the fall of political power go hand in hand. From this perspective, the key observation and argument is that political elites have not retreated from economic life as markets have spread. Instead, this group's members have both survived in political positions in the state apparatus and taken active roles in an increasingly market-oriented, privatized economy. The emergence, expansion, and growth of the private sector, according to this perspective, have all taken place in the shadow of the robust and influential bureaucratic system. The cultivation and maintenance of connections to local state officials have therefore been crucial for any private entrepreneur in the development of his or her business.

Bruun (1993, 1995) identified multiple types of entrepreneur-bureaucracy links: Private entrepreneurs build favor-exchange *guanxi* with SOE managers in order to obtain business opportunities; household businesses have one spouse registered as the owner while the other maintains employment in a local government office; owners of private enterprises perform temporary jobs for local bureaucratic units in order to win favors; and, most frequently, local officials are de facto partners with private entrepreneurs, from whom they regularly collect profit shares in the form of kickbacks for any business contracts they help establish. In sum, private entrepreneurs pursue connections with local state officials and SOE managers to gain valuable business information, investment opportunities, political security, and social esteem and recognition. Local officials, on the other hand, seek from these entrepreneur-bureaucracy connections such lucrative gains as taxes and levies from private businesses for the development of the local community. This pattern illustrates the "dependent development" nature of the private economy at local levels, suggesting that China may have, to a certain extent, returned to its pre-1949 pattern of "petty capitalism," a mode of production subordinate to and subsumed within the state-dominant economic system (Gates 1996).

While Bruun sees the growth of entrepreneurship as dependent upon a strong officialdom, Wank (1995, 1996, 1999) offers a different vision of interdependence between local state officials and private entrepreneurs. Wank has argued that the connections between entrepreneurs and bureaucrats are "symbiotic" patron-client ties. These ties characterized prereform SOEs—in which party secretaries exercised authority in a culture of "party clientelism" of particular instrumental ties with political activities on the shop floor (Walder 1986)—but in reform-era Xiamen such ties connect local bureaucratic patrons and private business clients (Wank 1995). "The intertwining of Communist legacies and new market activities created a distinct configuration of state power in China's emerging market economy that constrains commercial trade networks" (Wank 1999, 33). Although monopoly control of the state over factor resources (finance, labor, materials) is shrinking, the state influences the emerging market economy quite effectively through regulatory and administrative controls. When private entrepreneurs run businesses in markets, local government officials seek gains through various forms of control and influence, thereby lining their pockets and filling local government coffers. Mutually beneficial exchanges result in clientelist networks between these two groups. These clientelist ties are considered to facilitate efficiency enhancement, contract enforcement, and competition in an emerging market economy (Wank 1999, 37), all of which are, after all, positive for private entrepreneurs.

Wank's characterization of China's emerging private economy as "commercial clientelism" (1999, 35–39) or "clientelist capitalism" (1995, 229–31) offers a sharp contrast to the market transition perspective. The latter implies that the emerging market economy is full of horizontal trade ties among private businesses, but the clientelist capitalism view maintains that such horizontal ties cannot and will not replace vertical ties between entrepreneurs and officialdom. Unlike Bruun, Wank considers entrepreneur-bureaucracy ties to be a symbiosis rather than a one-way dependence; for Wank, entrepreneurs and officials survive and grow with interdependence, working together to capitalize on the business opportunities increasingly generated in the marketplace.

These two players in the emerging market economy are not only pursuing "utility-maximizing interest calculations but also the rationality of social trust" (Wank 1995, 31). Thus, clientelist capitalism implies neither the forcefulness of private property rights (as for Nee) nor the subjection of private entrepreneurs to government officials (as for Bruun); rather, it points to the relational nature of the emerging socioeconomic order. In the words of Boisot and Child (1996) and Sato (2003), China is on the road to "network capitalism."

While Bruun and Wank have focused on the impacts of the bureaucratic system on the new private sector, a more explicit view points to local governments' persistent control over public assets and TVEs. In the "local corporatism model" (Oi 1992, 1998, 1999; Walder 1995), local governments act as business corporations, exercising control rights over the enterprises under their jurisdictions to achieve economic and political benefits both for themselves and for the localities they lead. In this way, local government becomes the center for economic reform and development. Walder (1995) found that, compared to those in higher jurisdictions, governments in lower jurisdictions far from the central government are more capable of monitoring enterprises and of achieving good economic performance. These findings indicate that local governments have both the structures and the incentives to establish the local corporatism model.

The Social Roots Perspective

The social roots perspective attributes the rise of the private economy to the family-centered structure of Chinese society. Gold (1990) was among the first of the sociologists who studied the rise of household businesses in Chinese cities in the 1980s. He observed that, despite the three decades of socialism that dismissed and denounced the productive function of the family, the family immediately resumed that function, and even became the major form of private business, when the state again permitted individual/household businesses to operate in small commodity markets. In a more organized production system, such as the industrialized Daqiuzhuang Village in Tianjin, Lin (1995, Lin and Chen 1999) found that the managerial structure (the Daqiuzhuang Village Corporation) was rooted in the family and kinship structure of the villagers. There, many key corporate posts were occupied by members of the family of Yu Zuomin, then the paramount leader of the village, and the leader of the transformation of Daqiuzhuang from a poor village to a sizeable industrial center. In fact, many "industrial villages" have followed the same model. Along these lines, Zhou (2004) offers a detailed analysis of Huaxi Village in south Jiangsu Province.

Why would family-run firms be the major form of China's private businesses? Whyte (1995, 1996) took on this question and began with the observation that scholars differ in their judgments of whether the traditional Chinese family is an obstacle to or an engine of China's economic development. Whyte argued that Chinese families contain a mixture of positive and negative tendencies, and that the dominant influence of the tendencies hinges on outside factors. The transformation of Chinese families in the past, especially during Mao's era, gave rise to two important features: the weakening of the senior generation's power, and the survival of family solidarity and loyalty. This family structure provided the motivation and resources to mobilize family efforts, with innovative and productive results. Meanwhile, recent changes in the global economy that favor small enterprises have reinforced the economic potential of the Chinese family. Therefore, when economic reforms in China provided institutional support for private entrepreneurship, the potential of the Chinese family in economic undertakings became the real driver of a family-based economy (Peng 2004). Sun and Wong (2001) offered an extended family perspective in explaining the success of private enterprises. In contrast with the view regarding the trust network in China as family confined, Sun and Wong claimed that such relationships

Table 2.1

Sociological Accounts of Emerging Private Businesses in China

	Market transition perspective	Entrepreneur-bureaucracy connection perspective (network capitalism)	Social roots perspective (network capitalism)
Assumption of rationality	Instrumental	Social and instrumental value orientation	Instrumental and family-loyalty-oriented
Explanatory variable	Market institutions	Patron-client relationships	Family-centered loyalty and trust
Emphasized social network	Horizontal trade networks	Vertical clientelist ties	Family-centered networks
Prediction for social change	Standard capitalism	Petty capitalism/clientelist capitalism/local state corporatism	Family-based capitalism

extend beyond immediate family. Such extended trust networks make private enterprises better able to bridge the gaps related to productive resources and other supports that are fundamentally important to the growth of private enterprises.

The social roots perspective rests on the assumption that people do not merely pursue personal interests; instead, they conform to the ethics and norms of family, kinship, and social networks. In contrast to the two previously reviewed perspectives, the social roots perspective emphasizes family-based loyalty and trust rather than horizontal trade networks (the market transition perspective) or vertical ties between entrepreneurs and bureaucrats (the clientelist capitalism perspective). The social roots perspective implies that the emerging private economy is a form of family-based capitalism, one that is relevant to a Chinese culture of "familism" and characteristic of other Asian economies as well (Wong 1985, 1988, 1995).

Summary and Discussion

The three sociological perspectives just reviewed are based on different theoretical rationales, providing diverse explanations for the causes and consequences of China's emerging private economy. Table 2.1 summarizes the distinctive features of these perspectives.

The market transition perspective bridges two great historical events in transitional China—the revival of markets and the emergence of a private economy—and follows the logic of the "convergence school" of economic research in explaining China's transition (Woo 1999). The correlation between the growth of markets and the advancement of the private economy has been documented (Shi 1993, Zhang 1999). The motivations and initiatives of private entrepreneurs implied by the market transition perspective are observed in studies of the Wenzhou model and elsewhere (Parries 1993, Zhang 1999). The market transition perspective is, however, challenged by the view that political power ought not to decline as markets expand (Bian and Logan 1996, Parrish and Michelson 1996, Walder 2003, Zhou 2000). Crucial to the market transition perspective is the question of the changing nature of political power and local officials' strategies of adjustment and adaptation to an increasingly "marketized" and privatized Chinese economy.

The entrepreneur-bureaucracy connection perspective views the emerging private economy as born of and continuing to depend on business-government ties, and it offers three versions of the nature of these ties. Bruun's dependent-entrepreneur account points to the continuity of an official-centered Chinese culture under marketization; Wank's clientelist capitalism takes into account the cosurvival of local state bureaucracies and officials on the one hand and private entrepreneurs on the other; and Oi and Walder's local state corporatism points to the local state as an engine of local economic reform and development. These different views are broadly based (Pieke 1998, 260; Yang 1989, 1994), suggesting that researchers must take a local approach to examining what Walder (1996) first called "property rights regimes." Central to the entrepreneur-bureaucracy connection perspective is a judgment about the consequences of the commercialization of state power, which is not unique to China but phenomenal in all market economies (Wolf 1993). Why has Chinese state power been commercialized to an extent that fosters symbiotic clientelist networks or the patterns depicted by the local state corporatism model? And to what extent do such networks and patterns continue to characterize the Chinese private economy since China's entry into the WTO?

The social roots account grasps the distinctive pattern of Chinese social structure, namely family life. This perspective links economies such as those of Hong Kong, Taiwan, and Singapore with Chinese family traditions (Luo 1997, Tu 1991, Wong 1995). Within China, this perspective is broadly based (Entwisle et al. 1995), and it is true that the private economy has more social support (Peng 2004) and is more likely to grow (Zhe and Chan 2000) in a village community with a high concentration of people with a single family surname. The social roots perspective notwithstanding, it remains to be seen whether the success of the Chinese family-run business is transitory. In this light, it will be useful to compare China with Taiwan and Hong Kong, where wisdom and evidence regarding family enterprises have had more time to accumulate (Hamilton and Kao 1990, Weidenbaum 1996, Wong 1985).

RISING PROPERTY CLASSES

Parallel to the surge of the private economy has been the emergence and fast growth of the property classes, or bourgeoisie. As of 2002, China had more than six million registered private enterprise owners, and the real number is perhaps greater than ten million.[7] Sociologists have studied the three social groups—private business owners, individual/household business owners, and bureaucratic elites—that are the most likely components of China's rising bourgeoisie.

Private Business Owners

In 1992, private business owners' capital assets averaged 940,000 renminbi (RMB), and their housing space measured five times the national average (Li 1995, 244–47). By the end of 2001, their average assets had grown to more than 2 million RMB.[8]

Backgrounds of private business owners are diverse. Surveys in 1993 and 1995 show that roughly one-third of private business owners were former cadres from urban or rural state apparatuses; another third were managers or were self-employed and/or craftspeople before; and the remaining third were ordinary workers and peasants (Li 2000, 326–29). This breakdown means that market reforms have opened up avenues for a new propertied class. A recent tendency has been for more and more professionals and technicians to engage in private business (Li 1995, 236–37), signifying that the professional elite has begun to be an important source of this class.

Private business owners have mobilized a variety of different forms of capital for their businesses. The human capital of private entrepreneurs is very important for their success (Li 1996b). Family ties, which can be regarded as a sort of social capital (Peng 2004), are most important to private entrepreneurs (Zhang and Ming 1999, 156–63). Connections with public organizations are significant for private undertakings (Li 1996a). Large proportions of managerial personnel and technicians of private enterprises have come from the state sector and the urban collective sector (Zhang and Ming 1999, 146–47).

Individual/Household Business Owners

Individual/household business owners were the first to enter post-Mao China's private sector (see a focused analysis of entry into individual/household businesses in chapter 3, by Wu, in this volume). They were the signs of China's reform, and they formed a relatively wealthy stratum in the early 1980s (Shi 1993). There is little evidence that these people were still rich in the 1990s (Bian and Zhang 2002), and a 1998 Tianjin-Shanghai-Wuhan-Shenzhen survey showed that they clearly lacked durable social networks and social capital (Bian and Li 2000). To be sure, self-employed people in cities were increasingly marginalized, as was evident in economic, political, and social measures (Bian et al. 2005; Davis 1999; Lu, Zhang, and Zhang 1992). To what extent do individual/household business owners constitute a middle class? And what has their political impact been in China? These questions are worthy of further empirical research.

The Bureaucratic Elite

Party and state bureaucratic cadres are being transformed from redistributors to regulators or market participants (business owners). The opportunism model (Nee and Lian 1994) suggests that these cadre elites often give up their political loyalty and ideology for market gains as entrepreneurs, and So (2003) showed that the *embourgeoisement* of the political and administrative elite is widespread. Both cadres and SOE managers have been involved in profit-seeking activities (Duckett 2001, Lin and Zhang 1999, J. Wong 1994) and have quietly converted public properties into private ownership through processes labeled "inside privatization" (Ding 2000a,b; He 1998) or "spontaneous privatization" (Blanchard et al. 1991, 34; Boycko, Schleifer, and Vishny 1995, 76–85; Peck and Richardson 1991, 161; Spulber 1997, 120). Both of these processes reveal that state cadres and managers have shifted public assets to their personal pockets by exercising their executive authority in SOEs. There have been other ways for bureaucratic elites to privatize: SOE managers receive revenues through helping foreign investors in China (Wu 1998, 205–21); local officials plunder private entrepreneurs (Rocca 1992); and even the military is operating businesses (Bickford 1994). By 2004, it was common for incumbent state managers to gain substantial shares of stocks in newly transformed shareholding companies, which made headline news everywhere in major Chinese cities.[9]

CONCLUSIONS AND LOOKING AHEAD

The sociological perspectives we have reviewed above shed some light on the causes and socioeconomic consequences of the emerging Chinese private economy. The market transition perspective and the clientelist capitalism perspective may be regarded as competing explanations.

Between them is the sharp contrast of judgments about how market institutions and interest politics interact with each other, and how the two central groups—state bureaucrats/managers and private business owners—interplay to make and remake the emerging socioeconomic order.

Drawing upon this review, we suggest four directions for further research into China's emerging private economy. First, we still need to develop our understanding of the transformation of the Chinese state, which is a key to the kind of private economy that continues to grow in China. While the notion of the "developmental state" seems to focus attention on the role played by the central state in economic development, Chinese experiences have revealed that both central and local governments are sources of information, norms, legitimacy, and finances that direct, regulate, and structure private businesses. State policy directives and their motivations are always a topic for empirical research.

Second, researchers should further explore the role of cadres and state managers in property-rights transformations. Importantly, informal privatization fosters entrepreneurship within the public sector, and spontaneous privatization—or capitalization of political power and abuses of office authority—gives rise to a bourgeoisie that bears little relevance to entrepreneurship. The first process seems to have gained primacy in most recent conversions of SOEs into shareholding companies, whereas the second process seems quickly to spread to both central and local levels of the state bureaucracy, despite an anticorruption campaign by the new Hu Jintao-Wen Jiabao administration. Thus, it will be a task of empirical research to explore the implications of these processes for the character of the Chinese market economy.

Third, it has become scholarly wisdom that China's private economy will one way or another follow a model of network capitalism (Boisot and Child 1996, Sato 2003). This view calls for empirical research on the types and roles of business networks and embedded social capital in business development; on interorganizational relations and their implications for organizational behaviors, private and public; on the contractual and informal ties between the public and private sectors in defining and exercising the property rights of economic enterprises; and on the thresholds by which networks of social and economic relationships succeed or fail to coordinate resource allocation efficiently and effectively. The study of these topics is crucial for deepening understanding of the nature, character, and developmental patterns of the Chinese private economy.

Finally, as the private sector grows rapidly, democratic politics and civil society may soon become a new field of intellectual interest. To what extent is the private sector a source of support for nongovernment organizations? To what extent would private entrepreneurs mobilize the cause of democratic politics under a self-adjusting communist state coupled with a growing market economy? To what extent would private businesses manage their capital-labor relations in light of China's entry into the World Trade Organization? And how do private entrepreneurs react to the emerging labor movement of the relatively deprived urban workers and migrant laborers? These are some new sociological questions about China's emerging socioeconomic order.

NOTES

We are grateful to have received a research assistance grant from the Hang Lung Center for Organizational Research. We would also like to express our thanks to Anne Tsui, Tom Gold, and Andy Walder for their comments on an earlier version of this chapter, and to Wang Jianping and Zhang Lijuan for their helpful assistance.

1. See *People's Daily* (*renmin ribao*), July 2, 2001.
2. China entered the World Trade Organization in December 2002.
3. According to Wu (2003, 169), economist Lin Zili was responsible for this rhetoric.

4. See *China Economic Times* (*zhongguo jingji shibao*), July 18, 2003, "Developing a Non-State Economy, Improving Basic Economic Institutions" (fazhan fei gongyou jingji, wanshan jiben jingji zhidu).

5. The source is the same one cited in note 4.

6. See *China Securities News* (*zhongguo zhengquan bao*), November 19, 2003, "China Pushes Economic Restructuring, Maximizing the Configuration of State-Owned Enterprises" (zhongguo jiada bingguo chongzu lidu, youhua guoyou jingji buju).

7. See *Economy* (*jing ji*), November 13, 2003, "An Eye-Opening New Stratum" (yige yaoyan de xinxing jieceng).

8. The source is the same one cited in note 5. The article cites data from China's Fifth National Sample Survey of Private Enterprise Owners.

9. See, for example, the headline about the property rights reform of China's leading SOEs in the *Economic Observer* (*jingji guancha bao*), a weekly newspaper, October 2004.

REFERENCES

Bian, Y. J.; R. Breiger; D. Davis; and J. Galaskiewicz. (2005). Occupation, class, and networks in urban China. *Social Forces,* 83 (June).

Bian, Y. J., and Y. Li. (2000). Social network capital of the Chinese family. *Hsinghua Sociological Review,* 2, 1–18.

Bian, Y. J., and J. R. Logan. (1996). Market transition and persistence of power: The changing stratification system in urban China. *American Sociological Review,* 61, 739–58.

Bian, Y. J., and Z. X. Zhang. (2002). Marketization and income distribution in urban China: 1988 and 1995. *Research in Social Stratification and Mobility,* 19, 377–415.

Bickford, T. J. (1994). The Chinese military and its business operations: The PLA as entrepreneur. *Asian Survey,* 345, 460–74.

Blanchard, O.; R. Dornbusch; P. Krugman; R. Layard; and L. H. Summers. (1991). *Reform in Eastern Europe.* Cambridge, MA: MIT Press.

Boisot, M., and J. Child. (1996). From fiefs to clans and network capitalism: Explaining China's emerging economic order. *Administrative Science Quarterly,* 41, 600–24.

Boycko, M.; A. Shleifer; and R. Vishny. (1995). *Privatizing Russia.* Cambridge, MA: MIT Press.

Bruun, O. (1993). Business and bureaucracy in a Chinese city: An ethnography of private business households. *Contemporary China, Chinese Research Monograph* 43. Berkeley: Institute of East Asian Studies, University of California.

———. (1995). Political hierarchy and private entrepreneurship in a Chinese neighborhood. In A. G. Walder (Ed.), *The waning of the communist state: Economic origins of political decline in China and Hungary,* pp. 184–212. Berkeley: University of California Press.

Byrd, W. A. (1990). Entrepreneurship, capital, and ownership. In A. B. Willian and Q. S. Lin (Eds.), *China's rural industry: Structure, development, and reform,* pp. 189–271. Oxford: World Bank, Oxford University Press.

Cao, Y. Z.; Y. Qian; and B. R. Weingast. (1998). From federalism, Chinese style, to privatization, Chinese style. *Economics of Transition,* 71, 103–31.

Dai, Z. T. (1998). *The research on regional economies with investigation on the issue of Wenzhou's growth.* (in Chinese). Beijing: Zhongguo jihua chubanshe.

Davis, D. S. (1999). Self-employment in Shanghai: A research note. *China Quarterly,* 157, 22–43.

Ding, X. L. (2000a). Systematic irregularity and spontaneous property transformation in the Chinese financial system. *China Quarterly,* 163, 655–76.

———. (2000b). The illicit asset stripping of Chinese state firms. *China Journal,* 43, 1–28.

Duckett, J. (2001). Bureaucrats in business, Chinese-style: The lessons of market reform and state entrepreneurialism in the People's Republic of China. *World Development,* 29(1), 23–37.

Entwisle, B.; G. E. Henderson; S. E. Short; J. E. Bouma; and F. Y. Zhai. (1995). Gender and family businesses in rural China. *American Sociological Review,* 60, 36–57.

Gates, H. (1996). *China's motor: A thousand years of petty capitalism.* Ithaca, NY: Cornell University Press.

Gold, T. B. (1990). Urban private business and social change. In D. Davis and E. F. Vogel (Eds.), *Chinese society on the eve of Tiananmen,* pp. 157–78. Cambridge, MA: Harvard University Press.

Gregory, N.; S. Tenev; and D. Wagle. (2000). *China's emerging private enterprises.* Washington, DC: International Finance Corporation.

Hamilton, G. G., and Kao, C. S. (1990). The institutional foundations of Chinese business: The family firm in Taiwan. *Comparative Social Research,* 12, 95–112.

He, Q. L. (1998). *The pitfall of modernization—economic and social problems in contemporary China* (in Chinese). Beijing: Jinri zhongguo chubanshe.

Hershkovitz, L. (1985). The fruits of ambivalence: China's urban individual economy. *Pacific Affairs,* 58, 427–50.

Ho, S.P.S. (1994). *Rural China in transition: Non-agricultural development in rural Jiangsu, 1978–1990.* Oxford: Clarendon Press.

Jefferson, G. H., and T. G. Rawski. (1994). Enterprise reform in Chinese industry. *Journal of Economic Perspective,* 8, 47–70.

Jia, T., and K. C. Wang. (1989). The rise and development of the private enterprise owner strata in China (in Chinese). *Chinese Social Science,* 2, 89–100.

Kraus, W. (1991). *Private business in China: Revival between ideology and pragmatism.* Honolulu: University of Hawaii Press.

Kung, J. (1999). The evolution of property rights in village enterprises: The case of Wuxi County. In J. C. Oi and A. G. Walder (Eds.), *Property rights and economic reform in China,* pp. 95–120. Stanford, CA: Stanford University Press.

Lau, R.W.K. (1998). *The 15th Congress of the Chinese Communist Party: Milestone in China's privatization.* Working paper, Division of Social Studies, City University of Hong Kong.

Li, L. L. (1996a). Private entrepreneurs in the transformation of social structure: "system capital" and the development of private firms (in Chinese). *Sociological research,* 2, 93–104.

———. (1996b). Human capital of private firms and their success (in Chinese). *Chinese Social Science Quarterly* (HK), 15, 32–43.

———. (2000). The transformation of social stratification mechanisms and the emergence of private enterprises in Mainland China. In Z. J. Liu (Ed.), *Markets, classes and politics: The transforming Chinese societies* (in Chinese), pp. 325–58. Hong Kong Institute of Asia-Pacific Studies, Chinese University of Hong Kong.

Li, P. L. (Ed.). (1995). *Reports on the classes and strata in China's new era* (in Chinese). Shenyang, China: Liaoning renmin shubanshe.

Li, Q. (1993). *Social stratification and mobility in contemporary China* (in Chinese). Beijing: Shehui kexue wenxian chubanshe.

Lin, N. (1995). Local market socialism: Local corporation in action in rural China. *Theory and Society,* 24, 301–54.

Lin, N., and J. C. Chen. (1999). Local elites as officials and owners: Shareholding and property rights in Daqiuchuang. In J. C. Oi and A. G. Walder (Eds.), *Property rights and economic reform in China,* pp. 1–24. Stanford, CA: Stanford University Press.

Lin, Q. S. (1990). Private enterprises: Their emergence, rapid growth, and problems. In A. B. Willian and Q. S. Lin (Eds.), *China's rural industry: Structure, development, and reform,* pp. 172–88. Oxford: World Bank, Oxford University Press.

Lin, Y. M. (2001). *Between politics and markets: Firms, competition, and institutional change in post-Mao China.* New York: Cambridge University Press.

Lin, Y. M., and Z. X. Zhang. (1999). Backyard profit centers: The private assets of public agencies. In J. C. Oi and A. Walder (Eds.), *Property rights and economic reform in China,* pp. 203–25. Stanford, CA: Stanford University Press.

Liu, Y. L. (1992). Reform from below: The private economy and local politics in the rural industrialization of Wenzhou. *China Quarterly,* 130, 293–316.

Lu, X. Y.; H. Y. Zhang; and Q. Z. Zhang. (1992). The partition of peasantry in the transitional period (in Chinese). *Chinese Social Science,* 4, 137–51.

Luo, J. (1997). The significance of networks in the initiation of small business in Taiwan. *Sociological Forum,* 12(2), 97–317.

Morita, K., and K. Zaiki. (1998). A comparative analysis of privatization: A Chinese way and a Polish way. In Z. Ilianna (Ed.), *Eastern Europe and the world economy: Challenges of transition and globalization,* pp. 97–101. Cheltenham, England, and Northampton, MA: Elgar.

Nee, V. (1989). Theory of market transition: From redistribution to market in state socialism. *American Sociological Review,* 54, 663–81.

———. (1991). Social inequalities in reforming state socialism: Between redistribution and markets in China. *American Sociological Review,* 56, 267–82.

————. (1992). Organizational dynamics of market transition: Hybrid forms, property rights, and mixed economy in China. *Administrative Science Quarterly,* 37, 1–27.

————. (1996a). The emergence of market society: Changing mechanisms of stratification in China. *American Journal of Sociology,* 101, 908–49.

————. (1996b). Market transformation and societal transformation in reforming state socialism. *Annual Review of Sociology,* 22, 401–35.

————. (2000). The role of the state in making a market economy. *Journal of Institutional and Theoretical Economics,* 156, 64–88.

Nee, V., and Y. Cao. (1999). Path dependent societal transformation: Stratification in mixed economies. *Theory and Society,* 28, 799–834.

————. (2002). Postsocialist inequality: The causes of continuity and discontinuity. *Research in Social Stratification and Mobility,* 19, 3–39.

Nee, V., and P. Lian. (1994). Sleeping with the enemy: A dynamic model of declining political commitment in state socialism. *Theory and Society,* 23, 253–96.

Nee, V., and R. Matthews. (1996). Market transition and societal transformation in reforming state socialism. *Annual Review of Sociology,* 22, 401–35.

Nee, V., and S. J. Su. (1996). Institutions, social ties, and commitment in China's corporatist transformation. In J. McMillan and B. Naugton (Eds.), *Reforming Asian socialism: The growth of market institutions,* pp. 111–34. Ann Arbor: The University of Michigan Press

————. (1998). Institutional foundations of robust economic performance: Public sector industrial growth in China. In J. Henderson (Ed.), *Industrial transformation in Eastern Europe in the light of the East Asian experience,* pp. 167–87. New York: St. Martin's Press

Oi, J. C. (1992). Fiscal reform and the economic foundations of local state corporatism in China. *World Politics,* 45, 99–126.

————. (1998) The evolution of local state corporatism. In A. G. Walder (Ed.), *Zouping in transition: The process of reform in rural North China,* pp. 35–61. Cambridge, MA: Harvard University Press

————. (1999). *Rural China takes off: Incentives for industrialization.* Berkeley and Los Angeles: University of California Press.

Parries, K. (1993). Local initiative and national reform: The Wenzhou model of development. *China Quarterly,* 134, 242–63.

Parrish, W. L., and E. Michelson, E. (1996). Politics and markets: Dual transformations. *American Journal of Sociology,* 101, 1024–59.

Peck, M. J., and T. J. Richardson. (Eds.). (1991). *What is to be done?—Proposals for the Soviet transition to the market.* New Haven, CT, and London: Yale University Press.

Peng, Y. S. (2001). Chinese villages and townships in industrial corporations: Ownership, governance, and market discipline. *American Journal of Sociology,* 106, 1338–70.

————. (2004). Kinship networks and entrepreneurs in China's transitional economy. *American Journal of Sociology,* 109, 1045–74.

Pieke, F. N. (1998). Networks, groups, and the state in the rural economy of Raoyang County, Hebei Province. In E. B. Vermeer, F. N. Pieke, and W. L. Chong (Eds.), *Cooperative and collective in China's rural development: Between state and private interests,* pp. 256–72. Armonk, NY: M.E. Sharpe.

Rocca, J. L. (1992). Corruption and its shadow: An anthropological view of corruption in China. *China Quarterly,* 130, 402–16.

Sabin, L. (1994). New bosses in the workers' state: The growth of non-state sector employment in China. *China Quarterly,* 140, 944–70.

Sato, H. (2003). *The growth of market relations in post-reform rural China.* London and New York: Routledge Curzon.

Shi, X. M. (1993). *The breakthrough of the system* (in Chinese). Beijing: Zhongguo shehui kexue chubanshe.

So, A. Y. (2003). The changing patterns of classes and class conflict in China. *Journal of Contemporary Asia,* 33, 363–76.

Spulber, N. (1997). *Redefining the state: Privatization and welfare reform in industrial and transitional economies.* New York: Cambridge University Press.

Sun, W. B., and S. L. Wong. (2001). The development of private enterprise in contemporary China: Institutional foundations and limitations. *The China Review,* 2, 65–91.

Swartz, K. L. (1998). *Corporatization: A step towards privatization.* Thesis LL.M., University of Hong Kong.

Szelényi, I. (1978). Social inequalities in state socialist redistributive economies. *International Journal of Comparative Sociology,* 1–2, 63–87.

Tu, I. C. (1991). Family enterprises in Taiwan. In G. Hamilton (Ed.), *Business networks and economic development in Southeast Asia,* pp. 114–25. Hong Kong: University of Hong Kong, Centre of Asian Studies.

Walder, A. G. (1986). *Communist neo-traditionalism: Work and authority in Chinese industry.* Berkeley: University of California.

———. (1995). Local governments as industrial firms: An organizational analysis of China's transitional economy. *American Journal of Sociology,* 101, 263–301.

———. (1996). Markets and inequality in transitional economies: Toward testable theories. *American Journal of Sociology,* 101, 1060–73.

———. (2003). Elite opportunity in transitional economies. *American Sociological Review,* 68, 899–916.

Wang, H. S. (1994). The industrialization and structural change of the elite in Chinese rural areas in the reforming period. In Z. J. Liu (Ed.), *Development and inequality* (in Chinese), pp. 157–78. Hong Kong: Hong Kong Institute of Asia-Pacific Studies.

Wank, D. L. (1995). Bureaucratic patronage and private business: Changing networks of power in urban China. In A. G. Walder (Ed.), *The waning of the communist state: Economic origins of political decline in China and Hungary,* pp. 153–83. Berkeley: University of California Press.

———. (1996). The institutional process of market clientelism: Guanxi and private business in a South China city. *China Quarterly,* 29, 820–38.

———. (1999). *Commodifying communism: Business, trust and politics in a Chinese city.* Cambridge, England: The University of Cambridge.

Weidenbaum, M. (1996). The Chinese family business enterprise. *California Management Review,* 384, 141–56.

Whyte, M. K. (1995). The social roots of China's economic development. *China Quarterly,* 144, 999–1019.

———. (1996). The Chinese family and economic development: Obstacle or engine? *Economic Development and Cultural Change,* 45, 1–30.

Wolf, Charles, Jr. (1993). *Markets and government: Choosing between imperfect alternatives.* Cambridge, MA: MIT Press.

Wong, J. (1994). Power and market in mainland China: The danger of increasing government involvement in business. *Issues and Studies,* 301, 1–12.

Wong, S. L. (1985). The Chinese family firm: A model. *British Journal of Sociology,* 36(1), 158–72.

———. (1988). The applicability of Asian family values to other sociocultural settings. In P. Berger and H. H. M. Hsiao (Eds.), *In search of an East Asian development model,* pp. 134–52. New Brunswick, NJ: Transaction Books.

———. (1995). Business networks, cultural values, and the state in Hong Kong and Singapore. In R. A. Brown (Ed.), *Chinese business enterprise in Asia,* pp. 36–153. London and New York: Routledge.

Woo, W. T. (1999). The real reasons for China's growth. *The China Journal,* 41, 116–37.

Wu, J. L. (2003). *China's economic reform* (in Chinese). Shanghai: Shanghai Far East Press.

Wu, J. M. (1998). *Local property rights regime in socialist reform: A case study of China's informal privatization.* Unpublished doctoral thesis, Department of Political Science, Columbia University.

Yang, M. (1989). The gift economy and state power in China. *Comparative Studies in Society and History,* 31, 25–54.

Yang, M. (1994). *Gifts, favors and banquets: The art of social relationship in China.* Ithaca, NY: Cornell University Press.

Young, S. (1989). Policy, practice and the private sector in China. *Australian Journal of Chinese Affairs,* 21, 57–80.

———. (1992). Wealth but not security: Attitudes towards private business in the1980s. In A. Watson (Ed.), *Economic reform and social change in China,* pp. 63–87. London: Routledge.

———. (1995). *Private business and economic reform in China.* Armonk, NY: M.E. Sharpe.

———. (1998). The Chinese private sectors in two decades of reform. *Journal of the Asia Pacific Economy,* 31, 80–103.

Zhang, H. Y. (1999). The rising of another bloc—the restoration and growth of the private economy in the reforming and open-door time. In H. Y. Zhang and L. Z. Ming (Eds.), *Report on the development of Chinese private enterprises* (in Chinese), pp. 3–59. Beijing: Shehui kexue wenxian chubanshe.

Zhang, H. Y., and L. Z. Ming. (Eds.). (1999). *Report on the development of Chinese private enterprises* (in Chinese). Beijing: Shehui kexue wenxian chubanshe.

Zhe, X. Y., and Y. Y. Chan. (2000). Structure—actor relationship in institutional choices concerning property rights (in Chinese). *Sociological research,* 5, 64–81.

Zhou, X. G. (2000). Economic transformation and income inequality in urban China: Evidence from panel data. *American Journal of Sociology,* 105, 1135–74.

Zhou, Y. (2004). *Post-collectivism in a transitional economy: The logic of integration under the condition of radical differentiation in Huaxi Village.* Unpublished doctoral thesis, Department of Sociology, Chinese University of Hong Kong.

3

FAMILY BUSINESSES IN CHINA, 1978–96

ENTRY AND PERFORMANCE

Xiaogang Wu

The emergence of a private sector is an integral and crucial part of China's transition from a planned economy to a market economy. Private economic activity in China takes two forms: individual/household businesses *(geti gongshang hu* or *geti hu [getihu])* and private enterprises *(siying qiye)* (Gregory, Tenev, and Wagle 2000). Since 1978, Chinese reformers have adopted an incremental approach to expanding the private sector. In the early 1980s, only individual/household businesses were granted legal status, and a cap of seven was set on the number of workers a *getihu* could hire. Private enterprises *(siying qiye)* on larger scales, not sanctioned until 1988, had been developing rapidly since 1992, after Deng Xiaoping called for further market-oriented reforms in his famous tour of southern China. Private ownership was fully legitimized in the late 1990s, and since then has been playing an increasingly important role in China's economic growth and institutional transition (see detailed reviews in Bian and Zhang, chapter 2, this volume).

The historical development of the private sector in China can be confirmed by government statistical data. As Figures 3.1a and 3.1b show, the registered capital and revenues of both individual/household businesses and private enterprises have been growing rapidly since the 1980s, particularly after 1992. Private enterprises overtook individual/household businesses in total registered capital after 1994 and in revenues after 1998, and they have become the main growth engine of China's dynamic private sector.

Notwithstanding this fact, the role of individual/household businesses in China's economic transition should not be dismissed quickly. First, individual/household businesses continue to outnumber private enterprises in quantity and employment size. As of 1999, there were still 31,600,000 family businesses with 62,410,000 employed workers, but only 1,508,857 private enterprises with 20,220,000 employed workers (Lan 2002, Wang, 2002). Second, it was the emergence of individual/household businesses that initiated China's market transition and fostered the development of private enterprises a quarter century ago. For most of the reform period, until the late 1990s, only individual/household businesses were allowed to grow, and this growth facilitated the transformation of the state-planned economy.

The pace of the rise and subsequent expansion of the private sector has varied with institutional context in rural and urban China. Economic reforms brought about the revival of private ownership first in rural areas, where the implementation of the household responsibility system in 1978 unleashed a large amount of surplus labor, much of which came from nonagricultural busi-

Figure 3.1a   **Total Registered Capital (RMB): Individual/Household Businesses and Private Enterprises**

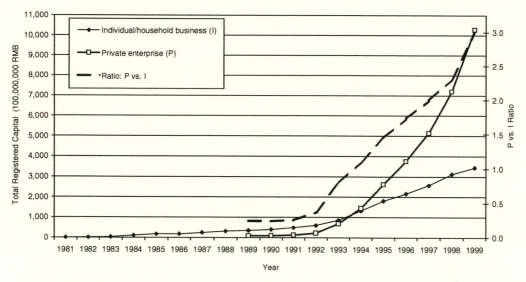
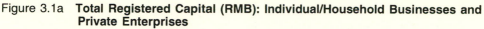

Source: Lan (2002); Wang (2002).

Figure 3.1b   **Total Revenues (RMB): Individual/Household Businesses and Private Enterprises**

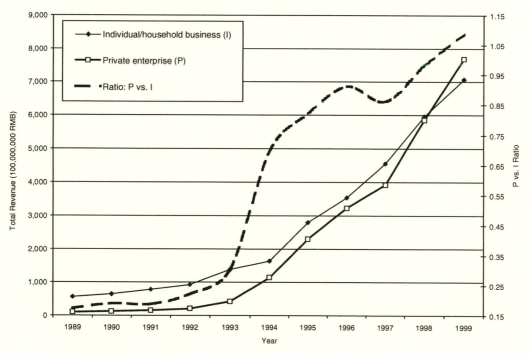
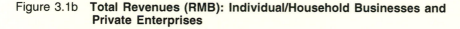

Source: Lan (2002); Wang (2002).

nesses (Qian 2000). Later, to solve unemployment problems, the government also encouraged urban residents to start individual/household businesses to create jobs on their own (Gold 1991). As Figures 3.2a and 3.2b show, rural individual/household businesses were developed long before their urban counterparts. While rural individual/household businesses continued to outnumber their urban counterparts in both quantity and employment size from 1989 to 1999, the gap has narrowed over time, particularly after 1992.

With the expansion of the private sector, Chinese workers have been afforded new market opportunities to achieve upward socioeconomic mobility (Sabin 1994). As entry into the private sector has served as an important mechanism through which the macro level institutional transition affects the change in income distribution among individuals, a close examination of the path to private businesses—namely, a close look at the backgrounds of those involved in private businesses—would be of particular interest to sociologists concerned with the social consequences of China's transition to a market economy.

In this chapter, I focus on two issues: (1) the path to family businesses—that is, what characteristics/backgrounds determine a family's entry into private economic activities—and (2) the performance of family businesses. I use the term "family business" to refer mainly to individual/household businesses employing fewer than eight workers, but also to refer to some small private enterprises whose operations resemble those of individual/household businesses but that are registered under a different category, according to Chinese laws (Entwisle et al. 1995). Both of these types of small businesses are run predominantly by family units, which have regained their economic functions since the reform (Entwisle et al. 2000).

Using data from the national survey *Life Histories and Social Change in Contemporary China* (Treiman and Walder 1996), I examine how the pattern of entry into family businesses varies between urban and rural areas and at different reform stages, and demonstrate how the divergent patterns of entry affect the economic performance of the family businesses. In the sections that follow, I first explain how the rise of private business has changed the opportunity structures faced by different Chinese families and derive several testable hypotheses, based on family characteristics, predicting the likelihood of business involvement in both urban and rural areas. I then describe the data and variables used for the analysis. I analyze 1996 cross-sectional data to test the hypotheses regarding rural–urban differences and use event-history data from 1978 to 1996 to examine the temporal trend of private business involvement. Finally, I examine how different paths of entry affect the performance of family businesses.

MARKET TRANSITION AND ENTRY INTO FAMILY BUSINESSES

In the transition from redistributive economies to market economies in former state socialist countries, private entrepreneurship has offered an alternative avenue of social mobility. As Nee (1996, 910) put it, "Whereas opportunities for advancement were previously centered on decisions made by redistributive bureaucracy and within the economy controlled by it, markets open up alternative avenues for mobility through emergent entrepreneurship and labor markets." With regard to its impact on social stratification, in such a dual structure of opportunities, "One could climb the rank order of the bureaucratic hierarchy, or one could try the market" (Szelényi 1988, 65).

A critical question up for debate is who has benefited more from the newly emergent market opportunities. Some scholars suggest that the main groups involved in private businesses are from the lower tiers of the social hierarchy. In his early study of Hungarian rural entrepreneurship, Szelényi (1988) demonstrated that cadres were less likely to participate in market-oriented businesses and that new economic elites were more likely to emerge from *less*-privileged groups.

Figure 3.2a   **Number of Individual/Household Businesses in Urban and Rural China**

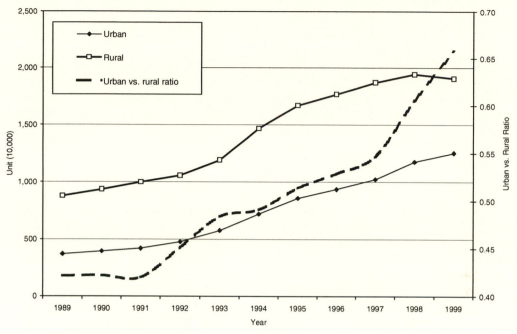

Source: Lan (2002); Wang (2002).

Figure 3.2b   **Total Employment of Individual/Household Businesses in Urban and Rural China**

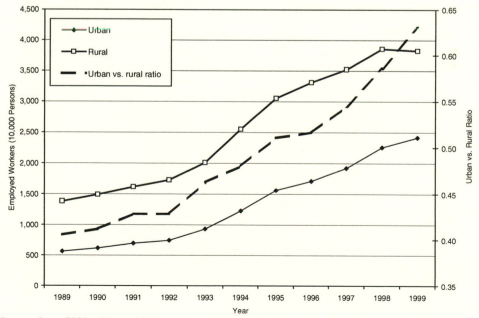

Source: Lan (2002); Wang (2002).

Drawing on survey data collected in rural Fujian Province, Nee (1989a) claimed that cadres in China had little or no net advantages in entering into private entrepreneurship; instead, direct producers (i.e., ordinary peasants and workers) with more human capital benefited from the market, and what they gained would undermine the privileges of the Communist cadres (Cao and Nee 2000; Nee 1989a, 1996).

Contrary to Nee's market transition theory (1989a), analyses of income distribution in China and other former state-socialist countries have reported that, as "marketization" proceeded, the advantages of redistributive power still persisted, and returns to human capital did not increase (e.g., Bian and Logan 1996, Gerber and Hout 1998, Parish and Michelson 1996, Xie and Hannum 1996). Róna-Tas (1994) found that, after the collapse of the Communist regime, former Hungarian cadres were able to maintain their advantages by successfully converting themselves into corporate entrepreneurs. Accordingly, his "power conversion" thesis argues that the growth of a private sector will actually enhance, rather than undermine, cadres' socioeconomic advantages.

Central to this scholarly debate is the fate of the Communist cadre elites—namely, how they fare compared to other social groups during eras of reform (Szelényi and Kostello 1996, Walder 1996). To look for answers, researchers need to direct their attention to the question of how different social groups (including cadres) respond to the expansion of the private sector. In other words, who has entered the private business sector? This dynamic process depends on specific institutional contexts. For example, the conversion of cadres to entrepreneurs may occur under certain circumstances (Róna-Tas 1994, 47), whereas the entry of less privileged groups described by Szelényi (1988) and Nee (1989b) could also occur under different circumstances. Wu and Xie (2003) pointed out that entrants into the market sector during different reform stages are likely to differ on human capital, political capital, and other observable and unobservable characteristics. The crucial mediating factor is the change in the opportunity structures faced by different social groups in the transitional labor markets.

Szelényi and Kostello (1996) provided a comprehensive picture of market transition and of the major players in the process. They identified three types of market penetration: local markets in redistributively integrated economies, socialist mixed economies, and capitalist-oriented economies. They argued that the major social actors in a market are fluid and dependent upon the specific type of market penetration. In the first type of market penetration—in which the market remains marginal to the entire economic system—most people involved in private business activities come from the lower tiers of the social hierarchy, as participation in the market is highly risky and requires little skill. In socialist mixed economies, private economic activities become legal and market competition plays a greater role in economic operations, resulting in a dual system of inequality. More qualified people start entering the market, pushing aside or even wiping out some of its early pioneers. In capitalist-oriented economies, when the market arises as the primary source of inequalities, those reliant on the redistributive mechanism completely lose their advantage, but a fraction of them may still manage to convert their old privileges into new ones. Hence, who wins and who loses depends upon the concrete institutional arrangements within which workers respond differently to market opportunities.

Unlike Szelényi and Kostello (1996), Walder (2003) proposed a theory of elite opportunity, focusing on how market reforms have injected new value into public properties and thereby created differential opportunities for elite insiders. He argued that advantaged groups in the redistributive sector need not become directly involved in private businesses. Instead, they may remain in the state sector and manage to appropriate public assets into their own pockets (Ding 2000a, b). Whether they are able to do so depends on the extent of regime change and legal barriers. Because the combinations of these two institutional circumstances vary from country to country and from time to time, market transition has no generic implications for changes in elite advantage in a postsocialist era.

Both Szelényi and Kostello (1996) and Walder (2003) emphasized the importance of changing opportunity structures for understanding the diverse stratification outcomes in postsocialist transitions. While each of these studies has captured one aspect of the transition process, the overall structure of opportunity faced by individual workers is defined simultaneously by both the transforming public sector and the expanding private sector. The large-scale changes in opportunity structures driven by institutional transition are reflected not only within the public sector or the private sector, but also in the relative strengths of the two sectors. Hence, to understand Chinese workers' different responses to private economic activities, we need to pay close attention to the overall opportunity structure they encounter. Individuals and their families make choices and decisions in adjusting themselves to changing political and economic environments, and their actions consequently reshape the order of social stratification in the postsocialist era.

Market transition in China's urban and rural areas started with different preexisting institutional legacies and then followed different paths. Under the household registration *(hukou)* system implemented in 1955 and still in place today, all Chinese citizens had to be registered in a place and categorized as having rural or urban status (Chan and Zhang 1999, 821–22). In the prereform era, rural residents—the majority of the national population—were prohibited from moving to cities without government approval and were entitled to a few rights and benefits (e.g., permanent employment, medical insurance, and pensions), all of which the socialist state also conferred on urban residents (Wu and Treiman 2004). Without an urban *hukou* status, even most cadres at the village and township level were not part of the state bureaucratic system, and thus were not as privileged as ordinary urban workers. In the reform era, despite the fact that geographic mobility and employment change became easier, the social concomitants of *hukou* status persisted. For instance, rural migrant workers in cities were still classified as "peasant workers" and discriminated against in the urban labor market (Wang, Zuo, and Ruan 2002).

Therefore, whereas the emergence of the private sector opened up a new window of opportunity, the social implications were different for rural and urban residents. Soon after the rural reform started, the collective farming system was sweepingly dismantled (Oi 1999), but the urban redistributive sector continued to exist and still exists to date (though it has shrunk substantially). Consequently, in rural areas private entrepreneurship provided a major avenue of mobility for those deprived of socioeconomic opportunities under socialism (Entwisle et al. 1995). Making money was the only way for rural householders/residents (including cadres) to reduce their disadvantages. In urban areas, a dual opportunity structure gradually evolved in the labor market. With the state still remaining the predominant employer—providing social security, fringe benefits, and political advancement—the private sector offers only an alternative (though an increasingly attractive) path to social mobility (Davis 1999).

HYPOTHESES

Given the different opportunity structures they faced, rural and urban families engaged in private businesses may have had different social backgrounds. Indeed, early studies reported that rural entrepreneurs were mainly from production team cadres, urban youth sent to work who stayed in the countryside, urbanites who returned to their villages, and discharged soldiers. These individuals possessed more human or political capital than the general rural population (Nee 1989b). In urban areas, according to several small surveys conducted in the mid 1980s, most urban family businesses were owned by members of marginal social groups—that is, migrant peasants, unemployed youth, dismissed employees, and retirees—who had little to lose and more to gain by entering into private businesses (Gold 1991; Young 1995, 37).

Therefore, I expected to find different patterns of entry into family businesses in urban and rural areas. *Urban families engaged in private businesses were more likely to come from disadvantaged backgrounds, whereas rural families engaged in private businesses were more likely to come from relatively advantaged backgrounds.*

I defined a family's advantage/disadvantage mainly in terms of its possession of human capital (education) and political capital (cadre status).[1] In urban areas, both educated people and cadres had other opportunities in professional or political careers (Walder, Li, and Treiman 2000); however, this was not the case in rural areas. Rural people's career opportunities were much more limited, unless they officially moved into cities and had their *hukou* status changed through a highly selective process (Wu and Treiman 2004). Those who stayed in rural areas (even as village cadres or managers in rural enterprises) were not as privileged as their urban counterparts, thereby increasing their motivation to venture into private businesses. Therefore, education and cadre status played different roles in families' private business involvement in urban and rural areas. Specifically, I tested the following two hypotheses:

Hypothesis 1. Families with higher education are less likely to engage in private businesses in urban areas, but they are more likely to do so in rural areas.

Hypothesis 2. Cadre families are less likely to engage in private businesses than noncadre families in urban areas, but they are more likely to do so in rural areas.

Family class background plays an important role in private business involvement. In the sociological literature, scholars argue that an entrepreneurial spirit can be inherited. For instance, Szelényi (1988) found that in rural Hungary, people from pre-Communist entrepreneurial families were more likely to start family businesses when economic reform started. In the recruitment of new economic elites in post-1989 Eastern Europe and Russia, "reproduction" rather than "circulation" dominated the process (Szelényi and Szelényi 1995). Similarly, during the first thirty years of the People's Republic of China, such an *embourgeoisement* process was also interrupted by the implementation of state socialism. As the "interruption" was more complete in full-fledged socialist urban than in rural China, family entrepreneurial history may have played different roles in the revival of the private sector in the two settings: social reproduction of new economic elites may be more prominent in rural areas than in urban areas. Hence,

Hypothesis 3. Families' business activities before 1949 may not help them engage in private businesses in urban areas, but may help them do so in rural areas.

Entry into family businesses is a dynamic process associated with China's economic transition. Opportunity structures not only differed between urban and rural labor markets, but also changed over the stages of reform. When the private economy was seen as merely peripheral to the redistributive economy, people involved in private economic activities mainly came from socially marginal groups that had little to lose. However, as the market gained legitimacy and came to play a greater role in economic operations, not only were market opportunities expanded substantially, but also people's perceptions of the private sector were significantly altered. Thus, I propose:

Hypothesis 4. The rate of entry into family businesses has increased over time in both urban and rural China.

With the expansion of market opportunities and the decline of political risks, growing numbers of capable people gave up on their career opportunities within the redistributive sector, "jumping into the sea" *(xia hai)* of private entrepreneurship (Wu and Xie 2003). Consequently, the social profile of families involved in private businesses has changed. For instance, research conducted by the Chinese Academy of Social Science reported that former cadres accounted for 11 percent of private entrepreneurs in 1997, 14.4 percent in 2000, and 15.3 percent in 2002 (Lu 2004, 253).

Since a large body of sociological literature has been devoted to the debate on whether (former) Communist cadres have benefited from market transition and become winners, I propose a specific hypothesis in regard to cadres:

Hypothesis 5. Cadre families are more likely to be engaged in private businesses over time in both urban and rural areas.

Hypotheses 1 and 2 suggest that the patterns of entry into family businesses differ diametrically between urban and rural areas, because the dual opportunity structure exists only in urban areas, deterring urban families with more human and political capital from involvement in private businesses. Hypothesis 3 implies that class backgrounds also play different roles in determining entry into family businesses in urban and rural areas.

Despite their differences, urban and rural transitions in China share some similarities. With market-oriented reforms proceeding further, the urban duality of opportunity has shifted more toward the private sector. As Hypotheses 4 and 5 suggest, more family businesses have emerged, and cadre families have been particularly active in seeking new entrepreneurial opportunities. Although urban cadre families are still less likely to be engaged in private businesses, they become more likely to do so over time. Urban and rural patterns of entry into family businesses may eventually converge.

Data and Variables

The hypotheses posed above were tested with data from a survey entitled *Life Histories and Social Change in Contemporary China* (Treiman and Walder 1996), a multistage, stratified national probability sample of 6,090 adults ages 20 to 69, from all regions of China (except Tibet). Samples from urban and rural areas were drawn separately, yielding 3,087 urban cases and 3,003 rural cases (Treiman 1998, Appendix D). The questionnaires included many questions about the respondents' families; thus, each individual can be treated as representing a family. The unit of analysis used in this research is households/families, rather than individuals.

I investigated the process of entry into family businesses in both urban and rural China during the period 1978–96. The dependent variable was based on the following question: "Do you or your family earn income from any nonagricultural business (for example, handicrafts, manufacturing, transport, a restaurant, or a store)?" The responses were: 1, "yes," 0, "no."

Loosely defined, family businesses include quite diverse economic activities, ranging from street peddling to running a factory. Family businesses can be categorized into three types: single-person businesses without employees, businesses with other family members, and businesses with nonfamily employees. As the upper panel of Table 3.1 shows, nationwide 21.3 percent of Chinese families are involved in private businesses; 9.0 percent of families have an individual in a single-person business; 8.7 percent have businesses that hire other family members; and only 3.6 percent have businesses that hire nonfamily members. Although the population survey dem-

Table 3.1

Summary Statistics for Variables in the Logit Models on Entry into Nonagricultural Family Businesses in Urban and Rural China, 1996[a]

	Overall			Family with sideline business	
	National	Urban	Rural	Urban	Rural
Dependent variables					
Family sideline business (%)	21.25	21.27	21.22	—	—
Without employees	8.98	7.82	10.81	36.77	50.94
With family employees only	8.68	9.18	7.51	43.16	35.39
With other employees	3.60	4.27	2.90	20.08	13.67
Income from family business (RMB)	—	—	—	18,657 (98,986)	8,125 (20,873)
Income from family business (logged)	—	—	—	8.74 (1.15)	8.20 (1.19)
Entry after 1991 (1 = "yes")				27.57	26.41
Independent variables					
Mean years of schooling	4.05 (2.12)	5.00 (2.35)	3.07 (1.68)	4.67 (2.01)	3.54 (1.52)
Cadre family (%)	12.82	22.09	3.34	11.35	5.82
Pre-1949 family business (%)	39.07	33.83	44.43	32.36	47.80
Mean age	45.69 (7.88)	46.40 (8.10)	44.94 (7.58)	44.19 (6.98)	43.44 (6.44)
Number of children under age 18	0.78 (0.92)	0.58 (0.72)	0.99 (1.04)	0.77 (0.86)	1.08 (1.03)
Number of cases	6,061	3,065	2,996	652	636

[a]The figures in parentheses are standard deviations for the continuous variables.

onstrates that most Chinese private businesses are quite small,[2] urban and rural areas differ slightly in the types of family businesses they contain: more urban private businesses than rural private businesses hire nonfamily employees (20.08 percent vs. 13.67 percent); and only about a third of urban private businesses are run by single persons, whereas this type of private business accounts for more than half of all private businesses in rural areas. Moreover, in terms of net business income in 1995, urban families earned 18,657 RMB, on average, while rural families earned less than half of that (8,125 RMB).

The year of entry into family business, reported in the survey, was recoded as a dummy variable representing reform stage, as opportunity structures with regard to the development of the private economy changed significantly over time. The period 1978–91 marked the first reform

Figure 3.3   **Rate of Entry into Family Business: Urban and Rural China, 1978–96**

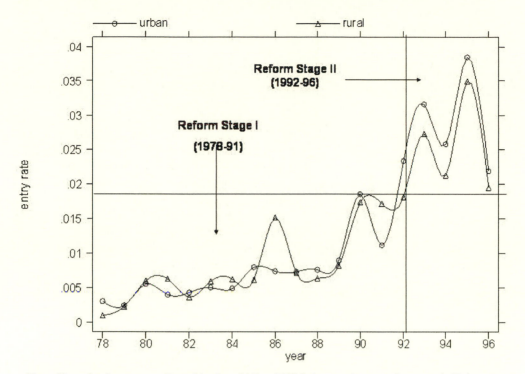

Note: Since the data were collected in the middle of 1996, that year's rate only covers half the year.

stage, during which the private sector emerged as a marginal element of the redistributive economy. Since 1992, substantial expansion of the private economy has prompted a new wave of private business start-ups *(xiahai),* as the growth trend shown in Figures 3.1a, 3.1b, 3.2a, and 3.2b indicates. Table 3.1 shows that 27.52 percent of urban private businesses and 26.41 percent of rural private businesses were started during the period 1992–96. Figure 3.3, which is based on the survey data, plots the annual rate of entry into private business during 1978–96 in urban and rural China: prior to 1992, the annual entry rate remained around 1 percent of all families for most years; from 1992 on, the entry rate jumped to 2–4 percent per year.

Independent variables measuring family characteristics in the following analyses included: the mean years of schooling and the mean age of all adult family members (20–69) living in a household; whether it was a cadre family (1, "yes," and 0, otherwise); whether the respondent's parents or grandparents owned any family business before 1949 (1, "yes," and 0, otherwise); and the number of family members under age 18.

The mean number of years of education, a continuous variable calculated from all adult family members' number of years of schooling, measured the human capital a family possessed. Whether a family had a cadre member captured both the political and the social capital necessary for starting a private business. Here, cadre status was coded slightly differently for the urban and rural samples. For the urban sample, I coded as "cadre" those who reported that they or a family member had held occupations such as "middle-rank manager/administrator" or "high-rank manager/administrator," as well as those who reported that they or another family member had held a position at the rank of section chief *(gu ji)*; rural cadres included both township cadres and village cadres, ranks that the respondents directly reported. A family with at least one cadre member was coded as a cadre family.

Family class background was defined on the basis of a respondent's parents' or grandparents' economic activities prior to 1949, when the Communists seized power. I used a dummy variable set equal to 1 for respondents whose parents/grandparents had owned land, hired someone to farm the land or rented the land to others, or owned a shop or other business prior to 1949, and set to 0 otherwise.

The remaining variables were standard family demographic characteristics, included in the analyses as controls. Mean family age was based on the information on all adult members. Although age is often used to approximate experience, it may not be favorable to involvement in private entrepreneurial activities, since starting a business requires more risk-taking spirit than accumulated experience. Instead, older people may be more risk-averse (Gerber 2002b). Meanwhile, to capture family age structure, I included another variable, the number of children under age 18, in the model. The lower panel of Table 3.1 shows the descriptive statistics for all the independent variables mentioned above.

I first tested the hypotheses regarding the urban–rural differences in entry into family businesses, using the cross-sectional 1996 data, and then examined how the pattern changed over the two reform stages in both urban and rural areas, using the event-history data for the period 1978–96. Finally, I examined how the pattern of entry into family businesses affected net income.

Because the samples are clustered within 100 city districts/counties (see details in Treiman 1998), an adjustment on standard errors was needed in logit models, hazard models, and linear selection models. All the models reported were estimated using Stata 8.0 (Stata Corp. 2001), with robust standard errors to correct the clustering on sampling units (districts/counties).

RESULTS

Cross-Sectional Analysis

I estimated binary logit models on whether a family was engaged in a private business in 1996, separating the urban and rural samples. The results in Table 3.2 show diametrically opposed patterns. First, although the effect of education on the likelihood of entry is significant both in urban and in rural areas, the directions of the coefficients are opposite one another. In urban areas, families with higher levels of education are less likely to be involved in private businesses. One year of schooling decreases the odds of entry by 11 percent (= $e^{-0.12}-1$, $p < .001$), if all other variables are held constant. In rural areas, in contrast, families with higher education are more likely to start private businesses: One year of schooling increases the net odds of business start-up by 19 percent ($e^{0.17}-1$, $p < .001$). Family members with high education levels have various career options in urban areas, such as employment as professionals or managers in large organizations, or as officials in government agencies. Such career options may "pull" them away from private businesses. Rural people with relatively high education levels have few alternatives (if they are unable to move into cities), and private businesses provide them with an important path to socioeconomic mobility. Hence, the evidence lends support to Hypothesis 1.

Second, the effects of a cadre in the family on the likelihood of entry into private business are also in opposition for urban and rural areas. In urban areas, cadre families are significantly less likely to start private businesses than are noncadre families. The net odds of doing so for cadre families are only 52 percent (= $e^{-0.73}-1$) of the odds for noncadre families, with all else held

Table 3.2

Coefficient Estimates for Binary Logit Model on Entry into Nonagricultural Family Businesses in Urban and Rural China, 1996

Variables	Urban	Rural
Family mean years of schooling	−0.12***	0.17***
	(0.03)	(0.03)
Cadre family (1 = "yes")	−0.73***	0.71**
	(0.16)	(0.24)
Family business before 1949 (1 = "yes")	−0.03	0.17*
	(0.12)	(0.08)
Mean age	−0.06***	−0.03***
	(0.01)	(0.01)
Children under age 18	0.35***	0.13**
	(0.08)	(0.06)
Constant	1.66***	−0.99**
	(0.40)	(0.36)
2 log likelihood	−2,984	−3,001
Number of cases	3,065	2,996

[a]Figures in parentheses are robust standard errors adjusted for clustering on principal sampling units (districts/counties).

*p < 0.05; **p < 0.01; ***p < 0.001; two-tailed tests.

constant ($p < .001$). In rural areas, the scenario is different; indeed, cadre families are significantly more likely than noncadre families to get involved in private businesses. The net odds for the former are more than double ($= e^{0.71}$) the odds for the latter ($p < .001$). The difference is understandable in view of the different opportunity structures that cadre families face in urban and rural areas. Thus, Hypothesis 2 is supported.

Third, class background also plays different roles in the two types of settings in driving a family's entry into private businesses. In urban areas, the effect of family background is statistically insignificant. However, in rural areas, families that had engaged in any business prior to 1949 were more likely to return to it following thirty years in the socialist collective-farming system. The net odds of starting a family private business after 1978 for those families with businesses prior to the People's Republic increased by 19 percent ($= e^{0.17}-1$) over the odds for those without this experience ($p < .001$). The finding on the intergenerational reproduction of private entrepreneurs in rural areas is a bit surprising, since the "normal" mechanisms of inheritance of capital and land had been blocked for three decades under socialism. Drawing on similar findings in rural Hungary, Szelényi (1988) proposed a Weberian explanation of the social origins of entrepreneurship: that cultural capital—the values and skills related to entrepreneurship—can be transferred across generations. Such values and skills remained relatively intact in rural China but were largely destroyed in the full-fledged socialist programs of urban China.

The effects of mean family age and number of children under 18, included in the models as standard demographic variables, were similar in both urban and rural areas: mean age is negatively associated with the likelihood of entry into private business, suggesting that families with older members are more risk-averse, as they may have invested in skills specific to socialist redistributive economies. A one-year increase in mean age reduces the net odds of engaging in private entrepreneurship by 6 percent (= $e^{-0.06}-1$) in urban areas and by 3 percent (= $e^{-0.03}-1$) in rural China.

The number of children under age 18 has a positive effect on family business involvement. For urban families, one additional child increases the net odds of getting involved in family private business by 42 percent (= $e^{0.35}-1$, $p < .001$); for rural families, it increases the net odds by 14 percent (= $e^{0.13}-1$, $p < .01$). The presence of young children may affect the likelihood of a family's business involvement in two ways: on the one hand, young children require substantial supervision (especially time), thus discouraging families from running a small business; on the other hand, the presence of young children demands more economic resources, thus pushing Chinese families into private businesses in order to earn money for their children's future (see also Short and Fengying 1996). The 1996 survey data support the latter proposition and are consistent with previous findings by other scholars (e.g., Entwisle et al. 1995).

Table 3.3 further illustrates the effects of education and cadre status on entry into different types of family businesses, presenting the results of multinomial logistic regression analyses of three types of entry: a single-person business without employees, a business with family employees only, and a business with both family employees and other, nonfamily, employees. The comparison group is families not involved in any type of private business. The first three columns of the table show that, although education deters entry into family businesses without employees or with family employees only in urban China, it has no significant effect on entry into private businesses with nonfamily employees—indeed, the coefficient becomes positive. An additional year of education significantly reduces the net odds of entering into a single-person business by 13 percent (= $e^{-0.14}-1$), and the net odds of entering into a business with family employees by 16 percent (= $e^{-0.17}-1$), but it increases the net odds of entering businesses with nonfamily employees by 1 percent (= $e^{0.01}-1$). Similarly, while urban cadre families are significantly less likely to start private businesses of either of the first two types, they do not show a significant difference from noncadre families in the likelihood of entry into private businesses with nonfamily employees. For cadre families, the odds of entering private businesses without employees are only about 50 percent (= $e^{-0.70}$) of those for noncadre families, with other factors held constant ($p < .01$); for cadre families, the net odds of entry into private businesses with family employees are only about 36 percent (= $e^{-1.03}$) of those for noncadre families ($p < .01$). As to entry into businesses with nonfamily employees, the corresponding figure is 71 percent (= $e^{-0.34}$).

In rural areas, education facilitates entry into all three types of family business. An additional year of education significantly increases the net odds of entering a single-person business by 22 percent (= $e^{0.20}-1$); a family-member-only business, by 14 percent (= $e^{0.13}-1$); and a business with nonfamily employees, by 22 percent (= $e^{0.20}-1$). Cadre families' advantages over noncadre families in entry into private businesses with nonfamily employees are particularly prominent. With other variables controlled, the odds of cadre families going into the third type of business are 4.9 times (= $e^{1.58}$) the odds for a noncadre family ($p < .001$). In comparison, the net odds of cadre families getting into single-person businesses are 1.7 times (= $e^{0.52}$) the odds for noncadre families ($p < .001$); the odds of cadre families going into businesses with family employees are 1.6 times (= $e^{0.46}$) the odds for noncadre families.

Figures 3.4a and 3.4b plot the effects of education on the probabilities of entry into the three types of family businesses in both urban and rural areas, setting the remaining variables at their respective sample means. Although the patterns of entry into private businesses without employ-

Table 3.3

Coefficient Estimates for Multinomial Logit Models of Entry into Different Types of Nonagricultural Family Business in Urban and Rural China, 1996[a]

	Urban			Rural		
	Without employee	With family employees only	With nonfamily employees	Without employee	With family employees only	With nonfamily employees
Mean years of schooling	-0.14*** (0.01)	-0.17*** (0.04)	0.01 (0.05)	0.20*** (0.04)	0.13* (0.05)	0.20** (0.07)
Cadre family	-0.70** (0.23)	-1.03*** (0.22)	-0.34 (0.30)	0.52* (0.23)	0.46 (0.50)	1.58*** (0.43)
Family business before 1949	-0.16 (0.17)	0.16 (0.18)	-0.24 (0.18)	0.04 (0.11)	0.31* (0.12)	0.26 (0.24)
Mean age	-0.04*** (0.01)	-0.08*** (0.01)	-0.04* (0.02)	-0.02* (0.01)	-0.04*** (0.01)	-0.02 (0.02)
Number of children under 18	0.35*** (0.10)	0.36** (0.12)	0.37** (0.12)	0.05 (0.05)	0.14† (0.08)	0.35** (0.12)
Constant	-0.15 (0.51)	2.04*** (0.49)	-1.17 (0.81)	-1.80*** (0.45)	-1.52*** (0.48)	-3.88*** (0.93)
-2 log likelihood	4,313			4,233		

[a]The comparison group is a family without any sideline business. The figures in the parentheses are standard errors adjusted for clustering on principal sampling units (districts/counties).

†p < 0.10; *p < 0.05; **p < 0.01; ***p < 0.001; two-tailed tests.

Figure 3.4a   **Determination of Education on Entry into Three Types of Private Businesses in Urban China**

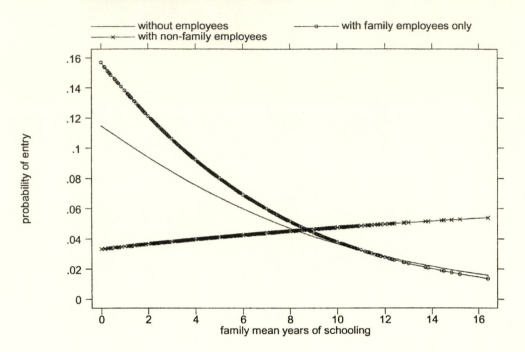

Figure 3.4b   **The Determination of Education on Entry into Three Types of Private Businesses in Rural China**

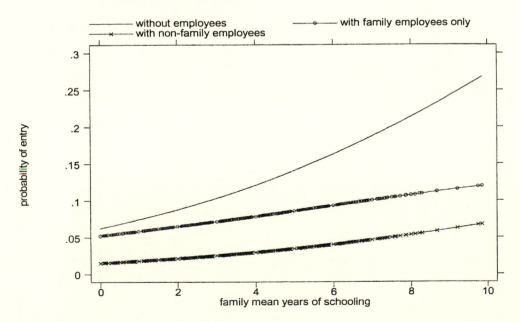

Figure 3.5   **Adjusted Odds Ratios Between Cadre Families and Noncadre Families on Entry into Different Types of Businesses in Urban and Rural China**

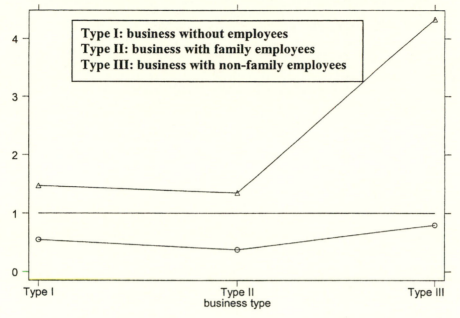

Type I: business without employees
Type II: business with family employees
Type III: business with non-family employees

Note: The other variables are set to the values of their respective sample mean in calculating the odds ratios. When the odds ratio is 1, it indicates that cadre families and noncadre families are equally likely to be involved in a business.

ees are completely different from those for businesses with family employees, the relationship between education and entry into businesses with nonfamily employees is to some extent similar for urban and rural China. Figure 3.5 plots the adjusted odds ratios between cadre families and noncadre families on entry into the different types of private business. Again, the odds ratio of entry into businesses with nonfamily employees is highest in both urban and rural areas, suggesting that among those involved in private businesses, cadre families are the most likely to get involved in enterprises with nonfamily employees.

Among the three types of businesses, the type with family employees only is closest to the ideal type of "family business." The inheritance of cultural capital works better in this type than in the others. Indeed, the family inheritance of entrepreneurship previously observed in rural areas (Table 3.2) is found only for this type of business ($p < .05$). Interestingly, even in urban areas, family background has a positive—though insignificant—effect on involvement in a private business with family employees only (for the other two types, the coefficients are negative and statistically insignificant).

With respect to the effects of the two demographic variables, mean family age has a negative and significant effect, and the number of children under 18 has a positive and significant effect on the likelihood of involvement in all three types of private business in urban areas. In rural areas, the effects of the two demographic variables vary with the type of enterprise a family is involved in: mean family age has no significant effect on the likelihood of involvement in businesses with nonfamily employees; the positive effect of the number of children under age 18 is not applicable to entry into the single-person businesses. Since I did not have any substantive research hypotheses regarding these demographic variables, examination of the difference found here is left for future research.

To summarize, the results shown in Table 3.2 present two quite different patterns of entry into private businesses in urban and rural areas, and they confirm the hypotheses regarding the effects of education, cadre status, and family class background. Generally, families of higher socioeconomic status—that is, those with less human capital and political influence—are less likely to get involved in private economic activities. Family entrepreneurial history prior to 1949 helped people start family businesses in the reform era. In contrast, in rural areas, where few alternative opportunities were available, families of advantaged status and entrepreneurial skill were more likely to seize entrepreneurial opportunities. The multinomial logistic regression results shown in Table 3.3 further clarify this urban–rural difference in that the effects of human capital or political influence on entry into businesses that hire nonfamily employees seem smaller than those on entry into single-person or family-employees-only businesses. Class reproduction of entrepreneurship in rural areas is found only for families involved in enterprises with family employees.

Event-History Analysis

As cross-sectional analyses cannot address temporal variations in patterns of entry into family businesses, I employed discrete hazard models in event-history analysis to examine how the entry patterns changed over time. A discrete hazard model involves a shift of the unit of analysis from respondent to event (i.e., entry into private business) at a specific time (i.e., a year). In this case, all families without nonagricultural sideline businesses were considered "at risk" of entry into private business in each year starting from 1978. Those who had not gone into business by 1996 were "right-censored." After restructuring the data, I could fit a discrete-time hazard model using conventional procedures for estimating binary logit models (Allison 1982). The dependent variable was entry into a sideline business in a specific year during the period 1978–96.

The effect of timing and cadre status are the focus of the models testing Hypotheses 4 and 5. Mean education, involvement in family business before 1949, mean age, and number of children under 18 remain in the model. To gauge temporal variations of entry rate, I coded the timing of entry into two periods (1978–91 and 1992–96) that reflect significant changes in opportunity structures with regard to the development of the private sector. This coding is included as a dummy variable in model 1 for the urban sample, and in model 3 for the rural sample.

The results shown in Table 3.4 are consistent with those found in the cross-sectional analysis and presented in Table 3.2. In urban areas, both education and cadre status deter families from entering into private business: A one-year increase in education reduces the odds of entry by 7 percent (= $e^{-0.07}-1$), with other variables held constant ($p < .05$). The net odds of entry into private businesses for cadre families are only 48 percent (= $e^{-0.73}$) of those for noncadre families ($p < .001$). In rural areas, the effect of education is positive and statistically significant: One year of schooling increases the net odds by 20 percent (= $e^{0.18}-1$) ($p < .001$), and the net odds of entry into private businesses for cadre families are only 59 percent (= $e^{0.46}-1$) higher than those of noncadre families ($p < .001$). The event-history analysis thus also confirms Hypotheses 1 and 2.

The hazard rate of involvement in family businesses increases with economic reform. In urban China, the net odds of involvement increased by more than three times (= $e^{1.41}-1$) between the first stage of reform (1978–91) and the second stage (1992–96) ($p < .001$). In rural areas, the net odds also increased, by more than twice (= $e^{1.1}-1$) ($p < .001$). This temporal pattern is consistent with the pattern plotted in Figure 3.3 and based on descriptive statistics. Hence, Hypothesis 4 is supported here.

To test the hypotheses concerning how the effect of cadre status on business involvement changes over time, I ran models with interactions between cadre status and reform stage sepa-

Table 3.4

Coefficient Estimates for Discrete-Time Hazard Models on Entry into Nonagricultural Family Businesses: Urban and Rural China, 1978–96

	Urban		Rural	
	Model 1	Model 2	Model 3	Model 4
Mean years of schooling	−0.07* (0.03)	−0.07* (0.03)	0.18*** (0.03)	0.18*** (0.03)
Cadre family	−0.73*** (0.152)	−1.13*** (0.24)	0.46** (0.17)	0.08 (0.23)
Family business before 1949	−0.03 (0.11)	−0.03 (0.11)	0.16* (0.07)	0.16* (0.07)
Mean age	−0.05*** (0.01)	−0.05*** (0.01)	−0.02* (0.01)	−0.02* (0.01)
Number of children under 18	0.26*** (0.07)	0.26*** (0.07)	0.09† (0.05)	0.08† (0.05)
Reform period I, 1978–91 (omitted)				
Reform period II, 1992–96	1.41*** (0.10)	1.34*** (0.11)	1.11*** (0.09)	1.08*** (0.09)
Interaction Reform II × cadre family	—	0.61† (0.34)	—	0.69* (0.31)
Constant	−2.30*** (0.35)	−2.26*** (0.35)	−4.52*** (0.32)	−4.50*** (0.32)
−2 log likelihood	6,095	6,090	6,085	6,082
Family-year at risk	47,137	48,035		

[a]Figures in parentheses are standard errors adjusted for clustering on districts/counties.
†p < .010; *p < .05; **p < .01; ***p < .001; two-tailed tests.

rately for the urban (model 2) and rural samples (model 4). Cadre families were more likely to enter private businesses in the second reform stage than in the first. In urban areas, the deterring effect of cadre status on entry into private business diminished in the second stage. In the first stage (1978–91), the odds of entry for cadre families were only 32 percent ($= e^{-1.13}$) of those for noncadre families; in the second stage, the odds for cadre families were 59 percent ($= e^{-1.13+0.61}$) of those for noncadre families, given controls for other variables. Statistical tests show that such a change is marginally significant ($p < .010$). In rural areas, I found a similar pattern: cadre families' advantages in private business involvement increased as the reforms proceeded. While the odds of entry into private business for cadre families were only 8 percent ($= e^{0.08}-1$) higher than those for noncadre families in the first stage (1978–91), the gap increased substantially in the second stage (1992–96), growing 1.2 times ($= e^{0.08+0.69}-1, p < .05$). Figure 3.6 plots the change in the effects of cadre status on entry into private business over the two reform stages.

Figure 3.6 **Adjusted Odds Ratios between Cadre Families and Noncadre Families on Entry into Businesses in Two Reform Stages in Urban and Rural China**

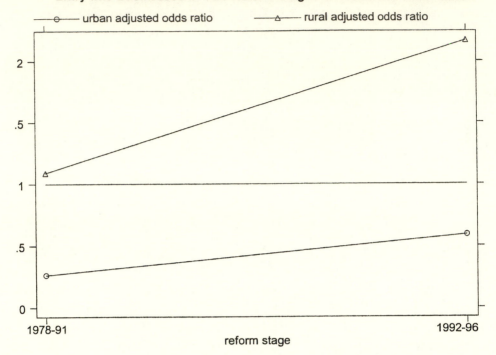

Note: The other variables are set to the values of their respective sample mean in calculating the odds ratios. When the odds ratio is 1, it indicates that cadre families and noncadre families are equally likely to be involved in a business.

To summarize, the event-history analysis reveals a somewhat similar pattern behind the divergence between urban and rural areas. As economic reform proceeded, both urban and rural Chinese families were more likely to get involved in private businesses. Cadre families were particularly more likely to take advantage of expanding opportunities as the private economy gained more legitimacy. While urban cadre families were less likely than noncadre families to be involved in private businesses during the first reform stage, they were increasingly more likely to do so in the second reform stage (1992–96). In rural China, cadre families enjoyed only a slight advantage over noncadre families in entrepreneurial activities prior to 1992, but the advantage has been significantly enhanced since then. The urban and rural patterns tend to approach a convergence.

Further Analysis: The Performance of Family Businesses

In urban China, cadre families are less likely to get involved in private business than noncadre families; but in rural China they are more likely to do so. How do the different paths of entry affect business performance in the market? In this section, I examine the performance of family businesses by taking into account the effect of selection into private businesses, which could have important implications for the fate of cadres and change in social stratification in the reform era.

In the survey, the respondents were asked, "How much net income did you or your family members receive from this business activity last year?" Those not involved in any business were censored on this question. I used this variable to measure business performance in relation to family income. On average, in 1995 urban family businesses received about 18,657 RMB, whereas rural family businesses received less than half that amount (8,125 RMB).

To account for the unobserved heterogeneity that may underlie both business entry and business income, I employed Heckman selection models to first deal with selection into family businesses from the full sample and then the determination of net business income among those with family businesses. Two equations were included in the selection model. The first is a standard probit model for the process of selection into family businesses, formulated as follows:

$$Z^* = \gamma'X_1 + u, \tag{1}$$

where Z^* is the latent variable for $z = 1$ (entry) if $Z^* > 0$, and $z = 0$ if $Z^* \leq 0$. Z^* is specified as a linear function of a set of explanatory variables X_1 plus a residual term u, which is assumed to follow a standard normal distribution ($u \sim N [0, 1]$).

The second equation is a linear function of business income determination:

$$\ln (Y) = \beta'X_2 + \varepsilon \qquad \text{observed only if } z = 1. \tag{2}$$

Equation 2 is restricted to families with private businesses. This equation could not be estimated via ordinary least squares (OLS) regression, since

$$E[\varepsilon \mid Y \text{ is observed}] = E[\varepsilon \mid z = 1] = E[\varepsilon \mid Z^* > 0] = E[\varepsilon \mid u > -\gamma'X] = 0$$

holds true only when the correlation (ρ) between the residual terms ε and u is equal to zero. OLS estimates are biased if the residual terms in the two equations are correlated.

Allowing for a potential correlation between the two residual terms (i.e., ρ is not equal to zero), one can estimate Equation 2 by adding to the OLS regression an additional predictor λ, calculated using the fitted values of Z^* from the estimation of the equation. The estimated coefficient for this term is equal to $\rho\sigma$, where ρ is the correlation between two residual terms u and ε, and σ is the standard deviation of ε (Greene, 2000; Winship and Mare 1992). Since σ is always positive, a negative correlation ($\rho < 0$) between the two residual terms would denote a negative selectivity: those families who entered private businesses had lower potential incomes than those who chose not to do so. In contrast, a positive correlation ($\rho > 0$) would suggest a positive selectivity.

To estimate the probit model of selection into family businesses, I included the variables used in cross-sectional and event-history analysis: family members' mean education, cadre status, parents'/grandparents' pre-1949 business ownership, mean family age, and number of children under age 18. For the income equation, I included three variables—family members' mean education, cadre status, and mean age—and focused on the effect of cadre status on business performance.

Table 3.5 presents the maximum likelihood estimation of coefficients for the two equations for both urban (models 1 and 2) and rural samples (models 3 and 4). Consistently with my cross-sectional and event-history findings, model 1 shows that both education and cadre status strongly deterred families from entering into private businesses in urban China; model 3 shows that the two factors facilitated entry into private businesses in rural China. Other things being equal, one year of schooling decreased the probit coefficient by 0.07 in urban China ($p < .001$) but increased it by 0.19 in rural China ($p < .001$); and cadre status decreased the probit coefficient by 0.39 in urban China ($p < .001$) but increased it by 0.35 in rural China ($p < .05$).

Table 3.5

Coefficient Estimates for Heckman Two-Stage Selection Models on Entry into Family Sideline Businesses and Profits in Urban and Rural China

	Model 1 (probit)	Model 2 (linear)	Model 3 (probit)	Model 4 (linear)
Mean years of schooling	−0.07*** (0.02)	0.11*** (0.02)	0.10*** (0.02)	0.06 (0.04)
Cadre family (1 = "yes")	−0.39*** (0.09)	0.48* (0.20)	0.35* (0.15)	0.17 (0.26)
Family business before 1948 (1 = "yes")	−0.03 (0.07)	— (0.05)	0.10*	—
Mean age	−0.03*** (0.00)	−0.01 (0.01)	−0.02*** (0.00)	0.01 (0.01)
Number of children under 18	0.23*** (0.04)	—	0.08* (0.04)	—
Constant	0.70** (0.25)	9.23*** (0.32)	−0.67** (0.22)	8.53*** (0.59)
Lamda (λ)	−0.57*** (0.13)	—	−0.45 (0.33)	—
Rho (ρ)	−0.47*** (0.08)	—	−0.37 (0.24)	—
N	3,065	—	2,996	—
Censored cases	2,483	—	2,416	—
Model χ^2	30.20		1.90	
df	3		3	

aFigures in parentheses are standard errors adjusted for clustering on districts/counties.
†p < 0.10; *p < 0.05; **p < 0.01; ***p < 0.001; two-tailed tests.

The significant coefficient for λ indicates that the OLS estimates for the income equation are biased for the urban sample. The estimated value of ρ (−0.47) for the urban sample indicates a strong negative selectivity (i.e., higher business income potential is associated with a lower likelihood of business entry). Models 2 and 4 of Table 3.5 present the unbiased estimates of OLS parameters in income equations for the urban and rural samples, respectively. In urban China, the net return to cadre status was significantly positive. After correcting the effect of negative selection, cadre families enjoyed a net income return of 62 percent (= $e^{0.48}-1$) higher than noncadre families, and the difference is statistically significant ($p < .05$). In the OLS regression (not reported here), the advantage enjoyed by cadre families is not only far lower (about 30 percent) but also statistically insignificant. Thus, the evidence indicates that urban families with observed characteristics (e.g., education and cadre status) and unobserved characteristics related to higher income potentials are less likely to get involved in private businesses. The effect of cadre status on business performance is underestimated, and so is the effect of education.[3] In rural areas the selection effect is insignificant, and the OLS regression results are not very biased.

A crucial point in the market transition debate pertains to the fate of cadres or former cadres in postsocialist stratification (Bian and Logan 1996, Nee 1989a, Róna-Tas 1994, Zhou 2000). Scholars have debated whether the stratification mechanism has been shifted from redistribution to markets, in view of evidence of the effect of political attributes (such as cadre status) on income. The example demonstrated here suggests that the market mechanism per se does not grant any advantage or disadvantage to cadre families (Gerber 2002a; Walder 2002, 2003; Wu and Xie 2003). The conversion of political advantage to economic advantage in the process of market transition essentially depends on the opportunity structures faced by different social groups and their route of access to market opportunities.

SUMMARY AND CONCLUSIONS

In this chapter I have examined patterns of entry into private businesses in urban and rural China and at different stages of reform, paying particular attention to cadre families' activity in the process of China's transition to a market economy. Results from urban and rural areas present almost diametrically opposed patterns: while both education and cadre status deter urban families' entry into private business, they promote rural families' entry (Hypotheses 1 and 2). Families engaged in private businesses before 1949 were more likely, during the reform era, to get involved in private businesses in rural areas (specifically, businesses with family employees only), but in urban China they were not more likely to get involved in business (Hypothesis 3). Furthermore, in terms of types of businesses entered, in both urban and rural areas families with more human capital and political influence were more likely to have businesses with nonfamily employees; these enterprises are presumably on larger scales and more formally structured than single-person and family-members-only businesses.

There is clear evidence that China's transition has afforded increasing entrepreneurial opportunities to its people in both urban and rural areas (Hypothesis 4), and particularly to cadres and their families (Hypothesis 5). In urban areas, although cadre families are still less likely to enter private businesses than noncadre families, they are increasingly more likely to do so over time. In rural areas, cadre families' advantages in seizing entrepreneurial opportunities were further enhanced during the late reform stage (1992–96).

Given the different opportunity structures and selection processes in urban and rural areas, families involved in private businesses may possess certain characteristics (observable or unobservable) that also pertain to their business performance. In urban areas, because families that are more likely to succeed in the market would have many other options and thus be less likely to get involved in private businesses, those who have done so actually earn less than they would have earned had there been no such selection effect. In rural areas, cadre families enjoy a substantial advantage in business earnings, which are likely to last for quite a long time as the reform proceeds.

Similar results have been reported in post-1989 Hungary and theorized as an ongoing process of "power conversion" in the postsocialist transition (Róna-Tas 1994). This chapter has demonstrated that the conversion process is conditioned upon the opportunity structures that the cadre elites and/or their families face. Whether certain social groups manage to maintain their advantage varies with different reform strategies and transition paths as well as with their responses. Those who can better situate themselves in a changing structure prevail, remaking themselves and regenerating a new social order.

The present analysis covers the period only up to the mid 1990s. Since the late 1990s, some fundamental changes have been underway in China's private sector. First, in the course of the property rights reform, many managers in the public sector (such as township and village enterprises) have legally converted themselves into private entrepreneurs (Oi 1999); cadres may illicitly strip state assets and set up their own enterprises (Ding 2000a, b). The entry of incorporated firms with limited liability into the private sector has been reshaping the social landscape of the Chinese private economy and possibly affecting the fate of Chinese family businesses. Second, as further reforms in state-owned enterprises have led to mass layoffs and rising unemployment, small-scale family businesses may provide "a refuge from poverty" rather than "a road to riches" (Hanley 2000). Lastly, once a family gets involved in a private business, whether it will grow bigger becomes even more problematic. As market competition has intensified, exits of private businesses have increased simultaneously with increases in entry rates.[4] Even though small family businesses can survive, they are most likely to stay small. Findings on these developments have been reported in postsocialist Eastern Europe (Hanley 2000, Róna-Tas 2002). Whether the development of Chinese private businesses will follow a similar trajectory and subsequently shape the process of class formation is a matter worth further exploration.

NOTES

The data collection was supported by grants from the National Science Foundation (SBR-9423453), the Luce Foundation, the Ford Foundation, and the University of California Pacific Rim Program. I thank Yanjie Bian and Tom Gold for helpful comments on an early draft.
    1. To be sure, as involvement in the private economy expands, strong social capital (strong connections to provide access to financial capital) is also an important requisite of success (Gold, Guthrie, and Wank 2002; Wank 1999). Here, I will not analyze the role of social capital in family business entry for two reasons. First, family cadre connections indeed capture a part of social capital that a family owns. Indeed, political capital can be seen as an institutionalized form of social capital (Eyal, Szelényi, and Townsley 1998). Second, there is no specific measure of social capital that is different from that of cadre connections in the survey data analyzed here.
    2. Among 1,288 reported family businesses, 42.2 percent have no employees; 51.5 percent employ one to seven workers, and only 5.3 percent employ eight or more workers. In other words, about 94.7 percent are categorized as individual/household businesses, and private enterprises account for only 5.3 percent of all family businesses.
    3. The net return to education is about 7.4 percent (the result is available upon request) lower than the return after correcting the selection effect (11.6 percent [$= e^{0.11}$] in model 2 of Table 3.5).
    4. The government statistical data show that, for private enterprises, the number of exits increased by 10.8 times, from 12,689 in 1993 to 136,407 in 1999, an increase of 5.1 percent to 8.3 percent within seven years (Lu 2004, 246). The 1996 survey data contain no information on private business exits.

REFERENCES

Allison, P. (1982). Discrete-time methods for the analysis of event histories. In S. Reinhardt (Ed.), *Sociological methodology*, pp. 61–98. San Francisco: Jossey-Bass.
Bian, Y., and J. Logan. (1996). Market transition and persistence of power: The changing stratification system in urban China. *American Sociological Review*, 61, 739–58.
Cao, Y., and V. Nee. (2000). Comment: Controversies and evidence in the market transition debate. *American Journal of Sociology*, 105, 1175–89.
Chan, K., and L. Zhang. (1999). The *hukou* system and rural-urban migration in China: Processes and changes. *China Quarterly*, 160, 818–55.
Davis, D. (1999). Self-employment in Shanghai: A research note. *China Quarterly*, 157, 22–43.
Ding, X. L. (2000a). Systematic irregularity and spontaneous property transformation in the Chinese financial system. *China Quarterly*, 163, 655–76.

———. (2000b). The illicit asset stripping of Chinese state firms. *China Journal*, 43, 1–28.

Entwisle, B.; G. E. Henderson; S. Short; and Z. Fengying. (1995). Gender and family businesses in rural China. *American Sociological Review*, 60, 36–57.

Entwisle, B.; S. Short; Z. Fengying; and M. Linmao. (2000). Household economies in transitional times. In B. Entwisle and G. E. Henderson (Eds.), *Re-drawing boundaries: Work, household, and gender in China*, pp. 261–83. Berkeley and Los Angeles: University of California Press.

Eyal, G.; I. Szelényi; and E. Townsley. (1998). *Making capitalism without capitalists: The new ruling elites in Eastern Europe*. London and New York: Verso.

Gerber, T. (2002a). Structural change and post-Socialist stratification: Labor market transitions in contemporary Russia. *American Sociological Review*, 67, 629–59.

———. (2002b). Joining the winners: Self-employment and stratification in post-Soviet Russia. In V. E. Bonnell and T. Gold (Eds.), *The new entrepreneurs of Europe and Asia: Patterns of business development in Russia, Eastern Europe, and China*, pp. 3–38. Armonk, NY: M.E. Sharpe.

Gerber, T., and M. Hout. (1998). More shock than therapy: Employment and income in Russia, 1991–1995. *American Journal of Sociology* 104, 1–50.

Gold, T. (1991). Urban private business and social change. In D. Davis and E. Vogel (Eds.), *Chinese society on the eve of Tiananmen: The impact of reform*, pp. 157–80. Cambridge, MA: Council on East Asian Studies, Harvard University.

Gold, T.; D. Guthrie; and D. Wank. (Eds.). (2002). *Social connections in China*. Cambridge, England: Cambridge University Press.

Greene, W. (2000). *Econometric analysis*. (4th ed.). Upper Saddle River, NJ: Prentice Hall.

Gregory, N.; S. Tenev; and D. Wagle. (2000). *China's emerging private enterprises*. Washington, DC: International Finance Corporation.

Hanley, E. (2000). Self-employment in post-Communist Eastern Europe: A refuge from poverty or road to riches? *Communist and Post-Communist Studies*, 33, 379–402.

Lan, S. (2002). The individually-owned business in China: 1989–1999 (in Chinese). In Z. Houyi, M. Lizhi, and L. Chuanyun (Eds.), *The blue book of private enterprises in China no. 3*, pp. 31–41. Beijing: Social Sciences Documentation Publishing House.

Lu, X. (Ed.). (2004). *Social mobility in contemporary China* (in Chinese). Beijing: Social Science Documentation Publishing House.

Nee, V. (1989a). A theory of market transition: From redistribution to markets in state socialism. *American Sociological Review*, 54, 663–81.

———. (1989b). Peasant entrepreneurship and the politics of regulation in China. In V. Nee and D. Stark (Eds.), *Remaking the economic institutions in socialism: China and Eastern Europe*, pp. 169–207. Palo Alto, CA: Stanford University Press.

———. (1996). The emergence of a market society: Changing mechanisms of stratification in China. *American Journal of Sociology*, 101, 908–49.

Oi, J. (1999). *Rural China takes off*. Berkeley and Los Angeles: University of California Press.

Parish, W. L., and E. Michelson. (1996). Politics and markets: Dual transformations. *American Journal of Sociology*, 101, 1042–59.

Qian, Y. (2000). The process of China's market transition (1978–1998): The evolutionary, historical, and comparative perspectives. *Journal of Institutional and Theoretical Economics*, 156, 151–71.

Róna-Tas, Á. (1994). The first shall be last? Entrepreneurship and communist cadre in the transition from socialism. *American Journal of Sociology*, 100, 40–69.

———. (2002). The worm and the caterpillar: The small private sector in the Czech Republic, Hungary, and Slovakia. In V. E. Bonnell and T. Gold (Eds.), *The new entrepreneurs of Europe and Asia: Patterns of business development in Russia, Eastern Europe, and China*, pp. 39–65. Armonk, NY: M.E. Sharpe.

Sabin, L. (1994). New bosses in the workers' state: The growth of non-state sector employment in China. *China Quarterly*, 140, 944–70.

Short, S., and Z. Fengying. (1996). Household production and household structure in the context of China's economic reforms. *Social Forces* 75, 691–717.

Stata Corp. (2001). *Stata reference manual. vol. 3*. College Station, TX: Stata Corporation.

Szelényi, I. (1988). *Socialist entrepreneurs*. Madison: University of Wisconsin Press.

Szelényi, I., and E. Kostello. (1996). The market transition debate: Toward a synthesis. *American Journal of Sociology*, 101, 1082–96.

Szelényi, I., and S. Szelényi. (1995). Circulation or reproduction of elites during the post-communist transformation of Eastern Europe. *Theory and Society*, 24, 615–38.

Treiman, D. J. (1998). *The code book for Chinese life history survey.* Berkeley and Los Angeles: ISSR UCLA.

Treiman, D. J., and A. G. Walder. (1996). *Life histories and social change in contemporary China.* Distributed by UCLA Social Science Data Archive (available at www.sscnet.ucla.edu/issr/da).

Walder, A. G. (1996). Markets and inequality in transitional economics: Toward testable theories. *American Journal of Sociology*, 101, 1060–73.

———. (2002). Markets, economic growth, and inequality in rural China in the 1990s. *American Sociological Review*, 67, 231–53.

———. (2003). Elite opportunity in transitional economies. *American Sociological Review*, 68, 899–916.

Walder, A. G.; B. Li; and D. Treiman. (2000). Politics and life chances in a state socialist regime: Dual career paths into the urban Chinese elite, 1949–1996. *American Sociological Review*, 65, 191–209.

Wang, X. (2002). The development and prospects of Chinese private enterprises (in Chinese). In Z. Houyi, M. Lizhi, and L. Chuanyun (Eds.), *The blue book of private enterprises in China no. 3*, pp. 3–30. Beijing: Social Sciences Documentation Publishing House.

Wang, F.; X. Zuo; and D. Ruan. (2002). Rural migrants in Shanghai: Living under the shadows of socialism. *International Migration Review*, 36, 520–45.

Wank, D. (1999). *Commodifying communism: Business, trust, and politics in a Chinese city.* Cambridge, England: Cambridge University Press.

Winship, C., and R. Mare. (1992). Models for selection bias. *Annual Review of Sociology*, 18, 327–50.

Wu, X., and D. Treiman. (2004). The household registration system and social stratification in China: 1949–1996. *Demography*, 41, 363–84.

Wu, X., and Y. Xie. (2003). Does market pay off? Earnings returns to education in urban China. *American Sociological Review*, 68, 425–42.

Xie, Y., and E. Hannum. (1996). Regional variation in earnings inequality in reform-era urban China. *American Journal of Sociology*, 102, 950–92.

Young, S. (1995). *Private business and economic reform in China.* Armonk, NY: M.E. Sharpe.

Zhou, X. (2000). Economic transformation and income inequality in urban China. *American Journal of Sociology*, 105, 1135–74.

4

TRANSNATIONAL OR SOCIAL CAPITAL?

RETURNEES VERSUS LOCAL ENTREPRENEURS

WILFRIED R. VANHONACKER, DAVID ZWEIG, AND SIU FUNG CHUNG

What is the impact of internationalization on the development of the private sector in China? China's planned entry into the World Trade Organization (WTO) built enormous pressure in China to expand the private sector (Lardy 2002), particularly in areas such as the privatization of state-owned enterprises (SOEs) and private foreign trade companies. Similarly, many new private firms are run by mainland entrepreneurs who returned from studying and/or working overseas (Ben 2002, Wei 2002), a phenomenon that combines privatization and internationalization. Returned entrepreneurs bring back global networks, knowledge of overseas markets, foreign technologies, and international management experience. Their strategic perspectives may reflect overseas business attitudes more than domestic views about management. They can, therefore, have advantages over people who have not gone overseas.

But does training in a Western business environment translate into success in an Asian one? While returnees may have earned "transnational capital"—the value added to one's human capital that accrues from time spent, networks established, and knowledge acquired overseas—is it an advantage in China's internal and external markets? Can returnee entrepreneurs establish successful business networks in China and translate the value-added gained overseas into success in China's complex business and political environment?

This chapter compares two groups of private entrepreneurs—those with foreign educational or professional experience and those who are locally trained—in order to answer these questions. This comparison allows us to measure the impact of overseas study and global experience on the development of the private sector and private enterprises in China. It may also help us understand the future of China's global economic links and its ability to compete in the international economy.

Since 1978, over 900,000 mainland Chinese have gone overseas to study. But for many years, the bulk of these scholars did not return. And those who did return in large part were people who went overseas as visiting scholars but who did not undergo graduate education overseas (Zweig 2002). While the impact of these early returnees was significant for the development of China's educational system and R&D sector, they had only limited impact on the industrial (private or public) or technological sector.

Since 1995, the number of returnees has increased at a yearly rate of about 13 percent. Many have graduate degrees, including a high percentage of Ph.D.s and M.B.A.s. Also, changes in the global and domestic context since 1997 have brought more returnees to China. In 1997, leadership in China passed smoothly from the Deng Xiaoping generation to the "Russian-returned" generation led by Jiang Zemin. In 1998, the dot-com boom hit China, while in 1999, at the second session of the Ninth National People's Congress, the private sector was heralded as "an important, integral part of China's socialist market economy," and not just ancillary to the state sector. Finally, in fall 2001, China joined the WTO, further integrating China's global and domestic economies.

These events increased the number of returnees with advanced technical knowledge who established themselves as private entrepreneurs. Officials in the Shanghai Personnel Bureau responsible for monitoring the returnees told one of the authors in 2002 that there were over 2,000 foreign-trained entrepreneurs running private businesses in Shanghai, and the number has since increased rapidly. A preliminary survey in 2001 of sixty-six returnees working in development zones in China indicated that 41 percent (twenty-seven of sixty-six) had foreign Ph.D.s, while 66 percent (forty-four of sixty-six) were running their own businesses (Zweig, Chen, and Rosen 2004). Western media have recognized the importance of this group (Chea 2002), but scholarly analysis has lagged, largely because this trend is new and difficult to study.

KEY THEORETICAL ISSUES AND RESEARCH QUESTIONS

The core issue in this chapter is whether transnational or social capital best explains the performance of entrepreneurs in China. International forces have been playing a more important role in China's economic development (Lardy 2002, Zweig 2002); therefore, people with transnational capital (human capital enhanced by time spent overseas and including foreign knowledge, technology, networks, and resources) should do well, relative to those who have not been abroad. Yet the impact of international forces on a country's development is constrained by the domestic structures, norms, and conditions of the society into which they are being transferred (Deutsch 1966, Garrett and Lange 1996).

Can managerial skills learned, knowledge of technology garnered, and networks established overseas guarantee success more than social capital accumulated by people who did not go abroad but built domestic businesses and political networks? According to Wank (1995), private entrepreneurs in China engage in "symbiotic corporatism," giving local government officials, and their families, special business opportunities in return for easier business relations.[1] Other studies have shown that social capital, in the form of membership in the Chinese Communist Party (CCP), has been among the best predictors of household income and upward mobility in Maoist and post-Maoist China (Bian, Shu, and Logan 2002; Cook 1998; Walder, Li, and Treiman 2000). Returnees may lack many of these political connections.

Finally, neither form of capital may definitively explain success; both local and returned entrepreneurs may have to build up their social capital to succeed within China, allowing both groups to succeed, or fail, in equal amounts. According to one report, 20 percent of all start-up companies in China run by returnees fail within the first year; another 70 percent just make ends meet; and only 10 percent continue to grow rapidly. However, this observer found similar results for local entrepreneurs (Ming 2002). Therefore, the core difference among our entrepreneurs may be their human capital—that is, their education, training, social background, age, and gender. Walder et al. (2000) found that, even in Maoist China, education was as important as ties to the CCP in explaining career paths. According to Gary Becker, "In the New Economy and our technologically more advanced world, skills conferred by college education have become more important. Although other factors may be at work, there are remarkable returns to be seen now" (Manville 2001).

To shed light on these issues, we sought answers to these three broad research questions: First, how much advantage do returnees gain from their overseas experience? Are there serious returns to their transnational capital? To what extent does access to foreign technology enhance the performance of entrepreneurs? Although some have asserted that returnees earn advantages from "symbolic capital," whereby institutions in China grant them advantages because it is *assumed* that they are better (Hayhoe and Sun 1989), we assert that time overseas, the quality of the technology to which a returnee has access, and possessing a foreign degree or an overseas network, all give returned entrepreneurs serious advantages in a Chinese market that is becoming more and more international. And, even if a returnee does not engage in foreign trade, possessing a new technology that is in short supply within China's domestic market will create important rents or "extranormal profits" for those returnees (Tollison 1982).

Second, do returnee entrepreneurs manage the domestic environment, particularly their relations with the government, differently than local entrepreneurs? Do they respond differently to the politics of doing business in China? One hypothesis is that, since returnee entrepreneurs have weaker social capital, but often set up shop in high-tech incubators run by local governments, they rely more on local government—particularly in the formative phase of their enterprises—than local entrepreneurs who, with stronger networks, eschew government support and involvement.

Related to this last issue is the question of whether returnees use different management styles because of their time overseas, and whether this strategy affects their performance. While local Chinese private firms are likely to rely on social capital—ascriptive, rather than professional, relations—in obtaining capital, management, and sales/suppliers, do returnees run their firms in a different way? Or is dependence on social capital necessary for success in China's personalized market (Solinger 1991)?

Finally, we may find that transnational capital plays little role, and that returnees are just as likely as locals to rely on social capital in the form of relatives, friends, and government ties. To that extent, human capital—the qualities that returnees, as individuals, possess—may be the most important predictor of their firms' success.

METHODOLOGY AND SAMPLING PROCEDURES

We created our database through face-to-face interviews at 200 firms: 100 run by returnees and 100 run by local entrepreneurs. To do our survey, we collaborated with the Chinese Private Enterprise Association (Zhongguo siying qiye xiehui) and its director, Zhang Houyi. Team members on the Chinese side included Dai Jianzhong, of the Beijing Academy of Social Sciences, and Dr. Chen Guangjin, of the Chinese Academy of Social Sciences. These three individuals were responsible for interviews in Guangzhou, Beijing, and Shanghai, respectively. Overall, we tried to insure diversity in sectors, including manufacturing and services. We also wanted to include returnees working outside the IT sector, particularly in manufacturing, as we hypothesized that returnees would excel at IT but be less effective than locals in manufacturing. Two other criteria were imposed on the sample: the firms had to have over 1 million RMB in revenue—otherwise we could not analyze their marketing strategy—and they had to have been in business for two years or more. The vast majority of interviewees met these criteria.

Throughout the data collection, we tried to get large lists of returnees, so we could select from them randomly. In Beijing, we approached the External Relations Department of the Beijing Science and Technology Commission. But while they had data on how many returnees there were in the fourteen high-tech zones established in Beijing, they did not have a comprehensive list of returnees within those zones. Also, too many firms on their list were in IT, and we wanted more diversification in the nature of our enterprises. So, we turned to the Returnee Association (gui guo renyuan xiehui) under the Industrial and Commercial Association (gong shang ye lianhehui)—the former Industrial and Commercial Bureau—which had a membership list of 350 people. From that list we chose ninety people in three different returnee incubators *(chuangye yuan)* and sent each a letter requesting an interview. Our goal of thirty-four interviews was achieved after eighty people had been contacted, a figure constituting a success rate of 42.5 percent.[2] In each zone, we also asked officials to introduce us to thirty local entrepreneurs. Among the locals, we had an acceptance rate of 64 percent (it took fifty contacts to get the thirty-four locals who were interviewed).

Shanghai and Guangzhou were more difficult. In Shanghai, we received twenty-nine names from the director of the Overseas Students Service Centre in Pudong's high-tech zone. After one month, we had completed just fifteen interviews. We then went back to the director, who gave us another thirty-seven names, allowing us to complete thirty-three interviews. The response rate, therefore, was 50 percent (33/66).

In Guangzhou we had more difficulties. While the head of the Guangzhou Returnees Association (Guangzhou liuxue gui guo renyuan xiehui) was helpful, the people he put us in contact with in the zones were less so. We worked with returnee service centers *(liuxue guiguo fuwu zhongxin)* in two urban districts, Huangpu and Zhongshan. After some hesitation, they gave us forty names; from that list, we arranged only six interviews, as many returnees were out of town. Zhongshan officials then gave us another twenty names, but Huangpu officials would not, asserting that the success rate would be equally low. So, the director of the Guangzhou Returnees Association introduced us to the Tianhe Software Zone, which gave us twenty-five names. Finally, through additional informal contacts, we completed thirty-three interviews. In the end, we contacted ninety-five people to get the thirty-three respondents—a response rate of 35 percent.

RESULTS

Sample Profile

Table 4.1 gives a profile of the 200 companies contained in the data set. Among the local companies, only 14 percent were located in an official high-technology zone, while 46 percent of the returnee companies were located in a zone. As for the year the companies were registered, 59 percent of the nonreturnee companies were registered prior to 2000, while only 37 percent of the returnee companies were, making the sampled returnee companies younger.

As for shareholding structure, there is great variance within both subgroups, but on average there is no significant difference in terms of equity held by a firm's founding entrepreneur (at the start of the company and at the time of our study). However, firms founded by returnees and those founded by local entrepreneurs differed in the relationship between the entrepreneur and the other shareholders. In returnee companies, 37 percent of the founding entrepreneurs have no ascriptive ties with other shareholders, whereas only 18 percent of the local companies' founders do not have these types of ties. Although family, friends, and classmates are shareholders in both subgroups, more professional relationships exist between shareholders in returnee companies than in local companies, where ascriptive ties may dominate.

Table 4.1 shows extensive reliance on personal funds and those of friends and family; other sources of external financing were limited. Privately earned income is by far the primary source of initial investment for both groups. For returnees, this 65 percent is income earned abroad; for locals, 64 percent is money earned in China. Family and friends are important secondary sources

Table 4.1

Profile of Companies

		Returnee companies	Local companies
Located in zone	Yes	46%	14%
	No	54	86
Company age since founding	Before 1990	2	6
	Before 2000	37	59
	After 2000	61	35
Shareholders	Number at start (range)	3 (1–8)	2 (0–7)
	Number now (range)	3 (0–10)	
	% equity held at start (range)	58 (1–100)	61 (5–100)
	% equity held now (range)	59 (1–100)	61 (5–100)
	Relationship		
	• Immediate family	19%	19%
	• Close family	12	16
	• Friends, schoolmates	60	56
	• No special relationships	37	18

Source of Initial Financial Investment (percent of investment funds)

	First	Second	Third	First	Second	Third
1 Foreign-earned income	65	4	8	3	1	0
2 China-earned income	11	35	6	64	16	7
3 Family members	8	27	14	15	41	24
4 Schoolmates/friends	1	12	31	9	16	42
5 Local government	1	8	14	1	0	2
6 Venture capitalist	3	1	8	0	0	0
7 Domestic bank or company	5	5	14	7	21	18
8 Foreign bank or entrepreneur	4	4	6	0	0	2
9 (other)	2	3	0	1	4	6

Registered capital (RMB 0000) (range)	511 (10–14,000)			223 (2–5,000)		
Employees (range)	54 (3–500)			74 (4–900)		
Turnover (RMB 0000) (range)	774 (11–6,000)			851	(0–20,000)	

Customer Profile	Retail	12%	22%
	Industrial:	88	78
	Mostly foreign companies in China	20	13
	Mostly Chinese private companies	44	65
	Mostly SOEs	36	22

Relationship to Distributors			
1	Former employees	12%	19%
2	Classmates	18	19
3	Relatives	17	21
4	Childhood friends	3	10
5	Same locality	22	24

Relationship to Suppliers			
1	Former employees	12%	14%
2	Classmates	28	24
3	Relatives	15	18
4	Childhood friends	19	14
5	Same locality	15	16

of finance for both returnees and locals, but the role of schoolmates and friends is more important for locals than for returnees. Local governments are investing in returnee firms—probably through the management company that runs the incubator in the zones—while for locals, only domestic banks, SOEs, and private firms are an important third source. Hence, very few nonreturnees relied on local government financing when their companies were created. Some, albeit few, returnees received private capital from abroad.

Table 4.1 also indicates to whom the firms sell and the importance of ascriptive ties to the local firms. As we can see, 28 percent of returnees have no personal relations with their distributors, while 93 percent of locals distribute their products through former employees (19 percent vs. 12 percent), former classmates (19 percent vs. 18 percent), relatives (21 percent vs. 17 percent), and childhood friends (10 percent vs. 3 percent). Both subgroups rely heavily on people who came from the same locality (24 percent vs. 22 percent). As for customer profile, 88 percent of the returnees are in industrial markets, whereas 78 percent of the locals are. Accordingly, the large majority of entrepreneurs in both subgroups are not in consumer goods. Looking at the profile of the industrial end-customer, for both subgroups of entrepreneurs Chinese private companies are the most important clients. This is particularly the case for locals, for whom 65 percent (relative to 44 percent for returnees) of their clients are Chinese private companies. In contrast, returnees do more business with foreign companies in China (20 percent of their clients relative to 13 percent for locals) and with SOEs (36 percent of their clients relative to 22 percent for locals).

Table 4.2 profiles the human capital of the entrepreneurs themselves. The majority are male (82 percent in both subgroups), and the age breakdown is almost identical for both subgroups, despite the fact that the local companies were established earlier than the returnee companies, and that returnees spent more time at university. There is a significant difference in social background. Returnees come more from intellectual families—which is how they went abroad—while locals are more often from worker or peasant families. Locals, relative to returnees, on average worked longer in leading management positions in China; and given that the age distribution in both subgroups is the same, the different length of managerial experience for locals reflects the time returnees spent abroad studying. In line with their social background, returnees attained a higher level of education in China; more than two-thirds of returnees finished university, compared to less than one-third of locals. In terms of highest degree earned (in China or abroad), 34 percent of the returnees received Ph.D.s, while no locals did. Twenty-two received Ph.D.s abroad. Finally, one measure of social capital is whether an individual has joined the Communist Party, as membership in the party enhances networks and incomes. About 20 percent of entrepreneurs in both subgroups were CCP members, a figure that is surprisingly high for returnees.

Defining Our Variables

In this part of the chapter, we analyze the transnational and social capital of our entrepreneurs, highlighting important differences. Then we present our findings from three multiple regression analyses, which compare the roles of these three forms of capital for the different subgroups in explaining firm performance, exports, and revenues.

The Role of Transnational Capital

Did people who went overseas acquire transnational capital that can be measured empirically, and that could give them advantages in business? Transnational capital is derived from overseas education, and, by definition, most returnees have acquired such capital. Among our returnees, 26

Table 4.2

Profile of Respondents

	Returnees	Locals
Gender		
Male	82	82
Female	18	18
Age		
≤ 30	8	11
31–40	45	43
41–50	38	38
51–60	8	8
> 60	0	0
Family social class		
Senior cadre	5	2
General cadre	21	20
Worker	17	40
Peasant	9	15
Intellectual/teacher	39	19
Businessman	6	2
Soldier	2	2
Other	1	0
Party member		
Yes	17	20
No	80	79
No response	3	1
Years in leading management position		
in China (range)	1.83 (0–12)	4.43 (0–25)
Education in China		
Below high school	2	5
High school diploma	7	32
Technical college or equivalent	18	35
Undergraduate	47	23
Master's	12	5
Ph.D.	12	0

percent had overseas Ph.D.s, while 43 percent had overseas M.A.s. Twelve percent had domestic Ph.D.s but had worked overseas as postdoctoral fellows. By definition, locals had no overseas degrees, though some had been on short-term training programs abroad. Like most entrepreneurs, who possess relatively low levels of formal education,[3] 37 percent of our local entrepreneurs never went beyond high school, and another 35 percent had only degrees from technical colleges or their equivalent. Thus, our two groups of entrepreneurs had significantly different levels of education and received that education in very different locations.

Among returnees, 81 percent had practical work experience abroad. And while half of the returnees had developed scientific skills abroad, a significant number supplemented that training

Table 4.3

Returnees Abroad

Quality of technology (percent in each category)	Returnees	Locals
Internationally the latest technology	34	9
Not the latest internationally, but new for China	46	30
Not latest for China, but new for the region	8	24
Not the latest even in the region	5	31
	93	94
Work experience abroad (percent)		
Postdoctoral fellowship	7	
Practical work experience	81	
None	12	
Skill developed abroad (percent)		
Teaching	4	
Scientific research	50	
Commercial R&D	16	
Sales and marketing	21	
Human resources	7	
Finance and accounting	4	
Project management	18	
Other	19	
Importance of overseas experience to business (mean and S.D.)	4.39 (0.83)	
Job related to skill developed abroad (mean and S.D.)	4.22 (1.24)	

with functional management skills (commercial R&D, sales and marketing, human resources, or project management). On average, returnees rated their experience abroad as extremely important to their businesses (4.39 on a 5-point scale), and believed that the skill they developed abroad was highly related to their current entrepreneurial work in China. They also believed that foreign language skills were critical to their businesses (94 percent vs. 74 percent).

An important aspect of transnational capital is the quality of the imported technology a product or firm possesses. But what types of technology did the sampled returnees bring? If it was not technology that was new for China, then there would be little value. So, we asked our informants whether "their" technologies were: (1) internationally leading-edge technologies; (2) not internationally leading-edge, but new for China; (3) not new for China, but new for their region of China; or (4) not new even for their region. If a technology fitted the fourth category, we could assume that the entrepreneur was relying primarily on marketing skills or social capital to make his or her business profitable; if the technology fitted the first two characteristics, an entrepreneur was employing transnational capital. For the third type of technology, the form of capital reliance could be mixed.

Our findings show that returnees possess a great degree of transnational capital (Table 4.3). They are four times as likely as locals to possess the latest international technology (34 percent vs. 9 percent), and almost 50 percent as likely (46 percent vs. 30 percent) to have technology that, while not the newest internationally, is new for China. Thus, while 34 percent of the returnees have a product that—given China's low labor costs—can be priced competitively in the international market, fully 80 percent of returnee entrepreneurs use technologies that are new for China, giving them a significant comparative advantage within the domestic market. Thus, these technologies could be an important explanation of their business success.

Local entrepreneurs, as expected, depend far more on social relations than on the technology in their product; 26 percent (twenty-four out of ninety-four) have technologies not new for China, and 33 percent (thirty-one out of ninety-four) have a technology that is not new for their region. If the local entrepreneurs' businesses are profitable, the quality of service or personal ties must bring in the customers. As for the sources of technology, only 16 percent of locals utilize externally developed technology, as compared to 46 percent of returnees. Thus, time abroad to master technology could be a factor increasing success. In fact, as shown above, the locals' distribution networks are based almost entirely on ascriptive ties.

One hypothesis confirmed by the data is that technology brings people back to China, precisely because they believe that it gives them an edge in the domestic market. When asked why they returned to China, 27 percent of returnees selected "I have a technology that I believe will have a good prospect in China" as their primary reason for returning, while another 28 percent chose it as their second reason. For these entrepreneurs, technology drives much of their activities.

Returnees' overseas contacts have created a different pattern of business partners. Among returnees, 67 percent had established networks of contacts while they were overseas, but overall they reported that they relied on their overseas networks to only a moderate degree. Still, 20 percent of returnees worked mostly with foreign companies operating in China, as compared to 13 percent of locals. Some of these returnees may have been employed by these foreign firms when they initially returned to China. Also, 17 percent of returnee firms have an overseas subsidiary (5 percent for local companies). Returnees are more involved in exports than locals (19 percent vs. 11 percent), and they expect to be more involved in exports five years down the road (33 percent vs. 21 percent). Returnees are also more likely to deal with the public sector than local firms; 36 percent of them did most of their business with SOEs, as compared to 22 percent of locals, while the vast majority of locals (65 percent) did business with other private firms, as compared to 41 percent of returnee entrepreneurs.

Social Capital: Entrepreneurs' Local Government Relations

An entrepreneur's ties to the local government are a good indicator of social capital because successful entrepreneurs work closely with the government, according to research findings (Wank 1995). Yet the need to rely on the local government may reflect a deficit in other forms of social capital. For example, returnees may rely on government ties precisely because they lack the social ties that facilitate competition in China's personalized market (Solinger 1991).

So we asked entrepreneurs the best strategy for dealing with the local government. We distinguished among five strategies, from having little or no contact with the local government to taking the local government as a business partner. Where 57 percent of the returnees indicated that establishing a cooperative relationship with the local government was the best strategy, 34 percent of the locals said so. Among locals, 36 percent preferred to deal with local government at arm's length (had little or no contact); the corresponding percentage for returnees was only 16 percent. Clearly, returnees prefer to be more engaged with their local governments, although few went as far as taking them as active partners in their businesses (4 percent).

The opinions of the locals on how to deal with the government vary more widely. For example, where 36 percent would want to keep the local government at arm's length, 11 percent indicated that taking the local government as a business partner is the best strategy. To some

Table 4.4

Entrepreneurs' Relations with Different Government Bureaus

		Importance		Rating		
		Returnees (n = 100)	Locals (n = 100)	Returnees (n = 100)[b]	Locals (n = 100)	t-test (significance)[c]
1	Personnel Department	30[a]	15	3.10*	2.33	−2.81 (0.01)
2	Science and Technology Bureau	52	12	2.83*	2.33	n.s.
3	Finance Bureau	20	23	2.30	2.60	n.s.
4	Office for New & High Technology	45	19	3.07*	2.00*	−3.65 (0.001)
5	Public Security Bureau	10	35	1.80*	2.20*	n.s.
6	Education Bureau	3	4	2.33	1.75	n.s.
7	Foreign Affairs Bureau	8	3	2.38	2.00	n.s.
8	Economic and Trade Bureau	14	21	2.57	2.38	n.s.
9	Commercial and Industrial Bureau	75	93	2.43	2.37	n.s.
10	Tax Bureau	76	96	2.43	2.36	n.s.
11	Information Bureau	13	18	2.23	2.61	n.s.
12	National Development and Reform Commission	1	2	4.00	1.50	n.s.
13	People's Bank, Branch	29	58	2.62	2.55	n.s.
14	United Front Department	3	0	4.00*	—	—
15	Overseas Chinese Office	8	0	3.13	—	—
16	Bureau of Foreign Trade, Import/ Export Office	10	6	2.10	2.17	n.s.
17	Patent Office	17	19	2.53	2.42	n.s.
18	Incubator Center Management Committee	6	1	2.83	2.00	n.s.
19	Land Bureau	4	3	2.75	2.00*	n.s.
20	Customs Office	23	23	2.35	2.48	n.s.
21	Foreign Exchange Office	15	3	2.13	1.67	n.s.
22	Office of local Party Secretary	2	2	2.50	1.00*	n.s.
23	Office of Municipal Government	17	36	2.59	1.92*	−2.38 (0.02)

[a]Number of respondents indicating that the bureau was one of the five most important for them.

[b]For those for which the bureau was important, mean rating of their relationship with the bureau (1 = "rather positive," 4 = "rather negative"). An asterisk (*) indicates whether the mean score is significantly different from 2.5 at a = 0.10 or higher.

[c]Two-sided t-test on mean ratings between returnees and locals.

extent, this divergence might reflect their longer experience with local governments (relative to returnees). Also, the fact that most of the local companies in our sample are not located in technology development zones, where local governments play a more active role, may explain the different levels of engagement.

We gauged the local governments' roles in the informants' businesses. Returnees indicated that their respective local governments had helped them with (1) finances; (2) land, office space, and/or equipment; and (3) import/export procedures. The local governments had helped locals get (1) land, office space, and/or equipment; (2) suppliers; and (3) financial resources. Very few people in either subgroup indicated that government agencies or government officials had interfered in their businesses (six returnees and five locals). This result suggests that such interference happens, but rarely.

We also looked at the entrepreneurs' experiences with twenty-three governmental bureaus, asking each to select the five most important bureaus and to evaluate the quality ("rather positive" to "rather negative") of their relationships with each of the five (Table 4.4). For both subgroups, the Commercial and Industrial Bureau and the Tax Bureau are the most important, but they are particularly important for nonreturnees, with virtually every local selecting them as being among the five most important bureaus. Beyond these two, some differences arise. For returnees, the Science and Technology Bureau is the third most important, which reflects the fact that returnees work with more advanced technology than the locals, and that they often work in technology zones. For locals, the third most important bureau is the People's Bank—44 percent of locals received investments from local banks or companies (Table 4.1).

As for the quality of these relations, three significant differences emerge. Returnees have more negative relationships than locals with the Personnel Department, the Office for New and High Technology, and the Office of the Municipal Government. But for the three most important bureaus for either subsample, we see no significant difference in the quality of the relationships between returnees and locals.

Looking at the quality of the relationships with the bureaus as a function of when a business was registered, more positive relations exist for older businesses, while more negative relations exist for newer businesses; this pattern is much stronger for returnees than for locals. Returnees who only recently registered their businesses were particularly unhappy with their relations with the bureaus that were most important to them and their businesses. In all likelihood, they were still uncomfortable with the administrative style of Chinese officialdom, an issue often raised by returnees in other surveys.

Both returnees and locals agreed equally that political support was necessary for them to succeed. However, locals agreed significantly more than returnees with the statement "good relations with government officials protects my business." Hence, locals (more than returnees) prefer good relations with the government (which in general they have); nevertheless, more than returnees, they prefer to keep the local government at arm's length.

MULTIVARIATE ANALYSIS

Here we present the results of three different regression analyses,[4] each of which had a different dependent variable. But first, we outline our independent variables.

Independent Variables

We selected several indicators of transnational capital from our data set (Table 4.5). These include the level of the technology an entrepreneur used in business, the number of years spent abroad, possession of an overseas degree, the importance of any overseas experience to their business, having an overseas subsidiary, and the level of reliance on an overseas network. We also considered whether a returnee's current job was related to what he or she studied overseas, since it was possible that a returnee had not activated transnational capital in any significant way.

Indicators of social capital encompass reliance on family, friends, and the local government. Drawing from our survey, we included family/friends investment in an entrepreneur's company, reliance on personal relations in selecting distributors and suppliers, the source of financing, Communist Party membership, and the nature of government relations. In the latter case, we created a single measure by averaging ratings of the quality of the five relationships with government offices that each entrepreneur selected as most important.

Finally, to measure the impact of the entrepreneurs' human capital, we included age, gender, education, family's socioeconomic background, and years of management experience. In total, we had twenty-one variables, but in some cases there were missing data.

Table 4.5

Variables and Coding

Variables	Coding (scales)
Dependent variables	
(1) Performance	Conglomerate scale using factor scores from the seven performance measures
(2) Revenues	Revenues in RMB 10,000.
(3) Export	Percent of revenues from exports
Independent variables	
(1) Year registered	Ordinal scale with 1 = "2004," 2 = "2003" . . .
(2) Level of technology	Ordinal scale with 1 = "most advanced," 4 = "not the latest technology even in the region"
(3) Transnational capital	
• Time spent abroad	Years, in total
• Degree abroad	Dummy variable; 1 = "yes," 0 = "no"
• Importance of overseas experience to business	Ordinal scale; 1 = "not important at all," 5 = "very important"
• Reliance on overseas network	Ordinal scale; 1 = "not at all," 5 = "very much"
• Job related to skill learned abroad	Ordinal scale; 1 = "not at all," 5 = "very much"
• Overseas subsidiary	Dummy variable; 1 = "yes," 0 = "no"
• Work experience abroad	Dummy variable; 1 = "yes," 0 = "no"
(4) Social capital	
• Friends/family as shareholders	Dummy variable; 1 = "yes," 0 = "no"
• Friends/family as suppliers	Dummy variable; 1 = "yes," 0 = "no"
• Friends/family as distributors	Dummy variable; 1 = "yes," 0 = "no"
• Friends/family as financiers	Dummy variable; 1 = "yes," 0 = "no"
• Government relations	Ordinal scale; mean of ratings on five most important bureaus; 1 = "rather positive," 4 = "rather negative"
• Strategy in dealing with government	Ordinal scale; 1 = "no contact at all," 5 = "government as partner"
• Member of CCP	Dummy variable; 1 = "yes," 0 = "no"
(5) Human capital	
• Age	Ordinal scale; 1 if <30, 5 if 61
• Gender	1 = male, 0 = female
• Education	1 = below high school, 6 = Ph.D.
• Social class	ISE scale
• Years of management experience	Years, in total

Dependent Variables

To estimate the impact of transnational capital, social capital, and human capital on the performance of the entrepreneurial firms, we estimated three regression models. One dependent variable is a composite of self-reported company performance.[5] All 200 companies were assessed on the basis of seven measures: (1) profitability (return on assets); (2) cash flow; (3) sales growth; (4) market share; (5) technical product/service design and development; (6) quality of product/service; and (7) employee satisfaction. The entrepreneurs reported how important each of these measures was to them and how they were performing relative to their industry average (1 = "much lower than industry average" and 5 = "much higher than industry average"). Hence, we need to keep in mind that performance was self-reported, or based on self-evaluation. Also, while some significant differences were apparent in the market focus and marketing practices of returnees and locals, those policies and their differences did not significantly impact self-reported performance. Locals do not report significantly better performance than returnees; in fact, both subgroups of entrepreneurs have a unique way of addressing the market but feel that they are equally successful in doing so.

Our second dependent variable is total revenues, which again was self-reported. While revenues need not reflect the health of a firm, as it could be running a huge deficit, we had no other empirical indicator that was not potentially heavily influenced by the informants' biased views of their own companies. Finally, we used foreign trade as a share of total revenue as our third performance indicator.

Results

Our findings are quite informative. As Table 4.6 shows, seven variables were significantly correlated with the self-reported performance of the firm at 0.10 or higher.[6] For both locals and returnees, the age of the company was positively correlated with performance. This finding is not surprising, suggesting that people who have been running their companies for a longer time feel more positive about their accomplishments.

Three transnational variables were significant. First, the level of technology was highly correlated with performance, but since 1 was the highest level of technology, and 4 was the lowest, the parameter estimate is negative. Even local firms did better if they had technology that was world class or at least unique for China. This finding again reinforces the assertion that global linkages are critical for success in an internationalizing China and that new technology creates "extra-normal profits."

A second transnational variable was an entrepreneur's reliance on an overseas network. The findings suggest that the more returnees and locals rely on overseas networks, the *less* positively they view their firm's performance. This relationship confirms the hypothesis that overseas networks are not considered to be enough and that returnees recognize that they must sink their feet into the domestic market if they are to succeed. Finally, overseas work experience is weakly correlated with performance ($p > .07$) for both subgroups, though locals had little overseas experience; otherwise, they would have been classified as returnees.

Two aspects of social capital were correlated with the perceived performance of a firm. Both locals and returnees who rely on ascriptive ties to develop their *distribution* networks view their firms' performances positively. Although this finding is not surprising for locals, one might have expected that returnees would have a negative view of relying on ascriptive ties when selecting distributors. Still, China's market is what it is, and returnees have to adapt to succeed. In fact,

Table 4.6

Performance[a]

Independent variables	Parameter estimates (significance)
(1) Year registered	0.06 (0.01)
(2) Level of technology	−0.18 (0.00)
(3) Transnational capital	
• Reliance on overseas network	−0.16 (0.01)
• Work experience abroad	0.61 (0.08)
(4) Social capital	
• Friends/family as distributors	0.59 (0.05)
• Friends/family as financiers	−0.64 (0.09)
(5) Differential effects[b]	
$D \times$ friends/family as suppliers	0.66 (0.09)

Model fit statistics
    R^2 = .21
    F (significance) = 1.84 (0.02)
    Condition Index[c] = 11.96

[a]Model with 21 variables; those significant at a = .10 or higher are shown.
[b]With $D = 1$ for returnee, $D = 0$ for local.
[c]Multicollinearity diagnostic.

while locals apparently do not need friends and relatives as suppliers to be successful, returnees apparently do—perhaps reflecting their weaker market positions and the fact that getting access to quality goods in China's domestic market may still depend on good personal ties. Finally, both groups show a correlation between relying on friends and relatives for financial support and problems in performance. In fact, earlier analysis showed that local firms, with finances from relatives, had difficulty keeping the relatives from interfering in the firm's activities, and thus scored rather poorly on "worker satisfaction."

Many of the variables used to explain variations in revenues were also significant (Table 4.7), and the model itself is quite powerful (R^2 = .39) in explaining the reported differences in revenues. Reported revenues were highly correlated with the age of a firm for both returnees and locals, which suggests that the link between age and performance, reported above, was real and not just perceived. Among our transnational variables, the level of technology was significant, albeit at the .09 level. Also, having an overseas subsidiary was positively correlated with revenues for locals, but negatively correlated for returnees. Local companies that were able to develop overseas subsidiaries were doing particularly well, and probably had a lot of revenue, which allowed them to reach out overseas. This finding fits well with the Chinese government's policy of encouraging successful domestic firms to do business overseas *(zou chu qu)*. But it remains difficult to understand why having an overseas subsidiary would lead to lower revenues for a returnee. Perhaps if their overseas subsidiary was their original firm, they were expending too much of their energies (and capital) to keep it going.

Table 4.7

Revenues[a]

Independent variables	Parameter estimates (significance)
(1) Year registered	134.960 (0.00)
(2) Level of technology	−217.313 (0.09)
(3) Transnational capital	
Overseas subsidiary	4,272.858 (0.00)
(4) Social capital	
Member of CCP	1,612.984 (0.00)
(5) Differential Effects[b]	
D × Overseas subsidiary	−4,545.277 (0.00)
D × Member of Communist Party	−1,944.471 (0.01)

Model fit statistics
    $R^2 = .39$
    F (significance) = 4.66 (0.00)
    Condition Index[c] = 10.59

[a]Model with 20 variables; those significant at a = .10 or higher are shown.
[b]With $D = 1$ for returnee, $D = 0$ for local.
[c]Multicollinearity diagnostic.

Interestingly, only one social capital variable was significant, but it is very important. Being a member of the CCP enhanced the revenue of a local firm, yet harmed revenue for returnees. In the latter case, returnees who were Communist Party members may have been poor businessmen or were constrained—in terms of black- or gray-market activity—by punishments they might receive, as party members, for corruption.

Only one variable—having an overseas subsidiary—is correlated with exports, and the levels of significance are .00 and .01 for locals and returnees, respectively. However, such a finding is not surprising, so we do not present it in tabular form. Any local with an overseas subsidiary should be an active exporter, unless the subsidiary is a front for laundering money overseas. In any case, the model for this regression is highly significant ($R^2 = .36$).

Finally, it is worth noting which variables are not significant. For example, level of education, gender, and length of time spent abroad do not affect reported performance or revenues, though work experience abroad does. Also, neither the strength of ties to local government nor the strategy employed to deal with the government affect the revenue or performance of these firms. We would have anticipated some relationship, as returnees often need the government's support to succeed at the start. Yet Table 4.4 showed that there were only minor differences in the nature of the ties to the government between locals and returnees, which explains why there was little impact on our indicators of success.

CONCLUSIONS

What can we say about our original research questions? First, returnees, more than locals, work closely with the government, a finding that runs counter to our expectations. We assumed that local private businessmen had woven a closely knit web with the local state as a form of protective *guanxi* (Wank 1995). But, in fact, local entrepreneurs keep their distance from the government, despite having good relations with it. But returnees, particularly those in the high-technology zones, depend on the local state for capital, land, and labor. As returnees to a China that has been transformed since they left, they need the help of various government bureaus to get started. Still, they remain uncomfortable with "capitalism with Chinese characteristics"—that is, with having to work closely with an annoying bureaucracy.

Second, we argued that technology is bringing people back, in anticipation that this form of transnational capital will facilitate success, and the data support our argument. We found a strong relationship between level of technology and subjective measures of success, but this was true for both returnees and locals. The findings also support the argument, however, that high-quality technology is not enough to succeed in China's politicized domestic market. Even returnees need to establish personal ties to ensure the supply and distribution of their products.

The result is that social capital is very important for all entrepreneurs. Local ones report that despite having technology that is not unique for China, they can succeed; hence, their social capital must be important. On the other hand, advanced world-class technology is not enough to guarantee success for returnees in the domestic market; they need ascriptive ties as well. But those ties must be personal—not ties to the government—as relations with the local government do not explain any of our success indicators.

Social capital, in the form of membership in the CCP, is very important to the success of our entrepreneurs. These findings mirror studies of political capital in China, which show that being a CCP member, or having a CCP member in one's family, contributes to one's income or life chances, even in the reform era. Still, for returnees, this type of social capital is more of a liability, though further research is necessary to explain why. And for both returnees and locals, social capital is problematic if family and relatives, who invest in the firm, interfere in its management and thereby generate low job satisfaction among employees.

Still, bringing a new technology into China is an important path to enrichment and remains a major force for returning. Such a finding is clearly a benefit to the Chinese government, which can spread this message as a way to attract more returnees, more foreign technology, and thereby upgrade the quality of the domestic market. By rewarding those who bring in technology, the government (as well as the Chinese market) is clearly creating the appropriate environment for China's openness to create a more technologically advanced Chinese state.

NOTES

Research funds were provided by the Hang Lung Center for Organizational Research, Hong Kong University of Science and Technology. Research assistance was provided by Vivian Lam. We thank Anne Tsui and Yanjie Bian for their very helpful comments on the previous draft.

1. A brief review of these various perspectives and empirical findings can be found in chapter 2 by Bian and Zhang in this book.

2. Returnees had a much higher refusal rate than locals, something that went against our expectations. Returnees are usually quite amenable to talk about their experiences. In this case, however, many returnees were on business trips out of town, if not out of the country.

3. Overall, domestic entrepreneurs have less education than returnees. However, according to national surveys, their level of education has increased significantly throughout the 1990s. Thus, while only 16.6 percent had a university education in 1993, by 1999, 35 percent did. See *Zhongguo siying jingji nianjian,* 2000, p. 362, cited in Guiheux (2002).

4. For those variables for which we had observations for returnees and locals, a slope dummy was introduced. For the independent variable *X,* we specified the model as $(\alpha + \beta D)X$, where D was a dummy variable indicating whether the observation was for a returnee ($D = 1$) or a local ($D = 0$). The α parameter

measured the pooled effect of X when $\beta = 0$ or the effect of X for locals when $\beta \neq 0$; the corresponding effect of X for returnees would then be $(\alpha + \beta)$. The parameter β measures the differential effect of X for returnees. In estimating the three models, we used multicollinearity diagnostics to derive the final model, taking extreme care to drive the condition index to a value of 10, considered a relatively low level of multicollinearity. We did this by dropping highly correlated independent variables. The resulting models are reported here, focusing on whether the parameter estimates one significant at .10 or higher.

5. The first measure, a conglomerate performance measure, was derived from the one-factor solution to a factor analysis of the seven performance measures included in the questionnaire.

6. The condition index for the final model equals 11.96, and the corresponding model retained twenty-one variables. The model is significant at the .02 level, and the $R^2 = .21$.

REFERENCES

Ben kan jizhe (This Journal's Reporter). (2002). The new debate about the wave of overseas students returning to start businesses (in Chinese). *Liaowang xinwen zhoukan* (Liaowang news monthly), 4, 6–9.

Bian, Y. J.; X.L. Shu; and J.R. Logan. (2002). Communist party membership and regime dynamics in China. *Social Forces,* 79, 805–41.

Chea, T. (2002). Looking homeward: Business, social opportunities await U.S.-educated Chinese. *Washington Post,* January 28, E01.

The China Market. (2003). How private firms are their own worst enemies. *South China Morning Post,* August 25, 11.

Cook, S. (1998). Work, wealth and power in agriculture: Do political connections affect the returns to household labor. In A. G. Walder (Ed.), *Zouping in transition: The process of reform in rural North China,* pp. 157–83. Cambridge, MA: Harvard University Press.

Deutsch, K. W. (1966). External influences on the internal behavior of states. In B. Farrell (Ed.), *Approaches to comparative and international politics,* pp. 5–26. Evanston, IL: Northwestern University Press.

Garrett, G., and P. Lange. (1996). Internationalization, institutions, and political change. In R. Keohane and H. Milner (Eds.), *Internationalization and domestic politics,* pp. 48–75. Cambridge, England: Cambridge University Press.

Guiheux, G. (2002). The social profile of private entrepreneurs: Socio-economic diversity and proximity to the party state. Paper presented at the conference "State Reforms and Social Stability in China," Chinese University of Hong Kong, July 5 and 6.

Hayhoe, R., and Y.L. Sun. (1989). China's scholars returned from abroad: A view from Shanghai, parts one and two. *China Exchange News,* no. 17, September–December.

Lardy, N. R. (2002). *Integrating China into the world economy.* Washington, DC: Brookings Institution Press.

Manville, B. (2001). Talking human capital with Professor Gary S. Becker, Nobel Laureate. *Learning from the human capital revolution* (Spring), at www.linezine.com/4.1/interviews/gbbmthc.htm.

Ming, R. (2002). Is a wave of Chinese scholars returning from overseas emerging? (in Chinese). *Qianxiao yuekan* (Qianxiao monthly), 3, 92–3.

Solinger, D. (1991). Urban reform and relational contracting in post-Mao China. In R. Baum (Ed.), *Reform and reaction in post-Mao China: The road to Tiananmen,* pp. 104–23. New York: Routledge.

Tollison, R. D. (1982). Rent seeking: A survey. *Kyklos,* 35, 575–602.

Walder, A. G.; B.B. Li; and D.J. Treiman. (2000). Politics and life chances in a state socialist regime: Dual career paths into the urban Chinese elite, 1949 to 1996. *American Sociological Review,* 65, 191–209.

Wank, D. (1995). Bureaucratic patronage and private business: Changing networks of power in urban China. In A. G. Walder (Ed.), *The waning of the communist state: Economic origins of political decline in China and Hungary,* pp. 153–83. Berkeley: University of California Press.

Wei, J. X. (2002). The road taken by Chinese overseas scholars in returning to China to set up businesses (in Chinese). *Ching pao,* 4, 30–2.

Zweig, D. (2002). *Internationalizing China: Domestic demand and global linkages.* Ithaca, NY: Cornell University Press.

Zweig, D.; C.G. Chen; and S. Rosen. (2004). Globalization and transnational human capital: Overseas and returnee scholars to China. *China Quarterly,* 179, 735–57.

5

THE SWEATSHOP AND BEYOND

AUTHORITY RELATIONS IN DOMESTIC PRIVATE ENTERPRISES

YI-MIN LIN

An important trend of economic change in post-Mao China is that the economy has become increasingly private. Although the Chinese government has never released comprehensive statistics on the full magnitude of private economic activities, there are clear signs that the once overwhelmingly dominant public sector has seriously eroded in the past twenty-five years. In 1980 state-owned units and collective enterprises made up 99 percent of the urban workforce; in 2003 their combined share went down to 31 percent (National Bureau of Statistics [NBS] 2004, 122–23). From 1984 to 2002 the share of collective enterprises in the workforce of the rural nonfarm sector decreased from 77 percent to 13 percent (Editorial Office [EO] 1989, 574; 2003, 130), whereas the entire workforce in the farming sector has been self-employed since the mid 1980s. In 2003 state-owned/-controlled enterprises and collectives contributed only 38 percent of the value added to the secondary sector, which includes industry and construction and accounted for 52 percent of China's gross domestic product in that year (NBS 2004, 53–54, 518–19, 578–79). The economic space vacated by public enterprises has been taken up by private or predominantly private economic entities.

As the significance of the private sector in employment and output increases, how the private workforce is governed becomes an important issue for those interested in China's economic transformation. A large and growing body of literature on the private sector exists (see, for example, the three review essays in this volume), yet in-depth research on the internal organization of private economic entities—especially domestically owned entities—remains scarce.

This chapter is a preliminary exploration for ways to narrow this gap. The starting point is a central finding of some widely noted studies of authority relations in foreign-invested enterprises, which are partly or predominantly privately owned. These studies reveal extensive use of coercive and abusive measures of labor control, which are akin to or amount to what is known in labor history as "sweatshop" practices. Comparing this finding with information that I collected from interviews with dozens of employees in domestic private enterprises, I find striking similarities in a few cases. But my fieldwork also reveals patterns of authority relations that do not closely fit the sweatshop model.

To conceptualize such similarities and differences and thereby facilitate further investigation into possibly diverse patterns of workplace practices in the private sector, I propose a simple descriptive scheme of authority relations, consisting of two basic dimensions: the extent of legal-rational regulation, and the breadth of the motivation/incentive system. I argue that this scheme may help define the ideal-typical sweatshop and illustrate its essential differences from other types of authority relations. To explore the usefulness of the two-dimensional construct, I analyze the data from a 1998 survey of 1,350 employees in 206 domestic private enterprises. The results provide provisional confirming evidence. They also show diversity in labor practices among different domestic private enterprises and suggest a need to look beyond the sweatshop model for a fuller view of the postsocialist reformation of authority in the workplace.

CAPITALIST LABOR RELATIONS IN THE WAKE OF STATE SOCIALISM

With the growth of private ownership and deepening of marketization, China is completing its journey toward capitalism. Historically, a trademark of early capitalist development is the predominance of sweatshop practices in the workplace. In both the West and the developing world, harsh working conditions, abusive treatment of workers, and extensive use of coercion have been common features of internal economic organization during the transformation from agriculture to industry (Burawoy 1985, Deyo 1989, Leupp 1992, Schmiechen 1984). Among the possible contributing factors to this are the slow pace of the construction of modern political institutions; manipulation of the state by powerful economic interests; lack of organization for collective action among workers; and destruction of traditional communities, as well as the agrarian moral economy, in which social normative pressures may constrain extremely rough treatment of workers (Murphy 1993, Powelson 1998, Thompson 1966).

On the other hand, uneven development, divergent paths of industrialization, and globalization may also have brought about conditions or countervailing forces that have the potential of limiting the scope, scale, and durability of sweatshop practices adopted in latecomers to capitalism (Clarke 1996, Silver 2003). These include, among other things, the spread of contemporary Western managerial practices and philosophies; the adoption of technologies that entail certain levels of adequacy in working conditions; the lingering influence of traditional norms, as well as institutional and cultural legacies carried over by countries that experienced socialist industrialization before embarking upon capitalism; and growing domestic pressures on multinational corporations to maintain "social performance" in their overseas operations.

During the transition from socialism, China has been undergoing a significant restructuring of authority relations in the workplace. What has emerged from the transformation, however, remains largely unclear. While much has been written about the changing and increasingly stormy industrial relations in public enterprises (e.g., Blecher 2002, O'Leary 1998, Solinger 2002), which are now rapidly disappearing, few in-depth studies are available on the internal organization of privately owned economic entities. Perhaps the closest accounts come from some recent works on labor relations in foreign-invested companies that are in the main also privately owned—mostly by expatriate Chinese—and operating in regulatory and market environments increasingly similar to those of domestic private firms (e.g., Chan 2001, Lee 1998, Pun 2005). A common finding of these studies is that various measures of coercion and inhumane treatment have been widely used to shape and control the behavior of employees. Such measures rely heavily on arbitrary use of personal authority and grossly violate basic labor rights, amounting to what some advocacy groups directly characterize as sweatshop practices (Varley 1998).

Whether or to what extent this finding represents the situation in the private sector at large is a question awaiting empirical investigation. There is evidence, though, that even among foreign-

Table 5.1

Profile of Case Study Sites

Case	Location	Products	Number of employees
1	Zhejiang	Paper	34
2	Guangdong	Fertilizers	26
3	Zhejiang	Cement	24
4	Shaanxi	Coal	19
5	Gansu	Coal	22
6	Guangdong	Plastic bags	17
7	Shaanxi	Printing	62
8	Shaanxi	Suitcases	41
9	Zhejiang	Buttons	16
10	Guangdong	Furniture	15
11	Guangdong	Garments	43
12	Zhejiang	Cotton weaving	1,488
13	Guangdong	Dried fruits	9
14	Gansu	Souvenirs	19
15	Zhejiang	Telecommunication devices	103
16	Beijing	Auto parts	377
17	Beijing	Lamps	56

invested enterprises, labor practices vary greatly (Frenkel 2001, Lin 1998; see also Chan 1995), and some companies initially adopting sweatshop practices may also change their management styles in the face of internal and external pressures. In the discussion below, I highlight contrasting findings from several case studies, and then recast them against a broader backdrop of conceptualization.

CASE STUDIES AND A BROAD VIEW OF AUTHORITY RELATIONS

In the summer and fall of 2003 I interviewed fifty-eight employees in seventeen domestic enterprises in Beijing, Zhejiang, Shaanxi, Gansu, and Guangdong. Table 5.1 provides a basic profile of these enterprises. In six of them I did find conditions quite similar to what Chan, Lee, and Pun depicted in their studies. In the workplace, employees were exposed to various kinds of hazards, such as noise; dust; foul air; high temperatures; extremely poor lighting; toxic, corrosive, and/or inflammatory materials; and dangerous tools and equipment. Protective measures against such hazards were either only minimally adopted or nonexistent. The average work time exceeded ten hours per day, yet there was little or no extra pay for work beyond the legal limit (of eight hours). After work hours, workers were confined to very crowded, prison-like dorms (most with very poor sanitary facilities) guarded by factory security personnel—and, in one case, attack dogs— and workers had to obtain special permission to leave the factory compound. Identity cards and travel documents were withheld by their employers, along with a deposit that had to be paid upon employment or deducted from wages during the first few months of work. There were no formal labor contracts or written rules regarding employment, wages, fringe benefits, and basic rights. Although there were strict standards for assessing work outcomes, the criteria for matching rewards with individual behavior and performance were opaque and shifting, subject to the arbitrary or even whimsical judgments of managers. The workloads approached the limits of the physical and mental capacities of workers, and the work processes were tightly paced and under close surveillance, with very little time to break for lunch, drink, rest, or even toilet. Verbal abuse by managers was commonplace; so was delay or irregularity in pay schedules. Fear prevailed among the workers, who faced such threats as blacklisting, pay cuts, fines, dismissal, confiscation of identity cards/travel documents, loss of deposits, ad hoc workload increases, and even physical punishment or assault.

Yet the situations in the remaining eleven enterprises where I interviewed employees were rather different. Working conditions were, in general, not as harsh as those highlighted above, and protection against work-related hazards was fairly adequate. Managers appeared to rely less (and in some cases much less) on arbitrary use of authority, and there appeared to be no apparent or frequent abuse of labor rights. There was at least nominal compliance with the basic requirements of China's 1994 Labor Law on labor contracts, work hours, and remuneration. Internal rules regarding work process, lines of command, individual and group responsibility, and performance evaluation were relatively clearly defined and conveyed to employees. While discipline was strictly enforced, naked coercion was not widespread. Instead, a range of incentives and benefits was used to motivate employees to achieve organizational goals. Performance-based bonuses were adopted to various degrees, and two highly profitable enterprises even granted a year-end bonus to all employees. Some "goodwill" gestures were also used. In one enterprise, for example, the afternoon of the last Saturday of each month was designated as time off with pay for employees whose birthdays fell in that month, and they could get a free, specially prepared birthday dinner from the factory canteen.

Table 5.2 summarizes the contrasting results of my interviews and observations. To be sure, the variations among the seventeen enterprises do not necessarily imply that sweatshop practices are indeed less prevalent than other types of practices. But it is important to ascertain what constitutes a sweatshop and to compare and make sense of the differences between sweatshop-style authority relations and the other styles of authority relations that also may represent impotant parts of reality in China.

From the vast empirical literature on labor exploitation and subjugation in early capitalist development (Deyo 1989, Silver 2003, Thompson 1966), one can discern three common features for the ideal-typical sweatshop: (1) abuse of or disregard for basic labor rights, including the right to be protected from work-related hazards; (2) arbitrary use by managers of organizational authority; and (3) heavy reliance on disciplinary action and punishment to maintain worker compliance. The first feature results from weak or inadequate state institutions for labor protection, a strong ability of firms to resist rules and norms adopted or accepted at the societal level, or a combination of both of these factors. The second feature reflects a low degree of adoption or enforcement of bureaucratic rules that emphasize the centrality of impersonal organizational authority. Together, these two features indicate an underdevelopment of legal-rational rules and regulation in the Weberian sense (Weber 1978), and thus can be seen as belonging to a common dimension. The third feature indicates an extremely narrow focus in the motivation system, which is confined to the use of intimidation and manufacturing of fear while ignoring the stimulating effects of such positive incentives as material rewards, opportunities for skill and/or position advancement, and symbolic goodwill gestures.

Extending the scales of measurement for the above two dimensions to the full, one can get a simple descriptive scheme, shown in Figure 5.1, that encompasses both the ideal-typical sweatshop and many other possible types of internal organization. In fact, the ideal-typical sweatshop may be viewed as an extreme case of what may be called "protocapitalist" approaches to management. Featuring a relatively low degree of legal-rational regulation and a rather limited range of incentives, these approaches figured prominently in early capitalist development in many economies where division of labor extended beyond the confines of family, kinship, and

Table 5.2

Characteristics of Labor Practices in Case Study Sites[a]

Case	Poor working conditions	Arbitrary use of authority	Reliance on coercion and fear
1	H	H	H
2	H	H	H
3	H	H	H
4	H	H	M
5	H	H	M
6	M	H	H
7	H	M	M
8	H	M	L
9	M	M	M
10	M	L	M
11	M	M	L
12	M	L	L
13	M	L	L
14	L	M	L
15	L	L	L
16	L	L	L
17	L	L	L

Note: The degree of consistency with the three conditions stated in the table is assessed as: H = high; M = medium; L = low.

[a]The assessments reported in this table are based on observations and information obtained during case visits. They reflect the subjective views of both the interviewer (this author) and the interviewees (fifty-eight employees). An aggregated score based on ratings from the respondents on a three-level scale and, where possible (e.g., with regard to the work environment), verified by the author was assigned to each case regarding the three issues noted above. Each issue covers more than one aspect. "Poor working conditions" covers employees' unprotected exposure to noise, foul air, dust, high temperature, toxic and/or inflammable materials, extremely poor lighting, and dangerous tools/equipment. "Arbitrary use of authority" concerns the degree of reliance on codified and consistent rules in hiring and firing, task assignment, work hours and scheduling, personnel appointment/deployment, and determination of wages and benefits. "Reliance on coercion and fear" concerns the use of threats and various obtrusive tactics of behavior control (e.g., pay cut/ withholding, fine, blacklisting, withholding of travel documents, and heavy surveillance) versus the use of positive incentives (e.g., material rewards, promotion opportunities, and goodwill gestures).

even community during the transformation from agriculture to industry (Burawoy 1985, Deyo 1989, Koo 1990). In contrast, many other approaches have become more important in industrial and postindustrial capitalism (Perrow 1986, Scott 1998). The essential features of these approaches can also be illustrated by the two-dimensional scheme. The upper left box in Figure 5.1 depicts what may be called "rationalist approaches," which commonly treat employees as purely economic animals and rely heavily on highly codified, impersonal rules and procedures to shape and regulate organizational behavior. The lower right box portrays what may be called "human relational approaches," which treat a firm as both an economic organization and a social unit and emphasize extensive use of both material and nonmaterial incentives to cultivate loyalty, induce and enhance work efforts, and sustain cooperation. The upper right box contains various approaches that may be characterized as "postrationalist," as they often repre-

Figure 5.1 **Categorization of Authority Relations**

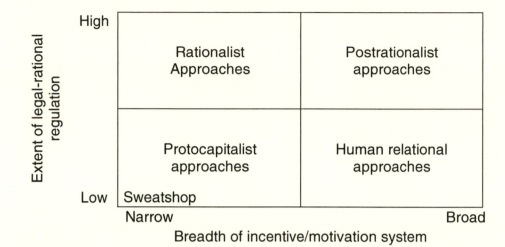

sent efforts to remedy the rigidity and dehumanizing effects of rationalist approaches by reconciling their inherent tension with human relational approaches, and by integrating the two for more optimal results.

It should be noted that the lines separating the four boxes are drawn for heuristic purposes, which also allow for the identification and examination of borderline cases. There is no fixed sequential relationship between the different types. The label "protocapitalist" that I use to denote the lower left box, for example, is intended to draw a parallel between contemporary situations and historical realities. It by no means implies that firms necessarily have to adopt these approaches before taking up other types of organizational design. Also, the protocapitalist approaches are not necessarily transient phenomena. They can persist in certain niches of "mature" capitalist economies (Portes, Castells, and Benton 1989). Moreover, while the two dimensions—within which the four types of authority relations are delineated—are not completely independent of one another (e.g., some regulatory rules may have motivational effects, whereas the use of certain incentives may be coupled with the enforcement or relaxation of such rules), their relationship is neither tautological nor necessarily causal in any uniform direction; if it were either of these, the usefulness of the scheme would greatly diminish.

The pivotal importance of the issues underlying these dimensions (i.e., the type of organizational rules and the scope of incentives) is nothing new in organization studies. The survival and success of organizations in modern society depend greatly on the extent to which they restrain opportunism, enhance cooperation, and cultivate productive efforts among organizational members. The basic rules of an organization are the nuts and bolts, whereas its motivation system is the motor that drives organizational behavior (Steers and Porter 1991). A large part of the economic literature on the "governance structure" of organizations, for example, is concerned with the costs and benefits of various formal rules and regulations—both internal and external—intended to tackle "agency problems" and locate and maintain a minimum floor for cooperation (Milgrom and Roberts 1992, Williamson 1985). A central issue in the management literature on organizational behavior is how to develop effective incentive schemes and management styles to motivate employees toward greater cooperation and increased work effort (Robbins 2001; Steers, Porter, and Bigley 1996). In the sociology of organization, considerable analytical attention has been devoted to the study of relationships between formal and informal organizational structures, and between internal rules and external institutional environments (Scott 1998).

For the study of organizational change in China's economic transition, the two-dimensional scheme proposed here may provide a useful template for mapping the landscape of industrial relations, which is not only rapidly changing but likely to diversify in the directions and outcomes of change. Other than those economic entities that resemble the ideal-typical sweatshop, significant numbers of firms may cluster around other ideal types of internal organization that can be defined and compared via this construct. In the borderline area between postrationalist approaches and human relational approaches, for example, one may locate an ideal type for the "Chinese capitalist" regime of management (Redding 1990) that combines a medium degree of legal-rational regulation and a comprehensive motivation system. One may also specify the ideal type of "Fordism" (Piore and Sabel 1984) with a medium-high degree of legal-rational regulation and a medium-low score on the incentive scale, which can be seen as a subcategory of the rationalist type.

Some caveats, however, should be stated here. The scheme presented above focuses on managerial strategies of behavioral control and leaves out many important aspects of industrial relations, especially those that involve interactions and counterstrategies from employees. An underlying assumption for the horizontal dimension of the construct is that material and nonmaterial incentives are complementary. In reality, different firms adopt different ranges and mixes of these incentives, though oftentimes material incentives have to be used as a floor on which to deploy nonmaterial incentives. Yet the scheme only focuses on the range of incentives and thus does not provide a direct way to differentiate clearly among different mixes/types of incentives. This is a major limitation. The same potential problem exists in the other dimension of the scheme, where two firms under study may demonstrate similar overall levels of legal-rational regulation that nevertheless result from combining different levels of internal and external rationalization. Where these variations are indeed present, further distinction is necessary to account for qualitative differences. Moreover, the scheme is simply a descriptive tool rather than an analytical model, as it does not specify any causal relationship. Its purpose is to provide a preliminary backdrop for the development of research questions and exploration for explanations.

ANALYSIS OF SURVEY DATA

To gauge the usefulness of the two-dimensional construct for comparative research and to explore whether there exist important patterns of authority relations that do not closely fit the sweatshop model but nonetheless merit further examination, I analyze the data from a 1998 questionnaire survey of private-enterprise employees.

The survey was conducted by the Center for the Study of Private Enterprises at the Chinese Academy of Social Sciences. It covered a random sample of 2,073 private-enterprise employees in twelve provincial entities (Anhui, Chongqing, Guangdong, Hebei, Henan, Hubei, Jiangxi, Shaanxi, Shandong, Shanxi, Tianjin, and Zhejiang). Since the data set includes both employees actively involved in production and those engaged in office work, I excluded the latter from the analysis. The remaining subset of data contains responses from 1,350 workers.

The data set contains answers to 189 questions on a variety of issues, including, among other things, the respondent's personal background, work experience, job searches, working conditions, wages and benefits, and relationship with management. From these answers, I derived eight variables that were most relevant to the two-dimensional construct specified above and included them for analysis. Table 5.3 provides the basic descriptive statistics of these variables aggregated to the firm level (see the discussion below).

Table 5.3

Means, Standard Deviations, and Correlations of Variables Used in Data Analysis (*n* = 216)

Variables	Mean	S.D.	1	2	3	4	5	6	7
1 Work–related hazards	1.28	1.39							
2 Sufficiency of protection	2.25	1.50	-0.53						
3 Arbitrary pay cuts	0.25	0.95	0.28	-0.19					
4 Assaults on workers	0.09	0.51	0.25	-0.13	0.80				
5 Deposits withheld	0.05	0.17	0.18	-0.11	0.24	0.27			
6 Adoption of bonus system	0.37	0.46	-0.08	0.08	-0.01	-0.05	-0.08		
7 Assistance for family problems	1.83	0.71	0.24	-0.25	0.17	0.06	0.15	-0.23	
8 Assessment of upward mobility	4.40	1.88	-0.10	0.17	-0.15	-0.05	-0.14	0.15	-0.23

Work-Related Hazards

This variable was constructed from answers to seven questions about whether the following types of hazards were present in the work environment: poor lighting, high temperature, dust, toxic air, loud noise, and inflammable or other harmful material. In the original data set, I coded a "yes" as 1 and a "no" as 0 and then created a new variable by summing the scores for the answers to the seven questions. The highest score was 7, for those indicating the presence of all the types of hazards, and the lowest score was 0, for those indicating no hazards at all. Those with higher scores were assumed to face more hazardous work environments than those with lower scores.

Sufficiency of Protection

This variable was based on answers to a question about whether the enterprises adopted sufficient measures to protect workers from work-related hazards. "No" was coded 1; agreement with the statement "There is no protection but workers are given an allowance for work-related hazard" was coded 2; "yes" was coded 3; and an indication of the absence of any hazard was coded 4. Like the previous variable, this one pertained to the working conditions of employees, which China's 1994 Labor Law requires to be hazard-free. Together, the two variables illustrated the extent of compliance with external legal institutions.

Arbitrary Pay Cuts

This variable was based on answers to a question about the frequency (to the best knowledge of the respondent) of incidents in which managers arbitrarily cut the pay of the employees (including the respondent) of the enterprise during the twelve months preceding the time of the survey The value of the variable corresponded to the number of incidents reported: 0, for example, represented "no occurrence," 1 represented "one occurrence," and so on. The assumption here was that the higher the frequency of arbitrary pay cuts, the greater the degree of arbitrary use of authority.

Assaults on Workers

This variable was based on answers to a question about the frequency (to the best of the respondent's knowledge) of incidents in which managers physically or verbally assaulted workers during the twelve months preceding the time of the survey. Assaults were coded in the same fashion as pay cuts, and higher frequency was again assumed to indicate greater abuse of authority, and vice versa.

Deposits Withheld

Requiring employees to pay a deposit upon employment is an illicit practice adopted by some private enterprises as a financial lever for behavior control. The survey contains a question about this practice. I surveyed a score of 0 to those indicating "no deposit was paid." For each respondent indicating a specific amount of deposit paid, I derived a score by dividing the amount by the respondent's annual wage. The higher the score, the greater the financial impact of the deposit and, presumably, the higher the degree of managerial reliance on extraordinary measures to control employees' behavior. What this and the preceding two variables had in common is that they provided information that could be used to gauge the extent to which managers relied on off-the-book, irregular, and coercive measures to regulate and control the behavior of employees.

Adoption of Bonus System

Each respondent was asked whether his/her enterprise had adopted a bonus system (1, "yes"; 0, "no"). This variable provided a proxy for the use of material incentives: firms adopting bonus systems are assumed to offer a wider range of material incentives than those not adopting such systems.

Assessment of Mobility

This variable was based on the question "Who among the employees are likely to be promoted?" The answers were scored as follows: 5 for "people achieving outstanding work results"; 4 for "anyone who works hard has a chance"; 3 for "people with strong abilities"; 2 for "people with better education"; 1 for "people with local household registration status," "people with good relations with the boss or having other special backers," or "workers will always remain workers, there are no promotion opportunities for them." The varying scores were assumed to reflect degrees of organizational mobility based on criteria with varying degrees of relevance to work outcomes. Since organizational mobility has both material and nonmaterial (self-actualization or aspiration-related) implications, this variable provided a proxy for mixed incentives.

Assistance for Family Problems

This variable was based on a question about whether the "boss" (which usually referred to the owner of a respondent's enterprise) provided special assistance to workers whose families encountered rather serious problems (1, "yes"; 2, "sometimes"; 3, "no"). Since employees' family problems per se are not work related, variations in this score could be seen as indicating varying intensity in the use of goodwill gestures, which are mainly a form of nonmaterial incentive.

Since the main purpose of the data analysis was to discern patterns of authority relations in different private firms rather than the characteristics of the specific work space that each respondent faced, it was necessary to aggregate the responses at the firm level. Unfortunately, the data set contained no definitive information about the enterprises in which the respondents were employed. To remedy this problem, I used two pieces of information available in the data set to identify the respondents' organizational affiliations: a five-digit postal code for each case, and the answer to a question about the economic sector in which a respondent's enterprise operated. I sorted those respondents who indicated the same postal code and economic sector into the same group. This classification resulted in the identification of 216 enterprises. On the basis of this information, for each group I computed the average scores of its members' responses to the eight questions noted above.

To ascertain whether it was appropriate to aggregate these variables at the firm level, I calculated single-item interrater agreement (r_{wg}) statistics (James, Demaree, and Wolf 1984, 1993). (Multiple-item r_{wg}s could not be calculated owing to variation in the scale of measurement among the variables.) The result showed that more than 80 percent of the groups had a single-item r_{wg} at 0.7 or above for each variable.

I performed a confirmatory factor analysis of the aggregated variables. Since the first two variables and the subsequent three variables described above are proxies for different aspects of the same latent dimension—legal-rational regulation—I ran a second-order analysis to examine their correlation both to the specific aspects in which they were respectively nested and to the common dimension. A comparison of the results of this analysis with those of a trial run of a first-

Table 5.4

Results (factor loadings) of Second-Order Confirmatory Factor Analysis of Internal Organization Variables[a]

	F1	F2	F3	F4
Work-related hazards	0.93			
Sufficiency of protection	−0.55			
Arbitrary pay cuts		0.89		
Assaults on workers		0.91		
Deposits withheld		0.29		
Adoption of bonus system			0.51	
Assessment of upward mobility			0.35	
Assistance for family problems			−0.54	
F1				0.68
F2				0.48

[a]$c^2 = 32$ ($df = 18$), $p < 0.05$; GFI adjusted for $df = 0.91$; RMSEA estimate $= 0.07$; normed fit index $= 0.9$.

Table 5.5

Results of k-Means Cluster Analysis[a]

	Cluster means		
Cluster category	Breadth of incentives (F3)	Legal-rational regulation (F4)	Number of cases
1 Human relational	0.57 (0.34)	−0.45 (0.24)	56
2 Protocapitalist	−0.50 (0.37)	−0.36 (0.28)	50
3 Rationalist	−0.69 (0.34)	0.51 (0.38)	32
4 Postrationalist	0.34 (0.40)	0.65 (0.40)	23

[a]Pseudo $F = 124.21$; cubic clustering criterion $= -3.9$; approximate expected overall $R^2 = 0.76$. Figures in parentheses are standard deviations.

order confirmatory factor analysis of these five variables as items in the same dimension showed that the second-order analysis markedly improved all the goodness-of-fit statistics (first-order analysis results are: $\chi^2 = 48$ [$df = 20$], $p < 0.0005$; GFI adjusted for $df = 0.88$; RMSEA estimate = 0.09; normed fit index = 0.85.) This pattern suggested that the second-order analysis represented a more appropriate model. I report the results of the analysis in Table 5.4.

To map out the patterns of authority relations more clearly, I obtained the composite scores for F3 and F4, which were approximations of the two key dimensions in the descriptive scheme developed above—that is, the breadth of the incentive/motivation system and the degree of legal-rational regulation, respectively. These scores were then included in a k-means cluster analysis using the PROC FASTCLUS procedure in SAS. Following the classification defined in the descriptive scheme, I set the maximum number of clusters at four. Fifty-five cases were omitted from the analysis owing to missing values. Table 5.5 contains the results of the analysis.

DISCUSSION

First, the factor loadings reported in Table 5.4 show that variables 1 and 2, work-related hazards and sufficiency of protection, are closely correlated with a common factor (F1), and variables 3 and 4, arbitrary pay cuts and assaults on workers, with another common factor (F2). The loading for the fifth variable, deposits withheld, is not as strong, though its inclusion results in improved goodness-of-fit statistics for the model (results from a trial run without this variable are not shown). These two factors in turn are significantly correlated with still another factor, F4, which, as noted above, proxies the degree of legal-rational regulation. On the other hand, variables 6–8, adoption of bonus system and assessment of upward mobility, bear moderate to strong correlation with a common factor (F3), which I characterize as the breadth of the motivation system. The goodness-of-fit measures reported at the bottom of the table indicate a generally adequate fit for the second-order analysis model. Overall, these findings provide moderate confirmation that the two-dimensional construct provides a useful descriptive tool to capture and classify the many-faceted variations in labor practice among different private enterprises.

Second, the results of the cluster analysis show that the cases included in the sample can be divided into four quadrants in a coordinate plane that resembles the two-dimensional scheme: quadrant 1 for "postrationalist" approaches, quadrant 2 for "rationalist" approaches, quadrant 3 for "protocapitalist" approaches, and quadrant 4 for "human relational" approaches. Clearly, there are quite a number of enterprises in the protocapitalist category, where the ideal-typical sweatshop represents an extreme situation. Yet, there are also significant numbers of cases in the other three categories, which together outnumber those akin to the sweatshop model. This pattern suggests that, while the sweatshop model may be a useful benchmark, it is necessary to look beyond it for a fuller view of the diverse landscape of industrial relations in China's private sector.

Third, and interestingly, the human relational category contains the largest number of cases. A further examination of the output data shows that for firms in this cluster, F4—the degree of legal-rational regulation—is significantly correlated with work-related hazards and sufficiency of protection (the Pearson correlations are 0.97 and –0.48, respectively), which concern working conditions, and insignificantly correlated with variables 3–5, which are primarily proxies for arbitrariness in the use of authority. This suggests that many firms in this category may have sought to use a broad range of incentives to offset the negative effects of harsh working conditions, which are not uncommon in early capitalist development and may be rather costly to fix quickly, especially for firms that have limited resources and operate in highly competitive environments.

Fourth, it is noteworthy that the postrationalist category contains the smallest number of cases. Also, the gap between the absolute values of the two cluster means for this category is wider than those for the other three categories, suggesting a possible disparity in the relative weight assigned to each of the two dimensions of organizational design. A case-by-case inspection of the output data reveals that none of the cases has similarly high scores in both dimensions. This may be due to the fact that, despite efforts to integrate rationalist and "natural" methods of management (Scott 1998), the intrinsic tension between them remains difficult to reconcile fully. Although China's private sector is still developing and thus may not provide sufficient factual and analytic ground for higher-level generalization, this provisional finding does raise the theoretical and empirical question of whether there exists a "zone of near impossibility" (at the upper right corner of the construct) in the internal organization of modern economic activity.

Finally, it should be pointed out that the data analyzed here have limitations. The questionnaire was not designed for this kind of investigation; as a result, only a small number of relevant variables could be used for the factor analysis and the cluster analysis. There is no information about the basic profile/background of the enterprises in which the employees worked, which limits further analysis of the forces that may have shaped the different patterns of authority relations. Nor are there any responses from enterprise managers to the same or similar questions that can be used to corroborate or be compared with the responses provided by the employees. Most of the variables are not on the ratio or interval scale, which may cause distortions in the factor analysis. What I report here, therefore, should be viewed as provisional findings.

CONCLUSIONS AND REFLECTIONS ON
FUTURE RESEARCH DIRECTIONS

Although the study reported in this chapter does not resolve the empirical question of whether the sweatshop is the predominant mode of internal organization among private enterprises in China, the findings reported above do suggest that other types of authority relations may not be trivial phenomena and thus are worth investigating. Using the sweatshop model as a heuristic tool, I developed a more encompassing scheme for mapping diverse patterns of internal organization in the fast-growing private sector. While there is provisional evidence confirming the plausibility of this scheme, much more needs to be done to ascertain its validity and operationalize its use.

If the diversity in the pattern of authority relations revealed by the data analysis is verified by data of more extensive coverage and better quality, it will be important to further explore where these different patterns are most likely to be found and what causes the variations among private enterprises. Before the reemergence of private economic activities in the post-Mao era, China was under the rule of state socialism. Privatization of public enterprises is a major avenue through which the private sector has grown, especially during the past decade. Many privatized enterprises not only have inherited a sizeable part of the old workforce along with their path-dependent perceptions and expectations about work, remuneration, and authority, but continue to make partial use of the preexisting internal rules and regulations. Some private owners are also former managers of state-owned enterprises (SOEs) or collective enterprises and continue to carry membership in the Communist Party, which may cast a moral and political constraint on their decision making. A question of great interest in this connection is whether the institutional and organizational legacies of the previous era have had any bearing on the construction or reconstruction of authority relations in private enterprises. For example, are employees with prior work experience in public enterprises less likely to be found in private firms adopting protocapitalist approaches to behavioral control? Are sweatshop practices less prevalent among privatized SOEs? Are private owners who used to be managers of public enterprises more inclined to avoid human relational approaches so as to eradicate any remnants of the "principled particularism" that was prevalent under the prereform system (Walder 1986)?

With the central planning system fading into history, government control over the economy has been increasingly decentralized. At the same time, the organizational health of the party-state has also deteriorated (Lin 2001). Since the state is the main external force that monitors organizational compliance with the Labor Law and related regulations, the relationship with local officials may assume great importance to private owners' strategies of behavior control over workers. On the other hand, the careers of officials continue to depend on the bureaucratic performance evaluation system, where maintaining social stability is used as one of the key criteria. Bad publicity about inhumane treatment of workers and/or labor unrest can be politically costly to leading local officials. A question that merits investigation is whether sweatshop practices are more likely to be found where private owners both have cozy relationships with local officials and operate in locales that are shielded, intentionally or unintentionally, from press coverage. (Incidentally, the mass media themselves have become more decentralized and competitive on the one hand, yet commercialized and prone to manipulation and corruption on the other.)

As in early capitalist development elsewhere, a significant portion of the workforce in China's reemerging private sector consists of rural migrants who are socially uprooted from their home communities. Yet, a peculiar feature of economic development in the reform era is rural industrialization driven by community-based enterprises, which mainly operated under public ownership in the 1980s but have subsequently become increasingly private and have continued to employ large numbers of locals. The bifurcation of the workforce into migrants and locally based workers provides an interesting case for studying the effects of communal norms and social pressures on the internal organization of capitalist production. Are migrants, for example, more likely than local residents to end up in sweatshops? Do age, education, gender, social networks, and labor market experience have any mediating effects on this? Are local employees more likely to work in firms adopting human relational approaches to management? Does family ownership, which is often associated with personalist styles of management in overseas Chinese business organizations (Redding 1990), make any difference in this regard?

Since the start of economic reforms, China has been increasingly integrated into the global economy. Economic internationalization has provided leapfrogging opportunities for some domestic private firms to adopt advanced technologies, which in turn may constrain the choice of strategies for internal organization (e.g., a chip maker cannot operate in dusty workshops with fluctuating temperatures, and a manufacturer using expensive precision equipment may have to confront the fact that it can be easily damaged by physically exhausted and/or mentally disturbed workers). If technological advancement indeed reduces the probability for sweatshop practices to survive, does it also have any directional impact on the selection and pursuit of alternatives among the three other broad types highlighted above? Moreover, as transaction partners, collaborators, and/or competitors of multinational corporations and/or foreign-invested companies, increasing numbers of domestic private firms are exposed to the influence of foreign managerial practices, which may manifest themselves through demonstration effect, decree (e.g., for compliance with internationally accepted labor practices as a precondition for transaction), and/or competitive pressures. Is this learning process more active in places (e.g., the coastal region and large cities) where foreign presence has reached a certain critical mass? Do the age, gender, education, and prior work and life experience of the owner of a firm matter to the resultant synthesis of strategies for organizational behavior control? What effects do the variations in labor practices adopted by different types of foreign companies (e.g., multinational corporations versus small firms based in economies like Hong Kong, South Korea, and Taiwan) have on organizational learning? Addressing these questions, as well as those noted above, will no doubt contribute to a better understanding of China's economic transformation.

REFERENCES

Blecher, M. J. (2002). Hegemony and workers' politics in China. *China Quarterly,* 170, 283–303.
Burawoy, M. (1985). *The politics of production: Factory regimes under capitalism and socialism.* London: Verso.
Chan, A. (1995). The emerging patterns of industrial relations in China and the rise of two new labor movements. *China Information, 9,* 36–59.
———. (2001). *China's workers under assault: The exploitation of labor in a globalizing economy.* Armonk, NY: M.E. Sharpe.

Clarke, S. (Ed.) (1996). *Conflict and change in the Russian industrial enterprise.* Cheltenham, England: Edward Elgar.

Deyo, F. (1989). *Beneath the miracle: Labor subordination in the new Asian industrialism.* Berkeley: University of California Press.

Editorial Office (EO). (1987–2003). *China township enterprise yearbook* (in Chinese). Beijing: Zhongguo nongye chubanshe.

Frenkel, S. J. (2001). Globalization, athletic footwear commodity chains and employment relations in China. *Organization Studies, 22,* 531–62.

James, L. R.; R. G. Demaree; and G. Wolf. (1984). Estimating within-group interrater reliability with and without response bias. *Journal of Applied Psychology, 69,* 85–98.

———. (1993). r_{wg}: an assessment of within-group interrater agreement. *Journal of Applied Psychology, 78,* 306–09.

Koo, H. (1990). From farm to factory: proletarianization in Korea. *American Sociological Review, 55,* 669–81.

Lee, C. K. (1998). *Gender and the South China miracle: Two worlds of factory women.* Berkeley: University of California Press.

Leupp, G. P. (1992). *Servants, shophands, and laborers in the cities of Tokugawa Japan.* Princeton, NJ: Princeton University Press.

Lin, Y. (1998). Governing the workplace: Regimes of labor control in foreign-invested enterprises in coastal China. Paper presented at the Annual Meeting of the Association for Asian Studies, March 28, Washington, DC.

———. (2001). *Between politics and markets: Firms, competition, and institutional change in post-Mao China.* Cambridge, England: Cambridge University Press.

Milgrom, P., and J. Roberts. (1992). *Economics, organization and management.* Englewood Cliffs, NJ: Prentice-Hall.

Murphy, J. B. (1993). *The moral economy of labor: Aristotelian themes in economic theory.* New Haven, CT: Yale University Press.

National Bureau of Statistics (NBS). (1990–2004). *China statistical yearbook* (in Chinese). Beijing: Zhongguo tongji chubanshe.

O'Leary, G. (Ed.) (1998). *Adjusting to capitalism: Chinese workers and the state.* Armonk, NY: M.E. Sharpe.

Perrow, C. (1986). *Complex organization: A critical essay.* New York: Random House.

Piore, M. J., and C. F. Sabel. (1984). *The second industrial divide: Possibilities for prosperity.* New York: Basic Books.

Portes, A.; M. Castells; and L. A. Benton. (Eds.) (1989). *The informal economy: Studies in advanced and less developed countries.* Baltimore, MD: Johns Hopkins University Press.

Powelson, J. P. (1998). *The moral economy.* Ann Arbor: University of Michigan Press.

Pun, N. (2005). *Made in China: Women factory workers in a global workplace.* Durham, NC: Duke University Press.

Redding, S. G. (1990). *The spirit of Chinese capitalism.* Berlin and New York: Walter de Gruyter.

Robbins, S. (2001). *Organizational behavior.* Upper Saddle River, NJ: Prentice-Hall.

Schmiechen, J. A. (1984). *Sweated industries and sweated labor: The London clothing trades, 1860–1914.* Urbana and Chicago: University of Illinois Press.

Scott, W. R. (1998). *Organizations: Rational, natural, and open systems.* Upper Saddle River, NJ: Prentice-Hall.

Silver, B. J. (2003). *Forces of labor: Workers' movements and globalization since 1870.* Cambridge, England: Cambridge University Press.

Solinger, D. (2002). Labor market reform and the plight of the laid-off proletariat. *China Quarterly, 170,* 304–26.

Steers, R. M., and L. W. Porter. (1991). *Motivation and work behavior.* New York: McGraw-Hill.

Steers, R. M.; L. W. Porter; and G. A. Bigley. (1996). *Motivation and leadership at work.* New York: McGraw-Hill.

Thompson, E. P. (1966). *The making of the English working class.* New York: Vintage Books.

Varley, P. (Ed.) (1998). *The sweatshop quandary: Corporate responsibility on the global frontier.* Washington, DC: Investor Responsibility Research Center.

Walder, A. (1986). *Communist neo-traditionalism: Work and authority in Chinese industry.* Berkeley: University of California Press.

Weber, M. (1978). *Economy and society.* Berkeley: University of California Press.

Williamson, O. E. (1985). *The economic institutions of capitalism.* New York: Free Press.

6

PROPERTY RIGHTS REGIMES AND FIRM BEHAVIOR

THEORY VERSUS EVIDENCE

Xueguang Zhou, He Cai, and Qiang Li

This book is about "domestic private firms" in China's transitional economy. This choice of subject matter already implies that the private sector has some distinct features that other, nonprivate sectors lack. This disposition invites a series of questions: What are the distinct behavioral characteristics, if any, of firms in the private sector? What are the mechanisms that generate these characteristics? These are the key issues we hope to explore in this chapter.

As it turns out, the very notion of "private firms" is muddy in the Chinese context. In the official classification system, "private firms" and "private entrepreneurs" belong to a specifically designated category, separate from other privately owned firms such as foreign firms or shareholding firms. Officially, *private entrepreneur (getihu)* refers to an individual- or family-based enterprise with eight or fewer employees; a *private firm* is a firm that is privately owned by an individual or partners and has more than eight employees. Excluded from this category are many so-called shareholding companies, or hybrid forms of organizations, which are to a great extent owned and operated as private firms. As many state or semistate firms are in the process of being brought into the private sector, the boundaries between the private sector and other nonprivate sectors become increasingly blurred.

This recognition leads us to the following question: What is the relationship between firm ownership and firm behavior? A central proposition in theories of property rights is that there is a strong association between the two. A close relationship between firm ownership and firm behavior is explicitly argued or implicitly assumed in various social science theories. Property rights/ ownership has also been routinely used as an analytical device in the study of Chinese economic and social institutions. Sociologists who study China make use of property rights/ownership to explain systematic variations across firms (Guthrie 1997; Lin 1995; Nee 1992; Walder 1995; Zhou, Zhao, Li, and Cai 2003) and the role of firms in the stratified social order (Bian and Logan 1996; Peng 1992; Walder 1992; Zhou 2000; Zhou, Tuma, and Moen 1997). For example, in our previous study, we made the following observations:

> Consequently, different types of firms may have distinctive behavioral patterns in contractual relationships. First, different firms experience different resource and regulatory constraints based on their institutional links. For example, state-owned firms are most sensitive

to state regulatory influences because of their close administrative and institutional ties to government agencies: Senior managers in these firms are appointed by the supervising agencies and internal operations are subject to routine inspections by the supervising agencies. In contrast, private firms tend to be much more remote from such influences because of their weak institutional links to the government. In between there are collective firms, which are often not under the direct control of the government but have close links with local governments. In the reform era, a new type of "hybrid firms" has emerged (e.g., "stock-sharing" firms) that has characteristics of transitional organizational forms; their behaviors are often similar to those of private firms.

Second, different property-right relationships (state or private ownership) also entail different incentive structures in managing business relations. Because they have close ties to political authorities, state firms may rely more on administrative channels in managing the business environment, whereas private firms may have a strong incentive to cultivate informal social relations. Therefore, we would expect systematic behavioral differences across types of firms. (Zhou et al. 2003, 79)

On the other hand, these studies also expose a glaring gap in knowledge: Although theoretical models of the importance of property rights abound (Nee 1992, Stark 1996, Walder 1995), few empirical studies look into the link between ownership and firm behavior, especially in a comparative framework (for recent developments, see Oi and Walder 1999). Our own statements quoted above were based more on impressionistic observations than on systematic empirical research—that is, the proposition about the relationship between property rights and firm behavior was largely based on theoretical ideas and has not been subjected to careful empirical scrutiny. As such, it should be treated as a theoretical speculation to be tested with data. This study explores the relationship between firm ownership and firm behavior empirically, with the aim of substantiating and qualifying our statements above.

CONTRASTING TWO THEORETICAL LOGICS

To guide presentation of our study, we first highlight and contrast two theoretical arguments on property rights, with special reference to the context of China's transitional economy. The first argument emphasizes distinct incentive mechanisms associated with property rights; the second is related to distinct business environments, especially institutional environments, encompassing firms exhibiting different property rights regimes.

Property Rights and Incentive Mechanisms

The key assumption in this line of argument is that individuals, including firm owners and employees, respond to incentives structured by the institutional arrangement of their firm. As Kornai (1980) showed, in a planned economy, in which production quotas and resource allocations are controlled by central authorities, and where soft budget constraints impose no consequences for inefficiency, firms have little incentive to gain efficiency. Rather, such an incentive structure induces firms to maximize inputs so as to meet production quotas, thereby generating chronic shortage problems under planned economies. Private owners in a market economy behave differently: the residual claim to profits based on private ownership provides a strong incentive for firms to pursue efficiency and improves marketplace competitiveness. This line of reasoning has been especially elaborated in economic studies of transitional economies.

According to this logic, then, one should expect distinct firm behaviors associated with different property rights/ownership in response to variations in the underlying incentive mechanisms. From internal authority structures to production processes to behaviors in the marketplace, one should expect to find significant, systematic variations in firm behavior that can be explained in light of the efficiency principle and the incentives associated with different property rights regimes. For example, this logic implies significant variations in interfirm contractual relationships across property rights regimes. The pursuit of efficiency is likely to induce private firms to adopt business practices that can maximize their profits. In contrast, the public ownership of state-owned firms gives managers less incentive to work for their firms; instead, they tend to pursue their own interests (e.g., accepting kickbacks or bribes) at the expense of the long-term firm interests.

Business Environment and Organizational Constraints

The second line of argument emphasizes that institutional arrangements in an economy lead to distinct patterns of distribution of resources, information, and political intervention and provide differential access to these resources for firms in different sectors or representing different forms of property rights. Firms with different forms of ownership (different property rights regimes) also experience different regulatory regimes and preferential policies or restrictions. As a result, firms are exposed to different business environments, especially institutional environments, that induce different behavioral patterns.

Although environmental constraints can be interpreted as incentives that motivate firms to adopt different behaviors, in our view it is more useful to treat environmental constraints as a distinct set of mechanisms. First, this conceptualization leads us to focus on organizational environments and on the analysis of interactions between firms and their environments. In contrast, an emphasis on incentives would direct our attention to individual firms and how they respond to such incentives. By highlighting the role of environments, we see firms not as merely reacting to incentives imposed by the environments; rather, we see them as engaging in a repeated game with other players in their environments (e.g., local governments). Second, a focus on environmental constraints may also lead us to identify new mechanisms that affect firm behavior. For example, state-owned firms' failure to acquire needed resources in their competition with private firms may not be due to a lack of incentives; rather, it may be a consequence of imposed institutional constraints. A focus on incentives would not easily shed light on the key mechanisms here.

However, neither of these logics can be accepted wholesale. First, consider the issue of incentives. In developing his model of "local government as industrial headquarters," Walder (1995) emphasized that, by aligning the interests of local authorities with those of local firms, the authorities can design effective monitoring mechanisms to ensure the performance of the firms. A broader issue underlying Walder's argument is this: Is it possible to devise institutional arrangements such that appropriate incentives are provided to align the interests of managers (in firms) with those of owners (central or local governments), if ownership and management are separate? That is, as Walder and Oi (1999, 3) put it: "To the extent that governments must exercise property rights over public firms, can incentives be created to make government officials behave in ways different than in years past?"

Second, institutional changes in recent years point to a decisive separation between governmental officials and the daily operation of firms, even in the state sector. In many respects, state-owned firms' involvement in market competition is not substantively different from that of private firms. Logically, one may infer that the behaviors of state-owned firms are increasingly disciplined by market mechanisms. The corresponding questions are: To what extent are state-owned firms governed by public/government property rights? Can market competition provide incentives for state firms to behave like private firms?

Third, there have been enormous changes in institutional environments in recent years. The rise of a variety of organizational forms—especially the transformation of state-owned firms into shareholding firms—has greatly blurred the boundaries of different types of firms and their corresponding institutional environments. The rise of shareholding companies, in which both the state and private owners share ownership, is permanently altering the traditional boundaries between public and private sectors.

These observations raise issues about the relationship between firm ownership and firm behavior. On the one hand, the theoretical ideas and logics in the literature are largely cast in terms of discrete institutional forms and distinct mechanisms; on the other hand, institutional forms and mechanisms are increasingly blended and intertwined in the real world. Even in industrialized market societies, the link between ownership and firm performance has been empirically elusive and subject to multiple interpretations (Kang and Sorensen 1999). As a result, the validity and usefulness of these ideas need to be carefully examined. To the best of our knowledge, there have not been careful, systematic comparisons of firm behavior across property rights regimes. In Chinese studies, most research focuses on one type of firm (e.g., state firms or private firms) rather than comparisons between types. Some studies have compared firms with different property rights regimes (Jefferson and Rawski 1994; Jefferson, Rawski, Li, and Zheng 2000), but their focus was on firm performance in terms of productivity or profits, which was heavily constrained by preexisting institutional arrangements.[1] We seek to examine firm behavior on more meaningful bases.

What is needed now is not another exercise in theoretical speculation; rather, researchers should begin careful detective work to understand what is really going on in China's transitional economy, to develop concepts and typologies that are sensible in mapping out recent changes. In this chapter, we take a step in this direction and focus on empirical patterns of firm behavior in the private sector. We propose to analyze firm behavior in a comparative framework; that is, we compare and contrast behaviors of firms in the private sector with the behaviors of firms under other property rights in order to assess the role of ownership in inducing behavioral patterns. In some cases, we will focus on comparing private firms with those in the state sector and the sector of hybrid firms. The state sector provides the sharpest contrast to the private sector in both incentive structures and institutional environments. Therefore, the comparison between the two allows us to assess variations across property rights regimes in a stark manner. We chose to examine the "hybrid firm sector"—mainly shareholding companies that were previously under state ownership—in order to assess how changes in property rights (from state ownership to market-based shareholding) affect firm behavior. In a sense, hybrid firms are a special case between state firms and private firms. In other cases, we compare private firms, state firms, and hybrid firms, as well as collective firms and foreign firms (including those of Hong Kong and Taiwan).

Our empirical study is organized around the following issues: (1) What are the relationships between ownership types and their environments? (2) What are the differences across property rights regimes in their formation of interfirm relationships? (3) What are the differences in internal management and structures across property rights regimes? The empirical evidence reported in this study is mainly based on data collected in our interfirm contract project and on our interviews with managers and salespersons in Beijing and Guangzhou between 2000 and 2002. For more information on the collection of the original data, see Appendix A in Zhou et al. (2003). We also draw additional examples and cases from media reports and research reports in the Chinese literature to illustrate these patterns.

Before we begin our empirical inquiry, we briefly discuss the measurement of ownership, which is the central issue of our study. In this study, interviewees from Chinese firms provided the ownership information in the interfirm contract data. We asked the respondents to choose the ownership structure that was most appropriate to describe his or her company from a list of nine types of property rights. We combined some of these categories in the analyses reported here. Given the complexity of the issue of property rights, one may question the reliability of the information provided by the respondents. In our judgment, the information provided by the respondents is more reliable than that reported in official statistics. For example, some firms may be officially labeled as "collective firms" but are in fact owned and operated as private firms. Firm members are more likely to convey truthful information about their firms' ownership in our interviews than in their reports to authorities. A more challenging issue is that many firms are in a transition phase or involve multiple property rights beyond the labels they adopted. For example, a small state firm may in fact be in the process of "secret" privatization. Or a large private firm may be having intensive interactions with political authorities. In such cases, self-labeled ownership categories may not match behaviors. We need to keep these issues in mind as we explore the empirical patterns in the rest of the chapter.

Throughout our discussions, we use *property rights regimes* to refer to the collective characteristics associated with ownership type, including institutional environment, internal structure, and behavioral patterns. This is a working conceptual construct based on the assumption that ownership type implies particular manifestations along these dimensions and that firms that share a type of ownership share common characteristics. Of course, the validity of this conceptual construct needs to be evaluated empirically, and we will revisit this set of issues toward the end of this chapter.

THE CONTEXT: CHANGES IN PROPERTY RIGHTS REGIMES IN CHINA'S TRANSITIONAL ECONOMY

Do property rights matter in the transformation of a state socialist economy? Judging by China's reform experience, the answer is an unambiguous "yes." As we noted above, a salient characteristic of China's economy is the presence of a variety of organizational ownership types—even before the economic transformation. Unlike the USSR, China has retained different forms of firm ownership since 1949: state-owned, collective, private, and mixed property rights. On the eve of the economic reform of the late 1970s, however, state owned and collective were the two dominant forms of firm ownership. In the processes of economic transformation over the last two decades, the reform of state-owned firms has involved changes in managerial incentives and ownership structures. Walder and Oi (1999, 7–10) reviewed several types of changes in China's reform processes: (1) changes in managerial incentive contracts; (2) onset of the contracted public asset involving government-management partnerships; (3) onset of leased public assets, and (4) privatization. Even in state-owned firms, there is the distinct possibility of "the hollowing out of public ownership."

We found a similar trend in our research on interfirm contractual relationships in two Chinese cities, Beijing and Guangzhou. Of the 621 firms in our data, 153 firms (about 25 percent) experienced changes in ownership. As Figure 6.1 shows, the transformation of firm ownership has accelerated since the 1990s, especially since the mid-1990s. Changes from state-owned firms to other types of firms accounted for 54 percent of all changes, and changes from collective firms accounted for another 20 percent. Among firms leaving state ownership, 78 percent became stockholding companies, and about 8 percent become foreign-owned firms. Among firms leaving collective ownership, 66 percent became stockholding compa-

Figure 6.1 **Number of Firms that Experienced Changes in Ownership**

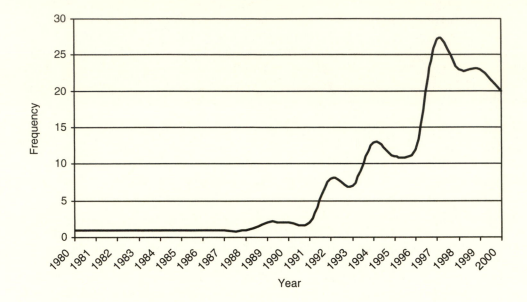

nies, 9 percent became private firms, and 22 percent became foreign-owned firms. Glimpses of these patterns reveal that changes in ownership have been extensive and gaining momentum in recent years.

Are there structural differences among firms across different property rights regimes? Table 6.1 reports descriptive statistics by ownership types for the firms in this study. Several characteristics are worth noting. First, state firms tend to be long established, large (in both size and sales volume), and in manufacturing industries; in contrast, private firms tend to be young, small firms in light industry and the retail sector. (Private entrepreneurs [*getihu*] are not included in our sample.) Second, in many respects, hybrid firms are similar to state firms (e.g., in size). This is not surprising, since a large proportion of hybrid firms were previously state firms. Their concentration in light industry and the retail sector is consistent with the fact that these sectors have experienced more rapid privatization in recent years. Third, collective firms also show similarities to state firms in age and industrial location, but they are much smaller. Finally, foreign firms tend to be large in production scale (sales volume), and they are heavily concentrated in light industry and the retail sector. These characteristics show that property rights relationships are associated with important institutional legacies and sectoral differences among firms. We need to keep these institutional contexts in mind as we interpret the relationship between property rights and firm behavior in the rest of this chapter.

FIRM BEHAVIORS ACROSS PROPERTY RIGHTS REGIMES: EMPIRICAL EVIDENCE

We now turn to assessing the association between firm ownership and firm behavior by contrasting private firms with other types of firms on several aspects. As we noted earlier, in this study we do not examine the link between firm ownership and firm economic performance (e.g., profitability or growth) for several reasons. First, an assessment of economic performance requires a differ-

Table 6.1

Descriptive Statistics of Firm Attributes, by Ownership Type

	State	Private	Hybrid	Collective	Foreign
Age in years	26.1	7.7	16.1	19.5	13.8
Size: number of employees	1,591	141	581	217	506
Sales (in 10,000 *yuan*)	61,787	3,329	16,345	6,417	53,187
Industry					
Heavy	29.3	2.9	7.8	15.4	7.0
Light	27.8	41.0	31.7	32.3	45.6
Construction	4.3	1.9	8.5	6.2	3.5
Retail	15.6	31.4	25.4	18.5	19.3
Banking, insurance, social service	10.9	4.8	8.5	10.8	12.3
Education, health, welfare	3.8	11.4	7.8	7.7	3.5
Other	8.5	6.7	10.6	9.2	8.8
Number of firms	214	117	141	62	57

ent research design, and it has been systematically carried out in other scholarly publications (e.g., Jefferson and Rawski 1994, Jefferson et al. 2000). Second, we also believe that comparisons of "performance" dimensions offer an incomplete or even misleading picture. This is because different types of firms are under different structural/institutional constraints and pursuing different goals. State firms, for example, are often directed by the government to pursue goals related to employment and welfare functions (e.g., providing benefits for their retirees) in the reform era, whereas private firms typically have no such institutional constraints. Therefore, to gauge the role of firm ownership, we propose to examine firm behavior in a variety of areas, specifically: (1) patterns of resource dependence; (2) patterns of interaction with other organizations; (3) relationships with political authorities; (4) patterns of interfirm contracting; and (5) employment relationships within organizations.

Patterns of Resource Dependence by Firm Ownership

We begin with an inquiry into patterns of resource dependence among firm types. This set of analyses, together with those below, allows us to identify and assess whether resource dependence is a key mechanism in generating behavioral differences across property rights regimes. Specifically, we ask, What are the channels through which firms acquire their factor resources? Are there any differences in resource dependence across property rights regimes? In an ideal marketplace, resources are transacted through price competition. In equilibrium, the principle of market efficiency dictates that resources flow to those firms that can make the best use of them (and are therefore willing to pay the highest price for them); by this logic, the issue of specific channels through which resources flow is a trivial one.

However, market mechanisms are but one of many channels through which a firm acquires resources. This is especially so in transitional economies. Different channels of access often decisively affect the survival chances of different types of firms. Ownership affects resource flows in two ways: First, ownership conditions access to channels of resource acquisition. Relative to other types of firms, for example, state-owned firms are more likely to have strong ties to political authorities and acquire resources through "rent-seeking." This relationship has evolved considerably in the reform era. Some evidence indicates that local governments play an increasingly important role in allocating business opportunities. For example, to assist the reforms initiated by state-owned firms, the Dalian municipal government was actively involved in providing institutional support for laid-off employees by channeling them to employment services; the government also provided special policies and financial resources to support these reform measures, according to the newspaper *Renmin Ribao* (RMRB) in an article published April 27, 2000. In contrast, private firms are heavily constrained in their access to financial resources and the use of land for development (RMRB, March 15, 2000). Although direct links between governments and firms have been greatly weakened in recent years, their current extent and effectiveness remains an empirical question. Second, ownership also affects resource channels by providing different incentives for firms to develop different strategies for resource acquisition. Private firms, lacking institution-based channels, are likely to adopt alternative means to secure resources. Distinct patterns of resource dependence based on ownership structures, if they exist, can provide an important means to explain and predict corresponding firm behaviors.

To explore this set of questions, we asked respondents interviewed in our interfirm contract study to indicate which of the three channels (government, marketplace, and social networks) was the *main channel* for their firms' acquisition of the following factor resources: (1) raw material supplies; (2) financial resources; (3) labor; and (4) product sales.[2] We tabulated the descriptive statistics by the conventional ownership types; Figures 6.2a–6.2d are graphs of these results.[3]

These patterns can be summarized as follows: First, there are noticeable variations in firms' resource dependencies, regardless of ownership type. It appears that the transaction of products and factor resources is to a large extent "marketized," as indicated by the fact that a majority (70–90 percent) of the firms in our sample identified the marketplace as the main channel for the acquisition of materials and for product sales. In contrast, the financial market is the least developed, with only 50–60 percent of the firms relying on markets for financial resources. As one can see, patterns of resource dependence are to a large extent a function of institutional legacies and of transformation in China. There is great unevenness in the extent to which market mechanisms have developed across different industries and arenas, as well as in the availability of other channels (e.g., social networks) for problem solving.

Second, the roles of the three channels—government, market, and network—vary in different areas, with noticeable variations across firm ownership. Not surprisingly, state firms are most affected by government arrangements, especially in the areas of financial resources, labor, and to a lesser extent, raw materials. For example, at the time of our interviews (around 2000), a significant proportion (about 10–20 percent) of state firms still identified "government" as their main channel for acquiring financial or labor resources, and to a lesser degree, raw materials. It is also worth noting that, where the government controls allocative channels, such as in the area of financial resources, social networks become a salient means of firms' gaining access to resources and overcoming institutional constraints. Interestingly, hybrid firms showed mixed patterns. They are closer to private firms in their acquisition of financial resources and in sales behavior, but they show more reliance on markets in their acquisition of labor and input supplies than either state firms or private firms. As the name implies, these hybrid firms indeed exhibit hybrid behavioral traits—and behaviors that are more complicated than those of other types of firms.

The extent of resource dependence along the market, government, and social network channels in Figures 6.2a–6.2d also indicates the distribution of political, market, and social resources across property rights regimes. When we combine all four factor resources, as

Figure 6.2a   **Channel of Inputs in the Last Year**

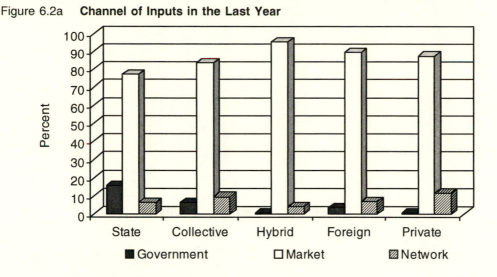

Figure 6.2b   **Channel of Sales in the Last Year**

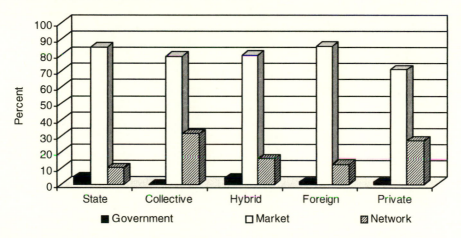

Figure 6.3 shows, state firms have the highest reliance on government channels, followed by hybrid firms and private firms.[4] The discrepancies in use of government channels are noticeably large. In contrast, this order is reversed in use of social networks, and the differences are relatively small.

We conducted a more rigorous test by estimating a negative binomial model for the acquisition of the four factor resources. In this model, we controlled for industry and firm size (sales) and city location. State firms have the highest probability of relying on government channels. In terms of their use of market mechanisms, there are no statistically significant differences among the types of firms (but foreign ownership has a positive and marginally significant effect). With regard to the use of networks, private firms used them the most, followed by collective firms and hybrid firms (marginally significant), and then state firms. And there are no statistical differences between state firms and foreign firms.

The overall pattern is that, as indicated in the middle of Figure 6.3, market channels are the

Figure 6.2c   **Channel of Finance in the Last Year**

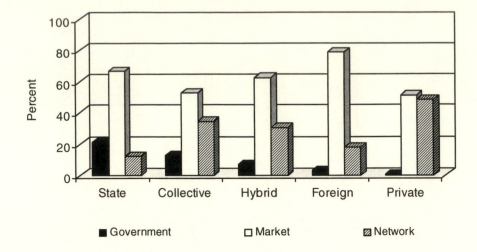

Figure 6.2d   **Channel of Labor Supply in the Last Year**

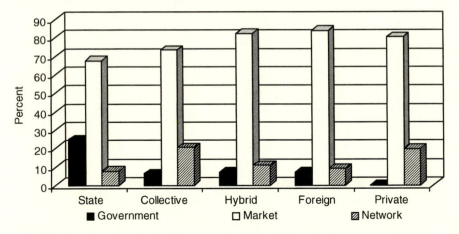

main mechanism through which all types of firms, including state-owned firms, exchange resources. In fact, taking all four resource factors together, we see no statistically significant difference in the probability of using market channels among firms under different property rights regimes—that is, all firms are equally likely to use the marketplace to acquire these resources. In contrast, government channels and social networks are two alternatives for resource acquisition for firms of different ownerships.

Although there are still some recognizable differences among types of firms in their patterns of resource dependence, overall the differences are becoming increasingly minor and narrow. These findings raise a critical question: If firms are facing similar market conditions in their resource dependence—or more accurately, if the differences in their patterns of resource dependence are increasingly narrow and insignificant—what are the bases upon which we should expect systematic differences in firm behavior across property rights regimes? We will return to this question in our discussion and conclusion section.

Figure 6.3 **Channel of Resource Dependence for Four Combined Factors**

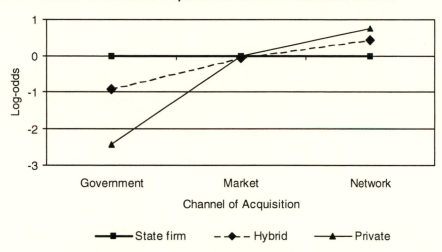

Interaction Among Different Types of Organizations

Our next set of analyses examines patterns of interaction among different types of organizations within their business environments. Scholars have different views about the role of *guanxi* ("interpersonal relationship" in Chinese) in interfirm relationships and in relationships between firms and local governments (Bian 1997; Gold, Guthrie, and Wank 2002; Guthrie 1999; Wank 1999). If property rights matter in providing distinct incentives and in channeling firms into distinct institutional environments, we should expect to find systematic differences in the interaction patterns between firms and other organizations across ownership regimes. If, on the other hand, firms are responding to similar incentives or business environments, then we would expect similar interaction patterns.

We asked respondents about how frequently their firms interacted with the following: (1) regulatory agencies; (2) supervising agencies; (3) firms within the same industry; and (4) other CEOs. Figure 6.4 plots the findings, using the state firm as the reference category for comparison.

We find some evidence that firms' behaviors vary with their ownership in terms of channels of resource dependence and in their interactions with other organizations. First, there are noticeable differences among different types of firms in their interactions with government agencies. The patterns indicate that state firms (the reference category) have significantly higher levels of interaction with both regulatory agencies and supervisory agencies, followed by collective firms and hybrid firms, whereas private firms have the lowest level of interaction. These patterns are consistent with their property rights relationships to the political authorities.

Second, hybrid firms and private firms are much more active in interacting with other CEOs, indicating that personal connections play an important role for these two types of firms. On the other hand, the relatively low level of interactions between these two types of firms and other firms in the same industry indicate that hybrid and private firms act more or less on their own, with fewer lateral relations among peers, as compared to state firms in the same industry.

Third, private firms stand out as a distinct group: except for interacting with other CEOs, they consistently have significantly lower interaction with both government agencies and other orga-

Figure 6.4 **Odds Ratio of Intensity of Interaction, by Firm Type**

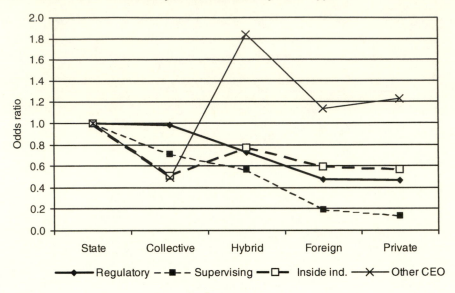

nizations. While networking is an important tool for private firms, as we discussed before, they are also least interested in generalized interactions such as those with other firms in the same industry. We interpret this pattern as indicating that private firms focus more on particular, relation-based ties rather than on general social interaction.

Property Rights and Government–Firm Relations

One of the key issues in the realm of property rights and firm behavior in China's transitional economy is the role of property rights in mediating government–firm relations. The empirical evidence presented in the preceding discussions suggests some identifiable patterns of property-rights-based variations in resource dependency and in interactions between firms and political authorities such as supervisory agencies and regulatory agencies. We now draw on our case studies and media reports to add institutional details of these relationships.

In keeping with the statistical patterns reported above, one salient finding in our interviews with managers of state firms is that, except in rare cases, the government has effectively withdrawn from the daily operation of these firms; nor does it play a substantive role in helping firms to acquire resources. This is consistent with the patterns of resource dependence revealed above. For example, the head of a medium-sized state-owned power equipment company said:

> In the planned economy, the production quotas were allocated by the government ministry. Today, except for special permits to manufacture power generators greater than 10,000 KW, one needs to find customers for all other products. . . . In terms of financial resources, it has been extremely difficult in recent years. We did not get one cent in loans from the bank. Our cash flow depends on the prepayment from the clients who purchase our products.

One state firm CEO made the following observation:

> Nowadays, there are huge differences among state firms. Old state firms carry lots of burdens left from the planned economy, they have unfair disadvantages. But new state firms are very similar in competitive conditions compared with other types of firms. The government no longer manages state-owned firms.

In other words, state firms face market competition similar to what exists for private firms, and they are likely to behave like private firms. Even for those large state-owned firms in which government intervention is most significant, managers perceive government assistance as limited and unreliable. One CEO of a large state firm remarked:

> Nowadays we face a market economy. The government no longer takes care of state-owned firms. In the past, the government had a strong interest in the development of state-owned firms, in guiding their business, and in demanding the improvement of internal management and efficiency. Now, the government no longer gets involved in these matters. We need to find our own market opportunities.

And a manager of another state-owned firm said:

> We used to have good relations with the government. But [for] historical reasons, we became a huge burden to the government, and it simply can no longer carry on this burden. This is like your attitude toward a product. You have a desire for it, if it is of high quality; but you want to get rid of it, if it is damaged.

Clearly, government–firm relationships have changed significantly in recent years.

However, it would be mistaken to infer that the governments, especially local governments, no longer significantly affect business behavior. Although the specific role of the government has changed significantly in recent years, its importance has not changed. In the past, local governments often directly intervened in firms' internal affairs, especially in state-owned firms. Our interviews revealed cases in which the government was deeply involved in bailing out large, failing firms; but such cases are more exceptions than the norm. Nowadays, only in extraordinary circumstances do state firms get such support from the government. More often, government agencies act like patrons or sponsors rather than like owners. For example, it is reported that the Wuxi municipal government has been actively involved in supporting local firms—state-owned ones as well as township-and-village enterprises (TVEs)—within its jurisdiction. As the CEO of a successful washing machine company put it, "We would not succeed without government assistance" (RMRB, January 29, 1996). On the other hand, the same report also observed that the role of government was being transformed from direct intervention to indirect management. For example, in the past, government agencies gave permission for state-owned firms to receive bank loans. Now, the government lets banks and firms deal directly with each other, thereby allowing performance-based loan decisions.

As state-owned firms were being privatized, local governments were heavily involved in the process, from choosing merger partners to setting up the terms of privatization (e.g., employment obligations). Moreover, there are continuous relationships between local governments and privatized firms. For example, a sugar-making company in one county used to be a state-owned firm governed by the county. In 2001, as part of a wave of privatization of small- and medium-sized state-owned firms per a directive from the central government, the county government organized the merger of two sugar companies and opened the bidding for the transfer of the merged company to private ownership. After negotiations with different parties, the county government carefully selected a local private entrepreneur (and his family) to be in charge of the newly formed firm, in which the government would hold 20 percent of shares and the family would hold 80 percent. Since then, the new company has kept close ties with the county government, which, in order to protect the interests of local firms, developed policies to guide the prices of raw materials for the whole county and organized police teams to enforce these policies. On the eve of the Chinese New Year, the county government sends a delegation to the company to present a special entertainment evening—an indication of a continuing intimate relationship. Thus, our data suggest that when state firms become privatized, government–firm relationships are carried over and extended into the private sector.

As the government shifts from the role of owner to that of regulator, the government–firm relationship evolves from resource dependence to regulatory protection/interference. There are numerous reports that local governments are actively setting up barriers to protect firms within their jurisdictions; likewise, the governments are facilitating mergers among firms as a way of stimulating local economic development or getting rid of state firms that incur losses. On the other hand, there are also frequent reports of local governments demanding excessive extra-tax fees to finance their local projects at the expense of local firms.

In this light, it appears that governments and firms are involved in a long-term symbiotic relationship (Wank 1999). The local government monitoring, as depicted in Walder (1995), has evolved, or is evolving, into informal and implicit collusion between governments and firms. In exchange for political protection and support, firms provide resources for and invest in public projects developed by their local governments. On the other hand, it seems that uneven government treatment of local firms has continued in one form or another; as a result, there are also salient tensions between firms and governments. The overall trend is that the distinction between state-owned firms and private ones is increasingly blurred, and government–business relationships are less governed by ownership than by other mechanisms.

Patterns of Interfirm Contracting

We now consider whether there are significant differences in firm behavior across property rights regimes in their interfirm contractual relationships. Following our previous study (Zhou et al. 2003), we consider such issues as patterns of search for contractual partners, forms of provisions in their contracts, and the intensity of social interactions after contract signing. The number of cases we had available was too small for us to conduct rigorous statistical analyses across property rights regimes, so we rely on descriptive statistics to compare and contrast these patterns, mainly among state firms, hybrid firms, and private firms.

The Search for Contractual Partners

We first ask, Do firms differ in the channels they use to search for contractual partners? The implications are obvious. If resources are located in different spheres (e.g., government-controlled versus price-based) that require different means of access, then resource dependence varies systematically with the search channels available to different types of firms. As Figure 6.5 shows, there are some interesting similarities as well as differences among the three types of firms with regard to the channels of search for contractual partners. Private firms are most likely to use

Figure 6.5 **Distribution of Search Channels Among Property Rights Regimes**

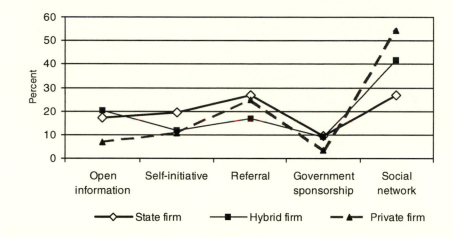

Table 6.2

Logistic Regression of Contractual Formality[a]

	Specificity	Volume	Quality	Price	Deadline	Safeguard
Private–private	0.76**	0.57*	0.87**	0.60*	0.66**	0.46
State–private	0.71*	0.35	0.55†	0.71**	0.64*	0.16
Hybrid–private	0.73*	0.51†	0.70*	0.54†	0.61*	0.43

[a]State firm–state firm contracts are the reference category. Because state firm–hybrid firm contracts show no statistically significant differences, this type of contract is also added to the reference category.
$†p < 0.10$; $*p < 0.05$; $**p < 0.01$

social networks and least likely to use open information, whereas state firms and hybrid firms are more likely to use government sponsorship. That is, private firms rely heavily on particularistic channels to search for contract partners, while state firms and hybrid firms rely more on traditional, institutional channels. However, these three types of firms are similar or mixed in their use of other channels. Overall, except for the use of social networks, the differences among types of firms are minor in their use of alternative search channels.

Forms and Provisions in Contracts

Our next question is, Do firms differ in the forms and provisions adopted in their contracts? In particular, we inquired about whether firms adopted formal or informal contracts concerning quality, product specificity, deadline, price, and safeguards. The results in Table 6.2 show some striking patterns. First, the state and hybrid firms show very similar patterns in the formality of interfirm contracting, indicating that they are operating under the same regulatory regime. Second, private firms show different patterns in that they tend to adopt informal (or no) provisions on the above items. The most striking observation is that both state-owned firms and hybrid firms, when interacting with private firms, also tend to adopt informal provisions. These patterns show

Table 6.3

Parameter Estimates of a Mixed Model Predicting the Intensity of Social Interaction in Contractual Relationships: 620 Firms in Beijing and Guangzhou, 1999–2000[a]

Covariate	State firm	Hybrid firm	Private firm
Intercept	2.13**	1.82**	2.53**
Guangzhou	0.06**	0.06	0.13*
Firm sales (log)	0.01	0.01	0.01
Industry			
Heavy industry	−0.09	−0.05	0.18
Retail	0.04	−0.13*	0.04
Construction	−0.04	0.13	0.03
Service	0.10	−0.08	−0.05
Other	−0.10	−0.06	−0.05
Prior acquaintance (1 = "yes")	0.19**	0.16*	0.15*
Duration of prior acquaintance	−0.00	0.00	−0.00
Search channel			
Government sponsorship	−0.04	−0.18	−0.08
Collegial referral	−0.11†	−0.06	−0.14
Social network	−0.00	0.06	−0.13
Self–initiative	−0.23**	0.03	−0.13
Type of contract			
Purchase	−0.20**	−0.09	−0.02
Service	−0.04	−0.06	0.04
Other	−0.19†	−0.24	−0.27†
Percent contract value	0.00	0.00	0.14*
Contract duration	0.01†	0.12*	−0.00
Number of contract partners	0.05	−0.02*	−0.01
Number of contracts	199	128	134
Log–likelihood	−137.9	−103.1	−78.7
Degrees of freedom	21	21	21

[a]Light industry is the reference category for industry; open information is the reference category for search channel; and sale is the reference category for type of contract. Three indicator variables for missing values for percent contract value, number of contract partners, and firm sales (log) are also included in the model.

†$p < 0.10$; *$p < 0.05$; **$p < 0.01$; two-tailed tests.

a polarized pattern: at the one end, private firms belong to a distinct regulatory regime; at the other end, all other firms behave similarly, presumably because they are all under similar regulatory pressures. This analysis controls for contract-specific factors.

The Intensity of Social Interaction After a Contract Is Established

By "social interaction" we mean a variety of activities that contractual partners take part in together, such as having dinner, visiting each other's families, helping each other in their private matters, attending the same parties, and so on. In our previous study, we found that the intensity of social interaction was instrumental in that it was proportional to the stake of the specific contract, independent of firm type. We sought here to explore this set of issues further by comparing the behavior of firms with the three types of ownership. As Table 6.3 shows, the effects of most variables are similar across the three property rights regimes. In particular, the intensity of social interaction for all three types of firms is higher among firms that have had prior contact. The main differences are related to the set of variables

Table 6.4

Logistic and Tobit Model Estimates of Payment Arrangements[a]

	Prepayment (1 = "yes")	Proportion of prepayment
Collective firm	0.70*	12.55**
Hybrid	0.31	6.37
Foreign	−0.21	−2.44
Private	0.52*	9.42*

[a]State firm is the reference category. This analysis also controls for contract characteristics and industrial location.
*$p < 0.05$; **$p < 0.01$.

on contract-specific risks: State-owned firms are sensitive to the duration of a contract, which has a marginally significant effect on the intensity of social interaction. The pattern is the same and even more salient for hybrid firms. However, for private firms, it is the proportion of contract value to the total sale that plays a significant role. How do we explain the observed differences? One possibility is that different types of firms may tend toward contracts of different durations. But the descriptive statistics do not support this interpretation. In our data, the mean contractual duration is 1.3 years (S.D. = 1.6) for state firms, 1.02 years (S.D. = 0.81) for hybrid firms, and 1.05 years (S.D. = 1.4) for private firms. Our interpretation is that private firms are more sensitive to risks in that the proportion of contractual value is a more direct measure of the stakes involved in a contract than is contract duration. Again, hybrid firms behave more like state-owned firms than like private firms.

Behavior in the Management of Risks

Do property rights affect firms' behavior in their response to risks? If property rights provide distinct incentives for firm behavior, we would expect significant differences based on ownership. But if the effect of firm ownership is mediated through resource dependence and other institutional processes, then these differences should be less salient, given the patterns that we observed above. To explore firm differences in their response to risk, we now examine payment arrangements. Delays in or the evasion of payment are major problems in economic transactions among firms in China. Therefore, payment arrangements in contract transactions reflect the management of risks. We analyzed two sets of issues: (1) whether there is prepayment or not, since prepayment is an important safeguard for reducing the risk of contract breach, and (2) what the proportion of prepayment is relative to the total contract value. The higher the proportion of prepayment, the lower the risk involved in contracting.

Table 6.4 shows that, after industrial and contractual characteristics are controlled for, private firms and collective firms are most risk averse in that they demand prepayments and ask for larger proportions of prepayment than other types of firms. On the other hand, there are no statistically significant differences among state firms, hybrid firms, and foreign firms.

There is an irony here. Recall that, as our previous analyses showed, collective and private firms are more prone to use social networks than other firms. Apparently, social networks do not ease their demands for safeguards. This is consistent with our findings in case studies—that social networks are often intertwined with market mechanisms. In terms of social relationships, an expression we frequently heard in our interviews was that "to deal with business you must first deal with [the] people involved." As one private firm owner put it, "There is an old saying: 'To make business you must first make people.'" But respondents also emphasized that network ties are often a means to initial contact, and one still needs to take precautions to safeguard one's interests. It seems that the main factor is the risks involved; or, as one respondent remarked, "Sometimes I ask for prepayment, sometimes I don't. It depends on the risks involved. If I worked with someone for a long time and know him well, I would not ask for prepayment. . . ." These remarks portray a more particularistic, instrumental view of social networks.

Employment Relationships Across Property Rights Regimes

In the final set of comparisons, we consider employment relationships across types of property rights regimes. Here, we draw on materials from our interviews, media reports, and research findings from previous studies.

That there are noticeable differences in employment relationship across property rights regimes in China is well known (Bian 1994, Walder, 1992). Until recently, state firms provided more stable employment, job security, better fringe benefits (e.g., housing), and closer management-worker interactions. In contrast, private firms tend to have arm's-length employment relationships and shorter durations of employment. What is more important are the significant differences in intersubjective perceptions among employees across these property rights regimes. Cai (1996, 1998) found that the public ownership of state firms created a strong sense of identity and entitlement among employees, who had strong moral expectations about the socialist managers and thereby exerted collective pressure to constrain managerial power. In contrast, employment relationships in private firms were distant, with a much stronger recognition and acceptance of managerial authority (e.g., in hiring and firing). In the consumer arena, Davis (2004) also found a significant role of what she called "logics of entitlement," in which social expectations and cognitions constrained the boundaries of property rights and provided the basis for the resolution of conflict.

The evidence mentioned in the previous paragraph reflects largely institutional changes before the mid 1990s. Since then, there have been tremendous changes in property rights reform. State firms, for example, pushed out a large number of idle workers in the late 1990s; the welfare system associated with state firms was also significantly weakened. Our question is, To what extent have these changes altered the patterns we observed earlier?

The empirical evidence we have come across in recent years shows that these patterns persist to various extents today. One constant complaint we heard in our interviews was that state firms are under much more severe regulatory pressures in the management of their internal organizational structures and employment relationships. For example, several media reports have advocated the "sunshine practice," in which decision making in state firms regarding employment, bonus allocation, and so on is transparent and open to employees' inspection (RMRB, April 19, 1999). This model of employment relationship is in stark contrast to those in private firms, where decisions about hiring, layoffs, and pay are solely in the hands of the owner and under little regulation. For example, in private firms, workers are pressured to work long hours with low compensation, and work environments lack adequate safety protections (RMRB, November 13, 1996).

There is also evidence that incentive structures differ across property rights regimes, which is consistent with the theoretical model on incentive mechanisms. In the sugar company discussed earlier, the internal organization and personnel were changed after the ownership change; as the CEO put it, "In state firms, the top managers act to impress their superiors so that they can get promoted and pursue their self-interests. They would make up accounting books and records. They don't care about the company or employees below. It is impossible for state firms to make such changes at all. Only privatization can make managers treat the company like their own family." Another salient piece of evidence from our interviews is the repeated claim that in inter-firm transactions with a state firm one needs to make sure that the "needs" of the salesperson from the state firm are "taken care of" before a business deal can be reached, indicating that problems in the alignment of incentives in state firms still persist and are widespread.

These accounts are consistent with the principal-agent arguments about the alignment of managerial incentives and ownership interests. Privatization, of course, makes the most unambiguous alignment. However, interpretation of these changes in property rights and ownership structures must be balanced by a different trend at the other side of the spectrum; that is, private firms have been striving to cultivate ties with political authorities for protection and privileged access. As a result, they are open to influence and regulation from local governments, and their autonomy in management may be undermined in this process.

DISCUSSION AND CONCLUSIONS

Few would take issue with the claim that fundamental changes in property rights are the key to the transformation of former state socialist economies and that the private sector plays an important role in the expansion of market economies in these societies (McMillan and Woodruff 2002). At the center of these discussions is the proposition that property rights and firm behavior are closely associated. Indeed, theoretical arguments on property rights become vacuous if such an empirical association is not established. In this study, we have aimed to assess this relationship by comparing and contrasting firm behaviors across property rights regimes in a variety of areas, in the context of China's transitional economy. Our goal was to identify empirical regularities that allow us to (1) evaluate this association empirically and (2) specify the mechanisms underlying this association. In this section, we take stock and summarize our main findings.

Overall, we did detect observable differences in patterns of resource dependence by property rights regime; patterns of interaction among types of organizations also systematically vary across property rights regimes. These patterns clearly reflect the institutional legacies of the command economy in China, in which state firms and collective firms were closer to the political authorities than are private firms.

However, it is worth pointing out that these differences are much less pronounced than one would expect on the basis of prevailing theories of property rights. In many cases, the differences across ownership types are relatively minor. There are mixed alignments among ownership types along different dimensions. For example, state firms and collective firms rely more on government channels, but collective firms and private firms are similarly dependent on network channels. And there are no differences in all firms' reliance on market channels with regard to acquisition of resources. In other words, the patterns across property rights regimes along these dimensions are often overlapping rather than distinct from each other.

A further question is, Do the differences in resource dependence, however small they are, affect firm behavior in any substantive way? In other words, does firm behavior vary systematically with patterns of resource dependence? The answer is a qualified "yes." For example, patterns of interaction with other types of organizations—as well as firms' responses to uncertainty —are consistent with these patterns of resource dependence: state firms and collective firms have stronger ties with government channels, while collective and private firms also show similarities in their reliance on social networks in their response to risks. Again, these differences across property rights regimes are much less pronounced than we anticipated, indicating that all firms are subject to similar pressures in their respective business environments.

An interesting finding emerging from these analyses is that, although state firms and private firms tend to behave differently, private firms do not always resort to market mechanisms; rather, they rely heavily on social networks to conduct their business. For example, our analyses show that private firms rely more on social network ties in acquiring scarce resources (e.g., financing), in searching for contractual partners, in forming contractual relationships (e.g., informal contracts), and in managing risks. In contrast, state firms—and especially foreign firms—tend to rely more on market mechanisms. This finding is at odds with the conventional wisdom that treats the private sector as the engine of market expansion. The behaviors of private firms seem to reinforce social network institutions, which at times function as substitutes for market mechanisms. Obviously, these patterns reflect the characteristics of ongoing institutional transformation in China, and it would be premature to draw any definite conclusions at this stage.

The fact that the behaviors of the firms that vary depending on property rights regime are often mixed, inconsistent, and without clear demarcation raises questions about underlying mechanisms. According to the "property-rights-as-incentive argument," different types of property rights/ ownership provide different incentive structures and induce corresponding firm behaviors. Although this relationship clearly exists—as revealed in both the statistical patterns and the qualitative data—the effectiveness of this mechanism depends on other factors, such as the extent to which firms are subject to the disciplines of market competition and incentive designs in organizations. One may argue that these overlapping patterns are due to the "transitional" nature of property rights reform. However, there are also good reasons to suspect that such overlapping property rights have persisted and are widespread in transitional economies (Francis 1999, Lin and Zhang 1999), and may be a more permanent feature of emerging economic institutions (Stark 1996, Zhou 2003). The increasingly blurred boundaries across property rights regimes greatly weaken the analytical power of the property-rights-as-incentive argument.

In our view, a focus on the link between organizational environment and organizational response provides a useful lens through which to view and understand the association between property rights and firm behavior. The central idea is that the distribution of resources, information, and political authority plays a significant role in shaping firm behavior. Along with changes in institutional transformation in China, business environments have also undergone tremendous changes. State firms, for example, are subject to market pressures similar to those on private firms. Furthermore, the institutional environments of governmental regulations also play an increasingly important role in shaping firms' behaviors across property rights regimes. Therefore, how these different types of environment evolve provides clues as to whether firms under different property rights regimes will become more similar or more different, hence providing the basis for understanding the association between property rights and firm behavior.

These multifaceted firm behaviors across property rights regimes undoubtedly reflect the fuzzy boundaries of property rights and how they are measured. In this study, we relied on self-reporting by respondents as to the property rights regimes of the firms in which they worked. The patterns based on this measurement are broadly consistent with our detailed case studies and numerous media reports. One needs to keep in mind that, in China's transitional economy, many firms are in a process of transforming from traditional (that is, state) ownership to more complex and less clear-cut ownership structures. The kinds of uncertainty in the conception and measurement of ownership regimes are intrinsic to the very transformation processes being studied here.

Given the ongoing processes of property rights reform in China, and the limited scope of our inquiry in both data sources and dimensions of analyses, the findings reported here are necessarily more suggestive than conclusive. We hope that future studies will further explore this set of issues. Above all, the power of theories of property rights depends on the empirical validity of the proposition regarding the relationship between property rights and firm behavior.

APPENDIX 6.1
INFORMATION ON "INTERFIRM CONTRACT" DATA COLLECTION

In this appendix, we provide information on the data collection process for the interfirm contract project (for more information, see Appendix A in Zhou et al. 2003).

1. DATA COLLECTION

In our initial research design, we planned to focus on two main industries, manufacturing and retail, in collecting information on interfirm contracts. However, because of difficulties in gaining access to confidential data and lack of information on the universe of business contracts, we were unable to follow random sampling procedures to select our sample. Instead, we adopted a convenient sampling method that led us to collect data in several industries.

We also collected information on the characteristics of the informants. Their average age was 37 at the time of interview; most of them were male (81 percent), and 70 percent of them had "some college" *(dazhuan)*. At the time of interview, 20 percent worked as "ordinary managers," 29 percent as "mid-level managers," and 39 percent as "high-level managers." An additional 10 percent held professional jobs in their companies (ordinary, mid-, or high-level professional). The median tenure in their current companies was six years (mean = eight years). The median tenure in their current managerial (professional) positions was four years (mean = five years).

Some studies have used more systematic sampling methods to draw samples of Chinese enterprises. But these surveys were aimed at collecting more general information on firms rather than detailed, sensitive information on business transactions, as was ours. Our own exploratory research experience taught us that we would be unable to collect detailed, reliable information on interfirm contracts through these conventional sampling methods. As we noted in the text, government sponsorship or the involvement of official research institutions may help researchers gain access to firms. But, given the sensitivities involved in business dealings (e.g., kickbacks), informants are less likely to provide honest information in interviews that are sponsored by official channels than through informal channels such as ours.

2. SAMPLE REPRESENTATIVENESS

Given that our sample was not random, we evaluated representativeness for studying contractual relationships. Two dimensions were examined: the distribution of firms with respect to (1) type as defined by property rights ownership and (2) industrial location.

Our sample contains a higher proportion of state firms and hybrid firms than the overall population of Chinese companies, per official statistics, and collective firms are underrepresented in our sample. The overrepresentation of state and hybrid firms reflects the fact that the researchers and interviewers have better access to these types of firms. The proportions of private firms and foreign firms are comparable between the sample and official statistics. The underrepresentation of collective firms is somewhat surprising. Our speculation is that, because of the rapid changes in China's organizational reforms, many officially labeled "collective firms" may in fact have been reported as private firms or hybrid firms by the managers interviewed in our data collection.

The category of "hybrid" includes firms whose property rights ownership is ambiguous and often involves both public (state-owned) and private (or foreign-investment) ownership. They are characteristic of transitional firms: some were previously state-owned firms but are now being privatized; some are nonstate firms jointly financed by several sources. As a whole, these hybrid firms have weaker administrative linkages with the government than state-owned firms.

With regard to types of industrial location, Beijing and Guangzhou show distinctive patterns in the official statistics, and these differences are also reflected in our sample. Heavy industry and light industry are overrepresented in our sample, relative to the official statistics. We suspect that this is partly because firms in these industries tend to be large and more accessible for data collection. The patterns across other industries are more or less comparable between the sample and official statistics, with some variations between the two cities and a higher proportion of "other industries" in official statistics.

Because our data are not drawn from a random sampling, the distribution of firms across types of ownership and across industrial settings shows patterns that reflect firms' accessibility. Overall, however, the distributions along these attributes do not indicate any serious bias in our sample. The overrepresentation of state firms, hybrid firms, and large firms (in heavy and light industries) also coincides with the fact that these firms tend to have durable, bilateral relations, owing to the nature of their products and institutional context.

NOTES

An earlier version of the paper was presented at Northwestern University, the University of Chicago, and the workshop "The Management and Performance of China's Domestic Private Firms: Multi-Disciplinary Perspectives" at Hong Kong University of Science and Technology, 2003. We thank Yanjie Bian, Tom Gold, and participants at these meetings for their helpful comments. We thank Dahai Hao, Xinping Lu, Shanhui Wu, and Wei Zhao for their assistance in collecting and preparing the data. This project is partly supported by a fund from the CCK Foundation to the first author. The first author also acknowledges financial support from Hong Kong University of Science and Technology in the preparation of this chapter.

1. The difficulty in evaluating profitability or other economic performance metrics across firms with different property rights regimes is that, as many studies have recognized, to a large extent the losses of state-owned firms were induced by state policies or institutional legacies, rather than by the firms' behaviors or incentive structures (Duan and Han 1999).

2. The distinctness of these channels is somewhat ambiguous. The channel "social networks," for example, may eventually lead to transactions in the marketplace (the "market channel"). Here, it is useful to think of an alternative as the main (rather than exclusive) channel that characterizes the transaction pattern in question.

3. In our questionnaire, we did not distinguish between central and local government. In most cases, government arrangements refer to the local governments in the region in which a firm is located.

4. We analyzed data using a negative binomial model that treated the four channels as a count variable; that is, the dependent variable was the probability of using one or more (up to four) channels along government, market, or network dimensions, with the characteristics of other covariates controlled.

REFERENCES

Bian, Y. (1994). *Work and inequality in urban China.* Albany: State University of New York Press.
———. (1997). Bringing strong ties back in: Indirect connection, bridges, and job search in China. *American Sociological Review, 62,* 266–85.
Bian, Y., and J. W. Logan. (1996). Market transition and the persistence of power: The changing stratification system in urban China. *American Sociological Review, 61,* 739–58.
Cai, H. (1996). The role of authority in state firms (in Chinese). *Shehuixue Yanjiu, 6,* 17–24.
———. (1998). Employee rights awareness and informal constraints across ownership types (in Chinese). *Guanli Shijie, 5,* 191–6.
Davis, D. (2004). *Talking about property in the new Chinese domestic property regime.* In F. Dobbin (Ed.), *The New Economic Sociology,* pp. 288–307. New York: Russell Sage Foundation.
Duan, W., and L. Han. (1999). Retrospects and prospects of the 20 years of state-firm reform (in Chinese). *Nankai Guanli Pinglun, 6,* 56–64.

Francis, C. (1999). Bargained property rights: The case of China's high-technology sector. In J. C. Oi and A. G. Walder (Eds.), *Property rights and economic reform in China*, pp. 226–47. Stanford, CA: Stanford University Press.

Gold, T.; D. Guthrie; and D. Wank. (2002). *Social connections in China: Institutions, culture, and the changing nature of guanxi*. New York: Cambridge University Press.

Guthrie, D. (1997). Between markets and politics: Organizational response to reform in China. *American Journal of Sociology*, 102, 1258–1303.

———. (1999). *Dragon in a three-piece suit: The emergence of capitalism in China*. Princeton, NJ: Princeton University Press.

Jefferson, G. H., and T. G. Rawski. (1994). Enterprise reform in Chinese industry. *Journal of Economic Perspectives*, 8, 47–70.

Jefferson, G. H.; T. G. Rawski; W. Li; and Y. Zheng. (2000). Ownership, productivity change, and financial performance in Chinese industry. *Journal of Comparative Economics*, 28, 786–813.

Kang, D. L., and A. B. Sorensen. (1999). Ownership organization and firm performance. *Annual Review of Sociology*, 25, 121–44.

Kornai, J. (1980). *Economics of shortage*. Amsterdam: North-Holland Pub. Co.

Lin, N. (1995). Local market socialism: Local corporatism in action in rural China. *Theory and Society*, 24, 301–54.

Lin, Y., and Z. Zhang. (1999). Backyard profit centers: The private assets of public agencies. In J. C. Oi and A. G. Walder (Eds.), *Property rights and economic reform in China*, pp. 203–25. Stanford, CA: Stanford University Press.

McMillan, J., and C. Woodruff. (2002). The central role of entrepreneurs in transition economies. *Journal of Economic Perspective*, 16, 153–70.

Nee, V. (1992). Organizational dynamics of market transition: Hybrid forms, property rights, and mixed economy in China. *Administrative Science Quarterly*, 37, 1–27.

Oi, J. C., and A. G. Walder. (1999). *Property rights and economic reform in China*. Stanford, CA: Stanford University Press.

Peng, Y. (1992). Wage determination in rural and urban industrial China. *American Sociological Review*, 57, 198–213.

Stark, D. (1996). Recombinant property in East European capitalism. *American Journal of Sociology*, 101, 993–1027.

Walder, A. G. (1992). Property rights and stratification in socialist redistributive economies. *American Sociological Review*, 57, 524–39.

———. (1995). Local governments as industrial firms. *American Journal of Sociology*, 101, 263–301.

Walder, A. G., and J. C. Oi. (1999). Property rights in the Chinese economy: Contours of the process of change. In J. C. Oi and A. G. Walder (Eds.), *Property rights and economic reform in China*, pp. 1–24. Stanford, CA: Stanford University Press.

Wank, D. L. (1999). *Commodifying communism: Business, trust, and politics in a Chinese city*. New York: Cambridge University Press.

Zhou, X. (2000). Economic transformation and income inequality in urban China: Evidence from panel data. *American Journal of Sociology*, 105, 1135–74.

———. (2003). *Rethinking property rights as a relational concept: Explorations in China's transitional economy*. Unpublished manuscript, Department of Sociology, Duke University.

Zhou, X.; N. B. Tuma; and P. Moen. (1997). Institutional change and patterns of job shifts in urban China: 1949–1994. *American Sociological Review*, 62, 339–65.

Zhou, X.; W. Zhao; Q. Li; and H. Cai. (2003). Embeddedness and contractual relationships in China's transitional economy. *American Sociological Review*, 68, 75–102.

7

OBSERVING PRIVATE BUSINESS IN CHINA

Thomas B. Gold

The fact that a private business sector had actually begun to emerge in urban China first struck me during a walkabout in Xiamen in the summer of 1984. I wandered down an alleyway and saw rows of stalls selling clothes, toys, shoes, housewares, and so on. There were food stalls and bicycle repairmen as well. In my year as an exchange student at Shanghai's Fudan University starting in February 1979, during which I traveled the length and breadth of the country, I had not noticed any private activity to speak of, save some farmers' markets and furtive peasants selling handicraft goods on city streets. But here was a vibrant and quite open market of city folk engaging in a range of retail and service business. It reminded me of street life in Taiwan during my first trip there in 1969.

From the perspective of 2006 this all sounds quite quaint, but it is a measure of how rapidly the private sector has expanded and evolved, of the extent to which it is now part of the landscape— a taken-for-granted aspect of life in urban China. Private entrepreneurs, who were a stratum of society universally denigrated as social marginals and misfits until very recently, have now achieved official recognition, including eligibility to enter the Chinese Communist Party (CCP), of all things.

When I began to investigate the *getihu* (micro entrepreneurs) systematically in the mid-1980s, I routinely drew puzzled reactions from Chinese colleagues: "But you're a sociologist; this is an economic topic. Why are you studying it?" they'd inquire.

I replied that as I saw it—and this may be an occupational hazard—the emergence of private business, however tentative, was more of a sociological than an economic phenomenon. The significance of economic issues took a back seat to the social ones, certainly until well into the 1990s. With all due modesty, I am gratified that the chapters in this section of this volume completely vindicate my point of view. Using diverse types of data that were not available until relatively recently, and an array of sophisticated methodologies, they draw attention to many issues of broader interest to sociologists, and to those of us studying the transformation of China in particular. These include, but are not limited to, such topics as class formation, labor, labor relations, stratification, mobility, social networks (*guanxi*), forms of authority, institutions, and organizations.

The matter of data is particularly striking. My research on *getihu* in the 1980s combined interviews arranged by research institutes, universities, and government agencies with what I called "guerilla interviewing" (Gold 1989), where I asked *getihu* a set of questions at their places of business in as systematic a way as I could, but did not write anything down until later, out of their sight. I did this in part because interviews arranged by the authorities—especially if they were present during the meeting—always carried the taint of being rather scripted discussions with carefully vetted "models." I also opted for guerrilla tactics because I wanted to speak with *getihu* unannounced and spontaneously while observing them at their places of business. At that time, their social status was still quite marginal, so they naturally were skittish about contacts with officialdom; therefore, I did not want to compromise them by involving them in awkward situations. If the encounter became uncomfortable, I would depart.

The chapters in this section all use surveys of some type, usually combined with in-depth interviews. Xiaogang Wu uses part of the massive 1996 *Life Histories and Social Change in Contemporary China*. Xueguang Zhou, He Cai, and Qiang Li gathered data from 621 firms in Beijing and Guangzhou. Yi-min Lin utilized a 1998 survey of 1,350 employees in 137 enterprises and, in 2003, interviewed fifty-eight employees in seventeen firms in five diverse locations. Wilfred R. Vanhonacker, David Zweig, and Siu Fung Chung, in collaboration with the China Private Enterprise Association, interviewed at 200 firms in Beijing, Guangzhou, and Shanghai. All are self-reflexive about their methodologies. Clearly, research on private business has come a long way, and the Chinese themselves realize that it is much more than an economic phenomenon.

One central sociological issue that the Chinese material can help address is whether or not "marketization," globalization (in the forms of direct foreign investment, membership in the World Trade Organization [WTO], and returnee entrepreneurs), and the emergence of a domestic capitalist class will help to bring about a shift from traditional-patrimonial forms of authority, as represented by the CCP, to authority based on rational-legal principles.

For instance, Lin's chapter, based on a survey of private enterprises, suggests ways to address this issue, although he is not able to come to firm conclusions at this point. His findings can be compared with those of Doug Guthrie, based on research in Shanghai conducted in 1995, which indicated, at least in his sample of state-owned enterprises, that the trend was in the direction of rational-legal authority (Guthrie 1999). Will private firms such as those Lin studied take the same road as Guthrie's state-owned enterprises (SOEs) claim to have taken? If so, will it be because of isomorphic inclinations to imitate the most successful firms they see around them (DiMaggio and Powell 1983)? Will it be because of state pressure, as the rule of law begins to bite and the arbitrary rule of party cadres recedes? Will it be because of WTO-imposed standards of behavior? Must firms reach a certain scale before authority relations can be expected to change in the desired direction? If the answer to this last question is yes, then China's tens of millions of micro enterprises may be able to claim that the laws should not apply to them. How would this impact the rule of law?

The chapter by Zhou, Cai, and Li, also based on an extensive survey, indicates that the role of *guanxi*—that is, particularistic connections—remains significant for all firms, especially private ones.[1] Ironically, state firms tend to rely more on the market than private ones! Here again, the work of Guthrie offers interesting comparative potential. In a very controversial article (1998), he argued that the significance of *guanxi* was declining in the state firms in his sample. He did not say it had disappeared, but that, although it might be important in establishing relations between firms, the final decisions about business contracts were based on economic, and not *guanxi*, considerations. Zhou et al.'s findings corroborate this view.

The fact that *guanxi* is still significant, as they found, may be attributed to the "institutional holes" that still exist in China's continuously transforming economy;[2] something has to be found in order to fill these gaps. Their data on hybrid firms are especially interesting in this regard. Of course, none of the data can address the question of whether or not private entrepreneurs actually want to see the development of rational-legal principles of authority. Maybe they prefer the more lawless environment and would see more laws as hindering or constraining their room to maneuver; state regulators would be interfering in their internal affairs. Vanhonacker, Zweig, and Chung draw attention to the fact that Chinese who have studied and worked abroad are returning and establishing private enterprises. One would assume that they would have a positive attitude toward a more predictable, law-based business environment. The study shows that they do realize, however, the need to have good personal relations with local officials—like it or not.

A related issue, noted by Wu, is the entry of cadres into the private sector. With the privatization of small and medium SOEs, many of their former managers utilized their position to strip assets or to buy the firms on the cheap, and then convert them into private enterprises with themselves as the bosses. At the same time, tens of millions of workers have been laid off (*xiagang*) or simply terminated, and then encouraged to start private businesses themselves. This account illustrates how the deck is stacked against many micro entrepreneurs from the get-go, especially these former state workers who have been suddenly compelled to take this road with little preparation.

These topics are interesting in their own right, but also help to bridge the still-existing gap between the discipline of sociology and China area studies. Data from China—which are now abundant and collected in an increasingly rigorous way—can and should be used to test and elaborate theories and concepts central to our discipline. For instance, the emergence and practices of mainland Chinese entrepreneurs offer extremely rich potential for examining the relation between culture and institutions. To answer this, one can compare mainland Chinese entrepreneurs with Chinese entrepreneurs as they exist in Chinese societies such as Taiwan and Hong Kong, as well as in Southeast Asia, where they comprise the dominant business class. They can also be compared to the private entrepreneurs who have emerged in former socialist countries such as Russia, Eastern and Central European nations, and Vietnam.[3]

The emergence of private entrepreneurs—first as truly *petit* business people (the Chinese term *getihu* literally means "individual household," and these firms could not initially have more than seven employees), and then as true capitalists employing, in some cases, thousands of people—is a truly extraordinary story. Here is a society whose members had been browbeaten for decades into banishing any thought of engaging in private business. "Tails of capitalism" were literally beaten during mass campaigns against alleged efforts to reestablish "capitalism," which had never really existed in the first place in China as the dominant mode of production. Their "crimes" amounted to little more than engaging in simple barter. Yet once the lid was lifted, millions of Chinese, most of whom had had no experience whatsoever with a market economy, began to engage in vibrant entrepreneurial activity, as if it were a suppressed genetic trait finally able to flourish. Entrepreneurship used to be a central topic in the study of modernization, and the experience of China since 1978—when the CCP officially changed its policies toward private business —certainly provides grounds for reopening this line of inquiry.

And as if the entrepreneurial revival weren't enough, the CCP, which was virulent in its attacks on private business and permitted it to reemerge only as a desperate tactic to help solve a number of serious social problems at the end of the Cultural Revolution, has constantly retreated before its onslaught. Private business has been granted social, legal, and ideological legitimacy, and leading entrepreneurs have been recruited into the Party.

A FIELD APPROACH TO THE STUDY OF PRIVATE BUSINESS

My own approach to thinking about private business in China builds on the theoretical work of Pierre Bourdieu and of Neil Fligstein, and it works well with the chapters under consideration here. I adopt Bourdieu's approach of conceiving of social life as comprising "an ensemble of relatively autonomous spheres of 'play' that cannot be collapsed under an overall societal logic, be it that of capitalism, modernity, or postmodernity" (Bourdieu and Wacquant 1992, 17). These "spheres of play" are called "fields":

> A field consists of a set of objective, historical relations between positions anchored in certain forms of power (or capital) . . . each of which prescribes its particular values and possesses its own regulative principles. . . . A field is a patterned system of objective forces (much in the manner of a magnetic field), a *relational configuration with a specific gravity* which it imposes on all the objects and agents which enter it. A field is simultaneously a *space of conflict and competition*, the analogy here being with a battlefield, in which participants vie to establish monopoly over the species of capital effective in it. In the course of these struggles, the very shape and divisions of the field become a central stake, because to alter the distribution and relative weight of forms of capital is tantamount to modifying the structure of the field. (Bourdieu and Wacquant 1992, 16–18; emphasis in the original)

I want to elaborate on a few of these points. First, fields have histories and they are malleable. They change, through a combination of "conflict and competition" among the actors within them and external influences, since each field is part of the larger "ensemble" of fields comprising society. Second, sets of rules govern behavior in each field; that is, rules govern each position in the field, as well as the engagement among actors. Third, the actors compete to gain whatever type of capital is the currency of the field—economic, political, cultural, and symbolic being the main varieties. And finally, there are principles of "convertibility" among the various types of capital; for instance, whether and how economic capital can be converted into political capital for use in the political field.

What are referred to as "regulative principles" in the long quote above can also be called institutions. In Neil Fligstein's words, "Institutions are rules and shared meanings (implying that people are aware of them or that they can be consciously known) that define social relationships, help define who occupies what position in those relationships, and guide interaction by giving actors cognitive frames or sets of meanings to interpret the behavior of others" (Fligstein 2001, 108). Institutions are created through social interaction. They may be consciously and proactively crafted, but it is more likely that they have evolved through practice and may then be codified in the form of commandments, or laws—or they may just be taken for granted. Institutions need to be maintained and reproduced over time. Clearly, there is an element of power involved here as regards institutionalizing and implementing these rules. The institutions very likely benefit some actors or groups in society while being detrimental to others. As the shapes of fields change through conflict and competition within and from outside, so do the institutions governing behavior within the fields. Actors may consciously challenge the rules or, for one reason or another, the behavior, or perhaps the entry of new actors into a field may compel a change. Again, these new rules may result in new formal regulations.

In the study of private business in China, the main focus is, of course, on the economic field, though it cannot be isolated from other fields, especially the political one. Several chapters here indicate the increased impact of the legal field on the practice of private business. After taking power in 1949, the CCP worked—at first gradually, then with admittedly reckless speed—to eliminate private businessmen from the economic field, and to establish a set of institutions, mostly in the form of taken-for-granted principles, making it well nigh impossible for them to reenter it. Beginning in the mid 1950s, virtually all of the actors in the economic field were organs and agents of the party-state (there being no distinction between the two). Economic capital was monopolized by the party-state and, as with all other forms of capital, closely interwoven with political capital, centralized through the monopoly of the CCP. Any attempts to engage in private business were dealt with most harshly by a combination of party and state power. The transformation in urban areas was more thorough than in the countryside, a circumstance that makes the revival in the cities a more dramatic story. Wu's comparison of urban and rural areas helps clarify this more.

Most of the changes in the economic field came first from the political field, where the CCP had an unassailable monopoly on power. Examples would be the socialist transformation of capitalist industry and commerce, and the Great Leap Forward. There is debate as to the origin of the post–Cultural Revolution return to the Agricultural Household Responsibility System. Some scholars say the initiative came from the party-state, whereas others argue that the party-state merely legitimized what the farmers were doing anyway.[4] In any case, the party-state has never relinquished its efforts to set and enforce the rules in the economic field, and it continues to be the dominant actor in the field, even though its ability to do so has weakened considerably.

As for the reintroduction of the private household sector in the urban areas (i.e., reintroducing private business actors into the economic field), my research indicates that it was initiated by the Party to address severe issues of unemployment, the return of millions of urban youth from the countryside, a rising crime rate, and disaffection with the quality of life, especially in the realm of consumption and services.[5] The Fifth National People's Congress in March 1978 reaffirmed the right of private enterprises to exist. Article 5 (p. 10) of *The Constitution of the People's Republic of China*, passed at that session, states:

> The state allows non-agricultural individual laborers to engage in individual labor involving no exploitation of others within the limits permitted by law and under unified arrangements and management by organizations at the basic level in cities and towns or in rural areas. At the same time, it guides these individual laborers step by step onto the road of socialist civilization.

The language used here is hardly enticing to an aspiring businessperson. There really were no laws, mostly just arrangements determined by local party and state cadres, something that would not inspire confidence. The rider that as these people take up private business they will simultaneously be guided toward "socialist collectivization" is a whopping disincentive. The economic field was virtually monopolized by the state and collective sectors, as the constitution's Article 5 (and also its Article 6), made clear.

Why did anyone in their right mind become a *getihu* under these circumstances? I found a range of responses from interviews I conducted in the mid 1980s. One glum fellow I met in Guangzhou in 1982 (very early in the game) said he did it because he had no *guanxi* with which to get a better position in the workforce, school, or army. Yet two bubbly, identically dressed young women I spoke with in Kunming in 1985 said they did it because they could be *"ziyou!"* or free. They complained that they found the *danwei* (work and welfare unit) system too stifling, and now they could manage their time and whereabouts by themselves. Being young, these women did not deem the attractions of the *danwei* in terms of housing, health care, and pensions a prime consideration. In any case, no one I interviewed in the mid 1980s saw private business as a long-term career prospect. The chap in Guangzhou was one of many who informed me that this was not really *gongzuo*, or "work," which was something he would do as soon as an opportunity presented itself.

Over the course of the 1980s—as the private sector did not deplete state funds and actually contributed tax revenues, in spite of rampant tax evasion; as it dramatically improved the quality of services in urban areas, thereby removing one source of popular discontent; and as it did not suffer state suppression—a wave of state workers took temporary leave from their jobs in order to make money through private business. There was thus an influx of new actors into the economic field as private entrepreneurs; the state began to promulgate laws to govern their activity, and the Party issued pronouncements confirming their legitimacy. When Premier Zhao Ziyang declared in 1987 that China was in the "primary stage of socialism," this signaled an ideological shift with regard to the rules governing all of the actors now competing in the field. Rather than a division of labor between the private and socialist sectors, head-on competition became permissible in many sectors, especially the service industry. Private restaurants, for instance, were known for better service, food, and ambience, and customers deserted the infirmary-like state eateries in droves.

Another high point was reached in 1988, when the constitution was amended to permit private companies to hire more than seven employees, thereby legitimizing a new category, *siying qiye*—literally, privately managed enterprises. With the turn of the decade, and especially after Deng Xiaoping's Southern Tour of early 1992, when he encouraged entrepreneurship, an influx of intellectuals and professionals "jumped into the sea" (*xiahai*) of the private sector. At the end of the decade, the main entrants into the burgeoning small-scale private sector were workers who had been laid off (*xiagang*) from the shrinking state sector and had no viable alternatives.

This quick review draws attention to an important fact about China's reforms: they were implemented gradually, in sharp contrast to the "big bang" approach in Russia and Eastern and Central Europe (Naughton 1995). This explains the high incidence of hybrid firms and fuzzy ownership rights, issues frequently raised in these chapters.

Clearly, private entrepreneurs have become legitimate actors in the economic field. The party-state has promulgated a number of laws and regulations to govern the activities of all actors in the field; the state and what remains of the collective sector are now, in theory at least, subject to the same rules as the private sector, domestic and foreign. As with much else in China, actually getting officials to implement the laws is another matter.[6] Although much business activity is still based on *guanxi*, corruption, Party favoritism, and so on, it is also clear that, in Bourdieu and Wacquant's (1992) phrase, a "specific gravity" is being imposed on all objects and agents in the field.

Turning to the question of convertibility of capital, it is known that many Party officials have utilized their social capital (i.e., *guanxi*) to buy out state firms at favorable prices, and have entered the economic field, as noted earlier. But the gradual nature of the process seems to have prevented the emergence of a class of oligarchs such as those seen in Russia. Some successful private entrepreneurs have been recruited into the CCP, or have joined the National People's Congress (NPC) or the Chinese People's Political Consultative Conference (CPPCC). According to the *New York Times*, more than 100 capitalist delegates attended the NPC meeting in March 2003, and they called for a constitutional amendment to protect private property (reported on March 12, 2003, on page A5). At the NPC meeting a year later, in 2004, this amendment actually passed (per the *Guardian* for March 14, 2004). In another case, Yin Mingshan, a producer of motorcycle components, joined the CCP and received an appointment as deputy chairman of an advisory body to the government of Chongqing, where he is based (reported in *The Economist*, March 29, 2003, page 62).

In these cases, private businessmen have played by the rules, converting economic capital to social capital, and social capital to political capital. There are other cases in which a capitalist attempted to convert economic capital to political capital prematurely, or without accumulating enough social capital in the process. One of the most notorious examples of this is Yang Bin, an orchid and property developer in Shenyang, who, to the great surprise of the Chinese authorities, was introduced by North Korea as the manager of a special free-trade zone at Sinuiju on the border between the two countries. The authorities have charged Yang with "various illegal activities," but another way to look at the case is that the charges were a pretext to rein in a capitalist who had gotten way ahead of himself in the political field.[7]

Clearly, as the chapters in this section demonstrate, the place of private business in the economic field continues to evolve, and the institutions governing the field do as well. Whether it is the social origin of the entrepreneurs, their experiences abroad, their ownership status, their relations with local authorities, or the types of capital they possess that is addressed, the situation remains dynamic, fluid, and interactive. One area of contention regards whether or not private investors can own banks. Once more, the direction appears to be for the state to retrench and permit private capital to expand into an area previously off-limits to it.

The preceding has been a sketchy overview of some ways in which a fields approach can be used to analyze the emergence and evolution of private business in China and draw together the empirical research. This is an approach and not a theory, to be sure, but its strength lies in its comprehensiveness and ability to help generate hypotheses. For instance, use of this approach can help researchers identify the actors in the economic field and map out their relations with each other, as this volume's authors have done.

As Marx pointed out, as history moves forward, the birthmarks of the old society do not disappear overnight. China's economic field is a work in progress, and a trove of empirical data now exists to indicate the state of play and its likely direction of unavoidable evolution.

NOTES

1. On the topic of *guanxi*, see Gold, Guthrie, and Wank (2002).
2. See Bian (2002) for a discussion of the role of *guanxi* in filling institutional holes in the labor market.
3. See Bonnell and Gold (2002) for case studies.
4. See, for instance, Kelliher (1992) and Zhou (1996).
5. I elaborated this point in Gold (1990).
6. For example, "The State Taketh, Chinese Entrepreneurs Say" reports on a private businessman in Xinjiang whose wealth was taken by officials linked to the CCP and People's Liberation Army with the collusion of the courts. (See www.latimes.com/news/nationworld/world/la-fg-ownersl lmar11,1,222185.story? coll=la-headlines-world.)
7. See discussions of Yang Bin's case in *Time* Asia, October 21, 2002 (accessed at www.time.com/time/ asia/magazine/printout/0,13675,501021021–3644) and the *Far Eastern Economic Review*, October 24, 2002, page 63.

REFERENCES

Bian, Y. (2002). Institutional holes and job mobility processes: Guanxi mechanisms in China's emergent labor markets. In T. Gold, D. Guthrie, and D. Wank (Eds.), *Social connections in China: Institutions, culture, and the changing nature of guanxi*, pp. 117–35. New York: Cambridge University Press.
Bonnell, V. E., and T. B. Gold. (2002). *The new entrepreneurs of Europe and Asia: Patterns of business development in Russia, Eastern Europe, and China*. Armonk, NY: M.E. Sharpe.
Bourdieu, P., and L. Wacquant. (1992). *An invitation to reflexive sociology*. Chicago: University of Chicago Press.
Constitution of the People's Republic of China. (1978). Peking: Foreign Languages Press.
DiMaggio, P., and W. Powell. (1983). The iron cage revisited: Institutional isomorphism and collective rationality in organizational fields. *American Sociological Review*, 48, 147–60.
Fligstein, N. (2001). Social skill and the theory of fields. *Sociological Theory*, 19, 105–25.

Gold, T. B. (1989). Guerilla interviewing among the *getihu*. In P. Link, R. Madsen, and P. Pickowicz (Eds.), *Unofficial China: Popular culture and thought in the People's Republic*, pp. 175–92. Boulder, CO: Westview Press.

———. (1990). Urban private business and social change. In D. Davis and E. F. Vogel (Eds.), *Chinese society on the eve of Tiananmen: The impact of reform*, pp. 157–78. Cambridge, MA: Harvard University Press.

Gold, T.; D. Guthrie; and D. Wank. (2002). *Social connections in China: Institutions, culture, and the changing nature of* guanxi. New York: Cambridge University Press.

Guthrie, D. (1998). The declining significance of *guanxi* in China's economic transition. *China Quarterly*, 154, 254–82.

———. (1999). *Dragon in a three-piece suit: The emergence of capitalism in China*. Princeton, NJ: Princeton University Press.

Kelliher, D. (1992). *Peasant power in China: The era of rural reform, 1979–1989*. New Haven, CT: Yale University Press.

Naughton, B. (1995). *Growing out of the plan: Chinese economic reform, 1978–1993*. Cambridge, UK: Cambridge University Press.

Zhou, K. X. (1996). *How the farmers changed China: Power of the people*. Boulder, CO: Westview Press.

8

A SURVEY OF THE ECONOMICS LITERATURE ON CHINA'S NONSTATE ENTERPRISES

DAVID DAOKUI LI

The term *nonstate enterprises* (or *nonstate sector*), as applied to China, refers to all production units that are not fully owned (or dominantly owned or fully controlled) by the state. It is a necessarily awkward and imprecise concept of research on the Chinese economy—and for good reason. Until very recently, the label of "private enterprise" or "private sector" carried negative social and political connotations and invited politically discriminatory treatment. As a consequence, many nonstate enterprises have chosen not to register as private enterprises, so that their formal ownership arrangements have been ambiguous. The distinctions among private, collective, and state-owned enterprises (SOEs) continue to be blurred.

It is difficult to exaggerate the important contributions of China's nonstate enterprises to the economy's development in the reform era. In the past two and a half decades, China's nonstate sector has achieved a growth record unparalleled by other transitional economies. With its growth far outpacing that of the state sector, the share of China's total industrial output produced by the nonstate sector rose from about 35 percent in 1985 to more than 66 percent in 2003. The nonstate sector's contribution to industrial growth was about 35 percent to 45 percent in the 1980s, about 60 percent to 70 percent in the 1990s, and about 80 percent in the early 2000s. The outstanding performance of the nonstate sector is indeed a feature distinguishing China's reform experience from those of other transitional economies. Given the share of the nonstate sector in China's economy, there is little doubt that this sector has become a determining factor of the overall performance of the country's economy (Bai, Li, and Wang, 2003).

China's nonstate enterprises have also made important contributions in another realm—namely, the knowledge of economics. Over the past two and a half decades, they have presented important intellectual challenges and stimulated academic research. Twenty-five years ago, few economists could have predicted the rapid growth of the nonstate sector in the face of the mounting restrictions placed on it. Few had imagined the extent of the flexibilities of the ownership and property rights arrangements of China's nonstate enterprises, enabling them to operate around such restrictions. Indeed, economists have been educated by the reality of China's nonstate enterprises, and some of the important lessons have been distilled into the literature of economic development and transition.

It is not an easy task to survey the large body of literature on China's nonstate enterprises over the past twenty-five years; hence, this survey is unavoidably nonexhaustive and cursory. For the sake of efficiency and clarity, I group the body of literature into three categories, each answering a key research question regarding China's nonstate enterprises. The first question is about their environ-

128

Table 8.1

The Share of Industrial Output: State Sector Versus Nonstate Sector[a]

Year[b]	State enterprises	Nonstate enterprises[c]
1985	64.90	35.10
1986	62.27	36.63
1987	59.72	40.28
1988	56.79	43.21
1989	56.06	43.94
1990	54.60	45.40
1991	56.17	43.83
1992	51.52	48.48
1993	46.95	53.05
1994	37.33	62.67
1995	33.97	66.03
1996	36.32	63.68
1997	31.62	68.38
1998	49.63	50.37
1999	48.92	51.08
2000	47.34	52.66
2001	44.43	55.57
2002	40.78	59.22
2003	33.04	66.96

[a]The values are percentages. Each year's total is scaled to 100. "Other types of enterprises" includes foreign investment firms and Sino-foreign joint ventures.

[b]*Source:* Table 13–6 of the 1998 *China Statistical Yearbook* (for data before 1990), Table 13–3 of the 2003 *China Statistical Yearbook* (for data from 1990 to 2002), and Table 14–2 of the 2004 *China Statistical Yearbook* (for data on 2003), which does not distinguish collectives from other enterprises.

[c]The share of industrial output of nonstate enterprises is calculated by 100 minus the share of industrial output of state-owned enterprises.

ment: What is the nature of the external environment that China's nonstate enterprises face? The second question is about their response: Given the external environment, how have China's nonstate enterprises responded with regard to the adoption of various organizational forms, including ownership and property rights arrangements? The third question is about their behavior: How different are China's nonstate enterprises from state-owned enterprises in behavior?

The survey proceeds in four parts; hence, the remaining sections of this chapter cover the following topics: environment, organization, behavior, and future research needed to advance knowledge of China's nonstate enterprises.

THE CHANGING ENVIRONMENT SURROUNDING CHINA'S NONSTATE ENTERPRISES

A Historical Perspective

A highly interesting but often neglected fact is that the steady emergence of China's nonstate sector in the reform era is almost a mirror image of the gradual fading away of China's private

Table 8.2

The Share of Contribution to Industrial Growth: State Sector Versus Nonstate Sector[a]

Year[b]	State enterprises	Nonstate enterprises[c]
1985	64.86	35.14
1986	62.27	37.71
1987	59.72	40.28
1988	56.79	43.21
1989	56.06	43.94
1990	54.60	45.40
1991	56.17	43.83
1992	51.52	48.48
1993	46.95	43.05
1994	37.33	62.67
1995	33.97	66.03
1996	36.32	63.68
1997	31.62	68.38
1998	28.24	71.76
1999	28.20	71.80
2000	11.10	88.90
2001	22.11	77.89
2002	17.73	82.27
2003	20.00	80.00

[a]The values are percentages. Each year's total increase in industrial output is scaled to 100. The negative share of contribution is partly due to changes in the ownership forms of many enterprises in 1998, from state-owned enterprises to collective enterprises and from collective enterprises to private enterprises. Calculated from Table 13–3 of the *China Statistical Yearbook* for 2000 and Table 14–2 of the *China Statistical Yearbook* of 2004.

[b]The source for the entries after 2000 does not distinguish collectives from other enterprises.

[c]Nonstate enterprises' share of contribution to industrial growth is calculated by 100 minus the share of state-owned enterprises' contribution.

sector from 1949 to early 1960. Both processes were gradually and carefully controlled by the government as a compromise between ideological correctness and economic pragmatism.

In 1949, when the Chinese Communist Party (CCP) took over political power in the country, it nationalized all foreign enterprises and SOEs of the previous regime, leaving intact the so-called national capitalist enterprises. Politically, the CCP needed the support of the national capitalists, many of whom were small proprietors and were sympathetic to the Party during its wars against the Japanese invaders and the Nationalist Party. More importantly, the new government understood very clearly that it needed the contributions of private enterprises for economic recovery, especially during the Korean War. Specifically, had these enterprises been quickly nationalized, the resulting capital flight and loss of managerial skills would have given rise to a major collapse of the nation's industrial production. One of the most notable manifestations of the ruling party's policy was a well-heeded speech in Tianjin by Liu Shaoqi, then the deputy chairman of the Chinese Communist Party. In that speech, Liu went so far as to say that the exploitation of workers by capitalists was a contribution to the country, that private enterprises should be encouraged to expand their operation, and that their expansion was a contribution to the country (Bo 1991, 49).

In 1953, the CCP published a document, *The Party's General Line and General Tasks,* which stated the following: "There is a transitional period starting from the foundation of the People's Republic to the complete establishment of the socialist institutions. During this fairly long period, the general line and general tasks of the Party are to gradually achieve industrialization and to gradually achieve the socialist transformation of agricultural, artisan, and capitalist industry and commerce." This gradualist approach to transforming private enterprises took three steps. The first step was for the state to take control of the product market, becoming the monopolist of major markets and restricting the market behavior of private enterprises. This step enabled the government to enter supply and procurement contracts with private enterprises. Second, the state enticed—and sometimes forced—capitalist owners to accept joint operation of their enterprises with government and labor participation. This process greatly constrained the decision rights of private owners. Third, the government converted private enterprises into SOEs by exchanging private ownership of the enterprises for fifteen-year annuities.

However, the actual implementation of the proclaimed gradualist approach was much shortened. Rather than taking at least fifteen years, as had been implied, the whole process was finished in five years, ending in 1958, during the Great Leap Forward. The hastened pace of the transformation was often cited as a breach of trust by the Party. In any case, it is still notable that the government made a deliberate decision to take a gradual approach to transition, which was driven by the practical consideration of assisting economic recovery at the end of the Civil War between the Communist Party and the Nationalist Party from 1946 to 1949. After the Civil War came the war in Korea, during which China sent millions of soldiers to fight against the United Nations army led by the United States.

In the years between the socialist transformation and the advent of reform, China's nonstate sector did exist, but fluctuated at the mercy of the country's political cycles. The nonstate sector existed in the form of small collective enterprises in urban residential communities and in townships and villages (at that time called "people's communes" and "production brigades," respectively). During years of intense political campaigns, the official ideology dominated government policy and called for harsh restrictions to be placed on the nonstate sector. In other years, pragmatic policies prevailed, permitting the development of such enterprises.

The reform era saw a reversal of the process of the gradual socialist transformation of the nonstate sector. Again, pragmatic concerns of economic stability, employment, and so on drove the step-by-step liberalization of the nonstate sector at the expense of official ideology. In 1982, the National People's Congress legislated a new state constitution. Of central importance to private businesses is Article 11, which states that "the individual businesses in urban and rural areas, operated within the limits prescribed by law, are complements to the socialist economy. The state protects the lawful rights and interests of the individual businesses by exercising administrative control." Meanwhile, there were many creative efforts by party theoreticians in reinterpreting Marxist doctrine to accommodate the development of the nonstate sector. For example, one scholar found evidence in Marx that hiring fewer than eight nonfamily members does not constitute exploitation. Laws and regulations were revised or drafted accordingly. In April 1988, the National People's Congress voted to allow private businessmen to hire more than the previously permitted seven nonfamily employees, officially creating and recognizing a new category of private business. In July 1988, it published a new set of regulations for these enterprises and also decreed that private entrepreneurs could sign contracts with foreign business concerns. During the mid 1980s, prohibitions on private long-distance transport and wholesale trade were removed, and access to raw materials was eased. The constitution was revised in March 1988 to add "privately run enterprises" *(siying qiye)* to the list of state, collective, and individual proprietorships making up the Chinese economy.

Changing Incentives of Local Governments

The most important changes in the environment of China's nonstate enterprises came from the governments. Before the start of the reform, government agencies—or, more specifically, government officials—were implementers of policies restrictive to nonstate enterprises. In the reform era, they have become increasingly enthusiastic about the establishment and growth of nonstate enterprises. What accounts for such changes?

The literature has identified two fundamental institutional reforms as responsible for the drastic changes of government agencies and officials toward the development of the nonstate sector. The first was a fundamental institutional reform in 1978, upon the resumption of power by Deng Xiaoping. Li (1998) argued that this is a political reform broadly defined, which came as a result of Deng's efforts to avoid future political disasters such as the Cultural Revolution. Being the most notable surviving victim of the Cultural Revolution, Deng was best positioned to initiate a fundamental reform of the institutions of personnel management within the government. The aim was to abolish life tenure by imposing age limits on all government positions and to include requirements for educational and professional knowledge in the appointment processes. Also, the reform called for administrative decentralization in the appointment of government officials. This reform, aided by providing incentives to retiring incumbent government officials, was sweeping. Within eighteen months, from mid 1978 to early 1980, the typical age of provincial and ministerial officials became much younger, and the education level much higher. Moreover, the idea of government officials quitting their positions in order to enter business began to be accepted. In brief, Li (1996) argued that the reform injected a prereform culture into the governments and diversified government officials' objectives from solely political to economic.

The second institutional change identified in the literature, which is closely related to the political reform discussed above, is fiscal decentralization. Starting in the mid-1980s, through a sequence of reforms, provincial governments were granted rights to collect and retain a large proportion of taxes from local enterprises. In many cases, provincial governments were only responsible for a fixed amount of tax contribution to the central government, leaving them with 100 percent of marginal tax revenue collected locally. Qian and Weingast (1992) called this federalism, Chinese style. The fiscal decentralization greatly stimulated local officials' interest in promoting rapid entry of enterprises into high-profit and high-tax-margin industries. In many cases, the entries took the form of nonstate enterprises. Oi (1999) called such entries local corporatism. This description is confirmed by Jin and Qian (1998), who showed that regions having a higher retention rate saw faster growth of nonstate enterprises.

Interestingly, the great fiscal decentralization of the mid 1980s was drastically reversed starting in 1994 by a fiscal reform that recentralized most of the tax collection rights, which reverted from provincial governments to the central government. Subsequently, from 1997 to 2002, the overall growth of the Chinese economy slowed, as official statistics show. According to much anecdotal evidence, tax recentralization caused the slowdown, because local governments' interest in sponsoring and supporting further entry of nonstate enterprises diminished sharply. Of course, this was also the situation during the Asian financial crises, which likely affected nonstate enterprises more severely than state-owned enterprises. In any case, there has been no systematic research to substantiate or falsify the connection.

A Tilted Playing Field

Despite continued relaxation of official ideology and major reforms of the government that have provided incentives for local government officials to promote economic development, the overall institutional setup of the economy is still not compatible with that of a conventional market economy. The environment facing China's nonstate—and especially its private—enterprises is in general nonsupportive.

Bai Li, and Wang (2003) summarized this situation by saying that the playing field is still tilted against nonstate enterprises. More specifically, that is true in three general areas. First, there still exist legal and administrative barriers to entry. Although individual local governments may have incentives to help remove these restrictions, the remaining ones are often nationwide and beyond the control of local governments. For example, defense industries, natural resource monopoly industries, and higher education are still closed to nonstate investors.

The second barrier is credit constraint. Since the late 1990s, local governments have had decreasing influence over commercial banks, which are dominated by the four big state-owned commercial banks. The state banks were institutionally configured to work with state-owned enterprises and therefore have limited ability to evaluate and lend to nonstate enterprises. As a result, according to a survey of the International Financial Corporation (2000), China's nonstate enterprises faced major credit rationing, which seemed to be even more severe in the early 2000s than a few years back.

The third aspect of the tilted field is poor legal protection. An independent judiciary system has yet to be established in China. Legal protection of rights is at best ad hoc. Nonstate enterprises—unlike state ones, which, as part of the government apparatus, have close relations with administrative branches—find this to be a big problem. Thus, it is difficult for a nonstate enterprise to get a fair ruling in a dispute with a state-owned enterprise. Because of this concern, nonstate enterprises typically try to avoid legal cases against state enterprises and yield to unfavorable settlements outside the legal system. Zhang and Ming (1999) found that when facing business disputes, the overwhelming majority of managers (71 percent) tried to deal with the disputes on their own. Only 6.5 percent of those surveyed said that they would resort to legal means.

ORGANIZATIONAL RESPONSES TO THE CHANGING ENVIRONMENT: OWNERSHIP AND PROPERTY RIGHTS ARRANGEMENTS OF CHINA'S NONSTATE ENTERPRISES

Responding to the challenges of this harsh environment, China's nonstate enterprises have adopted flexible and oftentimes unique organizational arrangements. The most outstanding innovation in this regard concerns property ownership and property rights. Very much contrary to the belief of many economists who have advocated well-defined and unequivocal private ownership as a necessary condition for good economic performance and rapid growth, until very recently, many rapidly growing nonstate enterprises in China did not have clear ownership arrangements. The question of who has what kinds of control rights has not been clearly answered either. Naturally, much research on China's nonstate enterprises has been devoted to reconciling these puzzling observations.

Is Chinese Culture a Substitute for Clearly Defined Property Rights?

One explanation of the unusual property rights situation of China's nonstate enterprises is that the Chinese culture is uniquely arranged in that there is no perceived need for clearly defined ownership and property rights in order for production and investment to be efficient. Weitzman and Xu (1994) first articulated this view in the context of China's township-and-village enterprises (TVEs). They argued that the basic precepts of standard property rights theory are wrong and that a transition strategy can be reliably based on the performance of vaguely defined cooperatives such as TVEs.

Weitzman and Xu (1994) proposed a general approach to property rights theory based on a notion of cooperative culture. They argued that standard property rights theories, which are generally viewed as universal or culture-free, rest on an explicit or implicit assumption—that all people are indiscriminately uncooperative. Thus, a major role of ownership, according to the standard theories, is to resolve conflicts and enforce cooperation in an economic organization. However, if in reality cooperative behavior varies among people of different societies, then the significance of ownership in solving conflicts in economic organizations may also vary. By using a fundamental concept of repeated game theory, it is possible to integrate formally the seemingly cultural element of a cooperative spirit with standard property rights theory to arrive at a more general version of the theory. This general approach may avoid the above-mentioned paradox, and it may have implications for understanding other interesting and puzzling phenomena, such as certain aspects of the Japanese economy.

Although the theoretical foundation of Weitzman and Xu (1994) is well understood and non-controversial (it is the so-called folk theorem of repeated games, which says that in a repeated game with sufficiently patient players, essentially any outcome can be an equilibrium), there is dispute about their theory's relevance. Is Chinese culture really more cooperative than others? If so, why are many state-owned enterprises and collective enterprises in China very inefficient? Are Chinese villagers and township residents cooperative with each other? If so, why did collective agriculture fail so badly in China that decollectivization became a popular and easy first item on the agenda of reform?

Weitzman and Xu (1994) sparked a debate on the nature of China's TVEs. One strand of literature emphasizes that they are private in nature and simply wear the hat of the collective enterprise (see the section "Discrimination against Private Enterprises and the 'Red Hat' Phenomenon" below). The other strand emphasizes that TVEs are different from private enterprises and have characteristics of collective enterprises with strong labor participation. Bowles and Dong (1999), in a small survey of a northeastern province, reported that township-and-village enterprises are different from private enterprises. TVEs put more weight on employment and motivate workers differently by providing higher employment security. Contrasting with these two strands of literature are two strands of theory focusing on the ambiguity of property rights as defined by residual control rights and local government control rights, respectively.

Ambiguous Property Rights in Imperfect Markets

In contrast with the cultural theory of vaguely defined cooperatives, there is a general line of literature that emphasizes imperfect market environments as a factor driving the ambiguity of property rights arrangements. The idea is that entrepreneurs and other involved parties endogenously chose property rights arrangements to cope with market imperfections. When a market is imperfect, after an initial investment in an enterprise has been made, certain agents may become useful to resolve uncertainties facing the enterprise. In this case, it is better to allow such agents to have control rights ex post, when they become productive in remedying market imperfection.

Li (1996) and Tian (2000) articulated this idea by using formal models. The Li model is close to the Grossman-Hart-Moore framework of property rights (Grossman and Hart 1986, Hart and

Moore 1990), with one explicit difference. In Li (1996), ambiguous property rights are defined as situations in which owners' rights are not guaranteed beforehand. Instead, owners have to fight for actual control, ex post. The key issue of the theory is to show why property rights arrangements make a difference. Suppose A and B are two investors contemplating two alternative arrangements. One is to let A (or B) be the sole property rights holder and therefore the sole decision maker when the enterprise is in operation. The other is to let A and B be ambiguous owners and, later on—when the market uncertainty is realized—renegotiate to decide who has the actual control rights. The key departure from the Grossman-Hart-Moore framework is that Li (1996) assumed that the information structure changes with property rights allocation. Thus, when A is the sole owner, B cannot check the firm's account books, so that A and B cannot efficiently negotiate when B turns out to be useful to the enterprise. On the other hand, when A and B are owners, they share inside information and therefore can more easily renegotiate to reallocate actual control rights. The conclusion is that if the marketplace is highly uncertain (i.e., it is hard to predict who will be more useful for the prosperity of the enterprise), it is better to keep both A and B as nominal (ambiguous) owners and then renegotiate to sort out actual control rights.

To be more specific, imagine A as a private entrepreneur and B a government official. If the market is fully liberalized, B is most likely to be of no use to the enterprise, since goods can be bought and sold without the intervention of B. In this case, the most efficient arrangement is for A to be the sole property rights holder. On the other hand, if markets for goods are not functioning very well, so that there is a high-enough chance that B will be useful to help resolve future problems, it will be better to keep B inside the firm as an ambiguous owner. When B turns out to be useful, A and B will be able to negotiate without information friction to allocate actual control to B.

The general implication of this line of theories of ambiguous property rights is that ownership and property rights arrangements are endogenous; they cannot be clarified without a properly functioning market. An unconditional call for clarifying the ownership and property rights of enterprises—a popular demand in China—may not be appropriate for transition economies. Given the abundance of imperfections in the market, a proper degree of ambiguity of property rights is perhaps necessary.

Discriminations Against Private Enterprises and the "Red Hat" Phenomenon

A common perception (that is, to a large extent, consistent with reality) is that many of the seemingly ambiguously owned enterprises and collective or community-owned enterprises in China are actually private enterprises in disguise. They simply wear the "red hat" of collective (or even state-owned) enterprises. This is often referred to as the "red hat phenomenon." In this vein, Young (1998) emphasized that the discriminatory environment caused China's private sector to develop hidden within the public sector, and that throughout the reform period it has been important for private entrepreneurs to widen their support base by cultivating good relations with local government officials. Because of the merging of ownership categories owing to the political constraints of the 1980s, it was not easy to delineate the "private sector."

From this perspective, Lo and Tian (2002) argued that the Chinese experience cannot, as Weitzman and Xu (1994) claimed, challenge the traditional property rights theory. The seemingly vaguely defined ownership is attributed to the discriminatory legal environment within which private property rights developed. Private property had to develop in the guise of the collective. Once the political and legal environments improved in the 1990s, the private sector achieved significant productivity gains and contributed more to economic growth than all other sectors. Accordingly, Weitzman and Xu argued, private property rights are crucial to economic performance; China is no exception.

Local Governments as Holders or Protectors of Property Rights

A prominent feature of China's nonstate enterprises, especially the township-and-village enterprises, is that they are under the strong influence or control of local governments. For example, Wen and Chang (1999) showed that local governments subsidized agriculture with profits made by TVEs, and argued that this policy has played an important role in maintaining stability and accelerating balanced economic growth in Chinese rural areas. These authors explained that this policy is unique in that it started at a very early stage of industrialization. Also, the policy has often been carried out voluntarily at the local level rather than at the national level. They attribute this fact to the power of the Chinese community governments.

Another line of literature takes on the extensive control rights of local governments to explain the property rights arrangements of China's nonstate enterprises. This line of reasoning has two premises. First, Chinese local governments have had strong incentives to promote local economic prosperity, given China's unique political institutional arrangements in the reform era, including administrative decentralization and fiscal contracting. These incentives make local governments particularly interested in supporting local enterprises that provide off-farm employment and increase local tax revenue. Second, to get effective help from a local government, entrepreneurs in the private sector are willing to be under its control or to register the enterprise as a collective one under the name of some branch of the government—that is, they are willing to wear a red hat.

Chang and Wang (1994) were among the first authors in this line of literature, and their focus is on China's township-and-village enterprises. They argued that a TVE is controlled by a township-village government, not by its nominal owners, the local citizens. Moreover, with explicit rules specified by the central government regarding profit distribution, the local citizens and the township-village government share residual benefits of the TVE. Further, the rationale for assigning control rights to the township-village government is cost minimization. Given the existing Chinese system of highly concentrated political power, private citizens may find it difficult to obtain key resources critical to the success of a TVE. Giving control to the citizens would thus give the enterprise a less-promising future. The more difficult question is why local citizens, rather than the township-village government, should be the nominal owners. Chang and Wang viewed the citizens' nominal ownership as a means by which the central government makes a commitment to policies and rules that guarantee that the main benefits from the operation of the TVE go to local players— the township-village government and local citizens. This commitment provides local agents with strong incentives to make sure that the TVE succeeds economically. Finally, to prevent the township-village government from appropriating excessive benefits, the central government makes some explicit rules as to how the profits of the TVE should be distributed. Chang and Wang (1994) claimed that it is natural and useful to view the ownership structure of TVEs as the central authority's solution to a design problem in which the objective is to improve the welfare of local citizens, subject to two constraints. One is that the present political system in China must be preserved. The other is that local agents must be provided with economic incentives. The first constraint explains why the government prefers TVEs to a genuine private sector. The second constraint explains why TVEs are locally, not nationally owned, as are the state-owned enterprises (SOEs).

Che and Qian (1998a, b) presented an analysis of the ownership of firms under insecure property rights. They argued that local government ownership can be perceived as an organizational response to state predation. When the local government controls two activities—government and business—together, the interests of the national and local governments become better aligned than the interests of the national government and a private owner. In the absence of revenue-based contracts, giving ownership rights to the local government provides an incentive, in that the local government can hide some revenue. Correspondingly, the national government finds it in its own interest to prey less on local-government-owned firms than on private firms. As a result, the local government (which owns the firm) may hide less revenue than what a private owner might hide. This analysis helps in understanding the relative success of local-government-owned enterprises in China in the absence of the rule of law.

One of the insights to come out of the study is that a certain type of government ownership has emerged as an organizational response to imperfect state institutions, which may work better than either conventional private or state ownership. Though not the first choice, this type of ownership can reduce the adverse effects of state predation in the absence of institutions to constrain the state. The positive role of the government identified here is not a cure for market failure; rather, local government ownership in this study is seen as overcoming "state failure."

In an empirical investigation, Jin and Qian (1998) examined a set of provincial data and verified that all the above theories carry some explanatory power. Specifically, they found that the share of TVEs relative to private enterprises is higher where the central government's influence is greater, the community government's power is stronger, and the level of market development is lower. TVEs helped community governments to increase revenue, rural nonfarm employment, and rural income. However, TVEs did not in fact increase rural income, given the levels of nonfarm employment and local public goods provision, indicating possible inefficiency as compared with private enterprises.

Privatization, or Clarification of Property Rights, of China's Nonstate Enterprises

A highly interesting observation that is extremely stimulating to students of economic institutions is that the property rights arrangements of China's nonstate enterprises have been undergoing continuous evolution during the era of reform. The general trend is for those nonstate enterprises with ambiguous ownership and property rights to be gradually clarified and for many (nominally) nonprivate enterprises to be privatized. Of course, there has been enormous regional and sectorial heterogeneity in the pace and fashion of the evolution. Why has this process of clarification of property rights occurred? How can one account for its heterogeneity? Why is the process of privatization often difficult, so much so that it is not complete in many cases? These stimulating questions have inspired a large body of literature.

Bai, Li, and Wang (2003) made a general point that although China's nonstate enterprises have benefited from a set of transitional institutions, such institutions cannot propel future growth of China's nonstate sector, since they are not only inadequate in today's economic conditions but also create distortions by themselves. Such transitional institutions are not real long-term solutions for the problems facing China's nonstate enterprises, especially when the enterprises are growing big and modern.

It is important to note that a near continuum of types of ownership arrangements has been evolved by China's nonstate enterprises over the past decades. Among these nonconventional ownership arrangements is one called the joint-stock cooperative (JSC) (*gufen hezuo qiye*), which was invented by entrepreneurs in Zhejiang province. A JSC is similar to an employee-shareholding enterprise with shares belonging to local government; its unique feature is that it has a block of collective shares that are not divided among individual persons, leaving a sense of ambiguity about collective ownership. Sun (2002) discussed this arrangement in detail, showing that the most striking feature of the ownership restructuring is the fading away of local government ownership. Sun also showed the adaptive efficiency of the new form.

Why Privatization?

Before discussing these results, an issue needs to be addressed; namely, is there need to privatize, or are there substitutes for ownership reform? Chang, McCall, and Wang (2003) answered this question by using data that trace the ten-year history of eighty TVEs. Studying the consequences of introducing managerial incentives and better-defined ownership for firms' financial performance, they found that managerial incentives had a positive but statistically insignificant effect on these firms' performance, as measured by returns on assets or on equity. Performance was significantly better under ownership forms with better-defined property rights than under community ownership, even when the latter was supplemented with managerial incentive contracts. Thus, the message is very clear: reforms of managerial incentives cannot replace ownership reform.

Li, Li, and Zhang (2000) provided a general answer based on product-market competition. They developed a theory focusing on how product-market competition induces institutional change through the interaction of bureaucrats and managers in regional government-controlled economies. When cross-regional competition is sufficiently intense, each region has to cut production costs. Given that the efforts of managers are not verifiable, local governments may have to grant total or partial residual shares to the managers. In general, intense product competition stimulates the rise of a private property system. Using a Chinese industrial census of over 400,000 firms, Li, Li, and Zhang (2000) conducted an empirical test of their theory. Ho, Bowles, and Dong (2003) answered this question in the context of China's rural industrial enterprises, relying upon interviews and survey data from three counties in the provinces of Jiangsu and Shandong. Their analysis shows that rapid privatization in these regions was driven by the desire to prevent further asset stripping; in order for the enterprises to operate efficiently, the privatization processes gave majority share ownership to enterprise managers. Furthermore, Ho and colleagues showed that privatization better served the interests of township governments and enterprise managers than those of workers.

Sun (2000) studied the ownership restructuring of TVEs in the 1990s. According to the analysis, many of these enterprises restructured their ownership for reasons other than as a response to crises. Instead, the restructuring was anticipatory. This observation illustrates that both market competition and interjurisdictional competition have induced such ownership reforms, and that the organization of the government matters in providing incentives for government officials to reform.

How Does Privatization Work?

Yao (2001) provided an explanation for the disparity among regions in China in the performance of privatization. He ascribed this disparity to the different degrees of local government commitment to privatization, claiming that to induce good privatization performance—or even to make privatization happen—local government officials have to make a credible commitment to limit their own power of interference and predation at the time of privatization. Therefore, reform of government is essential for the process. Yao presented the experience of government reform in the city of Shunde, in Guangdong Province, to illustrate his theory.

Dong, Bowles, and Ho (2002a) examined the determinants of employee share ownership in newly privatized TVEs in the provinces of Shandong and Jiangsu. They found that expected financial returns, job security, risk preference, and family wealth were important determinants of employee shareholdings. However, several other variables also affected the accessibility of share ownership to employees: local leaders' preferences for managerial buyouts relative to their concern for improving work incentives; their desire to maximize sales revenue; and the position, residential status, and gender of the employees.

Is there any special geographical pattern of privatization? Han and Pannell (1999) examined this question using descriptive statistics and correlation analysis to describe and explain the changing spatial dimensions of China's privatization process. They found that a complex spatial pattern of privatization has emerged, a pattern correlated with the legacy of prereform development and new economic opportunities in different regions. The analysis shows that unemployment was influential with respect to privatization in the late 1980s, but in the 1990s high state employment in commerce was associated with the growth of the urban private sector. Moreover, it is geographically significant that the stronger the private sector at the provincial level, the faster the province's economic growth.

What Is the Impact of Privatization?

What is the impact of privatization on regional economic performance? Tian (2001) used provincial data for the period 1985–97 and found that provinces with greater progress in privatization witnessed greater gains in marginal productivity of capital and more rapid economic growth. To test the robustness of the finding, Tian classified forms of ownership into different categories that represent various degrees of privatization. The findings suggest that China should pursue ownership reform in the direction of privatization in order to maintain growth momentum.

At the individual economic agent's level, what is the impact of privatization? Dong (2003) examined the impact of privatization of TVEs on earnings inequality, using a regression-based inequality decomposition technique and an employee survey undertaken in the provinces of Shandong and Jiangsu in 2000. He found that several factors have contributed, to various extents, to the rise of earnings inequality in postprivatization rural enterprises, including unequal distribution of share ownership among employees, increased returns to human capital, and widened gender wage gaps.

THE BEHAVIOR AND PERFORMANCE OF CHINA'S NONSTATE ENTERPRISES

Labor Participation

A line of scholarship studies the behavior of China's nonstate enterprises from the perspective of labor management, an arrangement in which labor actively participates in managerial decisions. Smith (1995) examined experiences of employee participation in equity ownership, profit sharing, and decision making in TVEs in China through eight case studies in Zhejiang Province. Such case-based studies are important complements to formal econometric research using a large amount of randomly sampled data. The evidence from the cases in the sample suggested that despite the accelerating moves toward formal and private ownership of TVEs in the 1980s and 1990s, TVEs retained a degree of employee financial participation and—to a lesser but significant degree—employee participation in decision making. In other words, clear traces of labor participation were present in postprivatization TVEs.

Dong, Bowles, and Ho (2002b) reported the impact of share ownership on employee attitudes in China's privatized rural industries, drawing on a survey administered in the provinces of Jiangsu and Shandong. The results indicated that, in general, employee shareholders had higher job satisfaction, perceived greater degrees of participation in enterprise decision making, displayed stronger organizational commitment, and had more positive attitudes toward the privatization process than nonshareholders in privatized firms.

It is interesting to note that China's nonstate enterprises are intrinsically different from labor-managed firms, although the two types of firms may share some characteristics. After all, local governments do exercise control rights over the enterprises, so that local governments' objectives are superimposed. For example, local governments' concern over employment—as opposed to the wage rate of those employed—is partly transmitted to nonstate enterprises. Empirical evidence shows this; for example, Dong (1998) examined the employment and wage behavior of TVEs, using a panel of data for the years 1984–90. She found that TVEs put positive weight on both employment and wage earnings.

Wage Determination and Income Inequality

Meng and Perkins (1998) conducted a comparative study of wage determination and related issues in different types of enterprises. They found that both the state-owned enterprises and the collective enterprises shared some behavioral similarities with labor-managed firms in their wage determination, while the private firms behaved more like profit-maximizing firms. The major difference lay in the objective function of these enterprises. While the private sector pursued profit maximization, the state and collective sectors appeared to be attempting to maximize income per employee. Further, the study showed that although both the state-owned and the collective enterprises pursued income maximization, profit sharing induced higher labor productivity growth in the collectives than in the state enterprises. The reason for this difference may be the different degree of separation of risk bearing and decision making in the various types of enterprises. Economic reforms have given SOEs significant autonomy in managerial decision making, while their assets are fully owned by the state, which still bears the major financial consequences of firms' decision making. This arrangement gives the managers of such firms an incentive to focus on the short-run welfare of their employees (including themselves) rather than the long-term value of the state assets they manage. The collective firms operate under relatively hard budget constraints and have to bear a certain degree of financial risk. Consequently, their decision making with regard to earnings is more cautious. Greater consideration is given to productivity growth when bonuses are distributed.

Gregory and Meng (1995) studied wage determination in rural enterprises in China, in which real wages had grown at around 11 percent per annum in the 1980s. Using data from interviews with about 500 male workers in forty-nine enterprises during 1986–87 in four counties, they found that experience was important for the wage rate and education was not, while for the subsample of market-matched rather than assigned jobs, education was positively significant for the wage rate. More generally, the relationship between wage, education, and occupational attainment for those who found jobs through their own efforts was similar to that in Western market economies. Employing a logit model to investigate the links between education and occupational attainment, they found that education was a significant factor in occupational attainment.

Dong (2003) used a matched sample of employees and enterprises to examine the effects of privatization on wage structures in rural industry in two provinces of China. She found that wage structures in transition economies usually diverged significantly from their centrally planned predecessors. Privatization was associated with increased wage and earnings inequality. She reported increased returns to education, increased returns to experience for middle-aged workers, and increases in gender wage discrimination. These aspects of wage structures were found to be similar in different types of private ownership emerging from the reform process.

Interestingly, the development of nonstate enterprises has implications for increases in income inequality. Walder (2002) found that in the second decade of market reform, rural cadre and entrepreneur households enjoyed large net income advantages of roughly equal magnitude. Cadre household incomes were primarily from salaries, and they did not decline with increasing levels of rural industrialization. An event-history analysis of occupational shifts reinforced these cross-sectional findings about income determination. With large income advantages based on salary income, at no point in market reform have cadres moved into self-employment or private entrepreneurship at higher rates than ordinary farmers. However, village cadres have become the most important source of collective enterprise managers, and collective enterprise managers in turn have become the most important source of new private entrepreneurs. Therefore, the thriving collective enterprise sector of the 1980s has served as a breeding ground for private enterprise in the 1990s.

The Relative Efficiency of China's Nonstate Enterprises

Perotti, Sun, and Zou (1999) presented a survey of the comparison between SOEs and TVEs in China. They argued that although TVEs were at a disadvantage in areas such as technology, labor skills, staff education levels, and access to bank loans and government support, they had important advantages in ownership and governance structure, personnel systems and labor relations, and institutional arrangements. These advantages apparently outweighed the disadvantages, allowing the TVEs to outperform SOEs and successfully expand their market shares. However, their analysis also reveals that SOEs would not have performed so badly if their broad social contributions other than reported profits also had been taken into account. In conclusion, the authors argued that both SOEs and TVEs need to reform their ownership and governance structures. The reason that TVEs also should carry out ownership reform is that their organizational advantages have been diminishing in those townships and villages where grassroots democratization has lagged behind TVEs' expansion in scale and market shares.

How do China's nonstate enterprises compare with those of comparable developing economies in technical efficiency? Using a sample of TVEs, Dong and Putterman (1997) addressed this question, studying technical efficiency and variations among TVEs during 1984–88. The average technical efficiency level among the sampled enterprises was found to resemble that of industrial enterprises in other developing countries.

Liu, Chew, and Li (1998) analyzed the productivity of different categories of labor and capital by estimating a production function using micro data on 140 industrial TVEs located in fifteen counties of Jiangsu Province during 1989–90. They estimated that the annual marginal productivity of labor was 19,282 RMB for tertiary-educated workers and 2,175 RMB for workers with lower education, at 1990 prices. There was not much difference in the marginal productivity of labor when work experience was considered. The estimated marginal productivity of capital was quite high; the rate of return on capital reached about 30 percent.

Using data on Chinese companies listed in the stock exchange, Wei and Varela (2003) examined the relation between state equity ownership and firm market performance among China's newly privatized firms in 1994 (164 firms), 1995 (175 firms), and 1996 (252 firms). The overall results showed that state ownership had a negative effect on firm value. Tobin's Q was convex with respect to state ownership, so that newly privatized firms gained capital and higher market values, with their increased size paying off in returns. The effect of international ownership was unpredictable, and domestic institutional ownership did not appear to improve performance, possibly because the latter lacked proper incentives to positively influence the firm management.

The results further showed that a firm's performance is not an important determinant of state ownership, but rather, its size and its strategic industry status are the main determinants of the state's equity ownership in China's newly privatized firms.

Financing and Contracting

In one of the first systematic attempts to take stock of the evolution of the Chinese private sector, through extensive surveys and interviews carried out in four locations (Beijing, Chengdu, Shunde, and Wenzhou), the International Financial Corporation (2000) provided evidence of private enterprises' difficulties gaining access to financing. It showed that, by far, the main source of initial investments in private enterprises has been family and social connections. The trend seems to have been strengthened for younger enterprises, implying that financing barriers to private enterprises in the formal financial market are becoming higher rather than lower over time.

In view of the apparent financing barriers to nonstate enterprises in the formal financial market, how have they managed to grow? How have they solved their financing problem? These are the questions that Tsai (2002) addressed. Through case studies in Fujian, Wenzhou, and Henan, she described how entrepreneurs created unofficial alternatives to state banks when the central government explicitly forbade private financial institutions, and she explained the tremendous variation in the scope and scale of informal finance throughout the country.

Examining the changing lending preferences of banks, Park and Shen (2003) presented a new explanation for the rise and fall of collectively owned enterprises. They explained that until the mid 1990s, bank loans to collective firms exhibited the key features of joint liability lending, supported by the sanctioning ability of local government leaders. However, subsequent changes in collateral, firm performance, interest rates, and financial competition led banks to prefer individual lending to private firms. This explanation is supported by empirical analysis of the determinants of bank lending preferences, the involvement of township leaders in lending, and the ability of firms to obtain loans.

On the issue of how nonstate enterprises make contractual choices, Zhu (1998) explained the pattern of contractual and ownership arrangements and their evolution in China's TVEs by constructing a formal model on the general lines of the rent-seeking theory. It was shown that, because local government officials are not the residual claimants of TVEs and are corruptible, they may have incentives to make inefficient choices. But market competition will increasingly force them to adopt efficient arrangements.

China's nonstate enterprises are commonly perceived to have low degrees of trust and credibility, making it difficult for them to honor and enter into contracts with other enterprises. In reality, however, it can be observed that both nonstate and state enterprises do have extensive business dealings that often involve multiperiod transactions requiring contracts. How can one explain this? Tao and Zhu (2001) offered an intriguing theory that looks for answers in the behavior of state enterprises. They observed that the agency problem was more severe in state enterprises. This was good, according to their analysis, when it came to contract enforcement, since managers of state enterprises, not being the owners of their firms, were less likely to breach a contract ex post when offered a relatively small private benefit on the side by nonstate enterprises. This explains why it is actually easier for a nonstate enterprise to contract with a state enterprise than with another nonstate enterprise.

How do China's nonstate enterprises design incentive contracts for their managers? Hsiao et al. (1998) argued that, unlike in conventional private enterprises, both employees and local governments are important contributors to the success of a nonstate enterprise. Thus, a double-sided moral hazard problem arises. Therefore, a profit-sharing system between employees and a local government is better than a quota profit system that leaves no profit share to one party. Using a national survey of 200 Chinese TVEs during 1985–90, Hsiao et al. (1999) verified their theory empirically.

UNDERRESEARCHED ISSUES

No doubt the literature on China's nonstate enterprises has made a significant contribution to knowledge of some fundamental issues of economic development and reform. Inasmuch as China's nonstate enterprises have been continuously evolving and their future development holds the key to the growth of the Chinese economy, research on them will likely attract ever more attention and expand ever faster. Although it is always difficult to predict in which direction research will advance, in the following paragraphs I list a few issues that seem to be underresearched so far and therefore may attract the attention of researchers in the future.

The first issue that has not been sufficiently studied so far is the so-called original sin that has attracted much attention among the general public in China. This refers to (perceived) illegal or immoral practices of entrepreneurs at the beginning of the establishment of their businesses. Of course, the definition of illegal or immoral is relative to the legal, regulatory, and moral standards at the time of the practices. One immediate implication of the discussion of original sin is whether a large amount of the assets of the nonstate enterprises should be forfeited to government agencies. A preliminary and very important question the literature needs to answer is how prevalent the issue of original sin is. What are the major types of "sins"? What are their proportions among all the nonstate enterprises? Without any such empirical evidence, discussions of the issue are not well grounded. Of course, these are very difficult research questions to tackle. But they are not impossible if one can creatively find some data set of special circumstances that help reveal important transaction information. Once these questions are addressed, further questions can be tackled. How does the uncertainty about the potential punishment of the original sin affect the behavior of the private owners of nonstate enterprises? Does this explain some sudden demise of China's nonstate enterprises? Does it explain the firms' unwillingness to expand beyond a certain size? How do we analyze alternative remedies for the original sin from the efficiency or welfare point of view? What would be the incentives of various parties involved in alternative remedies? These questions are not only of theoretical interest; they also have policy implications.

The second underresearched issue is the emerging pattern of ownership of China's nonstate enterprises, which are poised to be the absolute majority of China's enterprises in the future. Indeed, this is a fundamental issue that will determine what type of market economy China will have. Will the Chinese economy be like that of today's Hong Kong, with many dominant family-owned enterprises? Or will China evolve into a market economy like those of the United States and the United Kingdom, having mostly widely held corporations in which the founding families fade into passive shareholders? The pattern of corporate ownership structure has fundamental implications for regulations, lobbying, wealth distribution, and so on. However, research is needed to understand the current landscape of ownership of nonstate enterprises. Also important is to understand the competing forces driving the evolution of the ownership structure. For example, is China's political ecology conducive to the development of dominant family owners? Are there sufficient legal and social institutions to induce family owners to comfortably give up their control to professional managers without losing much of their future financial benefits? How do these two forces trade off with each other?

The third issue is corporate governance of China's nonstate enterprises. In today's Chinese economy, many nonstate enterprises are growing into large-scale businesses. How do the founding family owners and nonfamily owners differ in their exercise of control over their enterprises? What prevents the family of founding owners from transferring their control to professional managers? How do different types of nonstate enterprises attempt to grow in scale and expand in scope? What types tend to rely on investment within the enterprises? What types tend to go to the market for corporate control by conducting mergers and acquisitions? How efficient is China's market for corporate control? Do those emerging corporate empires that are assembled by private entrepreneurs through merger and acquisition in the securities markets operate as efficiently as comparable independent enterprises?

Last, but by no means least, is the question: How does the emergence of nonstate enterprises change the characteristics of the Chinese macroeconomy? Nonstate enterprises certainly behave very differently from state-owned enterprises. When the former emerge to replace the latter as the dominant component of the economy, China's macroeconomics will be very different. The micro-macro link is a critical issue, and existing research has been quite neglectful in this regard. Needless to say, these issues are of great concern to policymakers and the general public. Here are a few examples of research questions in this area: How do nonstate enterprises approach investment decisions differently from SOEs? To what extent does the investment behavior of nonstate enterprises give rise to fluctuations of aggregate investment in the Chinese economy? How would the nonstate enterprises react differently from the SOEs to administrative macroeconomic controls vis-à-vis market-based macroeconomic levers?

How do nonstate enterprises make labor employment decisions, and how different are they from state-owned enterprises in that regard? How does this difference generate new patterns of unemployment in the economy? How do nonstate enterprises approach the issue of price setting and competition differently from SOEs? How does this generate fluctuations in aggregate price level and output?

ACKNOWLEDGMENTS

This is part of a research project, entitled "China's Domestic Private Firms," of the Hang Lung Center for Organizational Research at Hong Kong University of Science and Technology. I am grateful for valuable research assistance from David W. Fan, Iris Pang, and Lanfang Wang. David Fan also participated in the early design of the survey. Financial support from Hong Kong Research Grant Council project HKUST 6224/02H, from the National Science Foundation of China project 70473048, and from the Chiang Jiang Scholars' Reward Program of the Ministry of Education of China is also gratefully acknowledged.

REFERENCES

Bai, C.; D. D. Li; and Y. Wang. (2003). Thriving in a tilted playing field: An analysis of Chinese non-state sector. In N. Hope, D. T. Yang, and M. Y. Li (Eds.), *How far across the river? China's policy reform at the millennium*, pp. 97–121. Stanford, CA: Stanford University Press.

Bo, Y. (1991). *Review of a few major decisions and events in retrospect* (in Chinese). Beijing: The Publisher of the Party School of The Central Committee of the Chinese Communist Party.

Bowles, P., X. Y. and Dong. (1999). Enterprise ownership, enterprise organisation, and worker attitudes in Chinese rural industry: Some new evidence. *Cambridge Journal of Economics*, 23, 1–20.

Chang, C., and Y. Wang. (1994). The nature of Chinese township-village enterprises. *Journal of Comparative Economics*, 19, 434–52.

Chang, C.; B. P. McCall; and Y. Wang. (2003). Incentive contracting versus ownership reforms: Evidence from China's township and village enterprises. *Journal of Comparative Economics*, 31, 414–28.

Che, J., and Y. Qian. (1998a). Insecure property rights and government ownership of firms. *Quarterly Journal of Economics*, 113, 467–96.

———. (1998b). Institutional environment, community government, and corporate governance: Understanding China's township-village enterprises. *Journal of Law, Economics, and Organization*, 14, 1–23.

Dong, X. (1998). Employment and wage determination in China's rural industry: Investigation using 1984–1990 panel data. *Journal of Comparative Economics*, 26, 485–501.

———. (2003). Privatization and rising earnings inequality in China's rural industries: Evidence from Shandong and Jiangsu. *China Economic Quarterly*, 2, 1–10.

Dong, X., and L. Putterman. (1997). Productivity and organization in China's rural industries: A stochastic frontier analysis. *Journal of Comparative Economics*, 24, 181–201.

Dong, X.; P. Bowles; and S. Ho. (2002a). The determinants of employee ownership in China's privatized rural industry: Evidence from Jiangsu and Shandong. *Journal of Comparative Economics*, 30, 415–37.

———. (2002b). Share ownership and employee attitudes: Some evidence from China's post-privatization rural industry. *Journal of Comparative Economics*, 30, 812–35.

Gregory, R. G., and X. Meng. (1995). Wage determination and occupational attainment in the rural industrial sector of China. *Journal of Comparative Economics*, 21, 353–74.

Grossman, S., and O. Hart. (1986). The costs and benefits of ownership: A theory of vertical and lateral integration. *Journal of Political Economy*, 94, 691–719.

Han, S., and C. Pannell, C. (1999). The geography of privatization in China, 1978–1996. *Economic Geography*, 75, 272–96.

Hart, O., and J. Moore. (1990). Property rights and the nature of the firm. *Journal of Political Economy*, 98, 1119–58.

Ho, S.; P. Bowles; and X. Dong. (2003). Letting go of the small: An analysis of the privatization of rural enterprises in Jiangsu and Shandong. *Journal of Development Studies*, 39, 1–26.

Hsiao, C.; J. Nugent; I. Perrigne; and J. Qiu. (1998). Shares versus residual claimant contracts: The case of Chinese TVEs. *Journal of Comparative Economics*, 26, 317–37.

International Financial Corporation (2000). *China's emerging private enterprises: Prospects for the new century*. Washington, DC.

Jin, H., and Y. Qian. (1998). Public versus private ownership of firms: Evidence from rural China. *Quarterly Journal of Economics*, 113, 773–808.

Li, D. D. (1996). A theory of ambiguous property rights in transition economies: The case of the Chinese non-state sector. *Journal of Comparative Economics*, 23, 1–23.

———. (1998). Changing incentives of the Chinese bureaucracy. *American Economic Review*, 88, 393–97.

Li, H. (2003). Government's budget constraint, competition, and privatization: Evidence from China's rural industry. *Journal of Comparative Economics*, 31, 486–502.

Li, S.; S. Li; and W. Zhang. (2000). The road to capitalism: Competition and institutional change in China. *Journal of Comparative Economics*, 28, 269–92.

Liu, Y.; S. B. Chew; W. and Li. (1998). Education, experience and productivity of labor in China's township and village enterprises: The case of Jiangsu province. *China Economic Review*, 9, 47–58.

Lo, V. I., and X. Tian. (2002). Property rights, productivity gains and economic growth: The Chinese experience. *Post Communist Economies*, 14, 245–58.

Meng, X., and F. Perkins. (1998). Wage determination differences between Chinese state and non-state firms. *Asian Economic Journal*, 12, 295–316.

Oi, J. (1999). *Rural China takes off: Institutional foundations of economic reform*. Berkeley: University of California Press.

Park, A., and M. Shen. (2003). Joint liability lending and the rise and fall of China's township and village enterprises. *Journal of Development Economics*, 71, 497–531.

Perotti, E.; L. Sun; and L. Zou. (1999). State-owned versus TVEs in China. *Comparative Economic Studies*, 41, 151–79.

Qian, Y., and B. Weingast. (1992). Federalism as a commitment to preserving market incentives. *Journal of Economic Perspectives*, 11, 83–92.

Smith, S. C. (1995). Employee participation in China's TVEs. *China Economic Review*, 6, 157–67.

Sun, L. (2000). Anticipatory ownership reform driven by competition: China's TVEs and private enterprises in the 1990s. *Comparative Economics Studies*, 42, 49–65.

———. (2002). Fading out of local government ownership: Recent ownership reform in China's township and village enterprises. *Economic Systems*, 26, 249–69.

Tao, Z., and T. Zhu. (2001). An agency theory of transactions without contract enforcement: The case of China. *China Economic Review*, 12, 1–14.

Tian, G. (2000). Property rights and the nature of Chinese collective enterprises. *Journal of Comparative Economics*, 28, 247–68.

Tian, X. (2001). Privatization and economic performance: Evidence from Chinese provinces. *Economic Systems*, 25, 65–77.

Tsai, K. (2002). *Back-alley banking: Private entrepreneurs in China*. Ithaca, NY, and London: Cornell University Press.

Walder, A. G. (2002). Income determination and market opportunity in rural China, 1978–1996. *Journal of Comparative Economics*, 30, 354–75.

Wei, Z., and O. Varela. (2003). State equity ownership and firm market performance: Evidence from China's newly privatized firms. *Global Finance Journal*, 14, 65–82.

Weitzman, M. L., and C. Xu. (1994). Chinese township-village enterprises as vaguely defined cooperatives. *Journal of Comparative Economics*, 18, 121–45.

Wen, G. J., and G. H. Chang. (1999). Communal duality: Agricultural subsidies from TVEs. *Contemporary Economic Policy*, 17, 79–86.

Yao, Y. (2001). *Government commitment and the results of privatization in China*. Mimeo, Chinese Center for Economic Research, Peking University.

Young, S. (1998). The Chinese private sector in two decades of reform. *Journal of the Asia Pacific Economy*, 3, 80–103.

Zhang, H., and L. Ming. (1999). A *report on China's private enterprises* (in Chinese). Beijing: Shehui Kexue Wenxian Chuban She.

Zhu, T. (1998). A theory of contract and ownership choice in public enterprises under reformed socialism: The case of China's TVEs. *China Economic Review*, 9, 59–71.

9

DECENTRALIZATION AND THE STRUCTURE OF CHINESE CORPORATE BOARDS

DO POLITICIANS JEOPARDIZE BOARD PROFESSIONALISM AND FIRM PERFORMANCE?

Dong-Hua Chen, Joseph P.H. Fan, and T.J. Wong

China's economic reform since 1978 has focused on the decentralization of decision rights, which have shifted from the central government to local governments, accompanied by the decentralization of control rights, which have shifted to business enterprises, although formal privatization of state ownership has not occurred. Continuous reform in the 1990s brought forth the corporatization of state enterprises and the creation of stock markets.

Table 9.1 presents evidence that China experienced a big boom in equity market development in the last decade of the twentieth century. The number of listed companies jumped to 1,088 in 2000, a level over twenty times higher than that in 1992. By the end of 2000, only about 5 percent of the total population of the country had become stock investors. If only the urban population is taken into account, this percentage is about 20 percent. In 2000, the total capitalization of the stock markets exceeded 50 percent of the country's total GDP, which was over US$1,000 billion. China's stock markets have expanded rapidly in the past ten years, ranking eighth among emerging markets and transition economies in market capitalization over GDP in 2001 (see Figure 9.1). In terms of this same statistic, China also ranked higher than almost all the Eastern European countries, whose stock markets started at almost the same time as China's.[1]

In the late 1980s, many critics argued that the establishment of stock markets would be against the ideology of socialism in China. To circumvent this political debate, which might have aborted the establishment of stock markets, a special style of stock markets with Chinese characteristics was created. These new stock markets are dominated by joint stock companies, which are reorganized from state-owned enterprises (SOEs). The process of reorganization, which allows the state to retain majority ownership, is known as corporatization (*gongsihua*), or more precisely, as partial privatization. Usually corporatization involves an initial public offering (IPO) of a minority portion of state shares to the private sector, while the majority of the shares of the newly listed company remain controlled by a parent state enterprise and are nontradable in the stock markets. Between 1994 and 2000, the average state shareholding was about 63 percent. This percentage shows an annual diminishing trend, going from 67 percent in 1994 to 61 percent in 2000 (Sun and Tong 2003).[2]

Table 9.1

Basic Descriptive Statistics of the Chinese Stock Market, 1992–2000

	1992	1993	1994	1995	1996	1997	1998	1999	2000
Domestic listed companies (A and B shares)	53	182	291	323	530	745	851	949	1088
Domestic listed companies with B shares	18	41	58	70	85	101	106	108	114
Foreign listed companies	0	6	15	18	25	42	43	46	52
Investor accounts (in thousands)	2,170	7,780	10,590	12,420	23,070	33,330	39,110	44,810	58,010
Market capitalization of all shares (in billions of RMB)	105	353	369	347	984	1,753	1,951	2,647	4,809
Market capitalization of all shares over GDP (%)	3.93	10.20	7.89	5.94	14.50	23.44	24.52	31.82	53.79
Market capitalization of tradable shares (in billions of RMB)	21	86	97	94	287	520	575	821	1609
Market capitalization of tradable shares over GDP (%)	0.78	2.49	2.06	1.60	4.22	6.96	7.22	9.87	17.99

Source: Data from *2001 Statistical Yearbook of China Securities and Futures*. China: Baihua Press, April 2001.

Figure 9.1 **Stock Market Capitalization over GDP for Emerging Markets and Countries (Economies) in Transition in 2001**

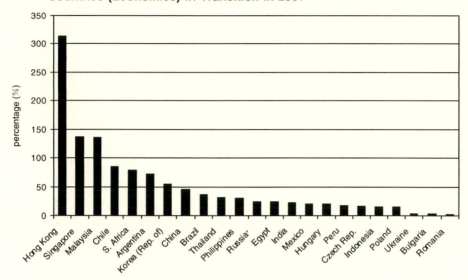

Source: China Economy database.

Although retaining majority ownership, the government has passed down most operating decision rights to the state enterprises and listed firms. By passing these control rights to listed companies and by encouraging market competition, the central government hopes that increased enterprise autonomy and market discipline will improve the efficiency of the listed companies. Increasing enterprise autonomy, however, comes with significant costs. Instead of promoting enterprise efficiency and competition, local governments may influence corporate resource allocation to support social objectives such as local development, reducing fiscal deficits, or protecting employment. Local politicians may also take bribes or divert corporate resources for their private benefit. In return, governments and politicians may bring benefits to companies, such as providing direct subsidies, protecting local markets by creating trade barriers, giving certain companies exclusive business rights, and rescuing financially distressed companies by injecting public resources into them. Knowing that politicians can strongly influence company profits, managers also have incentives to collude with them. The agency problem and the collusion of local politicians and managers thus weaken the competitive effects of decentralization.

This chapter addresses the roles of politicians in business activities in the context of China's partial privatization, examining the structure of the boards of directors of 621 companies that went public in China during the period 1993–2000. It focuses on the degree of politicians' presence on boards, and how that presence contributes to the professionalism of the boards and the firms' operational efficiency.

The remainder of the chapter proceeds as follows. We first provide the institutional background of China's decentralization and state enterprise reform, analyze the competitive and agency effects of the decentralization, and develop hypotheses about how the board presence of politicians affects board professionalism and other characteristics, government subsidies, employment, and firm performance. We then describe the sample and board characteristics, report empirical results, and offer our conclusion.

INSTITUTIONAL BACKGROUND AND HYPOTHESIS DEVELOPMENT

This section discusses two alternative views of the effects of decentralization on competition in China's product and capital markets and proposes hypotheses about how the competitive effects of decentralization shape human capital allocation, especially in the structure of boards and the performance of listed firms.

The History of Decentralization

Since 1978, China has decentralized by shifting various central government decision rights to local governments. The local governments have been allowed to retain substantial portions of their incomes instead of surrendering them to the central government, as in the past. The local governments' interest in profits and the promotion of markets has been enforced by harder budget constraints imposed by the central government, which tie expenditures with revenue generated, and by competition among local governments in different jurisdictions (Cao, Qian, and Weingast 1997; Qian and Roland 1998).

The central government also granted enterprise managers the right of control in production, pricing, sales, procurement, foreign trade, investment, use of retained funds, disposal of assets, merger and acquisition, labor, personnel management, wages and bonuses, internal organization, and refusal to pay unauthorized charges by the government (Qian 1994).

The reform resulted in significant economic benefits in the 1980s, including substantial improvement in the productivity of firms and industries (Rawski 1994). Economists have attributed the economic success to the improved incentives and information efficiency resulting from decentralization (Groves et al. 1994, Li 1997, Qian and Weingast 1997).

The Positive View

A positive view of China's decentralization is that it promotes sufficient competition to constrain governments' intervention in state enterprises. Governments may respond to the competitive pressure by lowering their intervention in state enterprises as it becomes increasingly counterproductive in a competitive marketplace. Competition arises from several dimensions. First, jurisdictional competition has become an incentive and monitoring mechanism of local governments. Qian and Weingast (1997) argued that the jurisdictional competition punishes inappropriate market intervention by lower government officials. Just as market competition pressures firm managers to reflect the interests of shareholders, competition among local governments helps to limit the governments' predatory behavior. Mobile resources can quickly leave jurisdictions that exhibit inappropriate behavior. Competition for mobile revenue sources prevents local politicians from imposing debilitating taxes or regulations (Buchanan 1995, Weingast 1995). Second, the shifting of control rights from the central government to state enterprises increases product-market competition. Third, the establishment of joint stock companies and the creation of stock markets secure greater enterprise autonomy and allow competition for funds in the capital markets.

The Negative View

While decentralization and market-based competition have brought about economic benefits, several features of China's enterprise reform have limited its effectiveness in promoting competition. First and foremost is an agency problem. Despite the process of decentralization, the central government still retains the ultimate rights to recentralize. This has created an agency problem between the central government on one side, and local governments and state enterprises on the other (Jefferson 1998; Lin, Cai, and Li 1998; Qian 1995).

The agency problem is manifested by collusion between local governments and state enterprises to regulate entry and relieve competitive pressure. Local governments have administrative power over the state enterprises under their jurisdiction and often want them to support objectives such as local development, reducing fiscal deficits, and protecting employment. The local governments can also exercise their administrative power to regulate local markets so as to shield the state enterprises from competition, resulting in regional protectionism. The state enterprises, knowing their profits depend on the local governments, will try to accommodate these objectives in return for a more relaxed competitive position.

Second is the anticompetitive effect of state-imposed policy burdens on state enterprises. Lin, Cai, and Li (1998) argued that the agency problems in state enterprises worsened after the enterprise reforms in spite of the intensification of competition. The root of the problem is state-imposed policy burdens, which put the state enterprises at a disadvantage in competing with nonstate enterprises. Because firms do not compete on a level playing field, the government is forced to provide soft budget constraints to support many of the state enterprises.

Third, when former bureaucrats quit their government positions and join new businesses where they share substantial residual control rights, they become effective lobbyists for reduced government intervention. On the other hand, a significant presence of former bureaucrats in businesses creates an environment where the government and the business are not separate, leading to government–business collusion and corruption.

Fourth is the perverse incentive associated with China's emerging capital markets. Local governments may treat the privilege of listing some state enterprises as a means to raise funds for fiscal projects and ailing state enterprises. To shore up the ability to raise funds, the local governments may provide direct subsidies or raise trade barriers to protect these listed companies. Again, this situation leads to increased economic regulation and increased collusion between listed state enterprises and government.

Hypotheses

The economic literature emphasizes that boards of directors are endogenously determined institutions (Hermalin and Weisbach 2001). The primary focus of this literature is the governance role of a board in mitigating conflicts of interest between managers and shareholders (Fama and Jensen 1983). Most prior works study how board composition (inside versus outside directors) is related to corporate policy and performance.[3] More recently Klein (1998) argues and provides evidence that directors are not randomly selected to boards but are appointed for their specific services. Several prior studies examine the roles of directors with experience in politics. Agrawal and Knoeber (2001) show evidence consistent with the view that political directors provide insight and advice to firms dealing with governments. Helland and Sykuta (2000) investigated the evolution of the board structures of listed natural gas companies in the United States during a period of deregulation. They found that a significant number of directors had a rent-seeking role: the former politicians used their political connections to get sweetheart deals for their new employers. The deregulation caused the firms to reduce the number of political directors on their boards.

Complementing this literature, we study boards of directors in the context of decentralization in a transitional economy where politics plays an active role in business activities. We specifically focus on the competitive and incentive effects of China's government decentralization on the human capital aspect of board structure. We develop several hypotheses pertaining to how politics affects board professionalism and geographical concentration, government subsidies, excess employment, and firm performance.

Board Professionalism

If the agency problem local governments pose is not effectively contained, they will actively intervene in local markets and enterprises to reduce competition. A strong presence of local politicians on the boards of listed companies is consistent with government intervention and associated rent seeking. Local politicians are sent by local governments to boards for the purpose of control and/or invited by the listed firms to facilitate their rent-seeking activities. We predict that the presence of politicians lowers board professionalism because directors with business and professional expertise may get in the way when governments trade favors with firms. Our formal hypothesis is,

> Hypothesis 1. The presence of politicians on a board is negatively associated with the level of professionalism of the board.

Board Geographical Concentration

Decentralization will not induce more competition among provinces, but rather will create incentives for local governments to set up trade barriers. If local governments and enterprises respond to the competitive pressure by colluding with each other to protect their local markets, boards will become more geographically concentrated. Therefore,

> Hypothesis 2. Politician presence on a board is positively associated with the number of directors from a single administrative region.

Government Subsidies, Employment, and Firm Performance

Having politician directors may be either beneficial or harmful to firms. On the one hand, if they serve as effective lobbyists, they can seek help from governments in times of financial distress or when the firms try to meet earnings targets prior to a new share issuance (Chen, Lee, and Li 2003). The government aid can come in the form of subsidies, which are directly credited to income. On the other hand, politician directors may pursue political and other social objectives that conflict with the share value maximization goal of outside shareholders. One of these political goals is to maintain social stability by providing full employment to a region.

Following up on the project reported in this chapter, Fan, Wong, and Zhang (forthcoming) documented that firms with politically connected CEOs are more likely to appoint other bureaucrats to boards of directors, while they appoint fewer directors with relevant professional backgrounds or prior business experience, and no representatives of minority shareholders. The presence of politically connected CEOs is related to the unemployment and fiscal conditions of the firms' regions while unrelated to most firm characteristics. The three-year post-IPO average stock returns of the sample underperformed the market by 20 percent, and the underperformance of firms with such politically connected CEOs exceeded those without politically connected CEOs by almost 30 percent. Overall, the results indicate that the appointment of politically connected CEOs does not enhance firm efficiency but, rather, fulfills the political goals of politicians.

In this chapter, we attempt to directly link the presence of politicians on boards to government subsidies, excess employment, and firm performance, which was assessed by an accounting-based measure. The arguments above lead to the following three hypotheses:

Hypothesis 3. The presence of politician directors on a firm's board is positively associated with government subsidies given to the firm.

Hypothesis 4. The presence of politician directors on a firm's board is positively associated with excess employment in the firm.

Hypothesis 5. The presence of politician directors on a firm's board is negatively associated with postlisting accounting returns.

METHODS

Sample

We manually collected board data from the IPO prospectuses of listed A-share companies in the Shanghai Stock Exchange and the Shenzhen Stock Exchange from 1993 to 2000.[4] From the "Introduction of the Board of Directors, Supervisors and Senior Managers" sections of the prospectuses, we obtained brief biographies of all directors. We searched other sections of the prospectuses to ascertain the backgrounds of the directors. For instance, we examined sections such as "History of Listed Company," "Background of Founding Investors," and "Background of Large Shareholders" to analyze whether the companies that the directors had worked for or were currently working for were affiliated with the listed companies. For some companies that went public prior to 1997, the information disclosed in the prospectuses was insufficient, owing to low disclosure standards and weak enforcement, a typical problem in emerging markets such as China. From the Shenzhen Genius Information Technology Company database we were able to obtain the IPO-year financial and ownership data for most of the companies.

The final sample consisted of 621 companies. Table 9.2 describes the sample. It represents 62 percent of the total number of IPO firms in China during the study period. Panel A of the table shows an uneven distribution of the IPO firms in our sample over the period of study, ranging from 131 and 173 firms in 1996 and 1997 to 11 and 10 firms in 1995 and 2000. The sample distribution largely reflects the overall IPO pattern in China: The IPO market was hot in 1996 and 1997 and cold in 1995.[5] In the year 2000, the sample was small relative to the population because most of the data for that year were not yet available to us. The sample coverage improves over time, from about 48 percent of the population in 1993 to 86 percent in 1999. This pattern reflects improved public disclosure of company information over time. Panel B of the table breaks down the sample by industry sector. Of the sample firms, 34 firms were in the natural resources sector, 386 in the manufacturing sector, 96 in the services and trade sector, 47 in the public utilities sector, 15 in the finance and real estate sector, and 43 were in multiple sectors and thus were classified as conglomerate. The sample displays similar degrees of coverage of the various sectors. It represents about 60 percent of the total IPO firms in each sector except for finance and real estate (40 percent).

Measures

We used the number of politician directors expressed as a percentage of all directors as a proxy for the degree of politician presence on a board, defining a politician as an individual who used to work or

Table 9.2

Distribution of IPO Firms by Year and Industry

	IPO firms in the sample	Total IPO firms in China	Sample as percentage of IPO firms in China
Panel A: Year			
1993	59	123	47.97
1994	65	110	59.09
1995	11	24	45.83
1996	131	203	64.53
1997	173	206	83.98
1998	89	105	84.76
1999	83	97	85.57
2000	10	136	7.35
Panel B: Industry sector			
Natural resources	34	56	60.71
Manufacturing	386	609	63.38
Services and trade	96	149	64.43
Public utilities	47	82	57.32
Finance and real estate	15	37	40.54
Conglomerate	43	71	60.56
Total	621	1,004	61.85

currently worked for the government, including the central government, local governments, and other governments. To test the effects of different types of *politicians*, we separated them into three categories: politicians from central government, local politicians, and politicians from other governments.

Board professionalism was measured by three variables. First, we deemed *directors from unaffiliated firms* (their former or current employees) to be business experts. The largest shareholder of a sample firm, the parent firm of the largest shareholder, other large shareholders, the firm existing prior to the IPO, and subsidiaries of the sample firm were considered affiliated firms. Second, consultants, lawyers, accountants, and finance professionals were considered *professionals*. Finally, we also considered *academics*, defined as individuals who formerly or currently worked for universities or research institutions, as directors with professional backgrounds.

Board geographical concentration was measured as the number of *directors from unaffiliated firms* who were *from a single region* over the total number of directors from all unaffiliated firms. The definitions of variables used for measuring subsidies, excess employment, and accounting performance will be discussed as we present the results.

RESULTS

In this section, we report a series of regression analyses examining the effects of politicians on board professionalism and other board characteristics, the level of government subsidies, firm excess employment, and firm performance.

Professionalism and Other Board Characteristics

Table 9.3 describes the variables collected in our study while Table 9.4 details characteristics of the sampled boards. The summary statistics in Panel A of Table 9.4 show that the board variables

Table 9.3

Definition of Variables

Board characteristics

Board size	Total number of directors on the board during the IPO.
Manager directors	Number of manager directors as a percentage of board size. Manager directors are directors who serve as senior managers of the firm during the IPO.
Largest shareholder	Number of largest shareholder directors as a percentage of board size. Largest shareholder directors are directors who used to work or are currently working for the largest shareholder of the listed firm.
Politicians	Number of politician directors as a percentage of board size. Politician directors are directors who used to work or are currently working for the government, including central government, local governments, and other governments.
Politicians from central government	Number of politician directors from central government as a percentage of board size. Politician directors from the central government are directors who used to work or are currently working for the central government.
Local politicians	Number of politician directors from local government as a percentage of board size. Politician directors from local governments are directors who used to work or are working for government agencies of the local administrative region where the listed firm is located, including government agencies at the provincial level and below. The level of autonomous regions and municipalities directly under the central government are considered equivalent to the provincial level.
Politicians from other governments	The number of politician directors from other governments as a percentage of board size. Politician directors from other governments are directors who used to work or are currently working for government agencies other than central and local governments defined above, e.g., army corps and other local governments outside of the administrative region where the listed firm is located.
Directors from unaffiliated firms	Number of directors with business experience from unaffiliated firms as a percentage of board size. These are directors who used to work or are currently working for any unaffiliated firms. The largest shareholder, parent firm of the largest shareholder, other large shareholders, preexisting firm prior to the IPO, and subsidiaries of the listed firm are considered as affiliated firms.
Unaffiliated directors from single administrative region	Number of unaffiliated directors from same administrative region as a percentage of total unaffiliated directors.
Professionals	Number of directors who are consultants or finance professionals as a percentage of board size. Directors who are consultants or finance professionals are those who used to work or are currently working for financial institutions or intermediaries, or who are accountants, lawyers, or auditors.

(continued)

Table 9.3 *(continued)*

Board characteristics	
Academics	Number of academic directors as a percentage of board size. Academic directors are those who used to work or are currently working for universities or research institutions.
Woman directors	Number of female directors as percentage of board size.
Age	Average age of directors on the board during the IPO.
Education	Average education level of the directors on the board during the IPO. If below junior college, the value is 0; if junior college, the value is 1; if graduated with bachelor's degree, the value is 2; if graduated with master's degree, the value is 3; and if graduated with doctorate, the value is 4.
Ownership and Financial information	
Log sales	Logarithm of sales in the IPO year.
Debt-to-sales	IPO-year-end debt divided by sales in the IPO year.
Information on industries	
Natural resources	SIC codes = 0100, 0200, 0700, 0800, 0900, 1000, 1200, 1300, 1400, 2900, or 4600.
Service and trade	SIC codes = 4700, 5000, 5100, 5300, 5400, 5800, 7000, 7200, 7300, or 7900.
Public utilities	SIC codes = 4000, 4100, 4200, 4300, 4400, 4500, 4800, or 4900.
Finance and real estate	SIC codes = 6000, 6100, 6200, 6300, 6400, 6500, or 6700.
Conglomerate	SIC code = 9900.

Note: Table 9.3 describes the variables collected for the 621 listed Chinese firms included in our study. The first column presents the variable names. The second column describes the variables. All the board data were collected manually from the IPO prospectuses of listed companies. The financial data are obtained from the Shenzhen Genius Information Technology Company database.

distribute evenly around their means while also exhibiting substantial variations across firms. The mean statistics reveal the following characteristics of a typical board in China. Such a board has about nine directors, 34 percent of whom are also managers of the company. Almost 49 percent of the directors are former or current employees of the company's largest shareholder, typically an affiliated firm in the immediate upper layer of the control pyramid in a business group. The prevalence of directors affiliated with the largest shareholder is not surprising, given that the major shareholder typically possesses a large equity stake in the sampled companies. The largest shareholder typically held nearly half of a sample company's outstanding equity.

About 32 percent of the directors in the sample were current or former government bureaucrats, referred to as politicians in this chapter. These politicians are affiliated with different levels of government but mainly with local governments: about 4 percent with the central government,

Table 9.4

Data on the Boards of Firms in the Sample[a]

Panel A: Summary statistics	Mean	s.e.	Lower quartile	Median	Upper quartile	Minimum	Maximum
Board size	9.22	2.60	7.00	9.00	11.00	5.00	19.00
Manager directors	33.68	17.40	20.00	33.33	45.45	0.00	100.00
Largest shareholder	48.58	19.10	33.95	49.93	64.32	6.67	88.35
Politicians	31.92	24.81	11.11	30.00	50.00	0.00	100.00
Politicians from central government	4.48	8.71	0.00	0.00	9.09	0.00	55.56
Local politicians	18.80	22.41	0.00	11.11	30.00	0.00	100.00
Politicians from other governments	9.27	15.44	0.00	0.00	14.29	0.00	85.71
Directors from unaffiliated firms	18.23	14.97	0.00	18.18	28.57	0.00	80.00
Professionals	5.23	10.57	0.00	0.00	9.09	0.00	51.74
Academics	13.94	19.88	0.00	9.09	18.18	0.00	100.00
Woman directors	5.00	7.62	0.00	0.00	10.00	0.00	44.44
Age	46.98	2.51	45.09	46.90	48.70	39.56	53.83
Education	1.67	0.43	1.38	1.67	2.00	0.67	2.86
Log sales	10.48	1.15	9.73	10.45	11.16	6.87	13.95
Debt-to-sales	1.05	3.00	0.40	0.66	1.06	0.00	67.28

[a]Table 9.3 describes the variables in detail

(continued)

Table 9.4 *(continued)*

Panel B: Pearson correlations

	Board size	Manager directors	Largest shareholder	Politicians	Politicians from central government	Local politicians
Board size	1.00 (0.00)	0.12 (0.33)	−0.04 (0.22)	−0.05 (0.77)	0.01 (0.38)	−0.04
Manager directors		1.00 (0.33)	0.04 (0.00)	−0.11 (0.08)	−0.07 (0.01)	−0.11
Largest shareholder			1.00 (0.68)	0.02 (0.79)	0.01 (0.64)	−0.02
Politicians				1.00 (<.01)	0.42 (<.01)	0.76
Politicians from central government					1.00 (<.01)	0.16 (<.01)
Local politicians						1.00
Politicians from other governments						
Directors from unaffiliated firms						
Professionals						
Academics						
Age						
Education						
Woman directors						
Log sales						
Debt-to-sales						

19 percent with local governments, and 9 percent with other governments, including the army and local governments outside the geographical area where a focal company was located.

The prevalence of politicians on the boards cannot be overlooked. One might think that they are also the same directors representing the largest shareholders of the company. This is not the case. As reported in Panel B of Table 9.4, the Pearson correlation coefficient between the fraction of directors affiliated with the largest shareholder and the fraction of directors affiliated with governments is only 1.6 percent. If the presence of politicians were a mirror image of the presence of directors representing the largest shareholder, the correlation coefficient would be highly positive. Breaking down politicians by type, the fraction of directors representing the largest shareholder is negatively correlated with the fraction of directors affiliated with the central and other governments (negative 28 percent and negative 26 percent, respectively). Although the presence of directors representing the largest shareholder is positively correlated with the fraction of directors affiliated with local governments, the correlation coefficient is significant only at the 10 percent level.

Table 9.4 (continued)

Politicians from other government	Directors from unaffiliated firms	Profes- sionals	Aca- demics	Age	Edu cation	Woman directors	Log sales	Debt-to- sales
−0.01	0.01	0.04	−0.03	−0.03	0.01	0.04	0.10	−0.01
(0.76)	(0.90)	(0.29)	(0.43)	(0.46)	(0.79)	(0.33)	(0.01)	(0.78)
0.02	−0.19	−0.13	−0.19	0.05	−0.12	−0.17	0.06	−0.02
(0.69)	(<.01)	(0.00)	(<.01)	(0.22)	(0.00)	(<.01)	(0.15)	(0.66)
0.04	−0.05	−0.07	0.04	0.02	0.06	0.00	0.31	0.01
(0.31)	(0.17)	(0.09)	(0.31)	(0.59)	(0.12)	(0.92)	(<.01)	(0.80)
0.32	−0.03	−0.25	−0.26	0.29	0.01	−0.21	−0.01	−0.01
(<.01)	(0.48)	(<.01)	(<.01)	(<.01)	(0.74)	(<.01)	(0.89)	(0.86)
−0.04	0.01	−0.12	0.10	0.07	0.18	−0.02	−0.01	0.07
(0.31)	(0.84)	(0.00)	(0.01)	(0.07)	(<.01)	(0.57)	(0.76)	(0.08)
−0.30	−0.09	−0.16	−0.31	0.16	−0.19	−0.08	−0.03	−0.02
(<.01)	(0.02)	(0.01)	(<.01)	(<.01)	(<.01)	(0.04)	(0.47)	(0.66)
1.00	0.08	−0.11	−0.03	0.21	0.21	−0.21	0.04	−0.03
	(0.06)	(0.01)	(0.48)	(<.01)	(<.01)	(<.01)	(0.34)	(0.53)
	1.00	0.27	−0.07	−0.06	0.10	0.09	−0.08	−0.07
		(<.01)	(0.09)	(0.17)	(0.01)	(0.03)	(0.06)	(0.07)
		1.00	−0.16	−0.28	−0.06	0.23	−0.10	0.02
			(<.01)	(<.01)	(0.16)	(<.01)	(0.01)	(0.64)
			1.00	0.19	0.61	−0.01	0.01	0.15
				(<.01)	(<.01)	(0.86)	(0.75)	(0.00)
				1.00	0.35	−0.29	0.03	0.09
					(<.01)	(<.01)	(0.45)	(0.03)
					1.00	−0.08	0.07	0.09
						(0.05)	(0.08)	(0.03)
						1.00	−0.04	−0.01
							(0.37)	(0.72)
							1.00	−0.15
							(0.00)	
							1.00	

Note: p-values are in parentheses.

It is interesting to note that the fraction of directors representing the largest shareholder is unrelated to the largest shareholder's shareholding. One would expect the owner to maintain directorship proportional to the owner's shareholding to safeguard its interest, but this is not the case in China. The absence of linkage between ownership and directorship reveals the unique feature of ownership and control of listed companies in China. The largest shareholder may exercise its administrative power, rather than ownership rights, to influence corporate policies. The use of administrative power in place of ownership rights is likely to be a result of the ambiguous property rights system in China.

It is not reported in the table that almost no directors represent minority shareholders, might they be institutional or individual investors. The lack of directors representing minority shareholders' interest is in stark contrast with the large percentages of directors affiliated with the largest shareholder and governments.

Next, we examined the general level of professionalism of a board as reflected in the directors' employment backgrounds, as shown in Panel A. Almost 18 percent of the directors were currently or had previously been employed in other unaffiliated companies in the same business sector or the same administrative region. The number is rather small relative to parallel numbers from more developed economies such as the United States, where outside directors typically dominate corporate boards (Hermalin and Weisbach 1988, Yermack 1996). The outside directors, often thought of as monitors of management (Fama and Jensen 1983), are usually decision makers in other organizations with expertise in capital markets, corporate law, or relevant technologies who support inside manager directors in dealing with specialized decision problems (Klein 1998). In China, the small fraction of directors with outside relevant business experience reflects the underdevelopment of the market for managerial professionals. Consistently, it also reflects the fact that the typical company tends to recruit managerial talent internally, either from within the company or from within the same business group. The sampled boards also lack legal, accounting, and finance professionals: only about 5 percent of the directors were accountants, lawyers, or current/past employees of financial institutions or securities intermediaries. By contrast, a surprisingly large fraction of directors had academic backgrounds. The mean value is 14 percent, and the median value is 9 percent. The large fraction of academicians on these boards suggests that they serve as substitutes for professional practitioners, who are scarce in Chinese businesses.

Turning to other board characteristics, we see that the average educational attainment was between a junior college and a college degree. The average age of the directors was 47. This generation of directors' education level is modest because various political movements such as the Cultural Revolution disrupted their formal education. Lastly, female directors accounted for 5 percent of the board members. Compared to the Fortune 1000 companies in the United States, in which less than 2 percent of the directors were women in 1990–91 (Farrell and Hersch 2001), China has a higher proportion of female directors, possibly because almost all women joined the workforce under the socialist regime.

In summary, the basic statistics reveal that directors representing the largest shareholders and directors who are politicians, especially politicians affiliated with local governments, dominate Chinese corporate boards. This pattern of domination reflects the fact that through decentralization, the largest shareholders and the local governments have been given control rights over the listed enterprises. The strong presence of local politicians on the boards in our sample indicates that local governments have exerted strong influence over corporate policies. By contrast, legal, accounting, and finance professionals and business experience from unaffiliated enterprises are generally lacking on these boards, suggesting a lack of professionalism. There are almost no directors representing minority shareholders, indicating that their interests may not be well protected.

Politicians and Board Professionalism

We conducted a number of regression analyses with our measures of board professionalism and other characteristics (board size; proportions of directors who were managers, or had unaffiliated business experience, or had legal, accounting, or finance backgrounds, or had academic backgrounds, or who were female; and average education level and age). The independent variables in each of the regressions were the fraction of directors affiliated with the largest shareholder, the fraction of directors affiliated with governments, the natural logarithm of firm sales in the IPO year, and total debt over sales measured in the IPO year. We used the log sales variable to control for the effects of firm size, a proxy for the complexity and the internal resource base of an organization. The debt over sales variable controlled for the effects of growth potential: lower-growth firms tend to have higher debt ratios (Smith and Watts 1992). We used sales instead of assets as the size measure and the scaling factor, because book values are often distorted owing to underdeveloped markets for assets in China. The regressions included industry sector dummy variables using the manufacturing sector as the base. Year dummy variables were also included but not reported. We estimated the regression models using the ordinary least squares method and the full sample of 621 firms. Note that the largest shareholder and politician directorship variables were at the right-hand side of the regression models, implying that they were assumed to be exogenous. This would not be too different from reality. In this early stage of capital market development in China, ownership structure and the degree of politician involvement of firms have been heavily influenced top-down by government policies; market forces, although increasingly important, have had secondary effects.

The regression results are reported in Table 9.5. In column 1, board size is negatively related to the degree of largest shareholder presence. The estimated coefficient is significant at the 1 percent level. Also, the presence of politicians is negatively associated with board size but is only statistically significant in the case of politicians affiliated with other governments (column 1), which were mainly local governments outside of the administrative region where the listed firms were located. Board size is positively related to firm size measured by log sales. This finding is consistent with the fact that board size and firm size both reflect the resource bases of the firms: larger firms are more complex and require more human capital on boards to help with monitoring and decision making. Firms in the natural resource sector also have larger board size.

In column 2, managerial directorship, as measured by the number of directors who serve as senior managers, is positively related to the degree of largest shareholder presence. However, the fraction of manager directors is strongly negatively related to the strength of local politician presence but unrelated to the presence of central and other governments. The evidence suggests that local politicians do not serve a managerial function or even substitute for the managerial function of the board.

As mentioned earlier, we used the numbers of directors from unaffiliated firms, directors with professional qualifications, and academic directors as proxies for professionalism. The fraction of directors with business experience from unaffiliated enterprises is negatively related to the largest shareholder presence but unrelated to politician presence, except for local politician presence (column 3). The evidence suggests that local politicians do not contribute relevant business experience to boards. They may also jeopardize the appointment of personnel with such experience to the boards, for fear of weakening their control of the boards, as these personnel are from districts outside of their jurisdictions. The evidence may also suggest that relevant business experience is not essential to firms heavily influenced by local politicians. This finding is consistent with our prediction that politician presence can hurt the professionalism of boards. On the other hand, the presence of politicians from the central and other governments does not crowd out relevant business experience.

From column 4, we find that the fraction of directors from the legal, accounting, and finance professions is negatively related to the degree of all types of politician presence, but unrelated to the degree of largest shareholder presence on a board. This evidence is consistent with our negative view of decentralization, which is that government influence still shapes the Chinese corporate board. Several complementary observations support this conjecture. First, politicians usually do not possess professional skills. Second, the large presence of politicians on boards suggests that political skills are important to the profitability of firms, which also implies that professionals add relatively less value to firms. Third, the large presence of politicians may also imply that the

Table 9.5

Regression Analysis Evidence on the Effects of Politician Presence on Board Structure[a]

Independent variables	Board size (1)	Manager directors (2)	Directors from unaffiliated firms (3)	Professionals (4)	Academics (5)	Education (6)	Age (7)	Woman directors (8)	Unaffiliated directors from single region (9)
Constant	7.37*** (6.88)	0.30*** (4.29)	0.36*** (5.94)	0.19*** (4.54)	0.02 (0.20)	1.09*** (6.70)	43.46*** (47.01)	0.13*** (4.14)	0.84*** (5.55)
Largest shareholder	-2.01*** (-4.64)	0.12*** (4.10)	-0.08*** (-3.35)	-0.01 (-0.40)	0.11*** (3.42)	0.45*** (6.82)	3.61*** (9.67)	-0.05*** (-3.76)	0.03 (0.41)
Politicians from central government	-1.45 (-1.14)	-0.02 (-0.18)	-0.02 (-0.30)	-0.12** (-2.39)	0.45*** (4.95)	1.45*** (7.55)	4.37*** (3.99)	-0.05 (-1.30)	-1.25*** (-7.58)
Local politicians	-0.36 (-0.72)	-0.10*** (-2.98)	-0.05* (-1.75)	-0.09*** (-4.48)	-0.34*** (-9.52)	-0.34*** (-4.57)	2.36*** (5.53)	-0.05*** (-3.46)	0.26*** (3.34)
Politicians from other governments	-1.32* (-1.80)	0.00 (0.03)	0.02 (0.68)	-0.11*** (-3.82)	-0.11** (-2.07)	0.69*** (6.21)	6.03*** (9.54)	-0.15*** (-7.02)	-0.53*** (-5.38)
Log sales	0.25*** (2.67)	0.00 (-0.12)	-0.01* (-1.66)	-0.01* (-1.89)	0.01 (0.95)	0.02 (1.59)	-0.02 (-0.22)	0.00 (-0.29)	-0.01 (-0.38)

	1	2	3	4	5	6	7	8	9
Debt-to-sales	0.01 (0.39)	0.00 (-0.25)	0.00* (-1.94)	0.00 (-0.26)	0.01*** (3.27)	0.01* (1.94)	0.07** (2.29)	0.00 (-0.63)	-0.01 (-0.43)
Natural resources	1.01** (2.19)	-0.02 (-0.50)	-0.05* (-1.88)	0.02 (0.89)	0.02 (0.60)	-0.05 (-0.73)	-0.86** (-2.16)	0.00 (0.20)	-0.10 (-1.59)
Service and trade	0.48 (1.62)	0.01 (0.69)	-0.01 (-0.59)	-0.01 (-0.65)	0.02 (0.89)	-0.01 (-0.14)	-0.08 (-0.31)	0.01 (0.60)	0.04 (0.90)
Public utilities	0.49 (1.18)	-0.02 (-0.87)	0.00 (-0.01)	0.00 (0.18)	0.02 (0.70)	-0.04 (-0.71)	-0.07 (-0.19)	0.00 (0.04)	0.05 (0.91)
Financial and real estate	-0.03 (-0.04)	-0.04 (-0.84)	-0.02 (-0.53)	0.02 (0.80)	0.00 (0.08)	-0.03 (-0.26)	-0.54 (-0.90)	-0.01 (-0.54)	0.22** (2.24)
Conglomerate	-0.28 (-0.66)	-0.10*** (-3.74)	0.05** (2.06)	0.04** (2.20)	0.03 (0.99)	0.01 (0.16)	-0.54 (-1.47)	0.03** (2.41)	0.04 (0.73)
Adjusted R^2	0.04	0.06	0.05	0.07	0.16	0.18	0.23	0.09	0.21

[a]Table 9.3 defines the dependent (columns 1–9) and independent (far–left) variables in detail. Values in parentheses are t–statistics.
$*p < 0.10$; $**p < 0.05$; $***p < 0.01$; two–tailed tests.

incentive to achieve political or social goals frequently surpasses the profit-seeking incentive, which leads to a lack of professionalism. Fourth, and by contrast, a strong largest shareholder presence on boards does not jeopardize professionalism.

Another measure of board professionalism is the fraction of academic directors. The results (column 5) show that academics' presence is strongly, positively related to the presence of politicians affiliated with the central government while strongly, negatively related to local and other politician presence. It can be argued that academician directors are more neutral and more likely than other directors to monitor managers and voice unbiased opinions on corporate policies. Academic directors are relatively neutral because they have no commercial conflicts of interest with the companies. Interpreting their role in this manner, the evidence here suggests that even academic knowledge is undesirable to boards populated with local politicians. The central government is an exception. Academic directors are more prevalent when the presence of politicians from the central government is large. Overall, the presented relations between academic directorship and directorship of the different levels of governments are consistent with the conflicts of interest between the central government and local governments.

Columns 6 through 8 present the regression results on the effects of the largest shareholder and politician presence on directors' education, sex, and age. We expected that the education level would be a proxy for the size of the knowledge base possessed by directors. We expected age to be less correlated with professionalism but more correlated with seniority. The lack of connection between age and professionalism is severe in China, because the various political movements from the 1950s to the 1970s disrupted the education and commercial activities of people now older than 40. The regression results show that average education level is highly, negatively related to local politicians' board presence. By contrast, the average education level is positively related to the presence of the other two types of politicians. Politician presence is generally associated with fewer women directors and higher average directors' age.

The debt-to-sales variable, measured as total year-end debt divided by total sales in the IPO year, is negatively related to the fractions of directors from unaffiliated enterprises and age, but positively related to the fraction of academic directors, and to directors' education levels. Conceivably, the demand for outside business expertise is lower for lower-growth firms. Lower-growth firms appoint more academic directors, perhaps because they offer a low-cost substitute for business professionals, as is evident in their negative correlation (Table 9.4, Panel B). By the same token, academics are attracted to the boards of low-growth firms because of their lower opportunity costs and perhaps because they are more risk averse than other professionals. The higher director education level of lower-growth firms reflects the tendency of the firms to hire academic directors.

Firm size is generally unrelated to board characteristics except that it is negatively related to the fraction of directors who are professionals and from unaffiliated firms, and positively related to board size. If firm size is a proxy for organizational complexity, this evidence suggests that complexity in a firm is unlikely to be a primary factor determining the appointment of professionals in China. However, the results for the industry sector dummy variables indicate that conglomerate firms are associated with lower managerial directorship, a higher fraction of directors possessing business experience from unaffiliated firms, a higher fraction of directors with legal or finance backgrounds, and more women directors. Operating in multiple sectors, conglomerate firms need expertise from various industry sectors. Conglomerate firms also need legal, accounting, and finance professionals to help the functioning of their internal markets for factors, products, and capital. Indeed, the evidence shows that the boards of conglomerate firms are composed of more outside business experts and legal, accounting, and finance professionals. This evidence is consistent with prior U.S. research indicating that the demand for professionals is larger in more complex organizations (Klein 1998).

Politicians and Board Geographical Concentration

The alternative argument for the effects of China's decentralization is that decentralization may give incentives to local governments and enterprises to create entry barriers that collectively result in fragmented markets. If this is true, we should observe geographically concentrated boards: directors' experience clustering within the same local administrative region. We examined a subset of directors who used to work or were working in unaffiliated firms ("unaffiliated directors," hereafter) and focused on the geographical profile of the directors: whether their former or current employers were located in the same administrative region as the companies where they served as directors.

The regression results are presented in Table 9.5, column 9. The dependent variable is the number of unaffiliated directors coming from the same administrative region as a percentage of the total number of unaffiliated directors on a board. We found that the negative effect of politicians is attributable to the politicians from the central and the other governments. By contrast, the estimated coefficient of the local politician directors is positive and statistically significant. The results are consistent with the hypothesis that local politicians contribute to geographically concentrated boards. On the other hand, the participation of the other types of politicians is associated with geographically diverse boards.

Politicians and Government Subsidies

In keeping with the prediction that politician presence can benefit a firm, the results in Table 9.6 show that the presence of political directors is associated with a higher level of government subsidies (as reported as a separate item in the income statements) in the year after an IPO (column 3), but not during the year of the IPO (column 1), and with a greater change in subsidies from the IPO year to the year after the IPO (column 5). When separating the political connections of directors into connections to central and local governments, we found that the political connection effects mainly came from local governments for the level (column 4) and the change results (column 6). This finding supports our argument that firms with more political directors on their boards will have a higher possibility of receiving subsidies from local governments. It further suggests that SOEs receive some benefits in exchange for bearing policy burdens. Our finding is also consistent with prior research, such as Faccio (2003) and Agrawal and Knoeber (2001), showing that firms with political connections facilitate their rent-seeking activities with the government.

Politicians and Excess Employment

In Table 9.7, column 1, we find that presence of politician directors on a board significantly increases the level of excess employment, measured by total employment over sales in the IPO year. The finding is consistent with the negative view that firms with more politician directors on their boards share more of the government policy burdens. Maintaining a high local employment rate is a key target for local governments. Our findings support the conjecture that firms with more political directors on their boards have more incentives to help governments to meet employment targets. Among the different types of politicians, local politicians have a dominant influence on firms' decisions to hire more workers (column 3). This is consistent with a negative

Table 9.6

Regression Analysis Evidence on the Effects of Politician Presence on Government Subsidies

Independent variables	Government subsidies over net income at IPO year		Government subsidies over net income one year after IPO		Change of the government subsidies over net income from IPO year to one year after IPO	
	(1)	(2)	(3)	(4)	(5)	(6)
Constant	0.04	0.04	0.01	0.01	−0.03	−0.03
	(0.59)	(0.59)	(0.08)	(0.06)	(−0.20)	(−0.22)
Politicians		0.00		0.10***		0.10***
		(−0.28)		(3.48)		(3.53)
Politicians from central government		−0.01		−0.03		−0.02
		(−0.30)		(−0.36)		(−0.21)
Local politicians		0.00		0.14***		0.14***
		(−0.01)		(4.06)		(3.96)
Politicians from other governments		−0.01		0.06		0.08
		(−0.57)		(1.37)		(1.61)
Log sales	0.00	0.00	0.00	0.00	0.00	0.00
	(0.50)	(0.52)	(0.05)	(0.09)	(−0.20)	(−0.16)
Debt–to–sales	0.00**	0.00**	0.00	0.00	0.00	0.00
	(2.32)	(2.34)	(0.35)	(0.51)	(−0.77)	(−0.63)
Adjusted R^2	0.09	0.09	0.05	0.05	0.04	0.05

[a]Table 9.3 defines the dependent (columns 1–6) and independent (far-left) variables in detail. Values in parentheses are t-statistics. The effects of industry and year were controlled but are not reported here.

*$p < 0.10$; **$p < 0.05$; ***$p < 0.01$; two-tailed tests.

view of decentralization indicating that the agency problem between central and local government reduces the efficiency of state firms.

Politicians and Firm Performance

The results seem to suggest that politician presence may sometimes benefit a firm through government subsidies and sometimes harm the firm through excess employment. Next, we used firm performance to evaluate the total net effects of politician presence on firms. As is reported in Table 9.8, we used three different dependent variables in three sets of regressions: return on assets (ROA) in columns 1 and 2, earnings before interest and taxes over total assets in columns 3 and 4, and gains from extraordinary items over total income in columns 5 and 6. The second dependent variable is an accounting returns measure that is less prone to earnings manipulation, while the third dependent variable is a proxy for the earnings component used for manipulation (Chen and Yuan 2004).

Table 9.7

Regression Analysis Evidence on the Effects of Politician Presence on Employment[a]

Independent variables	Employees per million in sales		
	(1)	(2)	(3)
Constant	3.02**	2.97**	2.72*
	(2.06)	(2.02)	(1.85)
Politicians	3.42*	3.01	
	(1.95)	(1.39)	
Politicians × the core income dummy			0.81
			(0.32)
Politicians from central government			−5.16
			(−0.68)
Local politicians			5.04*
			(1.89)
Politicians from other governments			2.91
			(0.68)
Politicians from central government × the core income dummy			11.27
			(1.14)
Local politicians × the core income dummy			−5.17
			(−1.51)
Politicians from other governments × the core income dummy			9.25*
			(1.75)
Debt-to-sales	0.16	0.16	0.15
	(1.23)	(1.20)	(1.14)
The profitability of core operation	5.11*	5.52*	5.84**
	(1.92)	(1.87)	(1.99)
Adjusted R^2	0.04	0.04	0.05

[a]Table 9.3 defines the dependent (columns 1–3) and independent (far-left) variables in detail. Values in parentheses are t-statistics. The core income dummy equals 1 if a firm's profitability from core operations was below the industry median, and otherwise zero. The effects of industry and year were controlled but not reported here.

*$p < 0.10$; **$p < 0.05$; ***$p < 0.01$; two-tailed tests.

In columns 1 and 3, we see that directors with political connections have a significantly negative effect on accounting performance. The result in column 3 confirms that the political connection is associated with lower accounting earnings that are not subject to manipulation. When we split the political connection measure into central and local governments, the results in columns 2 and 4 suggest that both central and local politicians have a negative effect on firm performance. In columns 5 and 6, our results show that the politician variables are not significantly associated with the earnings management proxy. The firm performance results indicate that politician presence on Chinese boards brings more harm than benefit to the firms.

Table 9.8

Evidence on the Effects of Politician Presence on Firm Performance[a]

Independent variable	Return on assets		Earnings before interest and tax over total assets		Gains from extraordinary items over total income	
	(1)	(2)	(3)	(4)	(5)	(6)
Constant	0.06*	0.06*	0.03	0.03	1.22***	1.11***
	(1.74)	(1.74)	(0.75)	(0.76)	(6.78)	(6.06)
Politicians	−0.02**		−0.02**		0.05	
	(−2.30)		(−2.50)		(1.38)	
Politicians from central governments		−0.04*		−0.03*		0.16
		(−1.94)		(−1.67)		(1.38)
Local politicians		−0.01		−0.02*		0.00
		(−1.38)		(−1.87)		(0.03)
Politicians from other governments		−0.02		−0.01		0.04
		(−1.30)		(−0.93)		(0.71)
Log sales	0.00	0.00	0.00*	0.00*	−0.05***	−0.05***
	(0.47)	(0.48)	(1.74)	(1.74)	(−6.17)	(−5.41)
Debt-to-sales	0.00***	0.00***	0.00***	0.00***	0.01***	0.01***
	(−3.32)	(−3.23)	(−3.26)	(−3.19)	(4.48)	(4.09)
Adjusted $R2$	0.06	0.06	0.08	0.08	0.13	0.12

[a]Table 9.3 defines the dependent (columns 1–6) and independent (far-left) variables in detail. Values in parentheses are t-statistics. The effects of industry and year were controlled but are not reported here.
*$p < 0.10$; ** $p < 0.05$; *** $p < 0.01$; two-tailed tests.

CONCLUSION AND FUTURE RESEARCH

We examined the board structure of a large sample of IPO firms in China. We report a strong politician presence on these Chinese boards. In contrast with directors from the firms' largest shareholders, the politician directors have more of a political than a managerial role. We argue that local politicians use their administrative power to influence both the markets and the firms under their jurisdictions. The firms in the resulting relationship-based markets benefit from the politicians' service in creating economic rents and enforcing transactions. In such markets, professionalism is in low demand. The demand for professionalism is even lower because professionals may leak sensitive information that could jeopardize the firms' rent-seeking activities. Consistent with this hypothesis, we found a negative relation between politician presence and professionalism, as revealed in various board characteristics. Consistent with politicians' roles in localizing their markets, we found that boards populated with local politicians were also more geographically concentrated. Consistent with the negative view of politician presence on boards, such firms end up hiring more employees and reporting lower accounting earnings, despite their ability to solicit more government subsidies. Overall, our evidence supports the view that, despite

China's efforts to decentralize, local governments' perverse incentives continue to plague state-owned firms.

Although the prevalence of politicians and the associated weak presence of professionals are a result of China's political economy, they are likely to become increasingly costly to listed companies in the future. China's markets are expected to become more open, since its recent entry into the World Trade Organization. The more competitive marketplace will weaken the role of politicians in the market as well as the boardrooms. On the other hand, firms' demand for experienced professionals will increase. Moreover, as the capital markets become more developed, companies will not be competitive in raising capital without improving corporate governance. That means they will restructure their boards by appointing representatives of minority shareholders and reducing the influence of politicians. The fundamental reason for politicians being important to listed companies in China is the ill-defined property rights and the separation of ownership and control of business enterprises. To market reformers, this study suggests that, if the property rights system cannot be overhauled, it is important to create effective incentive and monitoring mechanisms to induce local governments to deregulate their markets and decrease their involvement in business dealings.

There are a number of possible future extensions for the current research. First, researchers could examine the fundamental institutional factors that determine the presence of politicians on a board. Second, it is worthwhile to engage in more research on board and managerial professionalism. Is CEO or board member turnover related to firm performance? What fundamental factors, other than firm performance, affect the turnover? Finally, using politician presence as a measure of the degree of government intervention in a firm, researchers can investigate how it affects the corporate policies and transparency of the Chinese listed firm.

NOTES

The authors acknowledge the financial support of the High Impact Area Research Grant of HKUST and of NSF grant (No.70172008) of the Chinese government. Joseph Fan thanks the University of Queensland for research support during his visit. Donghua Chen acknowledges the financial support of the Research Grant of Shanghai Key Subjects and the Research Grant for Shanghai Excellent Young Scholar Candidates.

1. The shares of Chinese listed companies are divided into two categories: tradable shares and nontradable shares. If we used the percentage of the market capitalization of tradable shares over GDP for ranking, China would rank much lower.

2. Research by the European Bank for Reconstruction and Development (EBRD) and the World Bank using more than 3,000 firms with 100 or more employees in central Europe, eastern Europe, and central Asia indicates that the average state ownership of these firms is 51 percent for the Czech Republic, 53 percent for Hungary, 26 percent for Poland, 46 percent for Romania, 8 percent for Russia, and 21 percent for Ukraine (EBRD 1999). Compared with these ex-Communist states, the Chinese government retains more control over firms.

3. See Hermalin and Weisbach (2001) for a survey of this literature.

4. During the sample period, domestic investors traded A-shares, while foreign investors traded other classes of shares, such as B- and H-shares. Starting in 2001, domestic investors were allowed to trade B-shares.

5. The overheating economy and high inflation during the early 1990s resulted in central government policies to restrict the money supply, which caused the IPO market to collapse in 1995.

REFERENCES

Agrawal, A., and C. R. Knoeber. (2001). Do some outsider directors play a political role? *Journal of Law and Economics*, 64, 179–99.
Buchanan, J. (1995). Federalism as an ideal political order and an objective for constitutional reform. *Publius*, 25, 19–27.

170 DONG-HUA CHEN, JOSEPH P.H. FAN, AND T.J. WONG

Cao, Y.; Y. Qian; and B. R. Weingast. (1997). From federalism, Chinese style, to privatization, Chinese style. Manuscript, State Commission for Restructuring the Economic Systems, and Stanford University. Available at http://papers.ssrn.com/sol3/papers.cfm?abstract_id=57564.

Chen, X.; J. Lee; and J. Li. (2003). Chinese tango: Government assisted earnings management. Working Paper, Tsinghua University, Beijing. Available at http://papers.ssrn.com/sol3/papers.cfm?abstract_id=408800.

Chen, K. C. W., and H. Yuan. (2004). Earnings management and capital resource allocation: Evidence from China's accounting-based regulation of rights issues. *The Accounting Review*, 79, 3, 645–65.

European Bank for Reconstruction and Development (EBRD). (1999). *Transition report 1999; Ten years of transition.* London: EBRD.

Faccio, M. (2004). Politically connected firms. Working Paper, Vanderbilt University, Nashville, TN. Available at http://papers.ssrn.com/sol3/papers.cfm?abstract_id=444960.

Fama, E. F., and M. C. Jensen. (1983). Separation of ownership and control. *Journal of Law and Economics*, 26, 301–25.

Fan, J.P.H.; T. J. Wong; and T. Zhang (forthcoming). Politically connected CEOs, corporate governance and post-IPO performance of China's partially privatized firms. *Journal of Financial Economics.*

Farrell, K. A., and P. L. Hersch. (2001). Additions to corporate boards: Does gender matter? Manuscript, University of Nebraska-Lincoln. Available at http://papers.ssrn.com/sol3/papers.cfm?abstract_id=292281

Groves, T.; Y. Hong; J. McMillan; and B. Naughton. (1994). Autonomy and incentives in Chinese state enterprises. *Quarterly Journal of Economics*, 109, 183–209.

Helland, E., and M. Sykuta. (2000). Deregulation and board composition: Evidence on the value of the revolving door. Manuscript, Claremont-McKenna College and University of Missouri. Available at http://papers.ssrn.com/sol3/papers.cfm?abstract_id=291171.

Hermalin, B. E., and M. S. Weisbach. (1988). The determinants of board composition. *Rand Journal of Economics*, 19, 589–606.

———. (2001). Boards of directors as an endogenously determined institution: A survey of the economic literature. National Bureau of Economic Research Working Paper No. 8161, March.

Jefferson, G. H. (1998). China's state enterprises: Public goods, externalities, and coase. *American Economic Review*, 88, 428–32.

Klein, A. (1998). Affiliated directors: Puppets of management or effective directors? Manuscript, New York University. Available at http://papers.ssrn.com/sol3/papers.cfm?abstract_id=10569.

Li, W. (1997). The impact of economic reform on the performance of Chinese state enterprises, 1980–1989. *Journal of Political Economy*, 105, 1080–1106.

Lin, J. Y.; F. Cai; and Z. Li. (1998). Competition, policy burdens, and state-owned enterprise reform. *American Economic Review*, 88 (May), 422–27.

Qian, Y. (1994). A theory of shortage in socialist economies based on the 'soft budget constraint.' *American Economic Review*, 84, 145–56.

———. (1995). Reforming corporate governance and finance in China. In M. Aoki and H. K. Kim (Eds.), *Corporate governance in transitional economies:Insider control and the role of banks.* Washington, DC: World Bank, pp 215-52.

Qian, Y., and G. Roland. (1998). Federalism and the soft budget constraint. *American Economic Review*, 88, 5, 1143–62.

Qian, Y., and B. R. Weingast. (1997). Federalism as a commitment to preserving market incentives. *Journal of Economic Perspectives*, 11, 83–92.

Rawski, T. G. (1994). Chinese industrial reform: Accomplishments, prospects, and implications. *American Economic Review*, 84, 271–75.

Smith, C. W., and R. L. Watts. (1992). The investment opportunity set and corporate financing, dividend and compensation policies. *Journal of Financial Economics*, 32, 263–92.

Sun, Q., and W.H.S. Tong. (2003). China share issue privatization: The extent of its success. *Journal of Financial Economics*, 70, 183–222.

Weingast, B. (1995). The economic role of political institutions: Market-preserving federalism and economic growth. *Journal of Law, Economics and Organization*, 11, 1–31.

Yermack, D. (1996). Higher market valuation of companies with a small board of directors. *Journal of Financial Economics*, 40, 185–211.

10

FIRM BEHAVIOR IN A MIXED MARKET

THE CASE OF CHINA

CHANGQI WU AND DAVID DAOKUI LI

INTRODUCTION

One of the distinctive features of China's market environment is that firms under different owner-ships compete. These firms typically fall into three categories: private firms, state-owned enter-prises (SOEs), and subsidiaries of multinational enterprises.[1] The three types of firms possess different kinds of resources, pursue different objectives, face different operational constraints, follow different strategies, and subsequently have differences in economic performance. We call this kind of market structure *a mixed market* to reflect its unique characteristics.[2] As economic reform in China charges ahead, the behavior of firms in the marketplace and the interactions among them become important research topics in business strategy and public policy.

In the literature on China's enterprise reforms, most studies have focused on the comparative economic performance of non-state-owned and state-owned enterprises, measuring performance in terms of either productivity or profitability. The general consensus is that there are significant economic efficiency gaps between these two types of firms. The differences are reflected at both the level of change and the rate of change of total factor productivity and/or profitability. Lacking in the literature is a systematic study of how a firm's ownership influences its market behavior, and how that behavior in turn determines the firm's economic performance. Moreover, the ques-tion of how the composition of an industry by firms under different types of ownership influences the behavior of those firms remains unanswered.

This study aims to fill this gap and improve understanding of the nature and the consequences of competition among firms under different types of ownership in the same industry by studying firm behavior under different ownership types and market structures. Specifically, we address the fol-lowing questions: Do the state-owned firms behave differently in their marketing, financing, and operational activities than the private firms? If so, then how do they behave differently? How do market structure and industry composition influence a firm's behavior in such an environment?[3]

The issues we study here go beyond China's enterprise reforms. First of all, one cannot fail to notice that, in many transition economies, state-owned firms still play a significant role in a number of imperfectly competitive industries. In those economies, such a mixed market structure comes into existence from three transitional paths: The first is the entry of multinational enter-prises into industries traditionally controlled by SOEs, the second is the privatization of SOEs, and the third is the birth of many private firms. Moreover, even in some industrialized countries, both private firms and public enterprises exist in a number of industries; for example, the banking industry in Germany, the airline industry in Canada, and the mail services industry in the United States. Therefore, our study is relevant to any markets in which private firms compete against state-owned firms.

To address these issues, we adopt the conceptual framework of the industrial organization—in particular, its structure-conduct-performance paradigm. In this paradigm, market structure (e.g., the number of firms in an industry) determines the way firms act in the marketplace; the conduct of those firms in terms of pricing, competitive and innovative activities, and so on will influence the economic performance of both firms and industry, in terms of both economic efficiency and profitability.[4] Perfectly competitive markets are rare in the real world since the conditions of homogeneous goods are not satisfied in most markets. This market imperfection gives governments some justification to intervene through the SOEs. Therefore, we adopt here an imperfectly competitive market framework as the basis of our analysis.

To model the special characteristics of such a market structure, we deviate from the standard assumption of profit-maximizing firms and consider how firms under different ownership pursue different objectives and compete in the same market. Moreover, our analysis focuses on the relationship between market structure and a firm's conduct, as well as that between ownership and firm behavior. This approach differs from that of conventional studies of the relationship between ownership and economic performance in many works of transitional economics.[5]

Although the public economics literature contains some theoretical discussions on the possible behavioral deviations of public enterprises in a mixed market, see for instance Bos (1991), there is no systematic empirical study documenting the actual behavior of such deviations.

In this study, we used a database that contains information about a large number of firms from China's industries, which allowed us to address this issue empirically. The firm-level information for a large number of companies is contained in the data set of the industrial census compiled by the National Bureau of Statistics (NBS) of China. As our study shows, firms under different ownership indeed behave differently. Moreover, the particular mix of private and state-owned firms in a market also plays an important role in determining firm behavior, as does market structure, in terms of concentration.

LITERATURE REVIEW, THEORY, AND HYPOTHESES

There are two strands of literature on the relationship between firms' ownership and their strategies: the economics literature and the management literature.

In the early economics literature, public firms were modeled as instruments to regulate private firms and to correct market imperfections in an oligopolistic setting. The rivalry between welfare-maximizing public enterprises and profit-maximizing private firms were depicted as leading to an equilibrium output different from the standard setting—a competitive market in which profit-maximizing firms compete against each other. This rivalry was seen as providing policymakers with an additional instrument for intervening in an imperfect market to improve welfare. When a public enterprise was brought in, the equilibrium output might vary from that obtained under a standard oligopoly, depending on the objective functions of the public enterprises, and therefore might lead to a different level of social welfare (Bos 1991).

The experience of China's enterprise reform and the unsatisfactory performance of its SOEs have inspired some research on firm behavior and outcomes in mixed markets in the context of agency theory. Zhang and Ma (1999) analyzed the asymmetry between public enterprises and profit-maximizing private firms and examined the price levels and welfare consequences of such a mixed oligopoly. They concluded that the rivalry among the firms in mixed markets was more aggressive than that in a conventional oligopoly. Moreover, the agency problem that accompanies state ownership in public enterprises worsens the situation, in that there is excessive competition in which the public enterprises act as "loss leaders," setting prices below marginal costs.

From the perspective of comparative economics, a number of studies have compared the economic performance of industry competitors that are under alternative ownership arrangements. For instance, using total factor productivity as their measure, Ehrlich et al. (1994) showed that private firms in the Canadian airline industry and their state-owned counterparts differed in terms of total-factor productivity. Eckel and Vermaelen (1986) studied the economic performance of firms under various levels of state ownership in a number of industries and showed that firms with a high percentage of public ownership performed poorly.

Management scholars have also noticed the situation in China in which firms under different types of ownership compete. But their focus has been more on the relationship between ownership and strategy. Tan (2002), for instance, studied the influence of ownership type on environmental strategy, drawing on an analysis of 201 managers from four types of Chinese companies: state-owned, collectively owned, privately owned, and foreign joint ventures. Tan's results support the central notion that each ownership type exhibits a distinct environment-strategy configuration, which in turn has important performance implications for firms.

As we have stated above, despite an extensive literature studying the relationship between ownership and economic performance in transition economies, scholarly understanding of the nature of firms' behavior in a mixed market and its implications for competitive outcomes is definitely inadequate. What has not been well understood are the mechanisms that link the ownership and economic performance of those firms, or the role that market structure plays in this process. In the following section we outline the theoretical foundations of our study and derive a number of testable hypotheses.

To analyze firms' behavior in a mixed market, we start from the standard assumption of a private firm in a well-developed market. Such a firm faces competitive pressure in the product-market as well as in the market for productive input. The owner of the firm maximizes his or her profit. A state-owned firm differs from such a "standard" private firm in at least three dimensions: the state-owned firm is not a profit maximizer; its agency costs are higher; and it enjoys privileges. We will examine these dimensions in detail.

First, the state-owned firm may pursue objectives other than profitability. In a normative setting, public firms are supposed to maximize social welfare as opposed to their own profit. Because social welfare, by definition, includes both firm profit and consumer surplus, welfare-maximizing public firms tend to charge lower prices than do private firms. In an imperfectly competitive market, this typically means that a public enterprise produces more than a private firm in a mixed market at equilibrium, if they have similar cost structures.

Second, because a state-owned firm typically has a virtual owner instead of a real owner, as do private firms, the principal-agent problem is more serious, and agency costs are presumably higher than for private firms. Agency costs can lead to two opposite effects, as far as equilibrium outcomes are concerned. One possible effect is that, because of lack of proper supervision, managers of state-owned firms may tend toward "empire building." Therefore, state-owned firms may, for instance, charge a low price in order to pursue market share. Moreover, they may choose to maximize value-added factors, including both profits, from which they expect to obtain rents, and wages, which are part of costs. This maximization will also lead to more aggressive market behavior than that of a private firm.

On the other hand, it is equally plausible that SOEs are less aggressive competitively than are private enterprises because the managers of SOEs are less motivated and enjoy a quiet life. They can do so because the industries in which SOEs operate typically have high barriers to entry. These barriers shield state-owned firms (and their managers) from competitive pressure, allowing them to charge higher, noncompetitive prices. Therefore, these firms appear less aggressive.

Third, in a mixed market, firms under different types of ownership typically face an unlevel field. With government backing, state-owned firms enjoy favorable conditions in terms of finances and other resources. Because they face soft budget constraints, managers of state-owned firms have different perceptions of the cost of capital than the managers of private firms. The perceived low cost of capital encourages SOEs to invest in projects that are otherwise unprofitable, when evaluated by the risk-adjusted market-level cost of capital.

What is interesting is that these three fundamental differences in firm objectives, ownership arrangement, and resources between private firms and state-owed firms are bound to have implications for firms' behavior in such a mixed market. To assess empirically the differences in firms' behavior in a mixed market, we propose a set of testable hypotheses based on the theoretical arguments outlined above. We use these hypotheses to gauge the behavioral differences between SOEs and private firms.

Pricing

As we discussed earlier, SOEs charge lower prices than do private firms when they adopt social welfare maximization as their objective instead of profit maximization. State-owned firms will also charge lower prices than do private firms when they maximize value added. The existence of agency costs complicates prediction because state-owned firms may charge low prices when empire-building behavior prevails; conversely, they may charge high prices when competition is absent. SOEs with soft budget constraints tend to charge less when cost recovery is less of a concern to them. Therefore, we develop the following hypothesis.

Hypothesis 1. State-owned enterprises charge lower prices than do private firms.

The test of this hypothesis requires information on price levels of firms producing the same product under different ownership. It is difficult to compare prices absolutely because, first of all, price may vary with quality and other product characteristics. Moreover, direct comparison of prices for different products becomes almost meaningless in the case of a cross-industry comparison.

A plausible way to test the "underpricing hypothesis" is to compare price adjustment over time, an approach that is particularly interesting in view of the continuing process of SOE reform in China. Suppose that SOEs charge less than private firms, initially, because of the three fundamental differences between them. Over time, such differences tend to narrow as economic reforms occur. A natural extension of the underpricing hypothesis is that SOEs will raise prices more than private enterprises, regardless of the circumstances. Therefore, we modify hypothesis 1 as follows:

Hypothesis 1'. State-owned enterprises raise their prices to a greater degree than do private firms.

To capture the effect of price changes, we use the variable of *price adjustment,* which reflects the magnitude of price change in a year's time.

Innovation

A firm's competitiveness is to a certain degree reflected in its innovative effort. With profit maximization as their objective, private firms may be more aggressive in producing and marketing new products in order to create and capture new demand. For reasons already mentioned, SOEs have less incentive to be innovative. Therefore, we develop the following hypothesis:

Hypothesis 2. Private firms are more innovative than state-owned enterprises.

To capture the differences in degree of innovative effort, we adopt the variable of *new-product sales,* which measures a firm's total sales of new products. This variable reflects a firm's ability to produce and sell new products in the marketplace. It also reflects the innovation effort of the firm.

Marketing

It is often argued that SOEs are less successful in the marketplace because they are handicapped by the state's tight control of marketing expenses and rigid regulation of marketing behavior. It is commonly believed that the nonstate enterprises are more aggressive in marketing and eager to promote their products. Marketing effort should be reflected in cost structure. Greater marketing effort requires a higher percentage of sales costs in a firm's total revenue, all other things being equal. Therefore, we develop the following hypothesis:

Hypothesis 3. The sales expenses of private firms are higher than those of state-owned enterprises.

To test this hypothesis, we used the ratio of sales expenses to total sales in order to capture the degree of marketing aggressiveness of a firm. We consider that the more aggressive a firm is, the greater its marketing expenses will be, with the condition that the firm is efficiently run and acts as a profit maximizer. In the case of state-owned firms in transition, the situation can be more complicated, and at least two factors must be taken into consideration: first, state-owned firms may not be as efficient as private firms, in terms of marketing efficiency. Therefore, a high sales-to-cost ratio may be a reflection of such inefficiency. Second, managers of state-owned firms are prone to corruption, so they may use market expenses to hide personal benefits that they take from the companies.

Operations

There are a number of indicators of the efficiency of a firm's operation. One of them is its inventory level. Obviously, business cycles and market volatilities influence inventory level, but it may also depend on the nature of the firm. Here, we were interested in whether inventory level varies among firms under different ownership. As we have argued, agency costs in SOEs are high, so their managers care less about inventory level. Moreover, a high level of inventory may be a symptom of unsold goods, potentially a sign of managerial laziness. All these factors indicate that the inventories of state-owned firms will be higher than those of private firms. Hence, we develop the following hypothesis:

Hypothesis 4. The inventory levels of private firms are lower than those of state-owned enterprises.

To test this hypothesis, we used the ratio of the value of goods in inventory to the total annual sales.

Investment

SOEs are often blamed for their excessive and unproductive investments. Although such claims may be true, several factors may be accountable. First of all, SOEs must invest more aggressively than private firms if their objective is welfare maximization. Such investment requires greater output than that under profit maximization. The excessive investment can also be the result of the soft budget constraints facing state-owned firms. With such constraints, SOEs will invest more than private firms. Moreover, it is also plausible that the SOEs will use capital-intensive technology to produce the same quantity of the same product, given that their perceived cost of capital is lower than that of the market. Thus, we developed following hypothesis:

Hypothesis 5. State-owned enterprises invest more aggressively than private firms.

To test this hypothesis, we used the variable *investment,* calculated as the additional investment a firm undertakes in a particular year against its current fixed assets. We did not have information regarding whether additional investments were used to add capacity or to upgrade existing product line.

Capital Structure

When a firm has found a profitable investment project, it must decide how to finance it. In a competitive and uncertain environment, debt financing and equity financing have different taxation and incentive implications. For corporate managers, the greater the debt, the greater the risk of bankruptcy. This risk in turn increases the risk of loss of job and reputation; therefore, corporate managers perceive the need to keep their firm's debt level appropriate. In a mixed market in a transitional economy, the situation differs. Ownership also matters when it comes to financing decisions. Because state-owned banks favor SOEs, it is easier for them to get bank loans than it is for privately owned firms. When SOEs have such soft budget constraints, the discipline of bankruptcy does not apply. Therefore, we develop the following hypothesis:

Hypothesis 6. The financial leverage of private firms is lower than that of state-owned enterprises.

To test this hypothesis, we used the ratio of the sum of the long-term liability and current liability to the total fixed assets; this is an indicator of leverage. Like our variable for investment, this ratio reflects a firm's aggressiveness, but this leverage variable differs from the investment variable in the sense that the former measures the firm's financing decisions.

Clearly, these six hypotheses are based on the three fundamental theories describing the possible behavioral differences of SOEs and private firms. These hypotheses were tested with observable and operational indicators found in our data set.

All the above hypotheses focus on firm ownership type as an independent variable. It is plausible that variables that reflect the external environments of a firm, such as market structure and state dominance, may also influence the relationship between ownership and firm behavior. Hence, in addition to investigating the direct impact of firm ownership on firm behavior, we also wanted to learn more about the possible ways in which market structure and state–firm dominance in an industry could moderate the impact of ownership on firm behavior.

METHOD

Data

The data set that we used to test the above hypotheses is the industrial census data compiled by the NBS. The average number of firms is over 100,000 over a three-year period. The firms included in the census were above a minimum threshold size; specifically, they had to have annual sales of at least RMB200,000 within the survey period.

Although the NBS has been conducting this survey for a number of years, we found inconsistencies in the data collection. Some firms lack identification numbers; therefore, it is hard to match the data over time. We found the 1999–2001 data to have the best quality, so we chose these three years for our analysis, which provided us with a total of 394,556 observations. For each firm, the census data include over 70 entries. Table 10.1 lists the definitions of variables used in our analysis.

In Table 10.1, the first six items are dependent variables, and the remainder are explanatory (independent) variables.

Econometric Models

In this study, we used random-effects models to estimate the effects of the explanatory variables on the six dependent variables that we have discussed above.

$$y_{it} = \mu + \beta_1 ownership_{it} + \beta_2 Ratio - state_{it} + \beta_3 marketstructure_{it} + \beta_4 ownership_{it} *ratio - state_{it}$$

$$+ \beta_5 ownership_{it} *marketstructure_{it} + \beta_6 firmsize_{it} + \beta_7 dum99 + \beta_8 dum2000 + \alpha_i + \varepsilon_{it},$$

where:

y_{it} is a behavioral variable, namely, price adjustment, new product, sales cost, inventory, investment, or leverage; $ownership_{it}$ is the ownership type of firm i at time t;

$proportion\ of\ state\ firms$ is the proportion of SOEs in the industry that firm i is in at time t; $marketstructure_{it}$ is the Herfindahl index of the industry that firm i is in at time t;

$firmsize_{it}$ is the size of firm i at time t; $dum99$ is a dummy variable equal to 1 if t is equal to 1999, otherwise equal to 0; $dum2000$ is a dummy variable equal to 1 if t is equal to 2000, otherwise equal to 0; α_i is unobserved firm-specific effects;

and ε_{it} is the error term.

The basic regression model includes two interactive terms in addition to three key explanatory variables. These interactive terms are used to capture any possible interactions between firm ownership type and market structure, and dominance of state-owned firms and market structure.

Measurement

Because ownership type was an important explanatory variable, we measured it in two ways. One was using a dummy variable coded 1 for privately owned firms and 0 for state-owned firms. The other was to categorize firms into three types by the percentage of shares owned by the govern-

Table 10.1

Definition of Variables

Sales cost	Sales expenses/total sales
Investment	Long-term investments/total assets
Price adjustment	Present value of total output/fixed value of total output
New product	Present value of new-products output/present value of total output
Inventory	New-products inventory over the present value of total output
Leverage	Total debts/total assets
State share	The stated-owned capital over the total capital
Private firm	Dummy variable, equal to 1 if the firm is a private firm; 0 otherwise
d1	Dummy variable, equal to 1 if the state share < 0.3; 0 otherwise
d2	Dummy variable, equal to 1 if $0.3 <$ state share < 0.7; 0 otherwise
d3	Dummy variable, equal to 1 if state share > 0.7; 0 otherwise
Market structure	Herfindahl index, equal to the sum of the squares of the market shares in term of sales revenue
Firm size	Categorical variable for firm size from 1 to 6, 6 being largest and 1 being smallest
Employees	The logarithm of the number of employees
Proportion of state-owned firms	The number of firms with state shares $> 90\%$/total number of firms in the same industry
Dum00	Dummy variable, equal to 1 if the observation is from the year 2000; 0 otherwise
Dum99	Dummy variable, equal to 1 if the observation is from the year 1999; 0 otherwise

ment: the first category was firms with less than 30 percent stated-owned shares; the second, 30–70 percent state-owned shares; and third, more than 70 percent state-owned shares. Market structure was measured as a Herfindahl index. We also employed two measures for firm size. The first, a six-category measure adopted by the NBS in its census, applies two criteria: output in physical units and the book value of fixed assets. The threshold values for different industries varied. Only when a firm met both criteria was it put into a higher category. It is apparently a legacy of the centrally planned era to measure firm size in output units. Our second size measure, the logarithm of the number of laborers employed by a firm, is widely used in both economics and management. The descriptive statistics of these variables can be found in Table 10.2.

Table 10.2

Descriptive Statistics

Variables	Mean	S.D.
Sales cost	0.04	0.07
Investment	0.02	0.06
Price adjustment	1.32	1.92
Leverage	0.58	0.25
Inventory	0.11	0.16
New product	0.03	0.13
Private firm	0.29	0.45
State share	0.69	0.41
Proportion of state-owned firms	0.58	0.17
Market structure[a]	0.03	0.07
Firm size[b]	5.72	0.81
Employees	4.98	1.22

[a]Market structure is measured as a Herfindahl index.

[b]Firm size is a categorical variable ranging from 6 to 1, with 6 referring to large firms and 1 to small firms. The categories are specified by the National Bureau of Statistics of China.

RESULTS AND DISCUSSION

The regression results of various models are summarized in Tables 10.3–10.8. In each table, we report two sets of regression results that differ on ownership variables. The first four columns in Tables 10.3–10.8 are the regression results when the variable *private firm* is used to measure ownership type, with *state-owned firm* as the baseline case. The first model includes all explanatory variables, but without interaction terms (model 1 in Tables 10.3–10.8). The second model adds two interaction terms (model 2 in Tables 10.3–10.8). Firm size is measured via the six-category NBS indicator in the first two regressions, but we used *number of employees* in models 3 and 4. In the next four columns—models 1′, 2′, 3′, and 4′—we used three categories of ownership type to replace the private firm variable.

Price Adjustment (Hypothesis 1)

Table 10.3 summarizes the results of the price adjustment models that show the relationship between the magnitude of price adjustment and its determinants.

As we can see, the coefficients of the ownership dummy variable (private firm) all have a negative sign, meaning that private firms changed their prices more slowly than state-owned firms during the sample period. This result supports Hypothesis 1. In the process of economic reform, state-owned enterprises start deviating from welfare maximization and become more and more profit oriented. Hence, they behave more like private firms and start using their market power and raising prices.

If we look into the effects on the price adjustment of state shares measured in the three categories of ownership, we see that the influence of state share on a firm's price strategy varies. When the state-owned share is higher than 70 percent, the magnitudes of adjustments are larger and statistically more significant than in the other two cases.

Table 10.3

Regressions on Price Adjustment (hypothesis 1)[a]

	Dependent variable: Price adjustment							
	Model 1	Model 2	Model 3	Model 4	Model 1'	Model 2'	Model 3'	Model 4'
Private firm[b]	−0.03* (−2.57)	−0.03 (−1.77)	−0.02* (−2.20)	−0.01 (−1.5)				
d1state share					0.23** (2.74)	0.21* (2.48)	0.21* (2.47)	0.19* (2.19)
d2state share					0.09** (4.72)	0.09** (4.63)	0.08** (4.07)	0.07** (3.98)
d3state share					0.28** (31.44)	0.28** (31.46)	0.27** (30.36)	0.27** (30.41)
Proportion of state–owned firms	1.89** (87.94)	1.90** (78.23)	1.89** (87.94)	1.90** (78.24)	1.64** (73.25)	1.64** (65.85)	1.65** (73.36)	1.64** (65.92)
Market structure	−0.41** (−5.12)	−0.16 (−0.56)	−0.42** (−5.28)	−0.17 (−0.61)	−0.41** (−5.14)	−0.25 (−1)	−0.44** (−5.52)	−0.27 (−1.07)
Private firm × market structure		−0.15 (−0.84)		−0.13 (−0.75)				

	(1)	(2)	(3)	(4)	(5)	(6)	(7)	(8)
State share × market structure						-0.44* (-2.49)		-0.48** (-2.72)
Proportion of state–owned firms × market structure		-0.36 (-0.85)		-0.36 (-0.86)		0.26 (0.62)		0.29 (0.69)
Firm size	-0.01** (-3.20)	-0.01** (-3.22)			-0.03** (-7.84)	-0.03** (-7.78)		
Employees			0.011** (4.04)	0.011** (4.04)			0.004 (1.5)	0.004 (1.56)
Dum00	0.16** (23.97)	0.16** (23.98)	0.16** (24.03)	0.16** (24.03)	0.15** (23.02)	0.15** (22.98)	0.15** (22.9)	0.15** (22.94)
Dum99	0.05** (8.60)	0.05** (8.61)	0.05** (8.62)	0.05** (8.63)	0.05** (8.56)	0.05** (8.55)	0.05** (8.51)	0.05** (8.50)
Constant	0.10** (3.46)	0.09** (3.12)	0.12** (5.91)	0.12** (5.27)	0.05 (1.65)	0.05 (1.68)	0.23** (11.17)	0.23** (10.62)
χ^2	8,513**	8,514**	8,516**	8,517**	9,550**	9,556**	9,484**	9,492**
R^2	0.03	0.03	0.03	0.03	0.04	0.04	0.03	0.04

[a]All of the regressions use random-effects regression, so the values in parentheses are z-statistics.

[b]Ownership type is measured by the dummy variable *private firm* in models 1–4 and by three categorical variables, *d1state share, d2stateshare,* and *d3stateshare* in models 3–4 and 3'–4'. Firm size is measured by the six-category variable in models 1–2 and 1'–2' and is measured by the number of employees in models 3–4 and 3'–4'.

*Statistically significant at 5% confidence level.

**Statistically significant at 1% confidence level.

What is surprising is the negative sign of the coefficients of market concentration measured by the Herfindahl index. The results suggest that price adjustment is slower in concentrated industries than in less-concentrated industries. Given that the sample included only firms from manufacturing industries, not regulated monopolies, one plausible explanation is that sellers in competitive industries adjust their prices more quickly to reflect changes in input prices, while firms with some degree of market power increase their prices only partially and slowly.

For firm size, measured either as number of employees or as the NBS categorical indicator, the coefficients are positive and statistically significant, which shows that large firms adjust their prices more than smaller firms, even when the market structure remains the same. We also found that the greater the number of state-owned firms in the industry, the faster the price adjustment, as the coefficients of the variable measuring the proportion of state-owned firms indicate.

The above results remain unchanged after the interaction terms are added to the model. None of the coefficients of the interaction terms are significantly different from zero except that of market structure and proportion of state-owned firms in an industry. The negative signs of the coefficients imply that market concentration moderates the positive correlation between state ownership and price adjustment.

New-Product Sales (Hypothesis 2)

As we discussed earlier, we used the percentage of new-product sales as an indicator of firms' innovative efforts. The regression analysis results in Table 10.4 indicate that private firms produced and sold fewer new products than did state-owned enterprises. Therefore, Hypothesis 2 is rejected.

However, this result may not be totally surprising. It is well known that state-owned firms have easier access to research funding and personnel than do private enterprises. The unlevel field helps SOEs to develop and maintain their edge in terms of innovative capabilities. Hence, it is rational for private firms to enter a market by imitating existing products but offering them at much lower prices. When it comes to the impact of state ownership on new-product sales, we find that such sales do not rise proportionally with state ownership, as the magnitudes of the coefficients of the ownership category show. The coefficients for firms that are less than 30 percent state-owned are the largest of the three categories of state ownership, which means that the larger the share of state ownership in a firm, the lower the firm's new-product sales.

The results also show a positive relationship between market structure and new-product sales. The more concentrated an industry, the more new products are produced and sold in the marketplace. Interestingly, the coefficients of the two variables that measure firm size turn out to have opposite signs. While firms that are larger than others in terms of sales sell more new products, firms that are larger in terms of number of employees sell fewer new products. One possible explanation is that the production of mature-stage products tends to be more labor intensive than the production of early-stage products, which may be more capital intensive.

We also found that firms in industries with many SOEs sold fewer new products. We interpret this finding to mean that the less reformed an industry is, the lower the value of new products as a proportion of total sales.

Again, the inclusion of interaction terms does not change the significance of the effects of the explanatory variables. The coefficients of the interaction terms between the ratio of state-controlled firms in an industry to market concentration are all negative, which implies that in a highly concentrated industry, a higher proportion of SOEs in an industry had an even more negative impact on new products.

Table 10.4

Regressions on New–Product Sales (Hypothesis 2)[a]

	Dependent variable: New product							
	Model 1	Model 2	Model 3	Model 4	Model 1'	Model 2'	Model 3'	Model 4'
Private firm[b]	-0.003** (-5.44)	-0.002** (-3.81)	-0.004** (-7.22)	-0.003** (-5.15)				
d1state share				0.02** (4.18)	0.03** (4.53)	0.03** (4.86)	0.03** (5.26)	
d2state share				0.02** (14.42)	0.02** (14.50)	0.02** (16.81)	0.02** (16.89)	
d3state share				0.003** (4.80)	0.003** (4.06)	0.006** (10.37)	0.006** (9.46)	
Proportion of state-owned firms	-.05** (-33.59)	-0.05** (-26.44)	-0.05** (-30.7)	-0.04** (-23.45)	-0.05** (-31.60)	-0.05** (-25.11)	-0.05** (-30.23)	-0.04** (-23.52)
Market structure	0.13** (23.03)	0.27** (14.58)	0.14** (25.92)	0.31** (16.36)	0.13** (22.96)	0.24** (14.31)	0.14** (25.78)	0.27** (15.85)
Private firm × market structure		-0.02 (-1.69)		-0.02* (-2.05)				
State share × market structure						0.05** (4.29)		0.06** (4.92)
Proportion of state-owned firms × market structure		-0.23** (-8.46)		-0.26** (-9.43)		-0.25** (-9.16)		-0.28** (-10.13)
Firm size	0.02** (71.09)	0.02** (71.06)			0.02** (69.54)	0.02** (69.43)		

(continued)

Table 10.4 (continued)

	Dependent variable: New product							
	Model 1	Model 2	Model 3	Model 4	Model 1′	Model 2′	Model 3′	Model 4′
Employees			0.01** (51.62)	0.01** (51.74)			0.01** (50.60)	0.01** (50.66)
Dum00	−0.01** (−13.59)	−0.01** (−13.49)	−0.004** (−10.40)	−0.004** (−10.33)	−0.01** (−13.46)	−0.01** (−13.30)	−0.004** (−10.65)	−0.004** (−10.48)
Dum99	−0.003** (7.88)	−0.003** (−7.75)	−0.002** (−5.86)	−0.002** (−5.72)	−0.003** (−7.80)	−0.003** (−7.66)	−0.002** (−5.92)	−0.002** (−5.76)
Constant	0.19** (87.34)	0.18** (83.15)	0.001 (0.38)	−0.004* (−2.57)	0.18** (84.92)	0.18** (81.31)	−0.002 (−1.29)	−0.01** (−3.98)
χ^2	6,726**	6,802**	4,310**	4,404**	7,016**	4,616**	4,728**	
R^2	0.04	0.04	0.02	0.02	0.04	0.04	0.02	0.02

[a]All of the regressions use random–effects regression, so the values in parentheses are z–statistics.

[b]Ownership type is measured by the dummy variable *private firm* in models1–4 and by three categorical variables, *d1state share, d2stateshare,* and *d3stateshare* in models 1′–4′. Firm size is measured by the six–category variable in models 1–2 and 1′–2′ and is measured by the number of employees in models 3–4 and 3′–4′.

*Statistically significant at 5% confidence level.

**Statistically significant at 1% confidence level.

Sales Cost (Hypothesis 3)

Table 10.5 shows the results of the models that relate sales costs with ownership and market structure. The coefficients of the private firm variable are negative, indicating that firms with a large share of nonstate investment spent less of their total revenue on sales. The results of models 3 and 4 show the same pattern of influence as for the state-owned shares. This finding contradicts Hypothesis 3, which states that private firms spend more money on marketing. It also contradicts the common belief that because private firms are profit maximizers, they are more flexible when deciding how much money to spend on marketing.

One of the interpretations of this result is that SOEs, in response to market pressure, turn out to be more aggressive in marketing their products. They therefore spend more money on advertising- and sales-related activities. An alternative interpretation is that managers of SOEs are more likely to be corrupt and use marketing expenses as a means to embezzle funds from their companies. Our study cannot distinguish these two effects if both of them exist. More detailed studies of this issue are needed to attempt to separate these two effects.

In these models, the two variables measuring firm size all have negative and statistically significant coefficients. A straightforward interpretation is that large firms can benefit more from economies of scale in sales activities than can small firms.

There are significant interaction effects between the ratio of SOEs in an industry and the concentration of the industry. The positive correlation between sales cost and market concentration and that between sales cost and the ratio of SOEs in an industry are moderated for firms in highly concentrated industries that are also dominated by state-owned firms.

Inventory Levels (Hypothesis 4)

The coefficients of the private firm dummy variable in all models in Table 10.6 support the hypothesis that private firms maintain lower inventories than state-owned firms. But, as shown in model 3, in the category of firms with less than 30 percent of state ownership, the coefficient of state share is not significantly different from zero, while in the other two categories, the coefficients are significant and larger in the third category. This again sheds light on the fact that the influence of state shares is greater in firms that are highly controlled by the government.

The results in Table 10.6 also show that firms in highly concentrated industries have large inventories, as the coefficients of the Herfindahl index show. On the other hand, in those industries in which SOEs still dominate, the inventory level of the firms is low.

Investment (Hypothesis 5)

When coming to models on investment level, it is clear that private firms invest less than state-owned firms, as the negative coefficients of the private-firm variable show (see Table 10.7); hence, Hypothesis 5 is supported. This is the same as the previous results on inventory level: the coefficient of state shares of the second category is not significantly different from zero, which means that small state shares have only limited effects on a firm's behavior.

Moreover, firms in highly concentrated industries invest more than firms in less-concentrated industries. Speed of investment is also positively related to firm size, with large firms investing more than smaller ones. The dominance of state-owned firms also gives higher investment, as the coefficients of the proportion of SOEs show a positive sign.

Table 10.5

Regressions on Sales Cost (hypothesis 3)[a]

	Dependent variable: Sale cost							
	Model 1	Model 2	Model 3	Model 4	Model 1'	Model 2'	Model 3'	Model 4'
Private firm[b]	-0.0004 (-1.63)	-0.001* (-2.27)	-0.001* (-2.41)	-0.001** (-2.87)				
d1state share					0.02** (5.75)	0.02** (5.64)	0.02** (6.04)	0.02** (5.96)
d2state share					0.01** (10.41)	0.01** (10.34)	0.01** (11.05)	0.01** (10.99)
d3state share					0.004** (12.45)	0.004** (12.27)	0.01** (13.99)	0.01** (13.75)
Proportion of state-owned firms	0.02** (18.16)	0.02** (19.71)	0.02** (18.00)	0.02** (19.52)	0.014** (14.78)	0.02** (16.84)	0.013** (14.27)	0.02** (16.31)
Market structure	0.04** (11.53)	0.10** (9.95)	0.04** (11.70)	0.10** (9.94)	0.03** (11.48)	0.11** (11.58)	0.04** (11.57)	0.10** (11.38)
Private firm × market structure		0.01 (1.84)		0.01 (1.71)				
State share × market structure						-0.003 (-0.48)		-0.001 (-0.18)

Ratio × market structure		−0.11** (−7.62)		−0.11** (−7.52)		−0.12** (−7.80)		−0.11** (−7.71)
Firm size	0.001** (5.49)	0.001** (5.47)			0.001** (3.64)	0.001** (3.63)		
Private firm^b	−0.0004	−0.001*	−0.001**	−0.001**				
Employees			−0.001** (−12.30)	−0.001** (−12.14)			−0.002** (−13.40)	−0.002** (−13.29)
Dum00	0.002** (11.43)	0.002** (11.57)	0.002** (11.25)	0.002** (11.38)	0.002** (10.89)	0.002** (11.02)	0.002** (10.52)	0.002** (10.66)
Dum99	0.001** (8.31)	0.001** (8.46)	0.001** (8.24)	0.001** (8.38)	0.001** (8.15)	0.001** (8.29)	0.001** (7.98)	0.001** (8.12)
Constant	0.04** (31.53)	0.04** (29.27)	0.04** (47.19)	0.04** (42.80)	0.04** (29.92)	0.03** (27.73)	0.04** (48.74)	0.04** (44.38)
χ^2	586**	663**	705**	779**	826**	896**	993**	1,059**
R^2	0.003	0.003	0.003	0.004	0.004	0.005	0.005	0.005

[a]All of the regressions use random-effects regression, so the values in parentheses are z-statistics.

[b]Ownership type is measured by the dummy variable *private firm* in models 1–4 and by three categorical variables, *d1state share*, *d2stateshare*, and *d3stateshare* in models 1'–4'. Firm size is measured by the six-category variable in models 1–2 and 1'–2' and is measured by the number of employees in models 3–4 and 3'–4'.

*Statistically significant at 5% confidence level.

**Statistically significant at 1% confidence level.

Table 10.6

Regressions on Inventory (hypothesis 4)[a]

	Dependent variable: Inventory							
	Model 1	Model 2	Model 3	Model 4	Model 1′	Model 2′	Model 3′	Model 4′
Private firm[b]	-0.02** (-34.67)	-0.02** (-29.87)	-0.02** (-35.0)	-0.02** (-30.12)				
d1state share					-0.01 (-1.65)	-0.004 (-0.54)	-0.01 (-1.67)	-0.004 (-0.56)
d2state share					0.01** (5.35)	0.01** (5.71)	0.01** (5.70)	0.01** (6.05)
d3state share					0.05** (56.68)	0.04** (54.82)	0.05** (57.96)	0.04** (56.02)
Proportion of state-owned firms	-0.05** (-24.39)	-0.05** (-21.40)	-0.05** (-22.90)	-0.05** (-19.83)	-0.08** (-34.67)	-0.07** (-30.85)	-0.07** (-33.71)	-0.07** (-29.74)
Market structure	0.06** (7.97)	0.10** (4.10)	0.07** (9.30)	0.12** (5.07)	0.06** (7.94)	0.03 (1.41)	0.06** (9.08)	0.05* (2.29)
Private firm × market structure		-0.01 (-0.59)		-0.01 (-0.67)				

	(1)	(2)	(3)	(4)	(5)	(6)	(7)	(8)
State share × market structure						0.17** (11.91)		0.17** (11.99)
Proportion of state-owned firms × market structure		−0.06 (−1.78)		−0.08* (−2.41)		−0.15** (−4.50)		−0.17** (−5.07)
Firm size	0.01** (32.89)	0.01** (32.88)			0.01** (27.78)	0.01** (27.55)		
Employees			0.01** (39.41)	0.01** (39.43)			0.01** (36.88)	0.01** (36.76)
Dum00	−0.01** (−13.47)	−0.01** (−13.44)	−0.01** (−11.24)	−0.01** (−11.19)	−0.01** (−17.23)	−0.01** (−17.11)	−0.01* (−15.29)	−0.01* (−15.17)
Dum99	0.001* (2.08)	0.001* (2.11)	0.001** (3.56)	0.001** (3.60)	0.0002 (0.72)	0.0003 (0.77)	0.001 (2.01)	0.001 (2.07)
Constant	0.23** (80.15)	0.23** (77.84)	0.09** (46.93)	0.09** (43.99)	0.21** (75.10)	0.21** (73.07)	0.09** (48.33)	0.09** (45.72)
χ^2	2,890**	2,893**	3,370**	3,376**	4,974**	5,123**	44**	5,743**
R^2	0.02	0.02	0.02	0.02	0.03	0.03	0.03	0.03

[a]All of the regressions use random-effects regression, so the values in parentheses are z statistics.

[b]Ownership type is measured by the dummy variable *private firm* in models 1–4 and by three categorical variables, *d1state share*, *d2stateshare*, and *d3stateshare* in models 1′–4′. Firm size is measured by the six-category variable in models 1–2 and 1′–2′ and is measured by the number of employees in models 3–4 and 3′–4′.

*Statistically significant at 5% confidence level.
**Statistically significant at 1% confidence level.

Table 10.7

Regressions on Investment (hypothesis 5)[a]

	Dependent variable: Investment							
	Model 1	Model 2	Model 3	Model 4	Model 1'	Model 2'	Model 3'	Model 4'
Private firm[b]	-0.01** (-25.76)	-0.01** (-20.89)	-0.01** (-26.4)	-0.01** (-21.39)				
d1state share					-0.01** (-4.54)	-0.01** (-3.19)	-0.01** (-4.27)	-0.01** (-2.90)
d2state share					-0.000018 (-0.03)	0.0002 (0.4)	0.001 (1.13)	0.001 (1.55)
d3state share					0.003** (9.37)	0.002** (7.41)	0.003** (12.24)	0.003** (10.18)
Proportion of state-owned firms	0.001 (1.20)	0.002** (2.65)	0.002** (3.24)	0.004** (4.83)	0.003** (3.51)	0.004** (5.11)	0.004** (4.75)	0.01** (6.55)
Market structure	0.02** (8.53)	0.05** (6.31)	0.03** (10.53)	0.06** (7.64)	0.02** (8.49)	0.02** (2.96)	0.03** (10.47)	0.03** (4.23)
Private firm × market structure		-0.02** (-2.91)		-0.02** (-3.10)				
State share × market structure						0.07** (14.40)		0.07** (14.66)

Proportion of state-owned firms × market structure		-0.05** (-3.68)		-0.05** (-4.47)		-0.09** (-7.21)		-0.10** (-7.98)
Firm size	0.01** (48.02)	0.01** (47.98)			0.01** (47.75)	0.01** (47.47)		
Employees			0.004** (45.58)	0.004** (45.61)			0.004** (45.52)	0.004** (45.39)
Dum00	0.0004* (2.21)	0.0004* (2.26)	0.001** (4.85)	0.001** (4.91)	0.0002 (1.59)	0.0003 (1.78)	0.001** (4.07)	0.001** (4.27)
Dum99	0.0003* (1.98)	0.0003* (2.04)	0.001** (3.79)	0.001** (3.86)	0.0002 (1.79)	0.0003 (1.9)	0.001** (3.55)	0.001** (3.67)
Constant	0.06** (58.02)	0.06** (55.66)	-0.01** (-8.5)	-0.01** (-9.54)	0.05** (54.85)	0.05** (52.67)	-0.01** (-13.46)	-0.01** (-14.19)
χ^2	3,312**	3,330**	3,077**	3,101**	2,756**	2,977**	2,545**	2,780**
R^2	0.02	0.02	0.02	0.02	0.02	0.02	0.01	0.02

[a]All of the regressions use random-effects regression, so the values in parentheses are z-statistics.

[b]Ownership type is measured by the dummy variable *private firm* in models 1–4 and by three categorical variables, *d1state share*, *d2stateshare*, and *d3stateshare* in models 1′–4′. Firm size is measured by the six-category variable in models 1–2 and 1′–2′ and is measured by the number of employees in models 3–4 and models 3′–Reg4′.

*Statistically significant at 5% confidence level.

**Statistically significant at 1% confidence level.

Capital Structure (Hypothesis 6)

Table 10.8 summarizes the results on leverage. The coefficients of the state-share variables and the private-firm variables in those models indicate that leverage goes with state ownership; therefore, Hypothesis 6 is supported. Moreover, as shown in the third and fourth models, in categories with less than 70 percent of state shares, increase of state shares does not increase leverage. A possible reason for this is that with the reform of the banking industry, firms cannot obtain loans easily unless they have considerable state ownership.

The coefficients of firm size are all statistically significant, showing that large firms are more leveraged than small firms. Industry concentration has a negative coefficient, indicating that firms are less leveraged in more concentrated industries. But the coefficients become insignificant after the inclusion of interaction terms, implying that the significant effects of industry concentration might be due to interactive effects. What is surprising is the negative sign of the coefficients of proportion of state firms, which implies that firms in industries with a greater proportion of SOEs tend to borrow less when all other factors remain the same. The interaction terms between market structure and proportion of SOEs are negative and significantly different from zero, implying that the negative correlation between market concentration and leverage and that between the share of SOEs in an industry and leverage are both reinforced in industries that are both concentrated and dominated by SOEs.

CONCLUSION

Despite there being a large number of studies comparing the economic performance of state-owned and private firms in transition economies, few studies have looked closely at differences in firm behavior in mixed markets in which private firms and state-owned firms compete. As our study shows, private firms and SOEs indeed behave differently in many ways.

We found that Chinese state-owned firms are more aggressive in price adjustment and new-product introduction and marketing. They spend more on sales and borrow more from outside and invest more, although they maintain larger inventories. Moreover, when we classified firms into three types based on the proportion of their registered capital held by the state, we found variations in the effects of state shares on the firms' behavior.

The progress of SOE reform, measured by the ratio of state-controlled firms to private firms in an industry, also has an impact on firms' behavior. In addition, we found a positive interaction between the proportion of SOEs in an industry and the structure of the industry. A firm's behavior is influenced simultaneously by its ownership structure, by its market structure, and by the level of reform within SOEs.

The results of this study have improved our understanding of firms' behavior in China, a mixed market in which private firms and state-owned firms compete. Our results are based on unique industrial census data, which do have several limitations. For instance, the degree of market mix could be measured using the market share of SOEs or a market share–adjusted measure, instead of number of firms.

Moreover, the variables used in this study are from a single data source. As in a transitional economy, firms' behavior and performance are strongly influenced by external factors. We have not included in this study explicit policy variables capturing changes in the external operational environment, but only a dummy variable for time. Strategic choice variables such as diversification along other dimensions should be included in future studies.

This chapter is a first attempt to try to understand the behavior of different types of firms in

Table 10.8

Regressions on Leverage (hypothesis 6)[a]

	Dependent variable: Leverage							
	Model 1	Model 2	Model 3	Model 4	Model 1'	Model 2'	Model 3'	Model 4'
Private firm[b]	-0.02** (-19.25)	-0.02** (-17.98)	-0.02** (-18.6)	-0.02** (-17.48)				
d1state share					-0.04** (-4.67)	-0.04** (-4.20)	-0.05** (-5.17)	-0.04** (-4.73)
d2state share					-0.01** (-6.38)	-0.01** (-6.24)	-0.02** (-7.06)	-0.02** (-6.94)
d3state share					0.03** (23.77)	0.03** (22.97)	0.03** (22.57)	0.03** (21.77)
Proportion of state-owned firms	-0.02** (-6.32)		-0.02** (-4.91)	-0.01** (-3.07)	-0.03** (-10.15)	-0.03** (-7.86)	-0.03** (-8.63)	-0.02** (-6.15)
Market structure	-0.03** (-2.85)	-0.04 (-1.08)	-0.02* (-1.98)	0.07* (1.99)	-0.03** (-2.86)	0.04 (1.15)	-0.02* (-2.04)	0.07* (2.23)
Private × market structure		0.05* (2.45)		0.05* (2.56)				
State share × market structure						0.10** (5.05)		0.10** (4.82)
Proportion of state-owned firms × market structure		-0.13** (-2.65)		-0.17** (-3.40)		-0.22** (-4.60)		-0.26** (-5.32)
Firm size	0.01** (22.03)	0.01** (22.04)			0.01** (20.45)	0.01** (20.36)		

(continued)

194

Table 10.8 (continued)

| | Dependent variable: Leverage | | | | | | | |
	Model 1	Model 2	Model 3	Model 4	Model 1'	Model 2'	Model 3'	Model 4'
Employees			0.02** (58.91)	0.02** (58.98)			0.02** (58.17)	0.02** (58.17)
Dum00	−0.001 (−1.29)	−0.001 (−1.22)	0.001 (1.20)	0.001 (1.28)	−0.002** (−3.07)	−0.002** (−2.96)	−0.0004 (−0.59)	−0.0003 (−0.47)
Dum99	0.001* (2.28)	0.001* (2.34)	0.002** (3.96)	0.002** (4.04)	0.001 (1.61)	0.001 (1.69)	0.002** (3.27)	0.002** (3.37)
Constant	0.68** (161.38)	0.68** (157.29)	0.48** (165.3)	0.48** (156.99)	0.67** (159.75)	0.67** (156.01)	0.48** (167.66)	0.48** (159.81)
χ^2	917**	936**	3,916**	3,942**	1,243**	1,280**	4,226**	4,268**
R^2	0.01	0.01	0.02	0.02	0.01	0.01	0.02	0.02

[a]All of the regressions use random-effects regression, so the values in parentheses are z-statistics.
[b]Ownership type is measured by the dummy variable *private firm* in models 1–4 and by three categorical variables, *d1state share, d2stateshare,* and *d3stateshare* in models 1'–4'. Firm size is measured by the six-category variable in models 1–2 and 1'–2' and is measured by the number of employees in models 3–4 and 3'–4'.

*Statistically significant at 5% confidence level.
**Statistically significant at 1% confidence level.

a mixed market. The next step will be to identify the relationship between the differences in firms' behavior and their performance. Such future research should generate important performance implications.

NOTES

This chapter is part of a large research initiative, Private Firms in China, being conducted at the Hong Kong University of Science and Technology. Comments from participants in the Workshop on Private Firms in China at the Hong Kong University of Science and Technology and the 2004 Summer Workshop of Industrial Organization and Management Strategy at Peking University are gratefully acknowledged. The authors thank Leonard Cheng, Anne Tsui, and Yijiang Wang for their careful review and constructive comments on an early version of this chapter. We are also grateful for the financial support of the Hong Kong Research Grant Council, as well as the excellent research assistance of Zeng Yuping.

1. In the process of economic reform, the composition of firms also evolves under different ownership. In the early years of reform, private firms were virtually nonexistent. Instead, collectively owned enterprises, such as township-and-village enterprises, were the typical form of enterprise in the nonstate sector. As economic reform progresses, private firms have become the dominant force in the nonstate sector.

2. This term was coined to characterize an oligopoly in which public and private firms interact (Bos 1991).

3. Here "market structure" refers to the number of firms and the size distribution of those firms and "industry composition" refers to the distribution of the state and private firms in a market.

4. See, for instance, Scherer and Ross (1990).

5. Surveys of early literature on China's enterprise reforms can be found in Jefferson and Rawski (1994) and in Groves, Hong, McMillan, and Naughton (1994). More recent studies have shown that ownership reforms improve the efficiency of SOEs (Li and Wu 2004).

REFERENCES

Bos, D. (1991). *Economics of privatization.* Oxford: Oxford University Press.

Eckel, C., and T. Vermaelen. (1986). Internal regulation: The effect of government ownership on the value of the firm. *Journal of Law and Economics, 29,* 381–404.

Ehrlich, I.; G. Gallais-Hamonno; R. Lutter; and Z. Liu. (1994). Productivity growth and firm ownership. *Journal of Political Economy, 102,* 1006–38.

Groves, T.; Y. Hong; J. McMillan; and B. Naughton. (1994). Autonomy and incentives in Chinese state enterprises. *Quarterly Journal of Economics, 1,* 183–209.

Jefferson, G., and T. Rawski. (1994). Enterprise reforms in Chinese industry. *Journal of Economic Perspective, 8,* 47–70.

Li, D., and C. Wu. (2004). Privatization at the margin. Working paper, Hong Kong University of Science and Technology.

Scherer, F. M., and D. Ross. (1990). *Industrial market structure and economic performance* (3rd ed.). New York: Rand McNally.

Tan, J. (2002). Impact of ownership type on environment-strategy linkage and performance: Evidence from a transitional economy. *Journal of Management Studies, 39,* 333–55.

Zhang, W., and Ma, J. (1999). Ownership foundation of excessive competition (in Chinese). *Economic Research, 6,* 11–20.

11

IN MARKETPLACE AND BOARDROOM

WHAT DO WE KNOW AND NOT KNOW ABOUT CHINA'S NONSTATE ENTERPRISES?

Yijiang Wang

Each of the three chapters in this part of this book is very interesting and important in its own right, with an important perspective on China's nonstate enterprises (NSEs). The chapter by Li provides a quite broad and deep survey of the literature on NSEs, helping the reader to grasp the main issues regarding these enterprises within the context of China's political, legal, and social institutions and reform experiences. The chapter by Wu and Li studies how firms behave under different types of ownership and in different market structures, contributing a great deal to the question of what to expect of Chinese firms in the marketplace. The chapter by Chen, Fan, and Wong studies the composition of the boards of China's listed companies in terms of their proportions of politicians, experts, and professionals. It provides much insight into what happens inside the boardrooms of these listed firms. Together, the three chapters provide a rich picture of the history and the present situation of NSEs in China in the marketplace and the boardroom, and their implications for the economy.

This commentary is an effort first to review and evaluate the main points of each chapter, and then to discuss how the study of each topic might be extended.

LI: SURVEY OF THE NONSTATE ENTERPRISES LITERATURE

Setting the Tone

Being a veteran and renowned researcher in this area, David Li has done a superb job explaining both issues related to and research on NSEs. For anyone who is interested in NSEs for either research or practical purposes and wishes to become more familiar with the literature, this survey is an excellent place to start.

Li starts with a careful definition of NSEs, pointing out that, although in many aspects the NSEs are like private enterprises, the two types of enterprises are not exactly the same. Because private ownership of productive means used to—and to some extent still does—carry "negative social and political connotations and invite discriminatory policy treatment," private enterprises in China often disguise themselves in various forms. Consequently, the distinctions among private, collective, and state-owned enterprises (SOEs) are blurred. Much of the study of China's NSEs has centered around the question, What are the substantive implications of these various nominal forms of ownership arrangement? The question is not only interesting, but also very important practically. As Li's statistics show, the NSE has been the most dynamic force in China's reform process, and a pillar of the economy.

Topics Surveyed and Main Conclusions

After setting the tone, the main part of Li's survey covers three groups of issues in the literature. These issues are:

* the environment surrounding China's NSEs,
* NSEs' organizational responses to the environment,
* the behavior and performance of China's NSEs.

The Environment Surrounding China's NSEs

Li provides a historical review of the ideological, political, legal, and policy environment of NSEs. The time period the review covers spans from the Communist takeover of national political power in 1949 to the present. The review makes clear that the Chinese Communist Party (CCP) has a history of being very unfriendly or openly hostile to private enterprises. Outright hostility prevails when the Party's policies on NSEs are more ideologically and politically oriented. The hostility level drops when the Party has more pragmatic concerns—that is, when the Party and its local branches care more about economic development for employment, revenue, and other economic goods. However, even at the best of times, NSEs do not play with state enterprises on a level field: they are not allowed in certain key industries, they are more scrutinized when they apply for bank loans, and their legal rights are often violated.

NSEs' Organizational Responses to the Environment

Given an environment that swings between unfriendliness and outright hostility, China's NSEs would not have had a chance to grow if they could not find ways to obtain political protection and resources. Realizing that the solutions to both problems were actually in the same powerful hand—the CCP or, synonymously, the government—the majority of NSEs across the country all came to an unlikely organizational strategy for their businesses: teaming up with the government. To this purpose, various creative forms of ownership were devised, with township-and-village enterprises (TVEs) perhaps the best-known example. The essence of ownership in TVEs, as Chang and Wang (1994), Li (1996), and others have pointed out, is that an NSE yields part of its control and benefit rights to the local government in exchange for political protection and better access to resources. Che and Qian (1998a, b) further address the intriguing question of how teaming up with a township- or village-level government can protect a TVE from possible predation by a higher-level government.

Li's survey also covers ownership change in NSEs. Since nonconventional ownership arrangements are NSEs' responses to their environment, it follows that ownership forms continue to change with the environment. Privatization prevails when the environment becomes more market oriented and competitive.

The Behavior and Performance of China's NSEs

Government ownership in NSEs is not just nominal, but has behavioral implications as well. NSEs with a history of strong government intervention continue to have a high level of labor participation in finance and decision making, even after the withdrawal of government owner-ship. Being an owner or not, a local government is likely to superimpose some employment goal on an NSE within its jurisdiction. An important question here, then, is, What difference does privatization make when government gives up ownership? The empirical literature Li surveyed suggests that income inequality will increase. This is taken as a sign that privatization strengthens NSEs' profit motivation, leading them to reward different factors more according to the market values of these factors; for example, scarce managerial skills vis-à-vis unskilled labor.

The reports of more market-oriented behaviors of NSEs are consistent with those on NSEs' performance. Here, the findings of comparative studies from three different perspectives are most interesting and informative. First, NSEs are more efficient than SOEs. Second, the performance of China's NSEs is comparable with that of similar firms in other developing countries. Finally, NSEs can do even better when their ownership is further "clarified," which usually means that the government plays a more limited role in NSE governance and decision making.

Tao and Zhu (2001) noticed that, although it is generally good for efficiency and viewed positively by economists, a strong profit motivation might actually cause additional difficulty in NSEs' finances. Their insight is that—in an economy where the level of trust is low and contract enforcement is weak—stronger profit motivation means that an NSE is more likely to behave opportunistically; for example, it might be more inclined to breach a financial contract for short-term gain than an SOE.

Future Studies

Li lists a number of important topics regarding NSEs that are currently understudied.

- "Original sin," which refers to immoral or even illegal activities of owners of many NSEs for self-enrichment. The issue has recently received much publicity in China. Li points out the lack of empirical studies of the types and magnitudes of "sin" and questions the relevance of the issue to the study of NSEs.
- The emerging pattern of ownership of China's NSEs. Are they becoming more like firms in Hong Kong, with family-owned businesses as the dominant form, or Western-like public companies with dispersed ownership? Concerns on this issue could arise from its distributional and social implications.
- The pattern of corporate governance, which is an issue related to ownership. The chapter by Chen, Fan, and Wong falls under this topic.
- Macroeconomic implications of the emergence of NSEs, especially when they become dominant in the economy. To address this issue, researchers need to better understand the behavior of NSEs with regard with investment, pricing, and so on. The chapter by Wu and Li is a valuable effort to address this question.

Besides the issues mentioned by Li listed above, addressing the following issues and questions could also contribute to the study of NSEs, the Chinese economy, and mainstream economics.

1. What is the NSEs' optimization problem? Although theoretical and empirical explanations of the rise of the NSE in China and its nature have been plentiful, so far no rigorous theory of the

NSE has been constructed in terms of an optimization problem. Such an omission is neither trivial nor inconsequential. We are reminded of how much effort mainstream economists put into the study of optimization and the amount of insight such study provides. We also recall how much we have learned from the seminal work of Ward (1958) on labor-managed firms. The model of Bai, Li, and Wang (1997) on SOEs is in the same spirit. We are not denying that the neoclassical model of the firm—cast in terms of a profit-maximization problem—has never been completely satisfactory. It has been criticized by economists and experts in other disciplines, including prominent psychologists such as March and Simon, who proposed a "behavioral theory of the firm" in the 1960s. But this is not a reason for scholars not to build a baseline model of the NSE with its objective function and its optimization problem explicitly specified. Once a baseline model is in place, there will always be room for enrichment and extension by incorporating more realistic behavioral and institutional assumptions.

2. How do the study of and findings about NSEs relate to the logic and core ideas of mainstream economics? Certainly, the tools used in the study of NSEs (and other issues of the Chinese economy as well), such as contracting theory, statistics, and so on are usually drawn from modern economics. However, at a deeper level, the link is either not explicit or simply missing. For example, the study of ownership in NSEs has been extensive and fruitful in helping researchers understand NSEs' ownership features and the possible reasons for these features. However, it remains vague as to how the findings relate to such mainstream theories as those of, among others, Coase (1937), Grossman and Hart (1988), and Williamson (1985).

Does the success of China's NSEs with unconventional ownership forms suggest that mainstream theory is too limited and thus needs to be augmented? If so, how? My own answer to these questions is that the study of ownership in China's NSEs shares several key elements with the mainstream theory of ownership, and also departs from it in one important aspect. The shared elements are, first, ownership becomes relevant when contracting or contract enforcement is difficult. Second, control and benefit allocation involve costs and benefits. Ownership is arranged to find the best deal in a trade-off between the two sides. Finally, where the best trade-off is depends on a set of parameters, such as information and the relative importance of inputs. Given these shared core elements, findings on ownership in China's NSEs can only be seen as applications of the mainstream theory. However, an important deviation is that, in determining the relative importance of inputs and, thus, optimal ownership, the established theory focuses on various informational problems in contracting and contract enforcement in a fair court. In contrast, the study of ownership in NSEs points to problems in the legal institution itself—the lack of an unbiased court independent of political and, possibly, other influences. The significance of such a deviation cannot be overemphasized: In a typical developing country, the lack of market-supporting political and legal institutions is at least as prominent a problem as various informational problems.

3. How do we reconcile different theories with more sophisticated empirical work? It is generally believed that NSEs are discriminated against in obtaining bank loans. Tao and Zhu (2001), on the other hand, argued convincingly that NSEs tend (more than other types of firms) to breach financial contracts. This raises a challenging empirical question: How much is NSEs' difficulty in obtaining bank loans a result of discrimination, and how much is a result of banks' use of sound economic criteria? More meaningful policy recommendations for NSEs' finances need more solid empirical insight into this question.

4. Does the method used to privatize a firm—either changing it from an SOE to an NSE or further reducing the role of government in an existing NSE—matter? The concern here is twofold: First, how is postprivatization governance, conduct, and performance affected? Second,

how does the process affect income distribution and thus social and political stability in China? Here we are reminded of the effects of privatization in Eastern Europe and the former Soviet states on economies and social structures. Currently, managerial buyout has become a very sensitive issue in China, with its efficiency and equity implications heatedly debated.

5. What is the interactive relationship between NSEs and China's political and legal institutions? So far, the study of NSEs has focused mostly on how they emerged and grew under these institutions. It is most likely that the NSEs have also influenced the development of political and legal institutions in China and will continue to do so. The recent constitutional amendment to protect private property and the Party's effort to enlist members among NSE business owners—and even place them in Party leadership positions—are just some of the most visible examples. Recognizing the success of the NSEs and their critical role in dealing with many social and economic challenges in China, the more pragmatic side of the Party grew stronger and introduced these changes to encourage the further development of the NSEs. Since China's political and legal institutions greatly influence important variables such as ownership, governance, and, in turn, conduct and performance of the NSEs, how the interactive relationship will evolve and what cumulative effect the success of NSEs will have on China's institutions are necessarily questions of great importance. Their answers will help scholars understand both the future of NSEs and other important economic issues in China.

6. How does the integration of China into the global economy change the environment and thus future development of the NSEs? China is now a World Trade Organization (WTO) member and is integrating rapidly into the global economy in terms of trade, production, finance, technology, and other respects. Globalization has provided Chinese firms, NSEs included, a new and much larger platform. Besides all the explicit legal commitments the Chinese government has made, increased factor mobility in an open economy also gives NSEs new means to protect their interests and thereby greatly strengthen their bargaining positions in dealing with the government. The other side of the coin is that the indigenous Chinese NSEs now need to learn how to survive real competition in the global arena.

WU AND LI: FIRM BEHAVIOR IN A MIXED MARKET

Ownership, Structure, and Conduct

Wu and Li start with the observation that many industries in China contain firms under different types of ownership: NSEs, SOEs, and multinational corporations (MNCs). The question they ask and try to empirically answer is, How do firms in such a mixed market behave? The authors further observe that such a mixed structure of ownership in a market is not unique to China, but is fairly common in Western market economies, suggesting a rather general significance of their study. They mention banking in Germany, commercial aviation in Canada, and mail service in the United States as examples.

Wu and Li adopted the standard structure-conduct-performance paradigm to study the question, which implies that they assume oligopoly in the industries to be studied. The point of departure from other studies of oligopolistic competition is that they do not assume profit maximization for all firms. The departure is easily justified, since it is well known that SOEs have noneconomic objectives and are subject to soft budget constraints.

The data set they use is the industrial census compiled by the National Bureau of Statistics (NBS) of China, which contains data on 100,000 firms in manufacturing with annual sales above RMB 200,000 over a three-year period, from 1999 through 2001.

Major Findings

A set of very rich and sometimes surprising results emerged from this study.

- SOEs raise their prices more than private firms. This result is somewhat surprising because, with noneconomic objectives, SOEs are not supposed to be more responsive to market forces than private firms. The authors see this as evidence that over time the SOEs have become less like social welfare maximizers and more like profit maximizers.
- Larger firms adjust their prices more quickly than smaller firms, given market structure.
- Private firms produce and sell fewer new products than SOEs. The finding that SOEs are more innovative than private firms might be surprising at first glance. However, if we realize that SOEs control far more resources and are not subject to hard budget constraints, their generosity in R&D spending becomes easy to understand.
- Industries with greater SOE concentration sell fewer new products. The authors explain this finding by saying that the less reformed an industry is, the less the value of the new products in total sales. This explanation is plausible when it stands alone. However, it is not clear how one might reconcile it with the previous one that, within particular industries, SOEs sell more new products.
- A larger state-ownership share in a firm leads to a larger ratio of sales spending to revenue. The authors again explain this finding by soft budget constraints for SOEs, and possible corruption in using sales budgets.
- Private firms maintain lower inventories than SOEs. This finding is not surprising; it reflects the cost sensitivity of private firms, and its lack in SOEs. What is true within an industry, however, is again not true across industries. The study shows that industries still dominated by SOEs have lower inventory levels.
- Within industries, SOEs invest more than private firms. Across industries, those with greater SOE concentration invest more. Also contributing to more investment are firm size and higher concentration ratio in an industry.
- SOEs have greater leverage than private firms, borrowing more heavily from banks. This is particularly true if the government's ownership share is greater than 70 percent. However, the result does not carry across industries. When an industry has greater SOE concentration, its leverage actually goes down.

Further Discussion

Some of the empirical findings regarding the behavior of SOEs are not surprises—for example, compared with private firms, SOEs hold more inventory, borrow more, and spend more generously to promote sales and new products. Others are quite surprising: for example, SOEs respond more rapidly to market forces, as reflected in their price adjustment. Wu and Li try to explain both the surprises and the nonsurprises individually with various theories, such as noting the effects of soft budget constraints. However, the authors must have realized the lack of a coherent and consistent theory to explain all these—or at least several of these—empirical findings. By observing this fact, I am trying to make the point that, while empirical study of the conduct of firms in a mixed ownership structure is rare and much needed, so is a theory on the topic.

A model of competition in such a mixed industry should have the following specifications.

1. The SOE has an objective that is, say, a linear combination of profit and other motivation with parameterized weights.

2. The SOE has a budget with a parameter measuring its softness. For example, the participation constraint for the SOE is its profit being greater than a negative number.
3. The SOE competes with the NSE that pursues only profit and has a hard budget—that is,
   its participation constraint is nonnegative profit.
4. Possible choice variables in both firms' optimization problems in a competitive game
   include output level; price; sales expenditure represented by, say, advertisement expenditure; R&D; investment, inventory; and so on.

Among these features, points 3 and 4—the assumptions about private firms and competitive
variables—are conventional in industrial organization theories. However, points 1 and 2 deviate
from the conventions and incorporate our understanding of the SOE. What we would like to find
out are the following factors.

- What the equilibrium output, price, or other variables are like. If simultaneously studying
  several of these variables is technically too messy, the model can address one of them at a
  time, as is often done in industrial organization theory studies.
- How the relative weights of different objectives of the SOE affect the above equilibrium.
  The answer to this question can come from a comparative statics study of the objective
  weights mentioned in point 1.
- How the degree of budget softness affects the above equilibrium.
- How the findings of such a theoretical model would compare with those of an empirical
  study—for example, the one by Wu and Li.

CHEN, FAN, AND WONG: LOCAL GOVERNMENT AND BOARD
STRUCTURE IN CHINA'S LISTED FIRMS

Government and Board Structure: The Context and the
Significance of the Question

In Chapter 9 in this volume—"Decentralization and the Structure of Chinese Corporate Boards:
Do Politicians Jeopardize Board Professionalism and Firm Performance?"—Chen, Fan, and
Wong raise a very pointed and very important question: What individuals are on the boards
of China's listed companies? The study helps us to better see where government stands relative to human capital (expertise and professional skills) in running China's listed companies,
as well as how top personnel decisions in China's listed companies are influenced by the
political system.

In China's listed companies, the state has held the majority share: 67 percent in 1994 and
61 percent in 2000. A certain degree of separation of ownership and management does exist,
as the central government has granted much operational autonomy to these listed companies.
Autonomy from the central government, however, does not necessarily mean autonomy from
government. With local governments filling the vacancy left by the central government, a
new exchange relationship has emerged: corporations bribe local politicians in exchange for
favors in resource allocation and market protection. A formal, organizational arrangement to
facilitate this exchange relationship is the appointment of local politicians to the boards of
directors.

The data the authors used are from 621 companies that went public in China during 1993–
2000.

Major Findings

The authors present a set of rich and interesting findings. (In parentheses are Chen, Fan, and Wong's explanations for their empirical findings.)

- Board size in China's listed companies is negatively related to the degree of largest-shareholder presence and politician presence. (Small size allows the largest shareholder and politicians to more easily control a board.)
- Board size is positively related to firm size and complexity. (Larger and more complex firms need more professionals to manage them.)
- The fraction of directors with business experience is negatively related to largest-shareholder presence, but not related to politician presence. (The largest shareholder plays a management role, substituting for outside directors with business experience. Politicians typically do not.)
- The fraction of professional directors on a board is negatively related to the degree of politician presence, but not related to the degree of largest-shareholder presence on the board. (The presence of politicians on the board signals the firm's noneconomic goals and a lack of product-market competition that renders professional services not so valuable.)
- Largest-shareholder and politician presence lead to fewer women directors, and higher average education and age, with female presence a proxy for professionalism and age its opposite.
- When Chen, Fan, and Wong divided politicians into three categories—those associated with central, local, and other governments—they found that only politicians associated with "other" governments had a negative effect on board size. (Control of a board is most difficult for politicians from other than local government. A smaller board is easier to control.)
- The fraction of manager directors is strongly negatively related to the strength of local politician presence but unrelated to the presence of politicians connected with the central or other governments. (This is evidence of decentralization and local government control of listed firms.)
- The negative relationship of directors with business experience to politicians mainly concerns local politicians. The negative relationship of professional directors and politicians pertains for all three categories of politicians.
- Educational level is negatively related to the presence of local politicians. It is positively related to the presence of two other types of politicians. Politician presence is associated with fewer women directors and a higher average director's age.

Further Discussion

Why should we care about what is going on in the boardrooms of China's listed companies? The answer, as Chen, Fan, and Wong suggest with many descriptive statistics, is that the economy is being rapidly "corporatized." One can also add that for the Chinese government, to reform ailing, inefficient SOEs is often synonymous with turning them into publicly listed corporations, especially the larger and more important ones. Given the existing and anticipated greater importance of public corporations in China in the future, interest in their organizational features, conduct, and performance is fully justified.

How much do researchers know about the personnel, governance, and organizational features of China's listed companies? It is not much—far short of what we need to know. Many of the studies on China's listed companies have focused on their performance. The study by Chen, Fan, and Wong focuses on an important governance question and is a welcome and important contribution. But it is only a beginning. Empirical studies have yet to provide sufficient information regarding the mobility, compensation, and functioning of board members in China's listed companies. Particularly important is how the CCP and its Organization Department influence these variables, at different levels of the Party hierarchy. Empirical information in this regard will be critical for knowing to what extent China's business organizations and business leaders can and are basing decisions on sound economic and business criteria, rather than on criteria based on their political aspirations. It can be noted that mainstream economics lacks several potentially key theories: a theory of personnel when politics is a major factor, a theory of rational behavior of the politician-businessperson, and a theory of the implications of such politician-businesspeople for business organizations.

How do the executives of a listed company respond to strong political control by the Party? This is another very important empirical and theoretical question that has not received enough attention. Casual observations suggest that the executives of China's listed companies, especially those in which the government owns nontrivial shares, do not just wait for the political system to determine their fates. They also do many things to advance their careers in the political system. Below is a set of things they can and often will do.

- Work on their political ties and build political support in the government system. This is common sense and does not need much elaboration.
- Grow their firms to meet political criteria and thereby become model companies and model entrepreneurs. For example, an executive can receive much political glory and thereby become politically much better endowed by making his or her firm a "national pride." This can be achieved through extensive foreign investment and breaking into foreign product markets; however, the cost of doing so may be so high that it does not make much economic sense.
- Grow the firm as quickly as possible and make its internal relationships as complex as possible. A firm is internally more complex when it has many units (as independent legal units, if necessary) in a large number of different and unrelated industries, and these units have mutual ownership holdings, debt (e.g., heavy borrowing from state banks on each other's collateral), personnel, and supply-and-demand relations. A larger firm is more important for employment and for social stability, which is always a goal of utmost importance for the Party. When a large firm becomes so internally complex, removing a top executive becomes more difficult for the Party, for it realizes the risk of breaking the complex and delicate financial (and other) relations within the firm, which is bound to have undesirable employment and financial repercussions.

As one can easily see from these examples of what top executives of firms in China can and often will do to gain political leverage, the personnel and governance issues in these firms are important not only for their own sake, but also because they have profound implications for business decisions and efficiency. Study of these implications can help scholars to better understand Chinese firms' zeal for growth, heavy debt finance, and weak internal checks and balances; further, such studies could help scholars understand why so many firms have eventually been found to be "empty" and have suddenly collapsed after years of fame and glory based on self-claimed and Party-stamped successes.

There are certainly many reasons for the sudden deaths of many Chinese firms. Random adverse events can sometimes catch a firm off guard and cause its rapid demise. Another possibility is that some of the successful firms were opportunists to begin with. When they grew rapidly, however, they often failed to invest in the organizational structure and management teams able to deal with environmental changes, such as intensification in competition. Some companies have remained under the single-handed control of a visionary founder, with employees playing the simple role of taking orders from the omnipotent boss. When the boss is wrong, there is no system by which to contain the errors. Also, when the boss runs out of good ideas, the organization cannot generate its own. The lack of resiliency and sustainable power might be a problem for Chinese firms for many years to come. Continued political interference and the kinds of politically motivated responses that we described above can only aggravate the problem.

REFERENCES

Bai, C.; D. Li; and Y. Wang. (1997). Enterprise productivity and efficiency: When is up really down? *Journal of Comparative Economics,* 24, 265–80.

Chang, C., and Y. Wang. (1994). The nature of the township enterprises. *Journal of Comparative Economics,* 19, 434–52.

Che, J., and Y. Qian. (1998a). Institutional environment, community government, and corporate governance: Understanding China's township-village enterprises. *Journal of Law, Economics, and Organization,* 14, 1–23.

———. (1998b). Insecure property rights and government ownership of firms. *Quarterly Journal of Economics,* 113, 467–96.

Coase, R. (1937). The nature of the firm. *Economics,* 4, 368–405.

Grossman, S., and O. Hart. (1988). One share/one vote and the market for corporate control. *Journal of Financial Economics,* 20, 175–202.

Li, D. (1996). A theory of ambiguous property rights in transition economies: The case of the Chinese non-state sector. *Journal of Comparative Economics,* 23, 1–19.

Tao, Z., and T. Zhu. (2001). An agency theory of transactions without contract enforcement: The case of China. *China Economic Review,* 12, 1–14.

Ward, B. (1958). The firm in Illyria: Market syndicalism. *American Economic Review,* 48 (September), 566–89.

Williamson, O. E. (1985). *The economic institutions of capitalism: Firms, markets, relational contracting.* New York: Free Press.

12

CHINA'S DOMESTIC PRIVATE FIRMS

A LITERATURE REVIEW AND
DIRECTIONS FOR FUTURE RESEARCH

Jiatao Li and Jing Yu Yang

China is the largest transitional economy in the world. After more than two decades of sustained economic reform, a significant domestic private business sector has reemerged as one of the key driving forces behind China's rapid economic development (Asian Development Bank, 2003). We define China's domestic private firms as those firms or organizations owned and managed by Chinese citizens, including township enterprises, collectives, and individual start-ups. These are by far the most important source of income and employment growth for China (the Asian Development Bank estimates that the nonstate sector accounted for over two-thirds of GDP in China in 2002). The increasing significance of the private sector in China underscores an urgent need for systematic knowledge of its growth and development. To date, scientific studies of management and organizations in China have focused mainly on state-owned firms and those with foreign direct investment. However, the domestic private firms, undoubtedly among the most dynamic entities of China's economy, have so far received limited research attention.

In this chapter, we provide an overview of the extant research on management and organization issues related to China's emerging domestic private sector. We review the literature published in twenty-four leading English-language academic journals over the eighteen years from 1986 through 2003. From this review, we identify ninety-two articles related to China's private businesses and characterize them along two dimensions: the subject of study and the research methods employed. We have three objectives for this literature survey. The first is to provide scholars with knowledge about the types of management and organization research that have been done on China's domestic private business since 1986, the research issues or topics addressed, and the research methods used in these studies. The second objective is to map the contributions of this literature by reviewing key findings and conclusions, identifying research opportunities in the literature, and synthesizing these findings and opportunities from a strategic management perspective. Our third objective is to delineate important areas for future research.

The chapter is organized as follows. First, we identify a set of leading English-language academic journals that publish China-related management and organization research. Second, from these leading English journals, we develop a comprehensive database of articles related to management and organization issues of China's domestic private business over the 1986–2003 period. Third, we analyze the research issues, methods, and key conclusions of these studies. Drawing on the above substantive analysis, we clarify gaps in the literature and suggest some areas for future research.

A SURVEY OF MANAGEMENT AND ORGANIZATION RESEARCH ON CHINA'S PRIVATE FIRMS

Journal Sources and Article Selection

We considered four key factors when choosing the academic journals to be included in the literature survey. First, we sought to include management and organization journals that previous studies of levels of influence indicated were in the top tier (e.g., Johnson and Podsakoff 1994, Li and Tsui 2002, Park and Gordon 1996, Peng et al. 2001, Tahai and Meyer 1999). Second, we included entrepreneurship and small business journals as well as journals emphasizing international and cross-cultural research that have contributed to understanding of both macro, organization-level and micro, individual-level management issues related to China's private business and entrepreneurial development (e.g., Johnson and Podsakoff 1994, Shane 1997). Third, given that research on China appeared initially in area studies journals (e.g., Li and Tsui 2002, Peng et al. 2001), we included three Chinese journals. Finally, we focused primarily on academic journals that publish writings derived from rigorous scientific methods. Reviews of periodicals primarily for practicing managers and professionals, such as the *Harvard Business Review*, revealed only a few articles related to China's domestic private businesses. We thus excluded those managerial journals from the sample for the substantive review, but will discuss them in later sections in a supplementary analysis.

Twenty-four journals were selected for the sample; Table 12.1 identifies them. The sample includes sixteen leading academic journals in management, strategy, and organizational behavior (e.g., the *Academy of Management Journal*, *Strategic Management Journal*, and the *Journal of Applied Psychology*); five entrepreneurship and small business journals (e.g., *Entrepreneurship Theory and Practice*, the *Journal of Business Venturing*, and the *Journal of Small Business Management*); and three area-study journals (*China Quarterly*, *China Journal*,* and *Journal of Contemporary China*). These journals are published in Asia, Australia, Europe, and North America and represent the primary outlets for high-quality local and global organization and management research (Johnson and Podsakoff 1994, Li and Tsui 2002, Lohrke and Bruton 1997, Peng et al. 2001, Shane 1997, Tahai and Meyer 1999).

We used keywords such as "China," "Chinese," "private business," "private enterprise," "private sector," "township or village enterprise," "collective enterprise," and "family business" and relied on ABI/Inform within the ProQuest database service for the literature search. We selected 1986 as the starting year because both the International Finance Corporation (2000) and the Asian Development Bank (2003) describe 1984–86 as the beginning years of the development of the *siying qiye* (privately run enterprises) in China. To be included in the review an article had to address a theoretical or empirical issue related to China's domestic private business, either at the institutional/context, firm/strategy or psychological/micro level. Empirical studies had to include data based on companies or employees in the domestic private sector in China. We also cross-checked our database against the lists of China-related management and organization articles in several other published reviews (e.g., Li and Tsui 2002, Peng et al. 2001, White 2002).

---

*The *Australian Journal of Chinese Affairs* (1979–95) continues as the *China Journal* (1995–present). For details, refer to www.jstor.org/journals/13249347.html.

Table 12.1

**Management and Organization Research on China's Private Firms:
Survey of Twenty-Four Academic Journals, 1986–2003[a]**

	Number of articles		
Journal field and name	Subtotal	1986–94	1995–2003
Management	38	9	29
Asia Pacific Journal of Management	6	0	6
Organization Studies	4	1	3
Academy of Management Journal	3	0	3
Administrative Science Quarterly	3	2	1
Journal of Applied Psychology	3	2	1
Journal of International Business Studies	3	1	2
Academy of Management Review	2	0	2
Journal of Management Studies	2	0	2
Journal of Occupational and Organizational Psychology	2	1	1
Journal of Organizational Behavior	2	0	2
Organization Science	2	0	2
Strategic Management Journal	2	0	2
Human Relations	1	0	1
Industrial and Labor Relations Review	1	0	1
Journal of Management	1	1	0
Management Science	1	1	0
Entrepreneurship and Small Business	26	8	18
Journal of Business Venturing	8	3	5
Journal of Small Business Management	8	2	6
Entrepreneurship Theory and Practice	5	0	5
International Small Business Journal	4	3	1
Journal of Developmental Entrepreneurship	1	0	1
Area Studies	28	8	20
China Quarterly	16	5	11
China Journal or Australia Journal of Chinese Affairs[b]	7	3	4
Journal of Contemporary China	5	0	5
Total	92	25	67

[a]Details on all ninety-two articles are listed in Appendix 12.1.
[b]The *Australian Journal of Chinese Affairs* (1979–95) continues as the *China Journal* (1995–present). For details, refer to www.jstor.org/journals/13249347.html.

This review identifies a total of ninety-two articles on China's private business in the twenty-four journals that meet the criteria for inclusion, with twenty-five articles published in the first nine-year period (1986–94) and sixty-seven articles in the second nine-year period (1995–2003), more than double the number of studies in the first period. Table 12.1 lists the number of articles in each of the twenty-four journals over the two time periods.

Two observations can be made from Table 12.1. The first concerns the publication outlets. The table shows that thirty-eight articles (41%) were published in the sixteen management journals; twenty-six (28%), in the five entrepreneurship and small-business journals; and twenty-eight (31%) in the three area study journals. Only seven of the twenty-four journals had published five or more articles on China's private business in the past eighteen years, and of the seven, only one was a management journal (the *Asia Pacific Journal of Management*). The other six journals publishing at least five germane articles included three entrepreneurship and small-business periodicals (the *Journal of Business Venturing, Journal of Small Business Management*, and *Entrepreneurship Theory and Practice*) and three area study journals (*China Quarterly, China Journal*, and the *Journal of Contemporary China*).

A second and related observation from Table 12.1 is that over time the number of these articles appearing in mainstream, first-tier management journals such as the *Academy of Management Journal, Organization Science*, and the *Strategic Management Journal* has increased, although it is still small. This pattern again indicates a growing interest in management issues in the Chinese private business context among scholars and journal editors. With the continuing market transition and the proliferation of a dynamic private sector in the Chinese economy, we believe that this trend will continue and that high-quality research related to China's private businesses and management will appear more frequently in leading management journals in the future.

Research Issues and Methods

What are the issues that have received research attention in the literature so far? Have there been any changes in the research topics over the eighteen years of the review period? To answer these two questions, we classified the ninety-two articles on China's private business by their levels of analysis and by the research issues they studied. We included three levels of analysis in the review: institutional/context, firm strategy/structure, and psychological/micro. Each of the two authors first independently listed issues investigated in the ninety-two articles. Through subsequent comparisons and discussions, we reached consensus on ten general topics, which are identified in Table 12.2. Each article was then coded as to the primary topic addressed in its research questions.

Table 12.2 shows a clear trend toward more articles in all areas over time. Of the ninety-two articles, sixty-two (67%) are firm-level studies, sixteen (17%) are institutional/context studies, and the remaining fourteen (16%) are individual/psychological studies. Studies at the macro/ institutional level tend to treat "China" as an institutional context, implying a social, political, and economic structure that may impact the managerial decisions and behavior of firms and individuals. Firm-level studies focus on various strategies and structures and their implications for firm growth and performance. Individual/psychological studies tend to treat "China" as a social-cultural variable, a proxy for cultural values that may influence behavior and decisions at the individual level.

In addition, we grouped the ninety-two studies according to the research methods used, including survey/quantitative studies, case-based/qualitative studies, and conceptual development/ overview studies. Table 12.3 presents this breakdown. Thirty-four of the studies are survey-based, and two-thirds of these (twenty-two articles) examine firm-level issues. There are eighteen articles that use a case-based approach. Finally, forty articles are conceptual development or review papers, with about two-thirds of these (twenty-six articles) addressing firm-level issues, and the remaining one-third (thirteen articles) addressing institutional/context issues. These studies usually consider the effects of institutional environments when examining the strategy, structure, and performance of firms operating in the Chinese context.

In summary, the ninety-two articles published in the twenty-four leading English-language journals over the past eighteen years provide us with a snapshot of past and current research interests in China's domestic private business. The increasing appearance of such studies in pres-

Table 12.2

**Management and Organization Research on China's Private Firms:
Research Themes and Topics**

	Number of articles		
	Subtotal	1986–94	1995–2003
Institutional/context	16	3	13
Market transition/business system	13	2	11
Mobility/occupation/income	3	1	2
Firm strategy/structure	62	13	49
Business/institutions interactions	18	8	10
Firm strategy/performance	16	1	15
Entrepreneurship/venture creation	16	4	12
Interfirm relationship/networks	7	0	7
Corporate governance/ownership	2	0	2
Employment relationship/HRM	3	3	
Psychological/micro	14	9	5
Managerial behavior/values	11	9	2
Individual/group outcomes	3	0	3
Total	92	25	67

Table 12.3

**Management and Organization Research on China's Private Firms:
Research Methods and Themes**

	Number of articles		
	Subtotal	Survey/ quantitative	Case study/ qualitative	Conceptual/ overview
---	---	---	---	---
Institutional/context	**16**	**1**	**2**	**13**
Market transition/business system	13	0	1	12
Mobility/occupation/income	3	1	1	1
Firm strategy/structure	**62**	**22**	**14**	**26**
Business/institutions interactions	18	0	6	12
Firm strategy/performance	16	10	1	5
Entrepreneurship/venture creation	16	4	5	7
Interfirm relationship/networks	7	4	1	2
Corporate governance/ownership	2	2	0	0
Employment relationship/HRM	3	2	1	0
Psychological/micro	**14**	**11**	**2**	**1**
Managerial behavior/values	11	8	2	1
Individual/group outcomes	3	3	0	0
Total	92	34	18	40

tigious journals suggests their value to global scholarship on management and organizations. Given the above overview, we can conclude that research on management and organization issues in China's domestic private business has attracted growing attention among global scholars.

Mapping the Contributions of the Literature

In this section, we summarize the key issues/conclusions of each article under the ten general research themes at three different levels: institutional/context, firm strategy/structure, and psychological/micro studies. Table 12.4 gives an overview of the studies' issues and contributions, and Appendix 12.1 lists the bibliographical details of all ninety-two works. Given the integrated nature of many studies, the distinction among these areas is somewhat arbitrary. However, we believe that such an intuitive organizing framework allows us to capture the essence of this literature.

Institutional/Context

A majority of the institutional/context studies describe the changing institutional environments in China to explain the emergence of private firms or changes in the private sector (Table 12.4a). The literature tends to treat "China" as an institutional context, encompassing social, political, and economic elements that have impacted the emergence of private business, as well as the evolution of business systems, social stratifications, labor markets, employment structures, and income and inequality.

Within this broad area, we identify two research themes: market transition/business system change, and mobility/occupation/inequality. Studies with the first research theme focus on the emergence of private business in China (Anderson et al. 2003; Anyansi-Archibong, Danenburg, and Tan 1989; Dana 1999; Liu 1992; Parries 1993), ownership and property rights reform (Guo 2003, Putterman 1995), and business system changes and implications (Child and Tse 2001, Francis 1996, Wei 2002). The mobility/occupation studies focus on issues such as the emergence of labor markets, employment structure change, and wage determination (Davis 1999 Parish, Zhe, and Li 1995; Sabin 1994).

Individual/Psychological

At this level we again identify two research themes: managerial behavior/values, and individual/group outcomes (Table 12.4b). Studies of the first theme include cultural and cross-cultural analyses of differences in managerial behavior/values (McGrath, MacMillan, and Tsai 1992; Okechuku 1994; Ralston 1992; Ralston et al.1993; Vertinsky et al. 1990), and entrepreneurial traits, role structures, characteristics, and patterns of Chinese managerial behavior (Boisot and Liang 1992, Holt 1997, Miner 1991, Shenkar et al. 1998, Siu 1995). For example, Holt (1997) explores whether there is a significant difference between Chinese entrepreneurs and managers with respect to systems of values. Other studies focus on individual and group outcomes such as organizational citizenship behavior (OCB), turnover, and commitment (Chen, Hui, and Sego 1998; Chen, Tsui, and Farh 2002; Tjosvold et al. 2002).

Firm Strategy/Structure

We classify the firm-level studies into six broad research topics: business/institution interactions, interfirm relationship/networks, corporate governance/ownership, firm strategy/performance,

Table 12.4

**Management and Organization Research on China's Private Firms:
Detailed Research Topics**

A. Institutional/Context Studies: Detailed Research Topics

Market Transition/Business system change	• Emergence of private business in China (Anderson et al. 2003, Anyansi-Archibong et al. 1989, Dana 1999, Liu 1992, Parries 1993)
	• Ownership and property rights reform (Guo 2003, Putterman 1995)
	• Business system change and implications (Child and Tse 2001, Francis 1996, Wei 2002)
Mobility/occupation/inequality	• Emergence of labor market, employment structure change, and wage determination (Davis 1999, Parish et al. 1995, Sabin 1994)

B. Psychological/Micro Studies: Detailed Research Topics

Managerial behavior/Values	• Cultural and cross-cultural analyses of differences in managerial behavior (McGrath et al. 1992, Okechuku 1994, Ralston 1992, Ralston et al.1993, Vertinsky et al. 1990)
	• Entrepreneurial traits, role structures, characteristics, and patterns of Chinese managerial behavior (Boisot and Liang 1992, Holt 1997, Miner 1991, Shenkar et al. 1998, Siu 1995)
Individual/group outcomes	• Individual outcomes: OCB, turnover, and commitment (Chen et al. 1998, 2002)
	• Group outcomes (Tjosvold et al. 2002)

C. Firm-Level Studies: Detailed Research Topics

Business/Institution Interactions	• Hybrid form, network capitalism, local corporatism, local government intervention in economic activities (Blecher and Shue 2001; Boisot and Child 1988, 1996; Danenburg and Tan 1989; Jiang and Ha11 1996; Unger and Chan 1999; Kwong 2000; Nee 1992; Oi 1995)
	• Conditions, threats/opportunities, social attitudes toward private business (Snell and Tseng 2002, Tsang 1994, Young 1991)
	• Private business associations (Nevitt 1996, Unger 1996)
	• Cultural value and business system (Redding 2002, Shenkar and von Glinow 1994, Whyte 1995)
Interfirm Relationships/Networks	• Cultural, institutional, and organizational factors on *guanxi* utilization and interorganizational network formation (Li 1998, Xin and Pearce 1996, Wank 1996)
	• Effects of *guanxi* network and interorganizational relationship on firm performance (Li and Atuahene-Gima 2002, Park and Luo 2001, Peng and Luo 2000)
Corporate Governance/Ownership	• Governance structure and firm performance (Tian and Lau 2001)
	• Ownership types and environment-strategy configurations (Tan 2002b)
Firm strategy/Performance	• Institutional transitions and organizational strategic choices; network-based strategy (Boisot and Child 1999, Peng 2003, Peng and Heath1996)

(continued)

Table 12.4 *(continued)*

Firm strategy/Performance	• Innovations, radical change, proactive strategies, risk-taking behavior (Keister 2002, Li and Atuahene-Gima 2001, Luo 1999)
	• Product diversification strategies, entry/exit decisions (Li and Wong 2003, Luo 1999, Wing 1996)
	• Environmental and organizational factors on firm growth, efficiency, and financial performance (Schlevogt 2001, Tong 2001, Tong and Chan 2003, Wing and Yiu 1996, 2000)
	• Organizational capability, transaction cost, and strategic choice (White and Liu 2001)
Entrepreneurship/Venture creation	• Institutional, cultural, economic influences on the emergence of entrepreneurs and the development of entrepreneurial ventures (Chang and MacMillan 1991, Cornwall 1998, Fan 1996, Matthews et al. 1996, Murphy 2000, Odgaard 1992, Siu 1992, Wing 1994, Zapalska 2001)
	• Entrepreneurial orientation such as proactiveness, risk-taking behavior, and growth intention (Tan 1996, 2001)
	• Entrepreneur networking (Wank 1996, Zhao and Aram 1995)
	• How entrepreneurs create, sustain, and manage organizations; strategic orientations (Ahlstrom and Bruton 2002, Lau and Busenitz 2001, Tan 2002a, Tsang 1996)
Employment relationship/HRM	• National, cultural comparisons of employment relations (Frenkel and Kuruvilla 2002)
	• Employment relationships/HRM and firm performance (Law et al. 2003, Wang et al. 2003)

entrepreneurship/venture creation, and employment relationship/human resource management (HRM) (Table 12.4c).

We focus our discussions below primarily on studies of firms in China's emerging domestic private business sector, including private firms, entrepreneurial start-ups, and township-and-village enterprises (TVEs), and examine their interactions with the institutional environments as well as strategy, structure, and performance consequences. We do not focus on the privatization and transformation of state-owned companies in this review.

When formulating and implementing its business strategies, a firm needs to consider its external environment, including the broader institutional influences (Oliver 1997, Powell and DiMaggio 1991). This is particularly important in transitional economies, where firms are more susceptible to the institutional influences and changes (Child 1994, Peng and Heath 1996, Shenkar and von Glinow 1994). This emphasis has been reflected in the studies in our review sample. For instance, many of the business/institution interactions studies have argued that the emergence of private firms and entrepreneurial activities in China suffers from institutional constraints and government interventions (Boisot and Child 1988, 1996; Jiang and Hall 1996; Nee 1992; Tsang 1994). Therefore, many of the studies, particularly those on private firms, have emphasized the importance of different types of strategies to manage institutional constraints, such as *guanxi* networks, interorganizational relationships, and public–private hybrid governance structures (Table 12.4c). In general, this emphasis differs from that of the strategic management literature (in the Western context), where the focus has been on achieving competitive advantages through building core competences and developing innovative capabilities (Barney 1991, Penrose 1959). We will return to this observation in later sections.

Other studies focus on new venture creation and entrepreneurship in China. Some of these examine the institutional, cultural, and economic influences on the emergence of entrepreneurs and the development of entrepreneurial ventures (Chang and MacMillan 1991; Cornwall 1998; Fan 1996; Matthews, Qin, and Franklin 1996; Murphy 2000; Odgaard 1992; Siu 1992; Wing 1994; Zapalska 2001). Others examine the entrepreneurial orientations in China's private sector, such as proactiveness, risk-taking behavior, and growth intentions (Tan 1996, 2001); entrepreneur networking (Wank 1996, Zhao and Aram 1995); and entrepreneurs' strategic orientations (Ahlstrom and Bruton 2002, Lau and Busenitz 2001, Tan 2002a, Tsang 1996). For example, recent studies show that, in addition to the "networking" and "boundary-blurring" strategies, China's private firms and entrepreneurs have begun to adopt alternative strategies such as "prospecting," in which a firm focuses on innovation and change within a changing market (Miles et al. 1978). Recent studies have further compared how differences between private and other types of firms, such as state-owned companies, affect their adopting proactive, innovative strategies and risk-taking behaviors (Keister 2002; Li and Atuahene-Gima 2001; Luo, Tan, and Shenkar 1998).

Among the remaining studies at the firm level, a number of them examine general corporate strategies and management topics, including product diversification (Li and Wong 2003, Luo 1999, Wing 1996); corporate governance and firm performance (Tian and Lau 2001); and employment relationships/HRM and firm performance (Law, Tse, and Zhou 2003; Wang et al. 2003). Other studies focus on identifying the environmental and organizational factors affecting private firm growth, efficiency, and financial performance (Schlevogt 2001; Tong 2001; Tong and Chan 2003; Wing and Yiu 1996, 2000).

As we discussed earlier, research focusing on firm strategy and structure mainly examines why, when, and how firms adopt various strategies and their implications for firm growth and performance outcomes. Table 12.4c provides a snapshot of studies with this focus.

AN ORGANIZING FRAMEWORK

To better integrate the literature and to help identify areas for future research on China's private business, we developed a coherent organizing framework, shown in Figure 12.1, to illustrate the linkages between institutional changes, three types of corporate strategies, and performance outcomes. In the following sections, we first review briefly the linkages investigated in our survey sample, which were those associated with the relationship- or network-based strategy and the price- or volume-based strategy. We then suggest that a third type of strategy—the capability-based strategy, which is emphasized in the strategic management literature—has been less studied in our sample and should be the focus of future research.

Link 1: Changing Institutional Environment and Relationship-Based or Network-Based Strategy

China's transitional economy, often characterized by its weak capital market structures, poorly specified property rights, and high institutional uncertainty, creates an institutional environment in which hybrid organizational forms and local corporatism enjoy advantages over alternative governance structures (Jiang and Hall 1996, Nee 1992). For example, China's collective firms incrementally transformed into a hybrid organizational form when the market-oriented economy began to grow rapidly in the 1980s. Such hybrids of the transitional economy, like hybrids in advanced capitalist economies, are organizational forms that "use resources and/or governance

Figure 12.1   **The Development of Private Firms in China: An Organizing Framework**

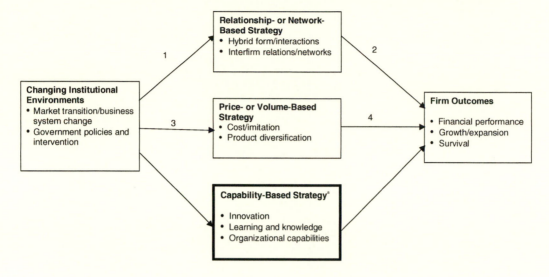

ᵃThe research studies in our survey sample have not focused on this key strategy dimension.

structures from more than one existing organization" (Borys and Jemison 1989, 235). The involvement of local governments or other collective bodies in business firms has been viewed as "local corporatism," which is regarded as crucial for economic development (Nee 1992). The advantages of hybrids and local corporatism in the transitional economy are emphasized in the literature because of their capacity to reduce uncertainty in interorganizational relationships involving bilateral dependency (Pfeffer and Salancik 1978). For example, local corporatism can enhance a firm's competitiveness in domestic and international markets by offering subsidies, facilitating horizontal and vertical economic integration, providing access to credit capital, and investing in supporting infrastructures and related services (Oi 1995).

Boisot and Child (1988, 1996) pointed out that it is quite common for Chinese firms to form alliances to provide horizontal and vertical integration. These alliances contribute to the development of quasi-market networks within China and have become a growing trend. Networks and interorganizational alliances offer greater capacities for generating and transmitting new information. And when sustained by trust-based relationships, they offer a cushion against the possibility of business failure.

However, the hybrid form, local corporatism, and the Chinese system of network capitalism lack the support of a well-specified structure of property rights and effective autonomy and therefore rely on personal ties rather than legal contracts to ensure parties will fulfill the terms of transactions. It is thus not surprising that many business transactions in China are settled through negotiations within a system of network relations based on interpersonal reciprocal obligations, especially *guanxi* ties with officials or cadres (e.g., Carroll, Goodstein, and Gyenes 1988; Xin and Pearce 1996). Xin and Pearce (1996) argue that an underdeveloped legal framework makes managers from private companies more dependent on *guanxi* than those in state-owned or collective/ hybrid companies. Executives in private companies consider business connections more important, rely more on connections for protection, have more government connections, present more unreciprocated gifts, and trust their connections more. Their results are consistent with findings from other countries where the legal and regulatory institutions are not well developed (e.g., Redding 1990).

Link 2: Relationship/Network Strategy and Performance Outcomes

Peng and Luo (2000) argue that Chinese managers cultivate two types of ties, one with executives at other firms, such as suppliers, buyers, and competitors, and the other with government officials. They examine the implications of these two types of ties on firm performance. Although the social capital argument supports a positive relationship between managerial ties and firm performance, there are no clear and consistent findings in the literature. In another study, Park and Luo (2001) demonstrate that institutional and strategic factors are critical for *guanxi* utilization with government authorities. In general, they conclude that *guanxi* leads to higher firm performance, but only in terms of increased sales growth, not profit growth; *guanxi* benefits market expansion and competitive positioning of firms, but does not enhance internal operations.

Some recent studies have begun to argue that with China's increasing market transformation, managerial ties and interorganizational networks may become "only necessary, but no longer sufficient" conditions for business success (Tsang 1998, 71). Guthrie (1998, 281) also comments on the declining economic importance of *guanxi* in China and the increasing realization that "*guanxi* only helps if you are competitive" (1998, 281).

Links 3 and 4: Changing Institutional Environment, Price- or Volume-Based Strategy, and Performance Consequences

The remaining studies on the strategies and structures of private firms are rather diverse. Some papers focus on traditional market competition variables (e.g., price, volume, and cost), and others examine the effects of changing institutional environments on such strategies and their performance consequences. In this section, we focus on our literature survey's implications for these two links.

Li and Atuahene-Gima (2001) examine the strategies of new technology ventures in China. They suggest that the competition in many industries in China could be best described as "dysfunctional"—firms are stuck on competing on volume and low price, rather than on developing innovative capabilities—so product innovation is minimal. Local firms are often simply imitating each other's products, without focusing on technological improvements. In addition, the weak enforcement of intellectual property rights protection leads companies to see product innovation as a highly risky and less profitable strategy, and thus discourages them from undertaking product innovations. Li and Atuahene-Gima (2001) did not show a clear linear relationship between the innovation strategy and the performance of new technology ventures in China, but suggested a need to consider environmental and relationship-based strategy factors as moderators of the innovation–performance relationship. However, others (e.g., Tan 1996, 2001) suggest that Chinese private companies tend to be more innovative and proactive than state-owned companies in response to the changing regulatory environments.

Diversification has been one of the main research areas in the strategy literature (Chandler 1962, Rumelt 1974). Recent studies have suggested that in emerging markets, because of the underdevelopment of such institutions as capital markets and legal frameworks, conglomeration (unrelated product diversification) and geographic expansion can help firms seek stability by spreading risk through investment in low-risk and fast-return markets (Guthrie 1997, Khanna and Palepu 1997). In addition, during the transition stage, when markets and institutions are developing, yet not fully developed, and customers are not sophisticated enough, the diversification strategy is often perceived as an efficient way to quickly exploit market potential and capture new business opportunities (Khanna and Palepu 1997). In our survey sample, Li and Wong (2003) empirically test the relationship between the product diversification strategy and firm performance in a sample of Chinese companies and find some support for this argument.

SUPPLEMENTARY ANALYSIS

The above review focuses on academic articles published in English-language journals, excluding books, managerial journals, or publications in other languages, such as Chinese. To supplement this analysis and provide some additional evidence, we also briefly reviewed some related books and articles in practitioner-focused journals, such as the *Harvard Business Review* (both English and Chinese editions).

Given the large number of books published on management issues in China over the last two decades, we decided to include only books that were reviewed in the book review section of at least one of the twenty-four source journals. Following that criterion, we identified thirty-eight China-related management books published during the study period. However, only a few of them focused exclusively on private firms in China and their management (Lu 1994; Wong, Ma, and Yang 1995). The majority of them focused on institutional transitions (Byrd 1991, Ho 1994, Nathan 1997, Young 1995), the management of foreign firms in China (e.g., Kelley and Shenkar 1993, Li 2001, Luo 2000) or of state-owned firms (e.g., Keister 2000), and general management issues across organizational forms (e.g., Chen 2001; Child 1994; Li, Tsui, and Weldon 2000; Peng 2000; Shenkar 1991).

Among managerial journals, we focused on the *Harvard Business Review*, which contained some short articles in the Chinese edition related to China's private businesses. These articles mostly concerned common business problems, challenges, and best practices for business practitioners. Our review of the issues identified in these short articles suggested that our conceptual model (Figure 12.1) indeed captured the main concerns of business practitioners in China as well.

THE DEVELOPMENT OF CHINA'S DOMESTIC PRIVATE FIRMS: A STRATEGIC MANAGEMENT PERSPECTIVE

Our survey of the management and organization literature over the past eighteen years suggests that, although the market transition in China in general is at a relatively early stage, especially regarding the reemergence of domestic private firms, a significant body of scholarship has been accumulated through the hard work of a global network of scholars. In particular, the institutional/business interactions studies have contributed greatly to understanding market transitions in general as well as their effects on strategies and behaviors of domestic private companies. The value of this research stream is particularly evident in its development of the idea of "network capitalism," a strategy that is clearly demonstrated by domestic private companies' emphasis on building interorganizational/network relationships.

Our survey results are in general consistent with work on market transaction structures. Researchers in economics (North 1990), sociology (Fukuyama 1995), and management (Moran and Ghoshal 1999, Peng 2003) commonly agree that transaction structures fall into two broad groups. The first transaction mode, "relational contracting" is the relationship-based, personalized exchange that "has characterized most of the economic history" (North 1990, 34). The second transaction mode, often termed "arm's-length transaction," is rule-based, impersonal exchange with third-party enforcement. As an economy expands, the scale, scope, and specificity of transactions rise exponentially, calling for the emergence of third-party enforcement through legal and regulatory regimes. The institutional transitions of these structures will have significant implications for firm-level strategic choices.

In this chapter, we argue that the institutional transition from a relationship-based transaction structure to a rule-based competition structure is already in progress in China. With the rapidly changing competitive landscapes in various industries in China today, many private companies have realized that they need to compete more on the basis of managerial and technological capabilities, rather than exclusively on the basis of informal social ties with government officials and others, or on the basis of low-price and imitation strategies. This is particularly so given the continuing expansions of multinational companies. Many of them are global leaders in their respective fields and are competing in China with their global scale, cutting-edge/proprietary technologies and global talents. How can small private companies in China compete with such dominant competitors? How can domestic private businesses prosper in the face of threats from foreign competitors? How can Chinese private companies develop their own capabilities and competitive advantages to ensure long-term survival in China?

So far, the China-related management and organization literature we have surveyed has little to say about these questions. One could argue that the past research on Chinese companies has been dominated by institutional, cultural, and related social explanations, with little research incorporating organizational capabilities into the analysis of firm-level strategic choices. However, several recent studies have noted that with China's increasing market transformation, the economic importance of *guanxi*, managerial ties, and interorganizational networks for firm growth and performance has declined, and they are becoming necessary but no longer sufficient conditions for business success (Child and Tse 2001, Guthrie 1998, Peng and Luo 2000, Tsang 1998). Others have recently suggested that competitive resources and capabilities will be of critical importance in response to the institutional transition into a rule-based market structure (Peng 2000, 2003).

However, the China-related literature that we survey in this study has not paid adequate attention to capability building in emerging economies. We propose that future research on the development of private firms in China should pay more attention to the organizational learning and capability building that will be fundamental to the success of these companies. We support this argument from the resource-based view (RBV) of the firm in the strategic management literature, which has received limited attention so far in management research on China's private business. Therefore, in addition to the other two types of strategies, we propose a new type of strategy, namely, the "capability-based strategy" (the bold-lined box in Figure 12.1), which emphasizes organizational learning and capability development. We suggest that future research should explore how the new strategy interacts with the changing institutional environment, the other two types of strategies found in the survey, and performance outcomes.

The strategic management perspective, particularly the literature on the resource-based view of the firm, has focused on understanding how companies achieve competitive advantage and how that advantage can be sustained over time (Barney 1991; Penrose 1959; Prahalad and Hamel 1990; Teece, Pisano, and Shuen 1997). According to this perspective, firms are bundles of resources, which are heterogeneously distributed across them, and resource differences can persist over time (Amit and Schoemaker 1993, Wernerfelt 1984). On the basis of these assumptions, researchers have theorized that when firms have resources that are valuable, rare, inimitable, and nonsubstitutable (i.e., the "VRIN attributes"), they can achieve sustainable competitive advantage by implementing value-creating strategies that cannot be easily replicated by competing firms (Nelson 1991, Peteraf 1993, Wernerfelt 1995).

Recently, scholars have extended the resource-based view of the firm to dynamic markets (Teece et al. 1997) and argued that the RBV has not adequately explained how and why certain firms have competitive advantages in situations of rapid and unpredictable changes. In these markets, where the competitive landscapes are shifting, the dynamic capabilities by which firms "integrate, build and reconfigure internal and external competencies to address rapidly changing environments" (Teece et al. 1997, 516) become the source of sustained competitive advantage. It is suggested that dynamic capabilities create and shape a firm's competitive positions (Eisenhardt and Martin 2000), knowledge resources (Kogut and Zander 1992), routines (Nelson 1991), and competitive strategies (Porter 1994). In turn, these variables will determine the firm's market position and its long-term performance.

The institutional transitions taking place in China today imply that a relationship-based, personalized transaction structure is giving way to a more rule-based market competition structure. Therefore, companies previously relying on a relationship- or network-based strategy will need to make the transition to a market-oriented, capability-based strategy in order to succeed.

But it will take time for local private firms in China to adapt to the institutional transitions and make strategic changes accordingly. How do Chinese private firms make a successful transition from competition based on relationships/networks to fully market-based competition, where achieving competitive advantage is the most fundamental factor for firm success? When is the appropriate time for launching such strategic changes? How do local private companies develop their organizational capabilities in order to achieve competitive advantages? We believe there is still a lot of work ahead for the global network of scholars interested in the development of private firms in China.

FUTURE RESEARCH DIRECTIONS: A THREE-STAGE MODEL OF MARKET TRANSITION AND STRATEGIC CHOICE

In view of the framework presented in Figure 12.1 and to integrate with research on market transitions, we propose a three-stage model of market transitions and strategic choices for private firms in China, along with a set of propositions to provide some directions for future research on China-related business issues.

Scholars have debated over the appropriate strategies for companies competing in transition economies. Some view competition based on networks and relationships as a winning strategy in the absence of formal institutional supports (e.g., Peng and Heath 1996; Spicer, McDermott, and Kogut 2000). However, others argue that too much emphasis has been put on personal ties and networks (White 2000, 339), which could be a hotbed of corruption and cronyism. Recent empirical studies have suggested that the importance of managerial ties and *guanxi* networks for firm growth and performance has declined (Guthrie 1998, Tsang 1998). Addressing this debate, Peng (2003) recently proposed a two-stage model of institutional transitions and argued that different types of strategies can be useful in different stages of the transitions.

Drawing on our own survey results, we extend Peng's work (2003) into a three-stage model with the aim of illustrating the nature of China's institutional transitions and their dynamic influences on private firms' strategic choices and performance consequences. Table 12.5 presents this model. We propose a more refined market transition process than that outlined by Peng (2003). We will first describe the beginning and ending stages of the market transition, and follow with our addition of a middle stage, which we believe could last for a long period of time, perhaps several decades.

Table 12.5

Market Transitions and Strategic Choices for Private Firms in China

	Phase I: Beginning of market transition (T1)	Phase II: Early stage of market transition (T2)	Phase III: Completion of market transition (T3)
Market transaction structure	Relationship-based, personalized	Late stage of relationship-based, personalized structure and early stage of rule-based, impersonal structure	Late stage of rule-based, impersonal structure
Bases for competition	• Markets not well developed (product, labor, and capital markets) • Institutions not well developed (government, legal, and financial institutions) • *Guanxi*/personal ties help reduce above uncertainties	• Markets and institutions still under development • Local players have weak technological capabilities • Absences of supporting and related industries • Local customers lacking sophistication • Local brand names and customer loyalty not established • Local intermediary markets not well established • Price/volume/cost/imitation become the competition base	• Markets and institutions well developed • Local players develop technological capabilities • Local supporting and related industries highly developed • Local customers become sophisticated • Entrepreneurship developed • Firm resources/capabilities/innovation become the competition base
Strategic choices	Relationship-/network-based strategy	Price-/volume-based strategy	Capability-based strategy
Performance consequences	Positive	Positive	Positive

Phase I (T1) is defined as the "beginning of market transition," a period when the relationship-based and personalized transaction mode dominates. China's economy during this period, characterized by various underdeveloped markets, weak capital structures, poorly specified property rights, and high institutional uncertainty, created an environment where personal ties, *guanxi* networks, and interfirm relationships enjoyed advantages in competition. Following the existing literature (Peng and Heath 1996, Xin and Pearce 1996), we argue that during this phase, private firms were more likely to compete on networks and relationships, and following such strategies resulted in better firm performance.

Phase III (T3) is defined as the "completion of market transition," a period when a rule-based and impersonalized transaction mode dominates the markets of an emerging economy, as in advanced economies. Markets and institutions are expected to be fully developed during this period. Leading local players will have developed technological capabilities, and the technical gap between local and multinational players would have been considerably narrowed. Customers in China will be sophisticated and diverse, requiring companies to provide innovative and differentiated products to meet their needs. At the same time, supporting and related industries, such as home-based suppliers, services, and intermediaries, will be well established. Drawing on the strategic management literature (Barney 1991; Eisenhardt and Martin 2000; Porter 1990, 1991; Teece et al. 1997), we argue that during this phase, private firms will be more likely to compete on resources and capabilities, and such a strategic focus can lead to firms' competitive advantage.

However, the beginning and ending stages described above do not capture the whole process of market transition, which could last for several decades. Therefore, we propose an intermediate stage, Phase II (T2), defined as the "early stage of market transition," when the relationship-based, personalized transaction structure begins to give way to a more rule-based and impersonalized transaction mode. During this transition period, a rule-based and impersonalized transaction structure begins to emerge but has not yet become the dominant market logic, while the importance of personal ties and *guanxi* networks as dominant sources of competitive advantages begins to decline. To ensure growth and survival in this transition phase, local firms begin to rely more on building market share with low prices and large volume.

With China's economy in this phase, it is still in transition, and the institutional infrastructures will take time to be fully developed to support firms fully adopting capability-based strategies. Porter (1990) suggests that a nation's economic development can be determined from four broad attributes (comprising the diamond model): factor conditions; demand conditions; related and supporting industries; and firm strategy, structure, and rivalry. These attributes shape the information firms have available to perceive opportunities; the pool of inputs, skills, and knowledge they can draw on; the goals that condition investment; and the pressures on firms to act (Porter, 1991, 111). As an emerging economy, China lacks specialized local factor pools, such as specialized skills, capital, and infrastructures, to support local firms developing innovative capabilities. Home market demand is suggested to play a disproportionate role in influencing the perception of buyer needs and the capacity of firms to improve products and services over time. Sophisticated and demanding home customers often stimulate firms' competitive success. The absence of demanding customers often discourages local companies from innovating or differentiating their products. Being in the early stage of the market transition from a command economy, China's customers need time to develop such sophistication. In addition, a nation's economic development is also strongly influenced by the presence of home-based suppliers and related industries (Porter 1990), which again will take time to develop. The general local suppliers or related industries in China have not been strong enough to confer potential advantages to other industries, and they therefore constrain the inputs and spillovers that are important and can be widely used to support firm innovations. Lastly, China's big market and the weak technological capabilities of local players during this stage offer a local rivalry with a quantity focus, which cannot stimulate a high rate of improvement, innovation, and ultimate success.

Given the above analysis, it is not surprising that many local firms are competing on price/volume during this phase of the market transition. On the one hand, relationships/personal ties are no longer sufficient for firm performance as market competition intensifies. On the other hand, local firms have not developed the necessary capabilities for innovation and product differentiation, even if they intend to do so. Therefore, many local companies are forced to compete on low prices and by imitating each other's products, in order to ensure survival in the short term.

We believe that this intermediate phase is distinct and should not be confused with the other two phases, either the beginning or the ending stages of the market transition. Unfortunately, the literature we have surveyed has not paid adequate attention to this important phase in the market transition process. In fact, we suggest that this stage is the essence of the market transition process and should be the focus of future research.

We propose the following propositions based on the above arguments:

Proposition 1. The Beginning of Market Transition (Phase I: T1)

Proposition 1a. In the beginning of market transition, when the relationship-based and personalized transaction mode of competition dominates (T1), private firms are more likely to employ the relationship-/network-based strategy.

Proposition 1b. The relationship-/network-based strategy is likely to lead to better firm performance during this phase (T1).

Proposition 2. The Early Stage of Market Transition (Phase II: T2)

Proposition 2a. During the early stage of market transition, when the relationship-based and personalized transaction mode of competition begins to decline, and the rule-based and impersonal transaction mode begins to appear (T2), private firms are more likely to employ the price- or volume-based strategy.

Proposition 2b. The price- or volume-based strategy is likely to lead to better firm performance during this phase (T2).

Proposition 3. The Later Stage of Market Transition (Phase III: T3)

Proposition 3a. During the later stage of market transition, when the rule-based and impersonal transaction mode of competition fully dominates (T3), private firms are more likely to employ the capability-based strategy.

Proposition 3b. The capability-based strategy is likely to lead to better firm performance during this phase (T3).

Proposition 4. Dynamic Change over the Three Phases of Market Transition (T1 → T2 → T3)

Proposition 4a. The impact of the relationship- or network-based strategy on firm performance decreases as a market transition moves from the relationship-based and personalized transaction mode (T1) to the rule-based and impersonal transaction mode (T2 + T3).

Proposition 4b. The impact of the price- or volume-based strategy on firm performance increases first as a market transition moves from the relationship-based and personalized transaction mode (T1) to the early stage of the rule-based and impersonal transaction mode (T2), but decreases as the market transition moves to the late stage of the rule-based and impersonal transaction mode (T3).

Proposition 4c. The impact of the capability-based strategy on firm performance increases as a market transition moves from the relationship-based and personalized transaction mode (T1) to the early stage of the rule-based and impersonal transaction mode (T2), and finally to the late stage of the rule-based and impersonal transaction mode (T3).

CONCLUSIONS

This chapter provides an overview of the extant research on management and organization issues in China's emerging private sector. We have reviewed ninety-two articles that were published in twenty-four leading English-language academic journals over eighteen years (1986–2003). In the review, we first identified and summarized existing research issues, and then synthesized this diverse and scattered body of literature according to rigorous selection criteria. Furthermore, we proposed a coherent framework from a strategic management perspective, outlining the three types of strategies in transitional economies: the relationship- or network-based strategy, the price- or volume-based strategy, and finally, the capability-based strategy. On the basis of the framework presented in Figure 12.1, and integrating with research on market transitions, we proposed a three-stage model of market transitions and strategic choices for private firms in China that may provide some guidance to future research on China. We have also provided a set of theoretical propositions, suggesting that different types of strategies are useful in different stages of the market transition, and that firms need to adopt appropriate strategies as the market transition evolves. These propositions need to be tested in future empirical research.

While the survey is intended to be helpful to researchers interested in management and organization issues related to China's domestic private business, it is necessary to acknowledge the constraints of such an undertaking. First, exactly what comprises the "private sector" in China is murky, and the lack of clarity is evident in the data on economic performance provided by official government statistics (e.g., *China Statistical Yearbook* 2002). Our initial rounds of literature review also evidenced the fuzzy definition of "private sector." In order to provide a coherent review in this study, we decided to include research on China's domestic privately run and collective firms, but excluded studies focusing on foreign-invested firms in China, which are also part of the private sector.

Second, given the youth of the emerging private domestic firms in China, it is not surprising that limited management research has focused exclusively on them. Many of these studies are comparative and include firms or employees under different types of ownership, including state-owned, foreign-owned, collective, and private firms. For instance, among the ninety-two studies in the survey sample, twenty-one articles (23%) focused on private (entrepreneur) firms, fifteen articles exclusively on township-and-village enterprises, and the remaining fifty-six studies were mixed in terms of focus on firm type.

Third, facing the trade-off between the depth and width of a review, we decided to review only research published in twenty-four English-language academic journals for a consistent and systematic analysis. While we have provided a brief review of related work appearing in books, edited volumes, and articles published in managerial journals in a supplementary analysis, future work is needed to conduct a more comprehensive survey of important work appearing in books and journals published in Chinese or other languages.

APPENDIX 12.1.
Bibliography of Management and Organization Research
Related to Private Business in China Published 1986–2003 in
Twenty-four Academic Journals Written in English

Ahlstrom, D., and G. D. Bruton. (2002). An institutional perspective on the role of culture in shaping strategic actions by technology-focused entrepreneurial firms in China. *Entrepreneurship Theory and Practice*, 26, 53–69.

Anderson, A. R.; J.-H. Li; R. T. Harrison; and P.J.A. Robson. (2003). The increasing role of small business in the Chinese economy. *Journal of Small Business Management*, 41, 310–16.

Anyansi-Archibong, C. B.; W. P. Danenburg; and Z. Y. Tan. (1989). Small business in China's Special Economic Zones. *Journal of Small Business Management*, 27, 56–62.

Blecher, M., and V. Shue. (2001). Into leather: State-led development and the private sector in Xinji. *China Quarterly*, 166, 368–93.

Boisot, M., and J. Child. (1988). The iron law of fiefs: Bureaucratic failure and the problem of governance in the Chinese economic reforms. *Administrative Science Quarterly*, 33, 507–27.

———. (1996). From fiefs to clans and network capitalism: Explaining China's emerging economic order. *Administrative Science Quarterly*, 41, 600–28.

———. (1999). Organizations as adaptive systems in complex environments: The case of China. *Organization Science*, 10, 237–52.

Boisot, M., and X. G. Liang. (1992). The nature of managerial work in the Chinese enterprise reforms: A study of six directors. *Organization Studies*, 13, 161–84.

Chang, W., and I. C. MacMillan. (1991). A review of entrepreneurial development in the People's Republic of China. *Journal of Business Venturing*, 6, 375–79.

Chen, X. P.; C. Hui; and D. J. Sego. (1998). The role of organizational citizenship behavior in turnover: Conceptualization and preliminary tests of key hypotheses. *Journal of Applied Psychology*, 83, 922–31.

Chen, Z. X.; A. S. Tsui; and J. L. Farh. (2002). Loyalty to supervisor vs. organizational commitment: Relationships to employee performance in China. *Journal of Occupational and Organizational Psychology*, 75, 339–56.

Cheng, Y.-S., and D. Lo. (2002). Explaining the financial performance of China's industrial enterprises: Beyond the competition-ownership controversy. *China Quarterly*, 170, 413–40.

Child, J., and D. K. Tse. (2001). China's transition and its implications for international business. *Journal of International Business Studies*, 32, 5–21.

Cornwall, J. R. (1998). The entrepreneur as a building block for community. *Journal of Developmental Entrepreneurship*, 3, 141–48.

Dana, L. P. (1999). Small business as a supplement in the People's Republic of China (PRC). *Journal of Small Business Management*, 37, 76–80.

Danenburg, W. P., and Z. Y. Tan. (1989). The "Sparking Program" and its effect on small business in the People's Republic of China. *Journal of Small Business Management*, 27, 60–62.

Davis, D. S. (1999). Self-employment in Shanghai: A research note. *China Quarterly*, 157, 22–43.

Fan, Y. (1996). Global perspectives: Chinese peasant entrepreneurs: An examination of township and village enterprises in rural China. *Journal of Small Business Management*, 34, 72–76.

Francis, C. B. (1996). Reproduction of danwei institutional features in the context of China's market economy: The case of Haidian district's high-tech sector. *China Quarterly*, 147, 839–59.

Frenkel, S., and S. Kuruvilla. (2002). Logics of action, globalization, and changing employment relations in China, India, Malaysia, and the Philippines. *Industrial and Labor Relations Review*, 55, 387–412.

Goldstein, S. M. (1995). China in transition: The political foundations of incremental reform. *China Quarterly*, 144, 1105–31.

Guo, S. (2003). The ownership reform in China: What direction and how far? *Journal of Contemporary China*, 12, 553–73.

Holt, D. H. (1997). A comparative study of values among Chinese and U.S. entrepreneurs: Pragmatic convergence between contrasting cultures. *Journal of Business Venturing*, 12, 483–505.

Jiang, S. H., and R. H. Hall. (1996). Local corporatism and rural enterprises in China's reform. *Organization Studies*, 17, 929–53.

Keister, L. A. (2002). Adapting to radical change: Strategy and environment in piece-rate adoption during China's transition. *Organization Science*, 13, 459–74.

Kwong, C.C.L. (2000). Business-government relations in industrializing rural China: A principal-agent perspective. *Journal of Contemporary China*, 9, 513–34.

Lau, C. M., and L.W. Busenitz. (2001). Growth intentions of entrepreneurs in a transitional economy: The People's Republi c of China. *Entrepreneurship Theory and Practice*, 26, 5–20.

Law, K. S.; D. K. Tse; and N. Zhou. (2003). Does human resource management matter in a transitional economy? China as an example. *Journal of International Business Studies*, 34, 255–65.

Li, P. P. (1998). Towards a geocentric framework of organizational form: A holistic, dynamic and paradoxical approach. *Organization Studies*, 19, 829–61.

Li, H. Y., and K. Atuahene-Gima. (2001). Product innovation strategy and the performance of new technology ventures in China. *Academy of Management Journal*, 44, 1123–34.

———. (2002). The adoption of agency business activity, product innovation, and performance in Chinese technology ventures. *Strategic Management Journal*, 23, 469–90.

Li, M. F., and Y. Y. Wong. (2003). Diversification and economic performance: An empirical assessment of Chinese firms. *Asia Pacific Journal of Management*, 20, 243–65.

Liu, Y. L. (1992). Reform from below: The private economy and local politics in the rural industrialization of Wenzhou. *China Quarterly*, 130, 293–316.

Luo, Y. D. (1999). Environment-strategy-performance relations in small businesses in China: A case of township and village enterprises in southern China. *Journal of Small Business Management*, 37, 37–52.

Luo, Y. D.; J. Tan; and O. Shenkar. (1998). Strategic responses to competitive pressure: The case of township and village enterprises in China. *Asia Pacific Journal of Management*, 15, 33–50.

Matthews, C. H.; X. D. Qin; and G. M. Franklin. (1996). Stepping toward prosperity: The development of entrepreneurial ventures in China and Russia. *Journal of Small Business Management*, 34, 75–85.

McGrath, R. G.; I. C. MacMillan; and W. Tsai. (1992). Does culture endure, or is it malleable? Issues for entrepreneurial economic development. *Journal of Business Venturing*, 7, 441–58.

Miner, J. B. (1991). Theory testing under adverse conditions: Motivation to manage in the People's Republic of China. *Journal of Applied Psychology*, 76, 343–49.

Murphy, R. (2000). Return migration, entrepreneurship and local state corporatism in rural China: The experience of two counties in south Jiangxi. *Journal of Contemporary China*, 9, 231–48.

Nee, V. (1992). Organizational dynamics of market transition: Hybrid forms, property rights, and mixed economy in China. *Administrative Science Quarterly*, 37, 1–27.

Nevitt, C. E. (1996). Private business associations in China: Evidence of civil society or local state power? *China Journal*, 36, 25–43.

Odgaard, O. (1992). Entrepreneurs and elite formation in rural China. *Australian Journal of Chinese Affairs*, 28, 89–108.

Oi, J. C. (1995). The role of the local state in China's transitional economy. *China Quarterly*, 144, 1132–59.

Okechuku, C. (1994). The relationship of six managerial characteristics to the assessment of managerial effectiveness in Canada, Hong Kong and People's Republic of China. *Journal of Occupational and Organizational Psychology*, 67, 79–86.

Parish, W. L.; X. Y. Zhe; and F. (1995). Nonfarm work and marketization of the Chinese countryside. *China Quarterly*, 143, 697–712.

Park, S. H., and Y. D. Luo. (2001). *Guanxi* and organizational dynamics: Organizational networking in Chinese firms. *Strategic Management Journal*, 22, 455–77.

Parries, K. (1993). Local initiative and national reform: The Wenzhou model of development. *China Quarterly*, 134, 242–63.

Peng, W. P. (2003). Institutional transitions and strategic choices. *Academy of Management Review*, 28, 275–93.

Peng, W. P., and P. S. Heath. (1996). The growth of the firm in planned economies in transition: Institutions, organizations, and strategic choice. *Academy of Management Review*, 2, 492–528.

Peng, M. W., and Y. D. Luo. (2000). Managerial ties and firm performance in a transition economy: The nature of a micro-macro link. *Academy of Management Journal*, 43, 486–501.

Putterman, L. (1995). The role of ownership and property rights in China's economic transition. *China Quarterly*, 144, 1047–64.

Ralston, D. A. (1992). Eastern values: A comparison of managers in the United States, Hong Kong, and the People's Republic of China. *Journal of Applied Psychology*, 77, 664–71.

Ralston, D. A.; D. J. Gustafson; F.M. Cheung; and R.H. Terpstra. (1993). Differences in managerial values: A study of U.S., Hong Kong and PRC managers. *Journal of International Business Studies*, 24, 249–75.

Redding, G. (2002). The capitalist business system of China and its rationale. *Asia Pacific Journal of Management*, 19, 221–49.

Sabin, L. (1994). New bosses in the workers' state: The growth of non-state sector employment in China. *China Quarterly*, 140, 944–70.

Schlevogt, K. A. (2001). Institutional and organizational factors affecting effectiveness: Geoeconomic comparison between Shanghai and Beijing. *Asia Pacific Journal of Management*, 18, 519–51.

Shenkar, O., and M. A. von Glinow. (1994). Paradoxes of organizational theory and research: Using the case of China to illustrate national contingency. *Management Science*, 40, 56–71.

Shenkar, O.; S. Ronen; E. Shefy; and I. H. Chow. (1998). The role structure of Chinese managers. *Human Relations*, 51, 51–72.

Siu, W. S. (1992). Corporate entrepreneurs in the People's Republic of China: Problems encountered and respective solutions. *International Small Business Journal*, 10, 26–33.

———. (1995). Entrepreneurial typology: The case of owner-managers in China. *International Small Business Journal*, 14, 53–64.

Snell, R., and C. S. Tseng. (2002). Moral atmosphere and moral influence under China's network capitalism. *Organization Studies*, 23, 449–78.

Tam, O. K. (1992). A private bank in China: Hui Tong Urban Co-operative Bank. *China Quarterly*, 131, 766–77.

Tan, J. (1996). Regulatory environment and strategic orientations in a transitional economy: A study of Chinese private enterprise. *Entrepreneurship Theory and Practice*, 21, 31–46.

———. (2001). Innovation and risk-taking in a transitional economy: A comparative study of Chinese managers and entrepreneurs. *Journal of Business Venturing*, 16, 359–76.

———. (2002a). Culture, nation, and entrepreneurial strategic orientations: Implications for an emerging economy. *Entrepreneurship Theory and Practice*, 26, 95–111.

———. (2002b). Impact of ownership type on environment-strategy linkage and performance: Evidence from a transitional economy. *Journal of Management Studies*, 39, 333–54.

Tian, J. J., and C.-M. Lau. (2001). Board composition, leadership structure and performance in Chinese shareholding companies. *Asia Pacific Journal of Management*, 18, 245–60.

Tjosvold, D.; C. Hui; Z. Ding; and J. H. Hu. (2002). Conflict values and team relationships: Conflict's contribution to team effectiveness and citizenship in China. *Journal of Organizational Behavior*, 24, 69–88.

Tong, C.E.N. (2001). Total factor productivity growth and its spatial disparity across China's township and village enterprises. *Journal of Contemporary China*, 10, 155–72.

Tong, C.S.P., and H.L. Chan. (2003). Disparity in production efficiency of China's TVEs across regions: A stochastic frontier production function approach. *Asia Pacific Journal of Management*, 20, 113–31.

Tsang, E.W.K. (1994). Threats and opportunities faced by private businesses in China. *Journal of Business Venturing*, 9, 451–68.

———. (1996). In search of legitimacy: The private entrepreneur in China. *Entrepreneurship Theory and Practice*, 21, 21–30.

Unger, J. (1996). Bridges: Private business, the Chinese government and the rise of new associations. *China Quarterly*, 147, 795–819.

Unger, J., and A. Chan. (1995). China, corporatism, and the East Asian model. *Australian Journal of Chinese Affairs*, 33, 29–53.

———. (1999). Inheritors of the boom: Private enterprise and the role of local government in a rural South China township. *China Journal*, 42, 45–74.

Vertinsky, I.; D. K. Tse; D. A. Wehrung; and K.-H. Lee. (1990). Organizational design and management norms: A comparative study of managers' perceptions in the People's Republic of China, Hong Kong, and Canada. *Journal of Management*, 16, 853–67.

Walder, A. G. (1989). Factory and manager in an era of reform. *China Quarterly*, 118, 242–64.

Wang, D. X.; A. S. Tsui; Y.C. Zhang; and L. Ma. (2003). Employment relationships and firm performance: Evidence from an emerging economy. *Journal of Organizational Behavior*, 24, 511–35.

Wank, D. (1995). Private business, bureaucracy, and political alliance in a Chinese city. *Australian Journal of Chinese Affairs*, 33, 55–71.

———. (1996). The institutional process of market clientelism: *Guanxi* and private business in a South China city. *China Quarterly*, 147, 820–38.

Wei, Y. D. (2002). Multiscale and multimechanisms of regional inequality in China: Implications for regional policy. *Journal of Contemporary China*, 11, 109–24.

White, S., and X. L. Liu. (2001). Transition trajectories for market structure and firm strategy in China. *Journal of Management Studies*, 38, 103–24.

Whyte, M. K. (1995). The social roots of China's economic development. *China Quarterly*, 144, 999–1019.

Wing, C.C.K. (1994). Entrepreneurs in China: Development, functions and problems. *International Small Business Journal*, 13, 63–77.

———. (1996). Entry and exit process of small businesses in P.R. China's retail sector. *International Small Business Journal*, 15, 41–58.

Wing, C.C.K., and M.F.K. Yiu. (1996). Firm dynamics and industrialization in the Chinese economy in transition: Implications for small business policy. *Journal of Business Venturing*, 11, 489–505.

———. (2000). Small business and liquidity constraints in financing business investment: Evidence from Shanghai's manufacturing sector. *Journal of Business Venturing*, 15, 363–83.

Xin, K. R., and J. L. Pearce. (1996). *Guanxi*: Connections as substitutes for formal institutional support. *Academy of Management Journal*, 39, 1641–58.

Young, S. (1989). Policy, practice and the private sector in China. *Australian Journal of Chinese Affairs*, 21, 57–80.

———. (1991). Wealth but not security: Attitudes towards private business in China in the 1980s. *Australian Journal of Chinese Affairs*, 25, 115–37.

Zapalska, A. M. (2001). Chinese entrepreneurship in a cultural and economic perspective. *Journal of Small Business Management*, 39, 286–92.

Zhao, L. M., and J. D. Aram. (1995). Networking and growth of young technology-intensive ventures in China. *Journal of Business Venturing*, 5, 349–71.

ACKNOWLEDGMENTS

We would like to thank Anne Tsui (the editor), Kaye Schoonhoven, and the participants at the Hang Lung Research Workshop for their helpful comments, and Song Chang and Jing Zhong for their excellent research assistance. We gratefully acknowledge the support from Hong Kong RGC Competitive Earmarked Grants (HKUST6150/02H; HKUST6196/ 04H) and a DAG grant (DAG03/04.BM48) at Hong Kong University of Science and Technology.

REFERENCES

Amit, R., and P.J.H. Schoemaker. (1993). Strategic assets and organizational rent. *Strategic Management Journal*, 14, 33–46.

Asian Development Bank. (2003). *The development of private enterprise in the People's Republic of China*. Manila, Philippines: Asian Development Bank.

Barney, J. (1991). Firm resources and sustained competitive advantage. *Journal of Management*, 17, 99–120.

Borys, B., and D. B. Jemison. (1989). Hybrid arrangements as strategic alliances: Theoretical issues in organizational combinations. *Academy of Management Review*, 14, 234–49.

Byrd, W. A. (1991). *The market mechanism and economic reforms in China*. Armonk, NY: M.E. Sharpe.

Carroll, G. R.; J. Goodstein; and A. Gyenes. (1988). Organizations and the state: Effects of the institutional environment on agricultural cooperatives in Hungary. *Administrative Science Quarterly*, 33, 233–56.

Chandler, A. (1962). *Strategy and structure*. Cambridge, MA: MIT Press.

Chen, M. (2001). *Inside Chinese business: A guide for managers worldwide*. Boston, MA: Harvard Business School Press.

Child, J. (1994). *Management in China during the age of reform*. Cambridge and New York: Cambridge University Press.

China Statistical Yearbook. (2002). Beijing: China Statistical Publishing House.

Eisenhardt, K. M., and J. A. Martin. (2000). Dynamic capabilities: What are they? *Strategic Management Journal*, 21, 1105–21.

Fukuyama, F. (1995). *Trust*. New York: Free Press.

Guthrie, D. (1997). Between markets and politics: Organizational responses to reform in China. *American Journal of Sociology*, 102, 1258–1304.

———. (1998). The declining significance of *guanxi* in China's economic transition. *China Quarterly*, 154, 254–83.

Ho, S.P.S. (1994). *Rural China in transition: Non-agricultural development in rural Jiansu, 1978–1990.* Oxford, England: Clarendon Press.

International Finance Corporation. (2000). *China's emerging private enterprises: Prospects for the new century.* Washington, DC: IFC.

Johnson, J. L., and P. M. Podsakoff. (1994). Journal influence in the field of management: An analysis using Salancik's index in a dependency network. *Academy of Management Journal*, 37, 1392–1407.

Keister, L. A. (2000). *Chinese business groups: The structure and impact of interfirm relations during economic development.* Oxford, England: Oxford University Press.

Kelley, L., and O. Shenkar. (1993). *International business in China.* London and New York: Routledge.

Khanna, T., and K. Palepu. (1997). Why focused strategies may be wrong for emerging markets. *Harvard Business Review*, 75(4), 41–51.

Kogut, B., and U. Zander. (1992). Knowledge of the firm, combinative capabilities, and the replication of technology. *Organization Science*, 3, 383–97.

Li, J. T. (2001). *Managing international business ventures in China.* Amsterdam: Pergamon.

Li, J. T., and A. S. Tsui. (2002). A citation analysis of management and organization research in the Chinese context: 1984–1999. *Asia Pacific Journal of Management*, 19, 87–107.

Li, J. T.; A. S. Tsui; and E. Weldon. (2000). *Management and organizations in the Chinese context.* New York: St. Martin's Press.

Lohrke, F., and G. Bruton. (1997). Contributions and gaps in international strategic management literature. *Journal of International Management*, 3, 25–57.

Lu, D. (1994). *Entrepreneurship in suppressed markets: Private-sector experience in China.* New York: Garland.

Luo, Y. (2000). *Multinational corporations in China: Benefiting from structural transformation.* Copenhagen: Copenhagen Business School Press.

Miles, R. E.; C. C. Snow; A. D. Meyer; and H. J. Coleman. (1978). Organizational strategy, structure, and process. *Academy of Management Review*, 3, 546–62.

Moran, P., and S. Ghoshal. (1999). Markets, firms and the process of economic development. *Academy of Management Review*, 24, 602–19.

Nathan, A. J. (1997). *China's transition.* New York: Columbia University Press.

Nelson, R. (1991). Why do firms differ, and how does it matter? *Strategic Management Journal*, 12, 61–74.

North, D. (1990). *Institutions, institutional change, and economic performance.* New York: Norton.

Oliver, C. (1997). Sustainable competitive advantage: Combining institutional and resource-based views. *Strategic Management Journal*, 18, 679–713.

Park, S. H., and M. E. Gordon. (1996). Publication records and tenure decisions in the field of strategic management. *Strategic Management Journal*, 17, 109–28.

Peng, M. W. (2000). *Business strategies in transition economies.* Thousand Oaks, CA: Sage Publications.

Peng, M. W.; Y. Lu; O. Shenkar; and D. Wang. (2001). Treasures in the China house: A review of management and organizational research on Greater China. *Journal of Business Research*, 52, 95–110.

Penrose, E. (1959). *The theory of the growth of the firm.* New York: John Wiley.

Peteraf, M. A. (1993). The cornerstones of competitive advantage. *Strategic Management Journal*, 14, 179–91.

Pfeffer, J., and G. Salancik. (1978). *The external control of organizations.* New York: Harper.

Porter, M. E. (1990). *The competitive advantage of nations.* New York: Free Press.

———. (1991). Towards a dynamic theory of strategy. *Strategic Management Journal*, 12, 95–117.

———. (1994). Toward a dynamic theory of strategy. In R. Rumelt, D. Schendel, and D. Teece (Eds.), *Fundamental issues in strategy: A research agenda*, pp. 423–61. Boston, Harvard Business School Press.

Powell, W., and P. DiMaggio (Eds.). (1991). *The new institutionalism in organizational analysis.* Chicago: University of Chicago Press.

Prahalad, C. K., and G. Hamel. (1990). The core competence of the corporation. *Harvard Business Review*, 68(3), 79–91.

Redding, S. G. (1990). *The spirit of Chinese capitalism.* New York: de Gruyter.

Rumelt, R. (1974). *Strategy, structure and economic performance.* Cambridge, MA: Harvard University Press.

Shane, S. (1997). Who is publishing entrepreneurship research? *Journal of Management*, 23, 83–95.

Shenkar, O. (1991). *Organization and management in China, 1979–1990.* Armonk, NY: M.E. Sharpe.

Spicer, A.; G. McDermott; and B. Kogut. (2000). Entrepreneurship and privatization in Central Europe: The tenuous balance between destruction and creation. *Academy of Management Review*, 25, 630–49.

Tahai, A., and M. J. Meyer. (1999). A revealed preference study of management journals' direct influences. *Strategic Management Journal*, 20, 276–96.

Teece, D.; G. Pisano; and A. Shuen. (1997). Dynamic capabilities and strategic management. *Strategic Management Journal*, 18, 509–33.

Tsang, E. (1998). Can *guanxi* be a source of sustainable competitive advantage for doing business in China? *Academy of Management Executive*, 12, 64–73.

Wernerfelt, B. (1984). A resource-based view of the firm. *Strategic Management Journal*, 5, 171–80.

———. (1995). The resource-based view of the firm: Ten years after. *Strategic Management Journal*, 16, 171–74.

White, S. (2000). Competition, capabilities, and the make, buy, or ally decisions of Chinese state-owned firms. *Academy of Management Journal*, 43, 324–41.

———. (2002). Rigor and relevance in Asian management research: Where are we and where can we go? *Asia Pacific Journal of Management*, 19, 287–352.

Wong, J.; R. Ma; and M. Yang. (1995). *China's rural entrepreneurs: Ten case studies*. Singapore: Times Academic Press.

Young, S. (1995). *Private business and economic reform in China*. Armonk, NY: M.E. Sharpe.

13

AUTHORITY AND BENEVOLENCE

EMPLOYEES' RESPONSES TO PATERNALISTIC LEADERSHIP IN CHINA

JIING-LIH FARH, BOR-SHIUAN CHENG, LI-FANG CHOU, AND XIAO-PING CHU

Leadership as a social influence process is a universal phenomenon that transcends national borders, but conceptions of it and the styles and practices associated with it have been found to vary widely across cultures (Farh and Cheng 2000). After all, leaders cannot choose their styles at will, and what works for a leader depends to a large extent on cultural context. Despite cautionary notes to this effect by cross-cultural researchers (Hofstede 1980b, 1994), contemporary theories and models of leadership continue to be dominated by the formulations of U.S. researchers.

In the Chinese context, much of the empirical research on leadership has relied on translated Western instruments to test the generality of popular Western leadership models to Chinese organizations (e.g., Chen and Farh 1999; Cheng 1990; Farh, Podsakoff, and Cheng 1987; Huang and Wang 1980). Although this research strategy is useful for identifying the boundary conditions of Western leadership theories, it is not fruitful for providing a comprehensive or valid understanding of leadership in Chinese organizations. As many writers have noted (e.g., Hsu 1981), the cultural differences between the East and the West (China and the United States in particular) are probably the deepest in the world. A study of indigenous Chinese leadership behavior in its own context not only should produce insights aiding understanding of the emic aspects of Chinese leadership, but also should contribute to etic knowledge about leadership in global contexts (Morris et al. 1999).

In the past three decades, the rapid rise of Asian economies dominated by overseas Chinese in Hong Kong, Singapore, Taiwan, and much of Southeast Asia has drawn researchers' attention to the management philosophy and practices of overseas Chinese businesses (e.g., Redding 1990, Whitley 1992, Wong 1988). Building on Silin's anthropological work (1976), several researchers have studied the leadership style and philosophy of owners/managers in overseas Chinese family businesses in Hong Kong, Indonesia, Singapore, and Taiwan (e.g., Cheng 1995a, b; Redding 1990). This stream of research has identified a pattern of leadership called paternalism or paternalistic leadership (PL). Broadly defined, PL is a fatherlike leadership style in which clear and strong authority is combined with concern and considerateness and elements of moral leadership (Westwood and Chan 1992).

The purpose of this chapter is to examine the applicability of PL to private businesses in the PRC. We first review the extant literature on PL to identify key areas of research. We then analyze the context of China's private sector and present hypotheses about the relationships between PL dimensions and subordinate responses. We finally describe tests of these hypotheses using a sample of 292 employees from 52 PRC private enterprises. The findings of the study are discussed in terms of their implications for leadership theories in general and management practices in China in particular.

THEORETICAL BACKGROUND AND HYPOTHESES

Authority and subordination in human relations as a research topic has fascinated Western social scientists for centuries. Max Weber (1864–1920) considered domination a critical subject in his analysis of societies. Domination occurs when a dominator asserts his or her will (command) on a subject (a dominated people), and the subject takes the command as the rules of conduct. Weber constructed three ideal types of domination or authority based on legitimacy: legal domination, traditional domination, and charismatic domination. Traditional domination occurs when legitimacy is claimed for the domination, and people believe in it by virtue of the sanctity of age-old rules and powers. Weber (1968, 231) described patriarchalism as one of the most elementary types of traditional domination; it is governance of a group (a household), which is usually organized on the basis of both economics and kinship, by a male individual who is designated by a definite rule of inheritance. Within such a social order, membership exists by tradition and not by enactment, and obedience is owed to the patriarch only by virtue of his traditional status. Weber (1968, 231) further pointed out that the decisive characteristic of patriarchalism is the belief of group/household members that domination, even though it is an inherent, traditional right of the master, must definitely be exercised in the interests of all members, and is thus not freely appropriated by the incumbent. In this sense, the patriarch is still largely dependent on the willingness of the members to comply with his orders.

Patriarchalism was common in traditional societies in China as well as in such societies in the West (such as those within Mediterranean culture). However, owing to differences in the sources of patriarchal power and to developmental history, patriarchalism continues to prevail in China, while its counterpart in the West has declined sharply over the last three centuries (Farh and Cheng 2000). Paternalistic leadership in overseas Chinese family businesses is a clear manifestation of China's patriarchal tradition in business organizations. Paternalistic leadership and philosophy have also been observed widely in Asian businesses and governments (e.g., Pye 1985).

Because of its strongly authoritarian tone and its reliance on subordinates' dependent mindsets, cross-cultural psychologists have reasoned that PL thrives only in high-power-distance cultures, in which people are used to and willing to accept high power differentials between hierarchies. Some cross-cultural psychologists have gone so far as to suggest that PL is ideal for high-power-distance societies. For example, Hofstede and Bond asserted the following: "The ideal leader in a culture in which Power Distances are small would be a resourceful democrat; on the other hand, the ideal leader in a culture in which Power Distances are large is a benevolent autocrat (or 'good father')" (1988, 14). Despite these bold predictions, cross-cultural research that compares the leadership style of Chinese leaders with that of their Western counterparts is rare. The limited evidence does show that Chinese societies as a whole tend to exhibit a larger power distance than many Western countries (Hofstede 1980a, Smith and Wang 1996); in comparison to their Western counterparts, Chinese leaders tend to be less participative (Xia 1987), much more likely to rely upon their superiors in handling events (Smith and Peterson 1988), and more likely to have a paternalistic attitude toward companies (Chang 1985).

Is PL an effective leadership strategy in China's private businesses? Do Chinese employees respond positively to PL exhibited by their supervisors? How does cultural change in the PRC as reflected by differences in the traditional value orientation of employees affect their reactions to PL? Does employees' dependence on their supervisors for resources affect their reactions to PL? This study sought to answer these key questions in the context of China's private businesses.

A Triad Model of Paternalistic Leadership and Its Cultural Origin

After an extensive review of the literature on PL in overseas Chinese family businesses, Farh and Cheng (2000) proposed a triad model of PL, conceptualizing it as consisting of three distinct leadership styles or elements or dimensions: authoritarianism, benevolence, and morality. Authoritarianism refers to leader behaviors that assert absolute authority and control over subordinates and demand unquestioning obedience from them. Benevolent leadership refers to leader behaviors that demonstrate individualized, holistic concern for subordinates' personal and family well-being. Moral leadership depicts leader behaviors that demonstrate superior personal virtues or qualities that provide legitimacy as well as arousing subordinates' identification with and respect for a leader. PL is thus defined as a style that combines strong discipline and authority with fatherly benevolence and moral integrity in a personalistic atmosphere (Farh and Cheng 2000, 94).

Furthermore, the three dimensions of PL are matched by three culturally prescribed subordinate responses. Under authoritarian leadership, subordinates will comply with and abide by leaders' requests without dissent. In response to leader benevolence, subordinates will feel deeply grateful and strongly obliged to repay when the situation allows. In response to moral leadership, subordinates will respect and identify with the leader's morality and integrity and try to imitate those qualities. Implicit in the model is the complementarity of leader and subordinate roles. Authoritarian leadership cannot work unless subordinates have been socialized to respect vertical hierarchy and have a dependent mind-set (Pye 1981, Redding 1990). Leader benevolence cannot be sustained if it does not engender feelings of indebtedness and a willingness to reciprocate in subordinates. Moral leadership works only if subordinates identify with their leader's moral superiority and are willing to imitate it. When both leaders and subordinates play their respective roles, social harmony exists. When a subordinate is not ready or willing to play his or her role, a leader's insistence on PL (especially authoritarian leadership) will be futile at best and may lead to strain, disharmony, and even a breakdown of the relationship at worst. In this sense, PL is based more on followership than on leadership.

Since some of the key elements of PL counter modern values of democracy, egalitarianism, and privacy, how could PL withstand the challenges of modern time and still prevail in contemporary Chinese business organizations? It has done so because it is deeply rooted in Chinese social cultural tradition (Farh and Cheng 2000, Redding 1990, Westwood 1997). For example, authoritarianism can be traced back to China's patriarchal family system, Confucian ethic of respect for vertical order, and long history of imperial rule. In Chinese tradition, the vertical bond between father and son is paramount and supersedes all other social relations, including the husband-wife relationship, and the father's authority over sons (and other family members) is absolute. China's imperial rulers took advantage of this ethic and defined the role relationship between an emperor and a minister (or a subject) as an extension of the father-son relationship. With the backing of the emperor, patriarchy was affirmed and embraced as the organizing principle of society for 2,000 years. Through the psychological process of "pan-familism" (Yang 1993), Chinese people generalize the experiences and habits acquired in the family to other groups so that the latter can be regarded as quasi-familial organizations. When the family model is applied in business, the owner/manager takes on the role of the father, and the subordinate the role of the son—that is, the all-powerful boss dictates, and the subordinate listens and complies.

The cultural roots of benevolent leadership originate from the Confucian ideal of the kind, gentle superior, and they are further cemented by practical concern for exchanging superior favors for subordinate indebtedness, personal loyalty, and obedience. In social relations, the Chinese strongly believe in reciprocity between one person and another. Favors done for others are often considered "social investments" for which handsome returns are expected. As Yang pointed out poignantly (1957, 291), although acceptance of the principle of reciprocity is required in practically every society, in China the principle is marked by its long history, the high degree of people's consciousness of its existence, and its wide application and tremendous influence in social institutions.

The importance of moral leadership also owes its origin to the Confucian philosophy of governance. Confucius emphasized the use of moral principles, moral examples, and moral persuasion in governing. He did not believe in the efficacy of law and punishment, which he thought could regulate overt behaviors only, not inner thought. The most effective form of governance was therefore leading by virtue and by moral example. China's weak legal tradition and the tradition of the rule of man further underscore the importance of the moral character of those who occupy positions of authority (Farh and Cheng 2000).

As a culture-based leadership style, PL and its associated culturally prescribed subordinate responses are embedded in a set of social-cultural and organizational factors. The key social-cultural factors are familism and Confucian values, which include respect for hierarchy, personalism/particularism, the norm of reciprocity *(bao)*, interpersonal harmony, and leadership by virtues. The organizational factors include family ownership, separation of ownership from management, entrepreneurial structure, simple task environment, and stable technology. In this model, the social-cultural and organizational factors provide the appropriate context for the practice of PL. Thus, PL is more likely to be practiced (and perhaps more likely to be effective) in family-owned and -managed businesses than in non-family-owned businesses. Individuals who identify with traditional Chinese cultural values (such as submission to authority) are more likely to respond positively to PL than those who do not. Paternalistic leadership will lead to more positive outcomes when it is practiced in a small organization with a limited product line, a simple task environment, and a stable technology than it will in a large organization with diverse product lines, a complex environment, and unstable technology.

Paternalistic Leadership and China's Private Businesses

How does the triad model of PL work in China in general and its private businesses in particular? This question depends to a large extent on whether the social-cultural forces of familism, the Confucian ethics of respect for hierarchy, particularism/personalism, the norm of reciprocity, and so forth are still in force in China. Existing research evidence seems to suggest that these cultural forces, once severely suppressed by the Communist Party, are fast coming back in contemporary China.

Let us use the traditional Chinese concept of *guanxi* (personal connection) as an example (Farh, Tsui, Xin, and Cheng 1998; King 1991; Tsui and Farh 1997). As soon as it gained control over the mainland in 1949, the Chinese Communist Party (CCP) launched a series of campaigns and movements intended to transform the traditional norms of personal relations in China from "friendship" to "comradeship" (Vogel 1965). Friendship, in Vogel's ideal form, invokes a particularistic or private morality, whereas comradeship draws on a universalistic ethic. Comradeship embodied a citizenship's public spirit in the new socialist state and was meant to transcend particularisms based on kinship and locality. This gigantic project of value transformation was achieved largely through fear. To control its citizenry, the party-state structured the society into all-inclusive, functional collectivities called *danwei* (work units). Almost every working adult belonged to a *danwei* that provided its members with the goods and services essential for survival. During the period of the Cultural Revolution (1966–76), the Party's domination over society reached its highest level. Under the concept of "all-round dictatorship over the bourgeoisie," the Party sought to bring all aspects of social life under its control. This irrational revolutionary fever boiled all over China and nearly brought the country to the brink of total collapse. The ensuing economic reform engineered by Deng in 1978 saw a steady retreat of political power from citizens' private lives. The long-suppressed concept of friendship sprang back to life with a vengeance. Using *guanxi* for personal gain in a semireformed economy was ubiquitous in China and had penetrated every sphere of life by the mid-1980s (Yang 1994).

The account above highlights the resiliency of traditional social-cultural forces in China. As the cultural and institutional fabric underpinning PL is deeply rooted in China, we have reason to believe that PL is probably as widely practiced in organizations in the PRC as in overseas Chinese firms. Indeed, drawing from research findings about the PRC, Ho and Si recently commented that "a strong sense of paternalism, or familism . . . is still widely shared by Chinese workers" (2001, 47).

The private sector of China's economy first reappeared in the early 1980s in forms such as small-scale curbside trading and smallhold farming, as the reforms of Deng took hold. It has grown now into most branches of industry, and is the fastest growing, most efficient, and most vibrant part of the economy (Smyth, Wang, and Kiang 2001). Patterns of ownership within the sector vary, but partnership and family appear to be the main formulae (Redding 2002). The centrality of family in Chinese social ethics seems now to be slowly reasserting itself on the mainland and, although severely weakened by Communist ideology and the one-child policy, the family is returning to act as the anchor to stabilize a still-turbulent period of change (Ho and Si 2001). In conditions of insecurity such as prevail in China, family remains the first, and often the only, resort (Redding 1990). In a recent study of fifty-six small- to medium-sized enterprises in China, Pistrui (2001) found that 89 percent of them were founded by their current entrepreneur-owners, 60 percent employed other family members, and 41 percent had family investors. Other studies have confirmed this tendency (Schlevogt 2001).

Paternalistic Leadership and Subordinates' Outcomes in the Modern Chinese Context

Although PL was observed to be prevalent in overseas Chinese family businesses in ideographical studies in the 1960s through the 1980s, the question remains as to how it will apply to supervisor-subordinate relationships in modern Chinese organizations in the face of drastic societal modernization (and Westernization). Recently, a series of four studies was conducted in Taiwan on the effects of PL on a variety of subordinate outcomes in different types of organizations, including financial services firms, automobile manufacturers, high-tech firms, and public schools. These studies were conducted using questionnaire items drawn from the paternalistic leadership scale (PLS) (Cheng, Chou, and Farh 2000). In each study, subordinates filled out surveys about the leadership styles of their immediate supervisors. The dependent variables included subordinates' self-reported responses to PL, organizational commitment, and satisfaction with supervision; and supervisory ratings of subordinate performance. Table 13.1 summarizes the key findings of the four studies as pertaining to PL. In terms of the main effects of the three dimensions of PL, the findings were quite consistent. First, authoritarianism was consistently, negatively correlated with subordinate outcomes. It evoked angry emotions (i.e., anger, indignation, agitation, tiredness) and also tended to suppress the expression of such negative emotion (Wu, Hsu, and Cheng 2002); it had a negative effect on team interaction and on team members' commitment to and satisfaction with team leaders (Cheng, Huang, Chou 2002); and it led to low loyalty toward leaders, trust in leaders, and organizational citizenship behavior (Cheng, Shieh, and Chou 2002). Cheng, Chou, Huang, Wu, and Farh (2004) reported the only exception to this pattern: authoritarianism was found to have a positive effect on subordinate identification, compliance, and gratitude in multiple regression analyses. In this case, suppression had occurred in the regression analysis (Cohen and Cohen 1983) because at the bivariate level, authoritarianism was negatively correlated with identification ($r = -.28$, $p < .01$) and gratitude ($r = -.17$, $p < .01$) and uncorrelated with compliance ($r = -.06$, $p > .05$).

Second, in contrast to authoritarianism, benevolence was found to have consistent, positive effects on subordinate outcomes. It had a positive effect on team interaction, team members' commitment, and team members' satisfaction with team leaders (Cheng, Huang, and Chou 2002); led to high levels of loyalty toward leaders, trust in leaders, and organizational citizenship behavior (Cheng, Shieh, and Chou 2002); and had a significant, positive effect on subordinate identification, compliance, and gratitude (Cheng et al., 2004).

Third, the findings regarding morality were quite similar to those for benevolence. That is, morality was found to have a consistent, positive effect on subordinate outcomes. It was associated with higher loyalty toward leader, trust in leader, and organizational citizenship behavior (Cheng, Shieh, and Chou 2002), and it had a positive effect on subordinate identification, compliance, and gratitude (Cheng et al., 2004).

The above findings suggest that despite sweeping changes in Chinese societies and organizations, two of the PL dimensions (benevolence and morality) have positive effects on subordinate outcomes, largely consistent with the predictions of the triad model of PL (Figure 13.1). The lone exception is authoritarian leadership. It no longer generates compliance and obedience on the part of subordinates as predicted by the triad model of PL, and it actually leads to negative subordinate emotions (e.g., anger, suppression of anger) and outcomes (e.g., dissatisfaction with supervision and lower organizational commitment).

In view of the above, we hypothesize:

Hypothesis 1.   Moral leadership and benevolent leadership are positively associated with subordinate identification with supervisor, with moral leadership having the stronger effect.

Hypothesis 2.   Moral leadership and benevolent leadership are positively associated with subordinate gratitude and repayment to supervisor, with benevolent leadership having the stronger effect.

Hypothesis 3.   Authoritarian leadership is positively associated with subordinate fear of supervisor.

Hypothesis 4.   Benevolent leadership and moral leadership are positively associated with subordinate compliance to supervision.

Hypothesis 5.   Authoritarian leadership is negatively associated with satisfaction with supervision and organizational commitment, whereas benevolent leadership and moral leadership are positively associated with satisfaction with supervision and organizational commitment.

Table 13.1

Summary of Four Studies on Paternalistic Leadership in Taiwan

Studies and samples	Independent variables	Outcome variables
Study 1. Cheng, Huang, and Chou (2002) 400 members from 71 work teams including electronic manufacturing (17),[1] food processing (13), automobile industry (8), sales service (10), medical service (15), and public service (8). The attributes of the teams include 30 general management teams, 18 total quality management teams, and 24 RandD teams.	Authoritarian leadership ($a = .85$) Benevolent leadership ($a = .89$)	Satisfaction with leader (single-item measure) Commitment to team ($a = .90$) Self-ratings of performance ($a = .86$) Intent to stay ($a = .89$)
Study 2. Cheng, Shieh, and Chou (2002) 509 principal-teacher dyads from 157 public county elementary schools in northern Taipei.	Paternalistic leadership: Authoritarian ($a = .85$), benevolent ($a = .89$), and moral leadership ($a = .89$) Transactional leadership: Task-related ($a = .94$) and people-related ($a = .95$) transformational leadership Contingent reward and punishment ($a = .90$); Noncontingent reward and punishment ($a = .71$)	Teacher's organizational citizenship behavior (OCB) rated by principals ($a = .91$) (dimensions only; rated by principals)
Study 3. Wu, Hsu, and Cheng (2002) 609 employees from a large automobile manufacturing company in Taiwan.	*Only* authoritarian leadership ($a = .82$)	Job satisfaction (single-item measure)
Study 4. Cheng, Chou, Huang, Wu, and Farh (2004) 605 managers and employees of a large private conglomerate (H) in Taiwan with 18,000 people in 2000. Its core business is financial services, but it also operates in a variety of other industries such as banking, import/export trade, telecommunication and communication services, and paper production.	Paternalistic leadership: Authoritarian ($a = .91$), benevolent ($a = .96$), and moral leadership ($a = .93$) Transformational leadership: High performance standard ($a = .75$) Individualized consideration ($a = .88$) Modeling ($a = .97$)	Subordinate response: Identification and imitation ($a = .93$) Compliance without dissent ($a = .81$) Gratitude and repayment ($a = .88$)

[1] The number in parentheses is the number of teams for this study.

Moderator/Mediator variables	Key findings related to paternalistic leadership
Intrateam interaction: Vertical interaction ($a = .90$) Horizontal interaction ($a = .89$)	1. Benevolence had positive effects on all mediator and outcome variables, whereas authoritarianism had negative effects on all mediator and outcome variables. 2. Authoritarianism and benevolence had positive interaction effects on vertical interaction and satisfaction with leader. 3. Intrateam interaction fully mediated the effects of benevolence and authoritarianism on self-rating of performance and intent to stay. 4. Intrateam interaction partially mediated the effects of benevolence and authoritarianism on satisfaction with team leader and commitment to team.
Affective loyalty to leader (identification and internalization) ($a = .96$) Obligatory loyalty to leader (sacrifice and dedication, business assistance, obedience, and coordinate actively) ($a = .93$) Trust in leader ($a = .98$)	1. After controlling for transformational leadership and demographics, benevolent and moral leadership had positive effects on all three mediators and OCB. 2. Authoritarian leadership was negatively associated with all three mediators and OCB. 3. Obligatory loyalty and interpersonal trust fully mediated the effects of benevolent and moral leadership on OCB. 4. The study did not test the interaction effects of PL dimensions on mediators or OCB.
Angry emotional feeling about leader ($a = .83$) Suppression of angry emotional feeling ($a = .85$)	1. Authoritarian leadership had a positive effect on angry emotional feelings (toward leader), and tended to suppress the expression of angry emotions. 2. Authoritarian leadership had a negative effect on work satisfaction, and this effect was fully mediated by angry emotional feelings.
Authority orientation of subordinate's traditionality ($a = .84$)	1. With corresponding transformational leadership dimensions, controlled, authoritarianism had a positive effect on compliance and gratitude, benevolence on gratitude and identification, and morality on identification and gratitude. 2. Benevolent and authoritarian leadership had positive interaction effects on all three subordinate responses, whereas negative interaction effects between authoritarianism and morality were found on all three subordinate responses. 3. Subordinate traditionality moderated the relationship between authoritarian leadership and all three subordinate responses.

Figure 13.1   **Paternalistic Leadership and Subordinate Responses**

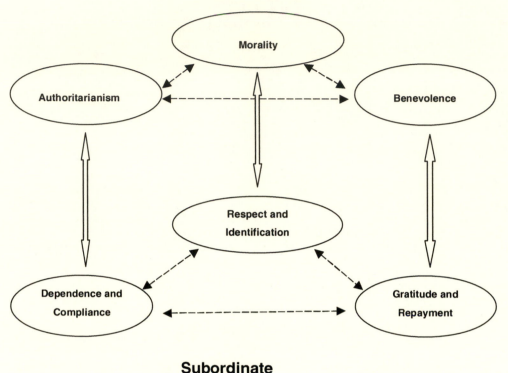

Source: Adapted from Farh and Cheng 2000.

The triad model does not include specific predictions about the interactive effects of the three PL dimensions on subordinate outcomes. However, according to a long tradition in China, an "ideal" leader is simultaneously benevolent and strict (in the sense of applying discipline). Two of the four studies examined the interactive effects of the three dimensions of PL on subordinate outcomes. In both studies, Cheng and his colleagues found a significant, positive interaction between authoritarianism and benevolence on subordinate outcomes. In Cheng, Huang, and Chou (2002), this effect was found on team vertical interaction and team member satisfaction with team leader. In Cheng et al. (2004), the effect was found on identification, compliance, and gratitude. The positive interaction effect between authoritarianism and benevolence, when graphed, reveals that when a leader was high in benevolence, authoritarianism had either a slight positive or no effect on subordinate outcomes; when the leader was low in benevolence, authoritarianism was negatively correlated with subordinate outcomes. This pattern of interaction supports the traditional idea of the "ideal" leader described above. Thus, we hypothesize:

Hypothesis 6. Authoritarian leadership and benevolent leadership interact positively to affect satisfaction with supervision.

The Contingent Effects of Subordinates' Traditionality and Resource Dependence

According to the triad model, subordinate responses to PL are contingent upon several factors. One of the factors is subordinate traditionality, which we define as the extent to which individuals are willing to respect hierarchy in society. Research has shown that individual differences in traditionality moderate the relationship between job attitudes and behavioral outcomes (Farh, Earley, and Lin 1997; Hui, Lee, and Rousseau 2004). Our general prediction is that subordinates who are high in traditionality will be more receptive to PL than those who are low in traditionality. Cheng et al. (2004) tested the moderating effects of traditionality on the relationship between PL dimensions and subordinate responses. Traditionality was found to moderate the relationships between authoritarianism and subordinate identification, compliance, and gratitude. For subordinates high in traditionality, authoritarianism was found to have a slight, positive relationship with identification, compliance, and gratitude, whereas for those who are low in traditionality, authoritarianism was negatively correlated with identification, compliance, and gratitude. Traditionality, however, was not found to interact with benevolence or morality to affect subordinate responses.

Besides traditionality, the dependence of subordinates on their supervisors may also affect subordinate responses to PL dimensions. In analyzing paternalism in overseas Chinese family businesses, Redding broke it down into seven themes, the first of which is "dependence of the subordinate as a mind-set" (Redding 1990, 130). The logic here is straightforward. Subordinates are likely to reject paternalism when they are independent and autonomous.

There are two different ways to conceptualize subordinate dependence. On the one hand, subordinate dependence may be construed as a psychological disposition of lack of need for independence (e.g., Kerr and Jermier 1978; Podsakoff et al. 1993). An alternative view is to construe it as resource-based dependence imposed by organizational structure. In analyzing worker behavior in state factories in China, Walder (1986) pointed out that the Communist Party deliberately created a culture of organized dependency in which workers were made to depend on the party-state for essential life needs. An unintended consequence of this resource dependency was the emergence of patron-client relationships between cadres and their loyal subordinates (i.e., "activists" and "backbones"). In such a "clientelist" exchange, the patron protected and cared for the needs of the clients, and the clients responded with personal loyalty and compliance. This resource-induced exchange was in essence a rebirth of China's paternalistic tradition. Thus, we expect that subordinates' dependence on their supervisors for valuable resources will serve as a key contingency for PL.

Our general prediction is that subordinates will respond to authoritarian and benevolent leadership more strongly when they are highly dependent on their supervisors for valuable resources than when they are not dependent on their supervisors. Resource dependence, however, should have little effect for moral leadership because moral leaders influence subordinates through personal character and integrity, not through power relationships or resource exchanges.

On the basis of the above discussion, we hypothesize:

Hypothesis 7. The effects of authoritarian leadership on subordinate outcomes vary according to the level of subordinate traditionality. Subordinates who are more traditional tend to respond to authoritarianism less negatively than those who are less traditional.

Hypothesis 8. The effects of authoritarian, benevolent leadership on subordinate responses vary according to the level of subordinate dependence. Subordinates who are more dependent on leaders tend to respond more strongly and favorably to authoritarianism and benevolence than those who are less dependent.

METHOD

Sample

Our sample consisted of 292 employees from 52 Chinese private enterprises in Suzhou, a major city located about 50 miles northwest of Shanghai. The enterprises represented a variety of industries popular in China, including electronics, communication, steel, textiles, restaurants, and manufacturing. The average size of these private enterprises was 207 employees (ranging from 20 to 735 employees), and the average company age was 6.92 years (ranging from 1 to 16 years, as measured until 2002). About one-third of these private businesses were family owned and run, with the remainder being various forms of joint ventures.

We obtained 292 valid surveys out of 400 distributed, achieving a return rate of 73 percent. The sample was balanced in gender (49 percent male) with an average age of 33.6 years (S.D. = 8.2). In terms of educational level, 30.4 percent of sample members had senior high school or vocational school degrees or below; 33.6 percent, professional training school degrees; 23.2 percent, bachelor's degrees; and 10.1 percent, graduate degrees. In terms of tenure, 17.9 percent of the respondents had worked in their current organizations for less than one year; 38.7 percent, one to three years; 16.8 percent, three to five years; 8.6 percent, five to seven years; and 18 percent, seven years or longer. In terms of position level, 62.5 percent of the respondents were nonsupervisory employees; 25.5 percent were first-line supervisors; and 12.0 percent were middle-level managers.

Procedure

A management professor at Suzhou University whom we hired as data collection consultant used his broad personal networks as well as the school's institutional networks to reach the HR managers of the sample enterprises to collect surveys. Respondents were given both oral and written instructions about the research purpose of the study and guarantees of the confidentiality of their responses.

Measures

Paternalistic leadership was measured using items from Cheng, Chou, and Farh (2000). The Cheng et al. (2000) scales imply a definition of PL that is broader than the original definition of the construct in Farh and Cheng (2000); we selected only items that corresponded tightly to the core definition of PL. Leader benevolence was measured by six items that specifically referred to leader behaviors that demonstrate individualized, holistic concern for subordinates' personal and family well-being. Moral leadership, or morality, was measured by four items that indicate that a supervisor is of exemplary moral character (honesty, integrity, and fairness) and willing to lead by example. Authoritarianism was measured by nine items describing the supervisor as one who centralizes decisions, demands obedience, keeps his or her true intentions purposely unclear, and acts in a dignified manner. The nineteen items of the PL scale were subjected to principal component factor analysis followed by promax rotation with Kaiser normalization. We found three factors with eigenvalues greater than one accounting for 56 percent of the total variance. All the PL items loaded properly on their designated dimensions (see Table 13.2 for survey items and factor loadings). The Cronbach alpha coefficients were .85, .84, and .83 for authoritarianism, benevolence, and morality, respectively.

Subordinate psychological responses to PL were measured on four dimensions: *identification, compliance, gratitude and repayment,* and *fear.* Items for measuring identification, compliance, and gratitude and repayment were taken from Cheng and Jiang's (2000) loyalty to supervisor scale. Identification included thirteen items expressing feelings of admiration toward and respect for the supervisor, and identification with supervisor values. Compliance was measured by three items indicating subordinate willingness to comply with supervisor work instructions without questioning. Gratitude and repayment was measured by seven items denoting that a subordinate was grateful for a supervisor's care and kindness and willing to make personal sacrifices for the benefit of the supervisor. Subordinate's fear of supervisor was measured by four items written for this study. We factor-analyzed the twenty-seven items using principal component analysis followed by promax rotation with Kaiser normalization and found four factors with eigenvalues greater than one and accounting for 61.2 percent of total item variance. All items loaded properly on their designated dimensions (see Table 13.3 for survey items and factor loadings). We deleted item thirteen from the identification scale because of its low factor loading. The Cronbach alpha coefficients were .93 for identification, .75 for compliance, .85 for fear, and .85 for gratitude and repayment.

Satisfaction with supervision was measured by a single item. Respondents were asked to indicate the extent to which they were satisfied with their direct supervisors on a 100-point scale. We did not use multiple items to measure satisfaction with supervision because previous research has shown that a single item adequately measures overall satisfaction (Negy 2002; Wanous, Reichers, and Hudy 1997). Subordinate *affective commitment* to an organization was measured by seven items drawn from previous research (Farh, Tsui, Xin, and Cheng 1998). Sample items included "My company's problems are like my own problems," "When someone praises my company, I also feel proud," and "I often tell my friends that my company is an ideal workplace." The Cronbach alpha coefficient for organizational commitment was .87.

Subordinate *dependence* on supervisor was measured by six items written for this study. We asked the respondents to indicate the extent to which their direct supervisors could determine their promotion, annual pay increase, work benefits, work resources (e.g., funding, equipment), and job content. *Traditionality* (defined as the extent to which one endorses traditional values of submission to authority) was measured by five items taken from Yang, Yu, and Yeh (1989). Since dependence was a new scale, we factor-analyzed its items along with our traditionality items using principal component analysis. We found two factors with eigenvalues greater than one accounting for 52.4 percent of variance. All items loaded properly on their designated dimensions (see Table 13.4 for survey items and factor loadings). We deleted item six from the dependence scale because of its low factor loading on dependence and cross-loading on traditionality. The Cronbach alpha coefficients were .80 for dependence and .77 for traditionality.

All of the survey items in the multi-item scales were measured on a six-point Likert scale. We used an even-numbered response format since previous research has shown that Chinese subjects tend to choose the midpoint on odd-numbered Likert scales (Chiu and Yang 1987). We hoped to reduce response bias by excluding the midpoint.

We included four demographic variables (respondent gender, age, education, and tenure) and respondent position level as controls in this study. These variables were included because they could be related to dependent variables in this study. Gender was dummy-coded (0 = female, 1 = male). Age had seven categories (1 = under 25, 2 = 26–30, etc.). Educational level had four catego-

Table 13.2

Results of Principal Component Factor Analysis of Paternalistic Leadership Scale
($N = 274$)

Paternalistic scale items	Authoritarianism	Benevolence	Morality
Authoritarianism			
1. In meetings, decisions are always made according to my supervisor's wish.	**0.77**	0.03	0.17
2. My supervisor determines all decisions in the work unit whether they are important or not.	**0.75**	−0.01	0.04
3. My supervisor does not let us know his true intention.	**0.74**	−0.03	−0.07
4. My supervisor asks me to obey his/her instructions completely.	**0.74**	−0.02	0.03
5. My supervisor scolds us when we can't accomplish our tasks.	**0.71**	−0.17	0.09
6. In my supervisor's mind, an ideal subordinate is one who always obeys his/her wishes.	**0.69**	0.09	−0.19
7. I feel a lot of pressure when working with my supervisor.	**0.62**	0.06	−0.22
8. My supervisor does not share information with us.	**0.54**	−0.10	0.20
9. In presence of us, my supervisor acts dignifiedly.	**0.53**	0.17	−0.08
Benevolence			
1. My supervisor shows concern about my private life and daily living.	−0.09	**0.78**	0.05
2. My supervisor ordinarily shows a kind concern for my comfort.	−0.11	**0.78**	0.05
3. My supervisor takes good care of my family members as well.	0.08	**0.78**	0.03
4. My supervisor takes very thoughtful care of subordinates who have spent a long time with him/her.	−0.01	**0.71**	0.13
5. My supervisor meets my needs according to my personal requests.	0.19	**0.70**	−0.21
6. My supervisor helps me resolve tough problems in my daily life.	−0.03	**0.67**	0.24
Morality			
1. My supervisor leads by example.	0.05	−0.02	**0.87**
2. My supervisor treats us fairly without bias.	0.00	−0.02	**0.86**
3. My supervisor is a role model for me in terms of moral character as well as way of doing things.	0.06	0.16	**0.75**
4. My supervisor is an honest person with integrity; he/she never promotes his/her private interests under the guise of serving the public.	−0.02	0.10	**0.66**

Table 13.3

Results of Principal Component Factor Analysis of Identification, Gratitude and Repayment, Fear, and Compliance (N = 264)

	Identification	Gratitude and repayment	Fear	Compliance
Identification				
1. I very much admire my supervisor's manner and behavior.	**0.90**	−0.21	0.01	−0.03
2. I identify with my supervisor in philosophy and methods of work.	**0.85**	−0.02	−0.05	−0.04
3. I have the greatest respect for my supervisor.	**0.82**	−0.13	0.00	0.09
4. I think my supervisor is a person of foresight.	**0.78**	−0.12	0.11	0.10
5. I tell my colleagues or friends about my supervisor's merits.	**0.75**	0.21	−0.16	−0.21
6. When my supervisor is treated unfairly, I will speak out for him/her.	**0.73**	−0.03	0.07	−0.12
7. I often tell my friends that my supervisor is a good boss.	**0.70**	0.13	−0.11	0.14
8. My values are becoming more similar to my supervisor's since starting to work here.	**0.67**	0.26	0.07	−0.10
9. I feel honored when my supervisor is praised.	**0.63**	0.05	0.01	0.20
10. When my supervisor is criticized, I feel as if I have been criticized personally.	**0.59**	0.24	0.15	0.03
11. My supervisor's success is my success.	**0.55**	0.33	−0.09	0.05
12. I find I always agree with my supervisor's opinions.	**0.52**	0.11	0.02	0.28
13. I think my supervisor is always right in his/her decisions.	**0.37**	0.24	0.14	0.23
Gratitude and Repayment				
1. When I get the opportunity, I'll repay my supervisor for the kindness shown.	0.12	**0.77**	−0.05	−0.19
2. I would sacrifice my own benefits to maintain my supervisor's benefits.	−0.02	**0.73**	−0.02	0.17
3. I am willing to help my supervisor perform his/her private business.	−0.02	**0.70**	−0.08	0.12
4. I am willing to take responsibility for the wrongs that my supervisor has done.	−0.21	**0.63**	0.23	0.10
5. I am willing to gather colleagues' information (e.g., plan, thoughts, opinions) to report to my supervisor.	−0.01	**0.61**	0.17	0.04
6. I am very grateful for my supervisor's kindness toward me.	0.30	**0.59**	−0.04	−0.09
7. I would work for my supervisor, even if I have to sacrifice my own interests to do so.	0.19	**0.45**	0.06	0.30

(continued)

Table 13.3 *(continued)*

	Identification	Gratitude and repayment	Fear	Compliance
Fear				
1. I feel tense when I am with my supervisor.	−0.05	0.08	**0.86**	−0.01
2. I try hard to keep distance from my supervisor.	0.02	0.07	**0.83**	−0.25
3. I always worry about my supervisor's criticism of my poor work performance.	0.16	−0.26	**0.80**	0.17
4. I am afraid of my supervisor.	−0.07	0.27	**0.75**	0.01
Compliance				
1. I comply with my supervisor's decisions even if I disagree.	−0.17	0.06	−0.04	**0.81**
2. I exactly abide by my supervisor's philosophy and methods for work.	0.18	0.05	−0.14	**0.70**
3. I completely obey my supervisor's instructions.	0.22	−0.02	0.07	**0.67**

Table 13.4

Results of Factor Analysis of Traditionality and Dependence ($N = 260$)

	Traditionality	Dependence
Traditionality		
1. The best way to avoid mistakes is to follow the instructions of senior persons.	**0.79**	0.03
2. To obey authority and respect elders are virtues that children should learn.	**0.78**	−0.15
3. When people are in dispute, they should ask the most senior person to decide who is right.	**0.78**	−0.04
4. Children should respect those people who are respected by their parents.	**0.67**	0.08
5. The chief government official is like the head of a family. Citizens should obey the chief's decisions on all state matters.	**0.67**	0.11
Dependence		
1. My promotion is pretty much decided by my direct supervisor.	−0.12	**0.79**
2. The size of my annual raise is heavily influenced by my direct supervisor's decision.	−0.10	**0.79**
3. I have to rely on my direct supervisor's support to obtain better benefits.	0.05	**0.79**
4. I have to rely on my direct supervisor to obtain necessary work resources (e.g., funding, equipment).	0.10	**0.67**
5. My job contents are assigned by my supervisor.	0.27	**0.44**
6. I have to rely on my direct supervisor's assistance to complete my work.	0.37	**0.37**

ries (1 = below junior high school, 2 = senior high school, 3 = bachelor's degree, and 4 = graduate school or above). Tenure had eight categories (1 = less than 1 year, 2 = 1–3 years, 3 = 3–5 years, 4 = 5–7 years, 5 = 7–9 years, 6 = 9–11 years, 7 = 11–13 years, and 8 = more than 13 years). Position level had three categories (1 = staff, 2 = first-line supervisor, 3 = second-line manager or above).

Analyses

We employed multiple regression analysis to test the effects of PL on subordinate outcomes, regressing each of these on the three PL components while controlling for subordinate demographics, position level, traditionality, and dependence. We used hierarchical regression analysis to examine the effects of interaction among the three components of PL on subordinate outcomes and the moderating effects of traditionality and dependence on the relationships between PL and subordinate outcomes. When a significant interaction or moderating effect was found, we used the procedure described in Cohen and Cohen (1983) to graph the effect. Since the various types of subordinate outcomes can be differentiated into proximal and distal outcomes, with tentative causal flows linking the former to the latter, we employed covariance structure analysis to test an overall causal model of PL effects on subordinate outcomes.

RESULTS

Correlational Analysis

Table 13.5 presents means, standard deviations, and intercorrelations among the study's variables. An examination of the table reveals several interesting patterns of relationships. First, while morality and benevolence were moderately correlated ($r = .48$), they were marginally correlated with authoritarianism ($r = -.16$ and .15, respectively). This correlation pattern suggests a fairly high degree of independence among the three components of PL. Second, although the six subordinate outcome variables (i.e., identification, compliance, fear, gratitude and repayment, satisfaction, and commitment) were significantly correlated, no two variables shared more than 38 percent of variance (the highest correlation was .61), suggesting that these outcome variables were relatively distinct. Third, subordinate traditionality and dependence were positively correlated with subordinate outcomes ($r = .07$ to .58) and three PL dimensions ($r = .20$ to .38). These values suggest that some of the correlations between PL and subordinate outcomes may be inflated owing to their correlations with subordinate disposition (i.e., traditionality) and a situational factor (i.e., subordinate dependence on a leader for resources). To control for this form of common method bias, we added traditionality and dependence to our list of control variables when we assessed the effects of PL dimensions on subordinate outcomes in multiple regression analyses.

Regression Analyses

To test Hypotheses 1–5 (i.e., the main effects of PL dimensions on subordinate outcomes), we regressed each subordinate outcome on the PL dimensions, along with control variables. Table 13.6 presents results of this analysis, showing a pair of models under each outcome variable. Each first column shows the effects of PL dimensions on subordinate outcomes we found while controlling for subordinate demographics and position only. Each second column shows results with traditionality and dependence added to the control variables to control for common method bias and the influence of the two moderating variables.

Table 13.5

Means, Standard Deviations, and Intercorrelations of Study Variables[a]

	Mean	S. D.	1	2	3	4	5	6	7	8	9	10	11	12	13	14	15	16
1. Identification	4.47	0.73	(0.93)															
2. Compliance	4.34	0.82	0.61	(0.75)														
3. Fear	3.59	1.02	0.17	0.25	(0.85)													
4. Gratitude	3.92	0.81	0.59	0.56	0.47	(0.85)												
5. Satisfaction	80.90	16.02	0.47	0.21	-0.12	0.14	—											
6. Commitment	4.51	0.73	0.61	0.40	0.01	0.35	0.36	(0.87)										
7. Age	3.81	1.65	0.07	0.05	0.13	0.19	0.08	0.07	—									
8. Sex	0.51	0.50	0.04	0.00	0.12	0.12	0.04	0.06	0.17	—								
9. Education	3.08	1.03	-0.05	0.05	0.03	0.04	-0.16	-0.16	-0.23	0.01	—							
10. Tenure	2.98	1.99	0.01	-0.07	0.01	-0.03	0.13	0.13	0.41	-0.08	-0.25	—						
11. Position	1.49	0.73	0.18	0.08	0.02	0.18	0.13	0.12	0.14	0.12	0.16	0.16	—					
12. Traditionality	3.90	0.93	0.43	0.45	0.34	0.42	0.15	0.38	0.05	-0.03	-0.06	0.02	0.02	(0.80)				
13. Dependence	4.20	0.77	0.47	0.49	0.46	0.58	0.07	0.27	-0.01	0.02	0.05	-0.04	0.06	0.36	(0.77)			
14. Authoritarianism	3.59	0.87	0.02	0.21	0.51	0.31	-0.14	-0.14	0.19	0.03	0.11	-0.01	0.02	0.26	0.37	(0.85)		
15. Benevolence	3.88	0.89	0.47	0.34	0.23	0.49	0.23	0.43	0.11	0.16	0.00	-0.06	0.10	0.38	0.34	0.15	(0.84)	
16. Morality	4.60	0.83	0.52	0.24	-0.12	0.18	0.43	0.54	-0.10	-0.03	-0.18	0.09	0.00	0.26	0.20	-0.17	0.48	(0.83)

Note: Numbers in parentheses on the diagonal are Cronbach alphas of the multi-item scale. $N = 244$, listwise deletion.
[a]When r is greater than 0.13 and 0.17, p is less than 0.05 and 0.01 (two-tailed), respectively.

Hypothesis 1 states that moral and benevolent leadership are positively associated with subordinate identification, with moral leadership having a stronger effect. As predicted, morality had a strong, positive effect on identification (columns 1 and 2). The effect of benevolence on identification was weaker (column 1) and became nonsignificant in column 2. Hypothesis 1 is supported. The same analysis also showed that authoritarianism had no effect on identification in column 1 but had a significant, negative effect in column 2, which signals its status as a suppressor variable in the equation.

Hypothesis 2 states that moral and benevolent leadership are positively associated with subordinate gratitude and repayment to a supervisor, with benevolent leadership having a stronger effect. As shown in columns 3 and 4 of Table 13.6, subordinate gratitude and repayment was strongly associated with leader benevolence but uncorrelated to morality. Hypothesis 2 was partially supported.

Hypothesis 3 states that authoritarian leadership is positively associated with subordinate fear of supervisor. As shown in both columns 5 and 6, fear was strongly, positively associated with authoritarianism. Hypothesis 3 was thus supported. Interestingly, benevolence was also found to be positively related to fear of supervisor, and, in contrast, leader morality tended to have a negative effect on fear of supervisor.

Hypothesis 4 states that benevolent and moral leadership are positively associated with subordinate compliance to supervision. As shown in column 7 in Table 13.6, compliance was significantly, positively correlated with all three PL dimensions. These significant effects dissipated, however, when traditionality and dependence were entered into the regression as controls. Hypothesis 4 was partially supported.

Hypothesis 5 states that authoritarian leadership is negatively associated with satisfaction with supervision and organizational commitment, whereas benevolent and moral leadership are positively associated with satisfaction with supervision and organizational commitment. As shown in columns 9–12, both morality and benevolence had significant, positive effects on organizational commitment, whereas authoritarianism had a significant, negative effect on commitment. The three PL dimensions together accounted for 24 percent of the variance in commitment beyond that accounted for by subordinate demographics, position level, traditionality, and dependence. Subordinate satisfaction with supervision was positively associated with morality only. Benevolence and authoritarianism had no effect on satisfaction, nor did subordinate traditionality and dependence. Hypothesis 5 was strongly supported with respect to organizational commitment but partially supported with respect to satisfaction with supervision.

Hypothesis 6 states that authoritarian and benevolent leadership interact positively to affect satisfaction with supervision. We tested this prediction by including the interaction of authoritarianism and benevolence in the regression equation, in addition to the PL dimensions and control variables. The interaction term was nonsignificant, and Hypothesis 6 was not supported.

Moderating Effects of Subordinate Traditionality and Dependence on Supervisor for Resources

Hypothesis 7 states that the effects of authoritarian leadership on subordinate outcomes vary according to the level of subordinate traditionality. Subordinates who are more traditional tend to respond to authoritarianism less negatively than those who are less traditional. We analyzed the effects of the interaction between traditionality and each of the three PL dimensions on subordinate outcomes using hierarchical multiple regression analysis. We found a significant interaction

248

Table 13.6

Multiple Regression Analysis of Effects of Paternalistic Leadership on Subordinate Outcomes (N = 244)

	Identification (H1)		Gratitude (H2)		Fear (H3)		Compliance (H4)		Satisfaction (H5)		Commitment (H5)	
	1	2	3	4	5	6	7	8	9	10	11	12
Step 1. Control variables												
Age	0.06	0.03	0.22**	0.20***	0.12	0.11	0.10	0.08	-0.01	-0.01	-0.02	-0.04
Gender	-0.02	-0.01	0.06	0.07	0.11	0.12*	-0.05	-0.04	0.03	0.03	0.03	0.05
Education	-0.08	-0.08	0.03	0.03	0.06	0.05	0.03	0.03	-0.16*	-0.16*	-0.17*	-0.15*
Tenure	-0.09	-0.06	-0.13	-0.10	0.00	0.03	-0.13	-0.10	0.07	0.08	0.06	0.08
Position	0.18**	0.15**	0.16*	0.13*	-0.01	-0.04	0.08	0.04	0.14*	0.14*	0.11	0.10
Traditionality		0.30***		0.24***		0.19**		0.32***		0.13		0.32***
Dependence		0.35***		0.48***		0.39***		0.36***		0.02		0.16*
ΔR²	**0.04**	**0.32***	**0.08****	**0.45***	**0.03**	**0.27***	**0.02**	**0.34***	**0.06***	**0.08***	**0.05**	**0.20***
Step 2. Paternalistic leadership												
Authoritarian	0.03	-0.15**	0.23***	0.03	0.45***	0.29***	0.19**	-0.01	-0.09	-0.10	-0.12*	-0.24***
Benevolent	0.22***	0.09	0.41***	0.27***	0.26***	0.15*	0.20**	0.04	0.03	0.01	0.23***	0.13*
Moral	0.45***	0.37***	0.04	-0.05	-0.19**	-0.26***	0.21***	0.12	0.39***	0.38***	0.41***	0.35***
ΔR²	**0.33***	**0.19***	**0.024****	**0.05***	**0.28***	**0.14***	**0.16***	**0.02**	**0.17***	**0.16***	**0.32***	**0.24***
Overall R^2	0.37	0.51	0.33	0.50	0.31	0.42	0.18	0.36	0.23	0.23	0.37	0.44
F-value	17.15***	23.87***	14.17***	22.89***	13.36***	16.56***	6.32***	12.98***	8.45***	6.83***	17.01***	18.39***

*$p < 0.05$; **$p < 0.01$; ***$p < 0.001$.

Table 13.7

Multiple Regression Analysis of the Interaction Effects of Paternalistic Leadership Dimensions, Subordinate Traditionality, and Dependence on Supervisor ($N = 244$)

	Moderation of traditionality		Moderation of dependence on supervisor for resources			
	Fear	Satis-faction	Fear	Compli-ance	Identi-fication	Commit-ment
Control variables						
Age	−0.03	0.08	−0.02	0.10	0.13*	0.07
Gender	0.10	0.06	0.10	−0.05	−0.02	0.03
Education	−0.03	−0.05	−0.04	0.04	0.00	−0.08
Tenure	0.08	0.05	0.08	−0.13*	−0.10	0.02
Position	−0.03	0.10	−0.02	0.06	0.15**	0.10*
Traditionality	−0.46	0.46	0.16**	0.27***	0.21***	0.22***
Dependence	0.30***	−0.01	−0.05	0.49	0.62	0.55
Paternalistic leadership						
Authoritarian (AU)	0.20	−0.66**	−0.31	−0.23	−0.06	−0.40
Benevolent (BE)	−0.42	0.22	0.21	−0.68*	−0.43	−0.82**
Moral (MO)	−0.26	0.87**	−0.23	0.94**	0.97**	1.52***
Two–way interactions						
AU * Traditionality	0.11	0.86*				
BE * Traditionality	1.00*	−0.36				
MO * Traditionality	−0.06	−0.93				
AU * Dependence			0.88*	0.31	−0.13	0.22
BE * Dependence			−0.10	1.12*	0.80*	1.46***
MO * Dependence			−0.07	−1.38*	−1.00*	−1.95***
ΔR^2	**0.02***	**0.04***	**0.01**	**0.03***	**0.01**	**0.05***
Overall R^2	0.44	0.27	0.43	0.39	0.52	0.49
F–value	13.68***	6.50***	13.22***	11.09***	18.93***	16.82***

$*p < 0.05; **p < 0.01; ***p < 0.001.$

between authoritarian leadership and traditionality on satisfaction with supervision. Somewhat unexpectedly, we also found a significant interaction between benevolent leadership and traditionality on fear. These results are shown in Table 13.7. Following Cohen and Cohen's (1983) recommended procedure, we plotted the two interaction effects in Figure 13.2a and Figure 13.2b. Consistent with Hypothesis 7, leader authoritarianism was more negatively associated with satisfaction with supervision for subordinates with low rather than high traditionality (Figure 13.2b). As the traditionality X authoritarian leadership interaction was found on one subordinate outcome only (i.e., satisfaction with supervison), Hypothesis 7 received partial support. Figure 13.2a shows that the relationship between benevolent leadership and fear was stronger for employees with high traditionality than for employees with low traditionality.

Hypothesis 8 states that the effects of authoritarian and benevolent leadership on subordinate

Figure 13.2 **Interactions Between Benevolent and Authoritarian
Leadership and Traditionality**

Figure 13.2a   Benevolent Leadership x Traditionality on Fear

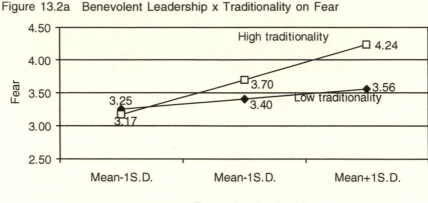

Figure 13.2b   Authoritarian Leadership x Traditionality on Satisfaction

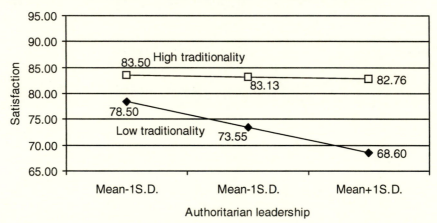

responses vary according to the level of subordinate dependence. Subordinates who are dependent on leaders tend to respond more strongly and favorably to authoritarianism and benevolence than those who are not dependent. We analyzed the interactive effects between dependence and PL dimensions using hierarchical multiple regression analysis. Seven of the eighteen interactions were significant. Results are in Table 13.7, and plots of the interaction effects are in Figures 13.3a–13.3g.

First, dependence was found to moderate the relationship between authoritarianism and fear. Supervisor authoritarianism had a stronger positive effect on fear of supervisor when subordinate dependence was high than when it was low (see Figure 13.3a). Second, dependence was also found to moderate the effects of benevolence on identification, compliance, and organizational commitment. Benevolence had a stronger positive effect on identification, compliance, and commitment when subordinate dependence was high than when it was low (Figures 13.3b–13.3d). Hypothesis 8 was partially supported.

Figure 13.3 **Interactions Between Paternalistic Leadership and Dependence**

Figure 13.3a   Authoritarian Leadership x Dependence on Fear

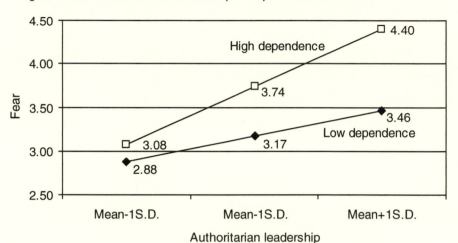

Figure 13.3b   Benevolent Leadership x Dependence on Identification

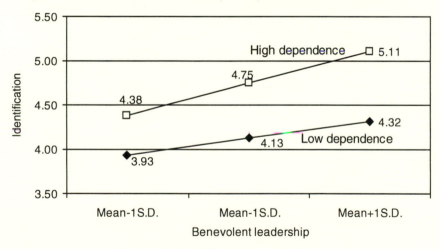

Unexpectedly, dependence was also found to moderate the effects of morality on identification, compliance, and commitment. The pattern of this effect was exactly the opposite of that for benevolence in that morality had a stronger positive effect on identification, compliance, and commitment when subordinate dependence was low than when it was high (Figures 13.3e–13.3g).

Supplementary Causal Analysis of PL Effects on Subordinate Outcomes

One of the major strengths of this study is that we examined PL effects on a variety of subordinate outcomes, some supervisor related (e.g., fear of supervisor) and others organization related (e.g., organizational commitment). We divided these six outcomes into two groups of three. The first group consists of immediate psychological responses directly impacted by PL dimensions, in-

Figure 13.3c   Benevolent Leadership x Dependence on Compliance

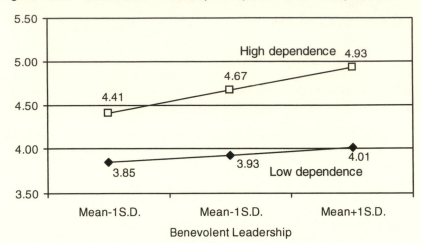

Figure 13.3d   Benevolent Leadership x Dependence on Organizational Commitment

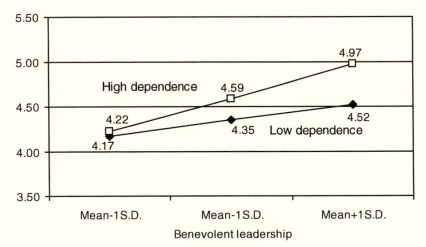

cluding fear, gratitude and repayment, and identification. The second group consists of more distal outcomes (i.e., compliance, satisfaction with supervision, and organizational commitment), which are linked with PL dimensions indirectly through the psychological states. We labeled the former "proximal outcomes" and the latter "distal outcomes." This data set provides an opportunity to conduct preliminary causal analysis of PL effects on these two layers of outcomes.

Figure 13.4 presents our exploratory causal model. The exogenous variables of this model are the three correlated PL dimensions. The three proximal outcomes immediately following the PL dimensions are fear of supervisor, gratitude and repayment to supervisor, and identification with supervisor. Drawing on the triad model (see Figure 13.1), we allowed direct causal paths linking the three PL dimensions to each of the three proximal outcomes: authoritarianism → fear; morality → identification; and benevolence → gratitude and repayment. We further introduced a causal path from gratitude and repayment to identification because psychological identification may

Figure 13.3e   Moral Leadership x Dependence on Identification

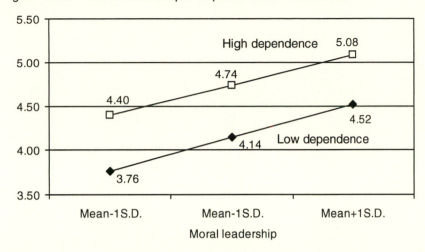

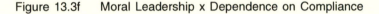

Figure 13.3f   Moral Leadership x Dependence on Compliance

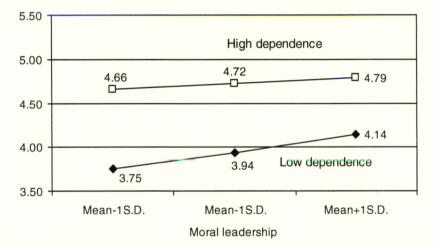

derive not only from respect for a leader's moral character, but also from gratitude for leader benevolence. Our model also included three distal outcomes (i.e., compliance, satisfaction with supervision, and organizational commitment), and all of them were impacted by the three PL dimensions through the three proximal variables (i.e., fear, gratitude and repayment, and identification). Thus, our model allows for direct paths from fear, gratitude and repayment, and identification to each of three distal outcomes. This setup is justifiable. For example, subordinates may comply with their supervisors' requests because of fear of reprisal by the supervisor, gratitude and felt obligation to repay past favors provided by the supervisor, and personal identification with the supervisor (cf. Etzioni 1961). In terms of satisfaction with supervision and organizational commitment, fear of supervisor should have a negative effect on both outcomes, whereas feelings that a supervisor deserves gratitude and repayment and personal identification with the supervisor should enhance both outcomes.

Figure 13.3g   Moral Leadership x Dependence on Organizational Commitment

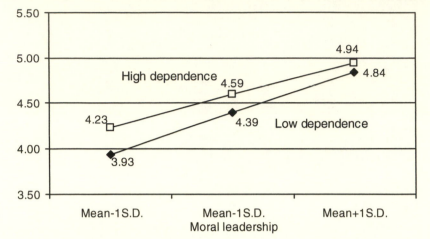

The exploratory causal model was estimated via the EQS 6.1 program using maximum likelihood techniques (Bentler 2004). Because of concern about the large number of parameters to be estimated in the measurement model, we collapsed multi-item scales into two indicators for each latent construct (Aryee, Budhwar, and Chen 2002; Bagozzi and Heatherton 1994). Ensuing covariance structure analysis indicated that the causal model fitted the data reasonably well (χ^2 = 352.38; d.f. = 120; RMSEA = .09; CFI = .92; NFI = .89). Figure 13.4 also presents the structural coefficients of this analysis, which confirmed most of the paths in the model. Authoritarianism had indirect negative effects on satisfaction with supervision and organizational commitment that were mainly mediated through fear. Authoritarianism also had a weak, indirect positive effect on compliance that was mediated through fear. Moral leadership's indirect effects on compliance, satisfaction with supervision, and organizational commitment were transmitted through identification. Benevolence had a positive indirect effect on compliance that was mediated through gratitude and repayment. Benevolence also had an indirect positive effect on satisfaction with supervision and organizational commitment, and its effects were mediated through gratitude and repayment, and then identification.

DISCUSSION

The primary purpose of this study was to investigate whether the PL model developed by Farh and Cheng (2000) could account for supervisor-subordinate relationships in China's private businesses. The overall findings from this study are supportive in that: (1) the three dimensions of PL had positive relationships with subordinate outcomes, per Hypotheses 1–4; (2) the relationships of PL to organizational commitment, satisfaction with supervision, and compliance with supervisor requests were mediated through the psychological responses of fear, gratitude and repayment, and identification; and (3) subordinate dependence on supervisor for resources and subordinate traditionality interacted with PL dimensions in affecting subordinate outcomes, as predicted by Farh and Cheng's (2000) model. These results not only replicate the core findings of prior research on PL conducted in Taiwan, but also extend them by linking PL dimen-

Figure 13.4 A Causal Model of Paternalistic Leadership on Subordinate Outcomes

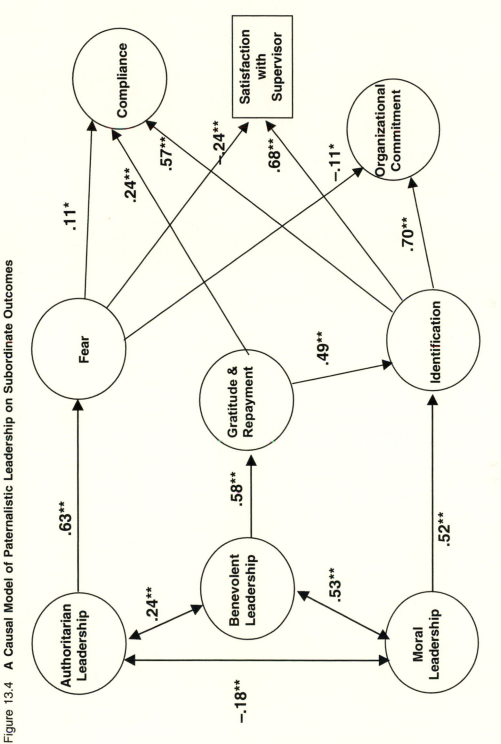

*$p < 0.05$; **$p < 0.01$; non-significant paths were omitted from the figure.

sions with satisfaction, commitment, and compliance through the psychological responses of identification, gratitude and repayment, and fear. In addition, this study demonstrated the importance of subordinate dependence on supervisor for resources as a key variable conditioning the effects of PL on subordinate outcomes.

One of the core findings of this study concerns the effects of authoritarianism on subordinate outcomes. In keeping with previous research, we found that authoritarianism led to a variety of negative outcomes, such as lower organizational commitment and lower satisfaction with supervision. Going beyond previous research, we found that subordinate fear of supervisor played a critical intervening role in accounting for the effects of authoritarianism. Fear was found to be positively related to compliance but negatively related to organizational commitment and satisfaction with supervision. This pattern suggests that authoritarian leaders may extract compliance from subordinates through fear, but their doing so has relational costs—lower satisfaction with supervision and lower organizational commitment.

We also found that authoritarianism interacted with subordinate traditionality in affecting subordinate satisfaction with supervision. For subordinates with traditional values, authoritarianism was not negatively related to satisfaction with supervision. For subordinates with less traditional values, authoritarianism evoked strong dissatisfaction with supervision. Authoritarianism was more strongly related to fear when subordinates were highly dependent on supervisors for resources than when they were not. These results suggest that subordinate responses to authoritarian leadership are contingent on their own personalities and their perceptions of dependence.

The negative effect of authoritarianism is of course not totally unexpected. The experience of Communist rule and economic reform in the PRC in the last five decades has weakened the very foundation of the traditional conception of authority. One can no longer assume that submission to authority is a universal value espoused by all Chinese.

With the deterioration of the traditional value of submission to authority in Chinese societies, authoritarian leadership in its present form may need to be revised before Chinese employees can accept it. This transformation could take two directions. First, authoritarian leadership could be transformed by purging leader behaviors that are particularly degrading to individual dignity (e.g., belittling subordinate contributions, tight personal control, insisting on absolute obedience). Other facets of authoritarian leadership (e.g., imposing strict work standards, insisting on following work rules, setting high performance standards) may still be retained and even reinforced in some organizational contexts. Indeed, a recent study by Wang (2002) showed that tight administrative control by CEOs was associated with higher firm performance. Second, instead of being fixated on building personal authority to inspire awe or fear in subordinates, supervisors could direct their attention toward building impersonal authority (e.g., upholding the *authority* of core principles or values that their companies cherish). When authority is transferred from a supervisor to core principles or values, subordinates are no longer obedient to "man" but to "law." They no longer experience the fear and awe associated with the exercise of personal authority but instead experience the *awe* associated with the core principles or values. Impersonal authority built on principles or values should be less likely to arouse employee resistance than personal authority in contemporary China. Impersonal authority also has the benefits of developing a strong, more enduring corporate culture, smoother managerial succession, and greater stability and continuity over time. Future research should look at these possibilities.

In contrast to authoritarianism, benevolence had a strong, positive relationship to gratitude and repayment to supervisor, through which benevolence had positive effects on identification, compliance, satisfaction, and commitment. Our study further showed that the positive impacts of benevolence on identification, compliance, and organizational commitment are stronger when subordinates depend on supervisors for resources. As our measure of dependence was a reverse measure of supervisor positional power, our finding suggests that when a powerful leader turns benevolent, he or she will have a particularly strong, positive effect on subordinates. In contrast, when a weak leader turns benevolent, his or her benevolent acts have little impact on subordinates. This finding is not inconsistent with findings in the leadership literature on position power (Yukl 1998). Although a powerful leader's benevolent acts may be seen as showing genuine care for subordinates, a weak leader's benevolent acts may be seen as a sign of weakness, which subordinates may not appreciate at all.

Among the three PL dimensions, morality emerged as the most influential on identification, satisfaction with supervision, and organizational commitment. Morality was also found to interact with dependence in affecting identification, compliance, and commitment. These interaction effects show that morality tended to have a stronger relationship to identification, compliance, and commitment when leaders had low position power than when they had high position power. This interaction pattern is exactly the opposite of the pattern for benevolent leadership. While benevolent leaders cultivate personal relationships with subordinates and influence them through reciprocity, moral leaders inspire subordinates through their integrity. Therefore, a benevolent leader holding a powerful position is especially influential, yet a moral leader influences despite lack of position power. These contrasting results are worth systematic replication in future research.

Unexpectedly, we did not find that PL dimensions interacted with each other to affect subordinate outcomes. In other word, there is no evidence that a leader who combines authoritarianism with benevolence is more effective in drawing out identification, compliance, gratitude and repayment, satisfaction, or commitment than an authoritarian leader who is not benevolent. Previous research has found such an interactive effect occasionally (see Table 13.1). Future research should examine why such combined effects occur in some samples but not in others.

Finally, we must hasten to add that our assessment of leadership effectiveness was limited to subordinate responses only. It is entirely possible that PL may produce positive outcomes at the organizational level that subordinate outcomes do not reflect. For example, PL at the executive rank tends to foster a single-person decision-making structure, which has the advantages of the gearing up on deeply informed intuitions, the great flexibility of strategy formulation, and the fast speed of response (Redding, 1990). These help the organization to become adaptive and flexible and are the strength of many Overseas Chinese organizations. In family-owned businesses, PL can certainly help the owner/managers maintain control. So in terms of maximizing the control of family wealth, PL may be a very effective strategy. Future research on PL needs to study its effects on organization-level outcomes.

LIMITATIONS

This study has several limitations that may raise concern about the interpretation of results. First, the PL data and subordinate responses were both drawn from the same group of subordinates, which might incur the problem of same-source bias or common method variance. However, some researchers have claimed that, methodologically, same-source bias does not necessarily have a serious impact on conclusions (Kline, Sulsky, and Rever-Moriyama 2000; Spector 1987). Despite these claims, future research should obtain independent and dependent variables from different sources.

Second, the cross-sectional nature of the study implies that our causal conclusions may be subject to alternative interpretations. Longitudinal design with measurement of the cause and effect at different intervals would enhance results.

Third, the target group whose leadership behaviors were described by our respondents comprised mid- and low-level managers. These findings may not generalize to top managers or to the owners of Chinese family businesses to whom the PL theory was intended to apply.

CONCLUSIONS

Paternalistic leadership (PL) is an indigenous Chinese leadership style rooted in China's patriarchal tradition and prevalent in overseas Chinese family businesses. This chapter reviewed the extant research on PL and then used a sample of 292 employees in 52 private enterprises to examine how PL applies to China's private businesses. We found a negative relationship between authoritarianism and employee outcomes of satisfaction with supervision and organizational commitment, and these effects were mediated by fear of supervisor. We further found benevolence and morality to be positively associated with subordinate compliance, satisfaction with supervision, and organizational commitment, and these effects were mediated by subordinate gratitude and repayment, and by identification with supervisor. Subordinate resource dependence and traditionality interacted with PL dimensions to affect several subordinate outcomes. We constructed a path model that shows tentative causal relationships between paternalistic leadership dimensions, subordinate psychological reactions, and attitudinal/behavioral outcomes. This chapter contributed to our understanding of leadership in China's private enterprises not only by identifying employees' underlying psychological responses to PL, but also by revealing the rich interplay among a leader's authoritarianism, benevolence, and moral character, and an employee's traditionality and resource dependence on the leader. We hope that this chapter has enhanced understanding of leadership in general and offered useful suggestions for managing employees in China.

REFERENCES

Aryee, S.; P. S. Budhwar; and Z. X. Chen. (2002). Trust as a mediator of the relationship between organizational justice and work outcomes: Test of a social exchange model. *Journal of Organizational Behavior,* 23, 267–85.
Bagozzi, R., and T. Heatherton. (1994). A general approach to representing multifaceted personality constructs: Application to self-esteem. *Structural Equation Modeling,* 1, 35–67.
Bentler, P. M. (2004). *EQS 6 for Windows Program Manual.* Encino, CA: Multivariate Software.
Chang, S. K. C. (1985). American and Chinese managers in U.S. companies in Taiwan: A comparison. *California Management Review,* 27, 4, 144–56.
Chen, X. P., and J. L. Farh. (1999). The effectiveness of transactional and transformational leader behaviours in Chinese organizations: Evidence from Taiwan. Paper presented at the annual meeting of the Academy of Management, Chicago.
Cheng, B. S. (1990). *Leadership and situation: An interactional psychology approach* (in Chinese). Taipei: Dayang.
———. (1995a). Paternalistic authority and leadership: A case study of a Taiwanese CEO (in Chinese). *Bulletin of the Institute of Ethnology Academic Sinica,* 79, 119–73.
———. (1995b). Hierarchical structure and Chinese organizational behavior (in Chinese). *Indigenous Psychological Research in Chinese Societies,* 3, 142–219.
Cheng, B. S.; L. F. Chou; and J. L. Farh. (2000). A triad model of paternalistic leadership: The constructs and measurement (in Chinese). *Indigenous Psychological Research in Chinese Societies,* 14, 3–64.
Cheng, B. S.; L. F. Chou; M.P. Huang; T. Y. Wu; and J. L. Farh (2004). Paternalistic leadership and subordinator responses: Evidence from Taiwan. *Asian Journal of Social Psychology,* 7(1), 89–117.

Cheng, B. S.; M. P. Huang; and L. F. Chou. (2002). Paternalistic leadership and its effectiveness: Evidence from Chinese organizational teams. *Journal of Psychology in Chinese Societies,* 3, 85–112.

Cheng, B. S., and D. Y. Jiang. (2000). Supervisory loyalty in Chinese business enterprises: The relative effects of emic and imposed-etic constructs on employee effectiveness (in Chinese). *Indigenous Psychological Research in Chinese Societies,* 14, 65–114.

Cheng, B. S.; P. Y. Shieh; and L. F. Chou. (2002). The principal's leadership, leader-member exchange quality, and the teacher's extra-role behavior: The effects of transformational and paternalistic leadership (in Chinese). *Indigenous Psychological Research in Chinese Societies,* 17, 105–61.

Chiu, C., and C. F. Yang. (1987). Chinese subjects' dilemmas: Humility and cognitive laziness as problems in using rating scales. *Bulletin of the Hong Kong Psychological Society,* 18, 39–50.

Cohen, J., and P. Cohen. (1983). *Applied multiple regression /correlation analysis for behavioral science.* Hillsdale, NJ: Lawrence Erlbaum Associates.

Etzioni, A. (1961). *Comparative analysis of complex organizations.* New York: Free Press.

Farh, J. L., and B. S. Cheng. (2000). A cultural analysis of paternalistic leadership in Chinese organizations. In J. T. Li, A. S. Tsui, and E. Weldon (Eds.), *Management and organizations in the Chinese Context,* pp. 94–127. London: Macmillan.

Farh, J. L.; P. C. Earley; and S. C. Lin. (1997). Impetus for action: A cultural analysis of justice and organizational citizenship behaviour in Chinese society. *Administrative Science Quarterly,* 42, 421–44.

Farh, J. L.; P. M. Podsakoff; and B. S. Cheng. (1987). Culture-free leadership effectiveness versus moderators of leadership behavior: An extension and test of Kerr and Jermier's substitutes for leadership model in Taiwan. *Journal of International Business Studies,* 18, 43–60.

Farh, J. L.; A. S. Tsui; K. Xin; and B. S. Cheng. (1998). The influence of relational demography and *guanxi:* The Chinese case. *Organization Science,* 9, 471–88.

Ho, Y. P., and S. X. Si. (2001). Employee responsibilities and rights in China. *Asia Pacific Business Review,* 7, 3, 34–56.

Hofstede, G. H. (1980a). *Culture's consequences: International differences in work-related values.* Beverly Hills, CA: Sage.

———. (1980b). Motivation, leadership, and organization: Do American theories apply abroad? *Organizational Dynamics,* 9, 1, 42–63.

———. (1994). Cultural constraints in management theories. In D.E. Hussey (Ed.), *International review of strategic management,* 5, pp. 27–48. Chichester, UK: Wiley.

Hofstede, G. H., and M. H. Bond. (1988). The Confucius connection: From cultural roots to economic growth. *Organizational Dynamics,* 16, 4, 4–21.

Hsu, F. L. K. (1981). *Americans and Chinese: Passage to differences* (3rd ed). Honolulu: University of Hawaii Press.

Huang, K. L., and I. F. Wang. (1980). The effects of leadership style and personality trait on worker job satisfaction (in Chinese). *Journal of Changchi University,* 41, 45–60.

Hui, C.; C. Lee; and D. M. Rousseau. (2004). Employment relationships in China: Do workers relate to the organization or to people? *Organization Science,* 15, 232–40.

Kerr, S., and J. M. Jermier. (1978). Substitutes for leadership: Their meaning and measurement. *Organizational Behavior and Human Performance,* 22, 375–403.

King, A. Y. (1991). Kuan-hsi and network building: A sociological interpretation. *Daedalus,* 120, 63–84.

Kline, T. J. B.; L. M. Sulsky; and S. D. Rever-Moriyama. (2000). Common method variance and specification errors: A practical approach to detection. *Journal of Psychology Interdisciplinary and Applied,* 134, 401–21.

Morris, M. W.; K. Leung; D. Ames; and B. Lickel. (1999). Views from inside and outside: Integrating emic and etic insights about culture and justice judgment. *Academy of Management Review,* 24, 781–96.

Negy, S. M. (2002). Using a single-item approach to measure facet job satisfaction. *Journal of Occupational and Organizational Psychology,* 75, 77–86.

Pistrui, D. (2001). Entrepreneurship in China: Characteristics, attributes and family forces shaping the emerging private sector. *Family Business Review,* 14, 141–52.

Podsakoff, P. M.; B. P. Niehoff; S. B. MacKenzie; and M. L. Williams. (1993). Do substitutes for leadership really substitute for leadership? An empirical examination of Kerr and Jermier's situational leadership model. *Organizational Behavior and Human Decision Processes,* 54, 1–44.

Pye, L. W. (1985). *Asian power and politics.* Cambridge, MA: Harvard University Press.

Redding, S. G. (1990). *The spirit of Chinese capitalism.* Berlin: Walter de Gruyter.

————. (2002). The capitalist business system of China and its rationale. *Asia Pacific Journal of Management,* 19, 221–49.

Schlevogt, K. A. (2001). The distinctive structure of Chinese private enterprises: State versus private sector. *Asian Pacific Business Review,* 7, 1, 1–33.

Silin, R. F. (1976). *Leadership and values.* Cambridge, MA: Harvard University Press.

Smith, P. B., and M. F. Peterson. (1988). *Leadership, organizations and culture: An event management model.* London: Sage.

Smith, P. B., and Z. M. Wang. (1996). Chinese leadership and organizational structures. In M.H. Bond (Ed.), *The handbook of Chinese psychology,* pp. 322–37. Hong Kong: Oxford University Press.

Smyth, R.; J. G. Wang; and Q. L. Kiang. (2001). Efficiency, performance and changing corporate governance in China's township-village enterprises since the 1990's. *Asian Pacific Economic Literature,* 15, 30–41.

Spector, P. E. (1987). Method variance as an artifact in self-reported affect and perceptions at work: Myth or significant problem. *Journal of Applied Psychology,* 72, 438–43.

Tsui, A. S., and J. L. Farh. (1997). Where *guanxi* matters: Relational demography and *guanxi* in the Chinese context. *Work and Occupations,* 24, 56–79.

Vogel, E. F. (1965). From friendship to comradeship. *China Quarterly,* 21, 46–60.

Walder, A. G. (1986). *Communist neo-traditionalism: Work and authority in Chinese industry.* Berkeley: University of California Press.

Wang, H. (2002). *Strategic leadership and organizational effectiveness: The role of situational uncertainty and organizational culture:* Doctoral dissertation, Hong Kong University of Science and Technology.

Wanous, J. P.; A. E. Reichers; and M. J. Hudy. (1997). Overall job satisfaction: How good are single-item measures? *Journal of Applied Psychology,* 82, 247–52.

Weber, M. (1968). *Economy and society.* Translated by G. Roth and C. Wittich (Eds.), Berkeley: University of California.

Westwood, R. I. (1997). Harmony and patriarchy: The cultural basis for "paternalistic headship" among the overseas Chinese. *Organization Studies,* 18, 445–80.

Westwood, R. I., and A. Chan. (1992). Headship and leadership. In R.I. Westwood (Ed.), *Organizational behaviour: A Southeast Asian perspective,* pp.123–39. Hong Kong: Longman.

Whitley, R. (1992). *Business systems in East Asia: Firms, markets and societies.* London: Sage.

Wong, S. L. (1988). *Emigrant entrepreneurs: Shanghai industrialists in Hong Kong.* Hong Kong: Oxford University Press.

Wu, T. Y.; W. L. Hsu; and B. S. Cheng. (2002). Expressing or suppressing anger: Subordinates' anger responses to supervisors' authoritarian behaviors in a Taiwan enterprise (in Chinese). *Indigenous Psychological Research in Chinese Societies,* 18, 3–49.

Xia, R. J. (1987). *Participative decision-making behaviour in industrial organizations* (in Chinese). Unpublished master's thesis, Institute of Psychology, Academy of Sciences, Beijing.

Yang, K. S. (1993). Chinese social orientation: An integrative analysis. In L.Y. Cheng, F.M.C. Cheung, and C.N. Chen (Eds.), *Psychotherapy for the Chinese* (selected papers from the first international conference), pp. 19–56. Hong Kong: Chinese University of Hong Kong.

Yang, K. S.; A. B. Yu; and M. H. Yeh. (1989). Chinese individual modernity and traditionality: Construct definition and measurement. In K. S. Yang and A. B. Yu (Eds.), *Chinese psychology and behavior* (in Chinese), pp. 241–306. Taipei: Laureat.

Yang, L. S. (1957). The concept of pao as a basis for social relations in China. In J.K. Fairbank (Ed.), *Chinese thought and institutions,* pp. 291–309. Chicago: University of Chicago Press.

Yang, M. M. (1994). *Gifts, favors and banquets: The art of social relationships in China.* Ithaca, NY: Cornell University Press.

Yukl, G. (1998). *Leadership in organizations* (2nd ed.). Englewood Cliffs, NJ: Prentice-Hall.

14

THE COMMITMENT-FOCUSED HRM SYSTEM

ADOPTION AND PERFORMANCE
IMPLICATIONS IN DOMESTIC PRIVATE FIRMS

YAPING GONG, KENNETH LAW, AND KATHERINE XIN

The transition from a centrally planned economy to a market economy has led to the phenomenal growth of domestic private firms in the People's Republic of China (PRC). In 1987, there were only 150,000 licensed domestic private firms (Warner 1995); by the end of 2001, there were over 2,000,000 (*China Private Economy Yearbook* 2002). Domestic private firms have contributed to the rapid growth of the Chinese economy and the expansion of employment (Ding, Lan, and Warner 2001). The total sales of domestic private firms reached 1,148.4 billion RMB, and the total number of employees working in domestic private firms reached 27.14 million by the end of 2001 (*China Private Economy Yearbook* 2002).

Within this macroeconomic background, we compare the utilization of a commitment-focused human resource management (HRM) system (Arthur 1994) in different types of firms in China and the impact of this commitment-focused HRM system on firm performance. HRM plays a key role in building a firm's human capital and enhancing firm performance (Wright, Dunford, and Snell 2001). Given that the future growth of the Chinese economy depends on the strength of domestic private firms, it is both theoretically and practically important to examine HRM practices in these firms. In this study, we define domestic private firms as those firms created and managed by private PRC citizens. Because of the convoluted property rights in many collective firms and township-and-village enterprises (Fan and Li 2001), we exclude these two types of firms from the category of domestic private firms in the current study. Instead, we compare the HRM practices in the domestic private firms to those in the state-owned and foreign-operated firms.

We intend for this study to make two major contributions. The China-related HRM literature has largely been focused on individual HR practices and outcomes at the individual level. First, in a shift away from this trend, we examine the system of commitment-focused HRM practices and its relationship to firm performance. Second, the strategic HRM literature has been largely focused on the HRM–firm performance relationship in countries with relatively stable and well-developed institutional environments. We examine not only the nature of HRM and its relationship to firm performance, but also the institutional antecedents (i.e., ownership types) of HRM practices, all within the fast-changing and diverse institutional environment of the PRC.

CONCEPTUAL BACKGROUND AND HYPOTHESES

The review by Li and Zhong in this book reveals that the management and organization literature on China's private sector has focused mainly on strategy, structure, interorganizational relationships, and social network issues. Among the published academic research on HRM in firms operating in China, the major focus has been on state-owned firms (e.g., Chow and Shenkar 1989; Warner 1997), joint ventures (e.g., Gong et al. 2001, 2005; Holton 1990; Von Glinow and Teagarden 1988), or comparisons between the two (e.g., Goodall and Warner 1999). A few studies have examined HRM in collective firms (e.g., Chow and Fu 2000, Ding et al. 2001). For example, Ding et al. (2001) conducted an in-depth case study of HRM issues in six township-and-village enterprises (TVES) in the Pearl River Delta area. They found that TVEs tended to evolve HRM practices different from state-owned firms. For example, TVEs tended to apply individual, rather than collective, contracts; adopt performance-driven reward systems; and have a moderate-to-low degree of unionization. Overall, scholarly understanding of management practices in domestic private firms in China is limited, and there is a great need to include domestic private firms in China-related HRM research.

Existing studies on China-related HRM issues tend to focus on individual HRM practices (e.g., Chen 1995) and give little attention to systems of HRM practices and their impacts on firm performance. A notable exception is Gong et al.'s (2005) study on HRM in China-based international joint ventures. In that study, Gong and his colleagues found that relational HR issues (i.e., a system of HR issues at the parent-venture interface) and within-venture HR issues (i.e., a system of HR issues mainly within the joint venture itself) had different effects on international-joint-venture performance in China. As another notable exception, Tsui, Wang, and Zhang (2002) found that domestic private firms were more likely to adopt organization-focused employment relationships (a system of HR practices that offers high commitment to and induces high commitment from employees). In another study, however, Wang et al. (2003) found that the domestic private firms adopting the mutual commitment type of employment relationship did not necessarily enjoy higher firm performance. Thus, the relationship between a commitment-focused HRM system and firm performance may not be straightforward in the different types of firms in China.

To summarize, while existing China-related HRM research provides useful insight into employment relationships and HRM practices in state-owned firms and joint ventures, we know relatively little about systems of HRM practices (i.e., bundles of internally consistent HR practices) utilized in other types of firms. In particular, we know little about the kind of HRM system that may enhance firm performance in China. Given that the sustained growth of the Chinese economy will depend heavily on firms not owned by the state, it is both theoretically and practically important to analyze the kinds of HRM systems that may enhance firm performance in different types of firms.

The strategic HRM literature suggests that a commitment-focused HRM system may enhance firm performance (e.g., Arthur 1994). A commitment-focused HRM system shapes desirable employee attitudes and behaviors by developing the employee's psychological attachment to an organization. It focuses on developing committed employees who have skills and can be trusted to use their discretion to perform tasks (Arthur 1992). Examples of commitment-focused HRM practices include employment security, selective hiring of new personnel, decentralized decision making, pay contingent on organizational performance, extensive training and development, and information sharing (Pfeffer 1998). Unfortunately, few researchers have examined the utilization of the commitment-focused HRM system and its relationship to performance in different types of firms in China.

In the sections below, we first discuss the use of a system of commitment-focused HRM practices at the management level, comparing these practices in China's domestic private firms to those in the state-owned firms, joint ventures, and wholly foreign-owned firms. We then discuss the relationship of the system of commitment-focused HRM practices to firm performance, and in particular whether the relationship is stronger or weaker in the domestic private firms. Our analyses focus on the system of commitment-focused HRM practices, its institutional antecedents, and its relationship to firm performance in the fast-changing and diverse institutional environment of China. We focus on managerial personnel because of their important role in strategic decision making and firm performance (Finkelstein and Hambrick 1996, Wang et al. 2003). How these managers are managed may have significant implications for firm performance.

COMMITMENT-FOCUSED HRM SYSTEMS IN
DIFFERENT TYPES OF FIRMS IN CHINA

Strategic HRM research suggests that a commitment-focused HRM system (e.g., Arthur 1994, Huselid 1995, Pfeffer 1998) may contribute to organizational effectiveness. A commitment-focused HRM system consists of HRM practices focused on inducing high levels of commitment from employees and shaping desirable employee attitudes and behaviors by developing employee skills and psychological attachment to organizations. It focuses on developing committed employees who can be trusted to use their discretion to perform jobs (Arthur 1992). In this study, we use the term "commitment-focused HRM system" to refer to these commitment-building HRM practices.

Traditional personnel management in China has been regarded as a controlling rather than an enabling mechanism, whereas a commitment-focused HRM system treats employees as valuable resources to be fully developed, empowered, and utilized for the purpose of enhancing organizational effectiveness (Goodall and Warner 1999, Warner 1995). The strategic HRM literature has documented the positive impact of commitment-focused HRM on firm performance in the United States (e.g., Arthur 1994, Huselid 1995, Pfeffer 1994). Given the institutional and cultural differences between China and the United States, the degree to which commitment-focused HRM practices have been utilized among different firm types—as well as whether such practices relate to firm performance in China—are still questions to be answered.

After two decades of reform, some Chinese firms have already adopted versions of the commitment-focused HRM system. For example, the management policy of Midea, a major manufacturer of household appliances in China, is to "secure the most capable personnel for positions throughout the country," "to bring employee potential into full play through the internal labor market," and "to encourage job rotation and provide training for at least 70 percent of employees in 2000" (Ding et al. 2001, 340). Meindl, Cheng, and Jun (1990) noted that managers in China were showing an increasing interest in using HRM techniques and motivational systems that emphasize productivity at individual, group, and firm levels. Further, commitment-focused HRM practices may be salient to Chinese firms and employees because of the Chinese culture of relationship orientation. However, given the early stage of modernization and corporate reform, and the diverse institutional environments in different types of firms, the use of a commitment-focused HRM system is unlikely to be uniform among firms operating in China.

Systematic evidence regarding HRM practices in Chinese domestic private firms is lacking. In general, we expect that domestic private firms are likely to utilize commitment-focused HRM practices at a level similar to what is used in state-owned firms. Some domestic private firms, especially smaller ones, may use short-term contracts and pay low wages to employees because of their lack of resources. Compared to state-owned firms, however, domestic private firms may face fewer institutional constraints in adopting commitment-focused HRM practices such as a performance-driven rewards system and extensive training for employees. In general, we expect that domestic private firms are likely to utilize a commitment-focused HRM system to a lesser extent than do foreign-operated firms. Relative to foreign-operated firms, the domestic private firms have less knowledge and fewer resources to implement a system of commitment-focused HRM practices. Some domestic private firms may not have in place a well-planned HR system of any kind due to resource constraints. In the paragraphs below, we elaborate on the rationale underlying our expectations.

State-owned firms are at the center of the traditional institutional environment in China. Owing to the greater embeddedness of state-owned firms in the traditional institutional environment (e.g., strict control over human resources by the state and its agents, norms of social stability, and principles of equality and seniority), state-owned firms are likely to face the greatest pressure from the traditional institutional environment and to experience institutional inertia (DiMaggio and Powell 1983, Greenwood and Hinings 1996, Lounsbury 2001, Scott 2001, Zucker 1987). As a result, state-owned firms are more resistant to change (i.e., they are unlikely to adopt commitment-focused HRM practices). As Tsui and her colleagues (2002) observed, a large number of state-owned firms are holding onto their traditional practices despite the dramatic changes introduced by the economic reforms. Domestic private firms, on the other hand, face fewer institutional constraints and therefore are freer to adopt commitment-focused HRM practices.

However, compared with domestic private firms, state-owned firms have easier access to financial resources. The state continues to provide financial capital to state-owned firms. Domestic private firms have long been discriminated against in the domestic capital market (Fan and Li 2001). Given that the implementation of commitment-focused HRM practices requires a great deal of resources, domestic private firms are likely to be less able to afford commitment-focused HRM practices than are state-owned firms. Taking into account institutional and resource factors, we expect that, on balance, the utilization of commitment-focused HRM is not significantly different between domestic private firms and state-owned firms.

Wholly foreign-owned firms and joint ventures are not embedded in traditional Chinese institutional environments and are directly subject to market pressures. Compared with domestic private firms, wholly foreign-owned firms are often able to gain financial resources from their foreign parent firms and also from foreign capital markets. The limited access to financial resources by domestic private firms suggests that domestic private firms may be less able to utilize commitment-focused HRM than would the wholly foreign-owned firms and joint ventures. Furthermore, wholly foreign-owned firms and joint ventures may have ready access to an advanced commitment-focused HRM system from their parent firms, which more often come from economies with advanced management practices. Therefore, these foreign firms, more than the Chinese domestic private firms, would be exposed to the knowledge to develop and implement such a system. To conclude, we propose,

Hypothesis 1. Domestic private firms are less likely to utilize commitment-focused HRM practices than are wholly foreign-owned firms and joint ventures, but they are likely to utilize such HRM practices at a level similar to those of state-owned firms.

COMMITMENT-FOCUSED HRM PRACTICES AND
FIRM PERFORMANCE

The resource-based view of the firm suggests that valuable, rare, and difficult-to-imitate resources provide firms with sustained competitive advantages (Barney 1991). Human resources, compared with financial and physical capital resources, are more difficult for competitors to imitate and therefore collectively can provide a unique source of competitive advantage (Barney and Wright 1998, Huselid 1995). Systems of HRM practices can affect a firm's human resource pool; for example, firms can use procedures to select high-quality individuals whose talents are rare and difficult to imitate (e.g., Huselid 1995; Huselid, Jackson, and Schuler 1997). Systems of HRM practices can also generate synergistic effects among individual HRM practices, which are also difficult for competitors to imitate.

From the perspective of the resource-based view, a commitment-focused HRM system may increase firm performance through enhanced employee motivation, better selection and development, and utilization of a firm's human capital resources (Arthur 1994, Barney 1991). Firms operating in China are in the process of rapid development. Commitment-focused HRM systems may enable managers to learn new skills to meet changing business needs. Under the commitment-focused HRM system, managers may be motivated to engage in extra role behaviors (Organ 1988) as reciprocity for organizational investment in them. This type of behavior is likely to be highly valuable in a fast-changing environment such as China, where roles are typically not well defined (Ilgen and Hollenbeck 1991). Commitment-focused HRM practices motivate managers to make suggestions for improving management and business activities. Decentralized decision making in a commitment-focused HRM system allows firms to tap into the creative potential of managers and motivate them to work harder for the firm. Extensive training and development enhance the managerial human capital pool of the firm and the creative potential of managerial personnel. A commitment-focused HRM system may also help establish a good corporate reputation for rewarding, respecting, and developing human resources. This reputation itself is difficult to imitate in China's transitional economy. For example, the human resource development approach at Midea has attracted many domestic and foreign university graduates, including M.B.A.s and Ph.D.s (Ding et al. 2001). To conclude, we propose,

Hypothesis 2.   The degree of utilization of commitment-focused HRM practices will be positively related to firm performance in China.

Because traditional cognitive, normative, and legal institutions persist in China, domestic private firms have yet to achieve a social and political standing equal to that of state-owned firms. Domestic private firms are often at their early stages of development, with uncertain performance outlook and survival potential (Wang et al. 2003). Domestic private firms are not popular employers for some managers because of the low social standing and the performance pressure of this type of institution (Sabin 1994). As a result, commitment-focused HRM practices in domestic private firms may not generate the same level of commitment and motivation as they do in other types of firms. In addition, domestic private firms tend to have less modern management knowledge and fewer resources to implement the commitment-focused HRM practices in an efficient way. To summarize, we hypothesize,

Hypothesis 3.   The positive relationship between commitment-focused HRM practices and firm performance will be weaker in domestic private firms than in other types of firms in China.

METHODS

Sample and Procedure

Our sample included firms whose managers attended executive education programs at a leading business school in Shanghai, China. Since this is a national business school, we had participants from all over China. At the end of each class, one of the authors explained this research project to the students and asked for voluntary participation. We then sent a package of surveys to the companies of those who agreed to participate. We initially contacted 374 companies. We color-coded two different surveys (blue for the middle manager survey and green for the human resources manager survey). To safeguard anonymity and confidentiality, we provided each respondent with an addressed and stamped envelope in which to return the survey.

After several rounds of follow-ups, HR managers from 125 firms responded to the HR manager survey. Middle managers from 146 firms responded to the middle manager survey. The number of middle managers per firm varied from one to six (mean = 2.57). Sixty-six percent of the firms had three middle managers who responded to our survey, and 20 percent of firms had two middle managers who responded to our survey. As a result of the matching process, we received responses from both HR and middle managers from 117 firms, representing a 31 percent response rate. Our sample consisted of 24 percent ($n = 28$) state-owned firms, 27 percent ($n = 32$) domestic private firms, 17 percent ($n = 20$) Sino-foreign joint ventures, and 15 percent ($n = 17$) wholly foreign-owned firms. About 22 percent of the firms were from the manufacturing sector, 33 percent were from the high-technology sector, and 36 percent were from the services sector.

Measures

Commitment-Focused HRM

We developed our commitment-focused HRM practices scale on the basis of a comprehensive review of the strategic HRM literature (e.g., Arthur 1994; Becker and Huselid 1998; Delery and Dotty 1996; Gerhart et al. 2000; Ichniowski, Shaw, and Prennushi 1997; Pfeffer 1994, 1998; Youndt, Dean, and Lepak 1996). The scale included eight dimensions: (a) selective hiring; (b) decentralized decision making through management teams; (c) compensation contingent on individual and organizational performance; (d) extensive cross-functional training; (e) regular objective performance appraisal for development, pay, and promotion purposes; (f) extensive information sharing; (g) reduction of status distinctions; and (h) employment security. HR managers rated the degree to which they agreed that commitment-focused HRM practices were implemented at the middle management level in their firms (1 = "strongly disagree," 7 = "strongly agree").

We conducted exploratory factor analyses using both HR and middle managers' ratings independently. Factor structures for dimensions (a)–(e) were consistent across HR and middle managers' responses. Therefore, we used dimensions (a)–(e) in subsequent analyses. Table 14.1 presents items in dimensions (a)–(e) and the exploratory factor analysis (EFA) results, with HR managers and the middle managers separately. The results are similar for the two groups of managers. We averaged responses to items within each dimension and obtained a score for each of the five HR dimensions. We further tested whether dimensions (a)–(e) loaded on the same second-order factor (i.e., the commitment-focused HRM construct) in a second-order factor analysis, and the result supported one overall factor structure. We used the HR managers' ratings of commitment-

Table 14.1

Factor Analysis Results for Five Dimensions of Commitment-Focused HRM

Items	Factor 1	Factor 2	Factor 3	Factor 4	Factor 5
A. Selective hiring					
1. All newly hired managers in our firm were selected based primarily on the results of validated selection tests.	**0.78** **(0.61)**	0.03 (0.00)	0.09 (0.03)	−0.02 (0.09)	−0.03 (0.09)
2. All managers were administered many assessment tools prior to employment in our firm.	**0.66** **(0.95)**	−0.01 (0.06)	−0.03 (−0.03)	0.07 (−0.06)	−0.02 (0.00)
3. A strict selection procedure was used in our firm to hire new managers.	**0.47** **(0.48)**	−0.03 (−0.14)	−0.03 (0.01)	0.07 (0.18)	−0.02 (0.06)
B. Decentralized decision making through management teams					
4. Managers in our firm meet on a regular basis in management committees to discuss critical company matters.	0.09 (0.07)	**0.87** **(0.95)**	−0.07 (−0.03)	0.03 (−0.03)	−0.04 (0.05)
5. Management committees in our firm can exert significant influence on major company decisions.	−0.05 (−0.04)	**0.62** **(0.70)**	0.11 (0.13)	0.03 (0.03)	0.06 (0.03)
6. The majority of managers in our firm are involved in formal or informal management committees or other related problem-solving activities.	−0.09 (−0.01)	0.51 **(0.53)**	0.04 (−0.03)	0.04 (0.08)	0.17 (0.02)
C. Pay contingent on individual and organizational performance					
7. The incentive pay of managers in our firm matches well with our firm's financial performance.	−0.04 (0.14)	−0.07 (−0.05)	**0.89** **(0.88)**	−0.01 (0.00)	−0.07 (−0.05)
8. In our firm, managerial merit increase is proportional to a manager's job performance.	−0.02 (0.00)	−0.01 (0.07)	**0.60** **(0.64)**	0.09 (0.16)	0.22 (0.13)
9. Managers are eligible for annual deferred incentive plans, profit–sharing plans, and/or gain–sharing plans in our firm.	0.09 (−0.24)	0.19 (−0.11)	**0.41** **(0.47)**	0.00 (−0.06)	−0.08 (−0.03
D. Extensive cross–functional training					
10. Managers often participate in cross-functional training or job rotation in our firm.	−0.09 (−0.09)	0.02 (−0.02)	−0.07 (0.03)	**0.91** **(0.89)**	−0.05 (−0.11)
11. A large proportion of managers in our firm are qualified to perform more than one job through training or job rotation.	−0.02 (0.05)	−0.06 (−0.02)	0.05 (−0.05)	**0.67** **(0.61)**	0.17 (0.14)

(continued)

Table 14.1 *(continued)*

Items	Factor 1	Factor 2	Factor 3	Factor 4	Factor 5
12. Managers in our firm often receive training outside their own functional areas.	0.21 (−0.06)	0.11 (−0.10)	0.07 (0.08)	**0.62** **(0.71)**	−0.07 (−0.06)
E. Regular objective performance appraisal for development, pay, and promotion purposes					
13. Managers frequently receive formal performance appraisals in our firm.	−0.04 (0.04)	−0.05 (−0.01)	0.06 (−0.01)	−0.02 (−0.08)	**0.89** **(0.90)**
14. Managers' performance appraisals are based on objective results in our firm.	0.04 (−0.01)	−0.02 (−0.08)	0.10 (0.04)	0.08 (−0.03)	**0.76** **(0.83)**
15. Managers often receive development-focused appraisals in our firm.	0.09 (0.12)	0.08 (0.07)	−0.11 (−0.06)	0.00 (−0.04)	**0.69** **(0.83)**
16. Managers often receive appraisals for pay purposes.	−0.02 (0.06)	0.01 (0.14)	0.14 (0.28)	0.04 (0.11)	**0.66** **(0.58)**
17. Managers often receive appraisals for promotion purposes.	0.00 (−0.06)	0.17 (0.02)	0.01 (0.01)	0.05 (0.12)	**0.60** **(0.73)**
18. Compared to our close competitors, our firm has a better-designed performance appraisal system.	0.11 (−0.02)	0.04 (−0.09)	0.03 (−0.02)	0.06 (0.05)	**0.57** **(0.73)**
Eigenvalue	1.14	1.68	1.14	6.36	1.74
Percentage of variance explained (%)	7.42	9.3	6.34	35.31	9.66

Note: Factor loadings are from HR managers and middle managers, with the latter included in parentheses.

focused HRM in our subsequent hypothesis testing because these managers were in a better position to understand the HRM practices of their firms.

Firm Performance

We measured firm performance using four indicators: total asset growth, after-tax return on total assets, after-tax return on total sales, and labor productivity. We asked the middle managers to compare their firms' current performances with those of close competitors on a five-point scale (1 = "lowest 20%," 5 = "highest 20%"). For the firms with multiple middle manager respondents, we averaged all respondents' ratings of firm performance. To make certain that data from different managers could be aggregated, we calculated the interrater agreement (r_{wg}; James, Demaree, and Wolf 1984, 1993), which was, on average, .80 for total asset growth, .77 for after-tax return on total assets, .76 for after-tax return on total sales, and .79 for labor productivity. All were greater than .70; thus, our aggregation was justified. Our EFA results indicated that the four performance indicators loaded on one factor (Table 14.2). In subsequent regression analyses, we examined overall performance as a latent factor underlying the four performance measures.

Table 14.2

Factor Analysis Results for Commitment-Focused HRM and Firm Performance

	Factor 1	Factor 2
Commitment-focused HRM (HR managers' ratings)		
1. Selective hiring	**0.38**	0.12
2. Decentralized decision making through management teams	**0.58**	−0.02
3. Pay contingent on individual and organizational performance	**0.65**	0.02
4. Extensive cross-functional training	**0.61**	−0.01
5. Regular objective performance appraisal for development, pay, and promotion purposes	**0.77**	−0.09
Firm Performance (middle managers' ratings)		
1. Total asset growth	0.08	**0.72**
2. After-tax return on total assets	−0.05	**0.93**
3. After-tax return on total sales	−0.08	**0.97**
4. Labor productivity	0.05	**0.68**
Eigenvalues	1.70	2.97
Percentage of variance explained (%)	18.87	33.01
Cronbach's α	0.73	0.89

Middle managers' ratings of firm performance were used for three reasons. First, we needed an independent source for the criterion variables to avoid the problem of common method variance. Second, line managers should know the performance of their firms better than staff managers. Third, we had multiple respondents from many firms. Random estimation errors on the criterion variables could be greatly reduced by averaging their estimates.

Lastly, we conducted an EFA on the five dimensions of the commitment-focused HRM scale (using HR managers' data) together with items for firm performance (using middle managers' data). Results indicated that all five HR dimensions loaded on one factor and the performance items loaded on a second factor. Table 14.2 presents these factor loadings. Cronbach's alpha was .73 for the commitment-focused HRM scale and .89 for the performance scale.

Control Variables

We also collected information about firm size (number of employees), industry (i.e., manufacturing, high technology, services, and others), and ownership types (state owned, domestic private firms, joint ventures, wholly foreign owned, and others). Both industry (three dummy variables) and ownership (four dummy variables) were dummy coded. We classified a small number of cases in which the ownership type could not be clearly categorized as "other."

RESULTS

Table 14.3 provides descriptive statistics for the major variables in our study. Consistent with our hypothesis, commitment-focused HRM was positively related to firm performance ($r = .26$, $p < .05$). Firm size (in terms of the number of employees) was also positively related to the use of commitment-focused HRM practices ($r = .21$, $p < .05$). Next, we present our regression analysis results.

Table 14.3

Means, Standard Deviations, and Zero-Order Correlations[a]

	Mean	S.D.	1	2	3	4	5	6	7	8	9	10
1. Employment size	1,023.96	2,286.87	—									
2. Manufacturing	0.22	0.42	0.22*	—								
3. High technology	0.33	0.47	-0.09	-0.38*	—							
4. Service	0.36	0.48	-0.17†	-0.41*	-0.53*	—						
5. Other	0.16	0.37	0.11	0.10	-0.16†	0.01	—					
6. Joint ventures	0.17	0.38	-0.05	0.14	-0.03	-0.06	-0.20*	—				
7. Wholly foreign owned	0.15	0.36	0.08	0.13	0.07	-0.11	-0.18*	-0.19*	—			
8. State owned	0.24	0.43	0.05	-0.11	-0.27*	0.25*	-0.25*	-0.26*	-0.23*	—		
9. Commitment HRM[b]	21.14	4.23	0.21*	0.02	-0.04	0.17†	-0.02	0.01	0.05	-0.12	—	
10. Firm performance[c]	13.54	3.49	0.08	-0.11	-0.07	0.19*	-0.06	-0.07	0.01	0.01	0.26*	—

[a]$N = 111–117$ (pairwise).
[b]Commitment-focused HRM data from HR managers.
[c]Firm performance data from middle managers.
† $p < 0.10$; * $p < 0.05$.

Table 14.4

Regression Results for Utilization of Commitment-Focused HRM[a]

Independent variables	Utilization of commitment-focused HRM	
	Model 1	Model 2
Step 1		
Log employment size[b]	0.28**	0.30**
Manufacturing	0.24†	0.15
High technology	0.32*	0.18
Services	0.41**	0.43**
Step 2 (H1)		
State owned		−0.21*
Wholly foreign owned		0.03
Joint venture		0.02
Others		−0.13
ΔR^2		0.10*
ΔF		4.10*
Degrees of freedom	4,107	8,103

[a]Standardized regression coefficients are presented in the table.
[b]Log transformation of employment size.
$^{†}p < 0.10$; $^{*} p < 0.05$; $^{**} p < 0.01$.

Utilization of Commitment-Focused HRM Practices

To test Hypothesis 1, we regressed commitment-focused HRM on ownership type. In the first step, we entered control variables in model 1 and then added our independent variables in model 2. Table 14.4 shows the results of these regression analyses. The regression coefficient for state-owned firms was significant ($\beta = -.21$, $p < .05$) in model 2, suggesting that compared to domestic private firms (the comparison group), utilization of commitment-focused HRM was lower in state-owned firms. Regression coefficients for wholly foreign-owned firms and joint ventures were not significant, suggesting that the use of commitment-focused HRM in domestic private firms was not significantly different from that of wholly foreign-owned firms and joint ventures. Thus, Hypothesis 1 was not supported. We elaborate on this finding in the discussion section.

Commitment-Focused HRM Practices and Firm Performance

To test Hypotheses 2 and 3, we coded domestic private firms as 1 and all other types of firms as 0. In our regression analyses, we entered control variables (i.e., logarithm of employment size, industry, and ownership type) in step 1, commitment-focused HRM in step 2, and the interaction between commitment-focused HRM and ownership in step 3. Table 14.5 presents our regression results. The result in step 2 indicates that commitment-focused HRM was significantly related to overall firm performance ($\beta = .25$, $p < .05$), lending support to Hypothesis 2. The sign for the interaction between commitment-focused HRM and ownership was in the hypothesized direction, but not statistically significant ($\beta = -10$, n.s.) in step 3. Hypothesis 3 was therefore not supported.

Table 14.5

Regression Results for Firm Performance

	Firm performance[a]		
Independent variables	Model 1	Model 2	Model 3
Step 1			
Log employment size[b]	0.07	−0.01	−0.01
Manufacturing	−0.07	−0.12	−0.13
High technology	−0.06	−0.12	−0.13
Services	0.15	0.04	0.03
Domestic private firms[c]	0.12	0.09	0.09
Step 2 (H2)			
Commitment-focused HRM[d]		0.25*	0.29*
Step 3 (H3)			
Commitment-focused HRM × domestic private firm		−0.10	
ΔR^2		0.05*	0.01
ΔF		5.63*	0.80
Degrees of freedom	5,102	6,101	7,100

[a]Standardized regression coefficients are presented in the table. Firm performance was rated by middle managers.

[b]Log transformation of employment size.

[c]Dummy coding with "1" = domestic private firms and "0" = all others.

[d]Commitment-focused HRM was rated by HR managers.

*$p < 0.05$.

DISCUSSION AND CONCLUSIONS

In the present study, we examined the relationship between ownership types and the use of commitment-focused HRM practices in firms operating in China. We further examined the relationship between use of commitment-focused HRM practices and firm performance. In keeping with the institutional argument, we found that the ownership structure did affect the utilization of commitment-focused HRM practices. Overall, domestic private firms used commitment-focused HRM practices to a greater extent than did state-owned firms. The utilization of commitment-focused HRM practices in domestic private firms was not significantly different from that in wholly foreign-owned firms and joint ventures. This finding is consistent with that of Tsui et al. (2002), who reported higher adoption of the mutual investment form of employment relationship with middle managers by private domestic firms, relative to other types of firms. One explanation is that the domestic private firms in our sample were relatively large ones with adequate resources (average sales of 549 million RMB). Resource availability, together with low institutional constraints, increases the adoption of a system of commitment-focused HRM practices. These private firms may use this HR strategy to attract managerial talents and gain competitive advantage. While state-owned firms generally have access to financial resources, they face greater institutional constraints in reforming their HRM practices.

We also found that use of commitment-focused HRM practices was positively related to firm performance. Contrary to Hypothesis 3, the positive relationship between commitment-focused HRM and firm performance was not significantly weaker in domestic private firms. This finding suggests that a commitment-oriented human resource system should work similarly for all kinds of organizations. We note that this result was free from common method bias because different sources provided the ratings of commitment-focused HRM and firm performance.

Our findings provide some support for the institutional prediction regarding utilization of a commitment-focused HRM system. The People's Republic of China is a country with diverse and rapidly evolving institutional environments. As state-owned firms are deeply embedded in/sheltered by traditional institutional environments and are subject to pressure from market institutions to a lesser degree, they are less likely to utilize commitment-focused HRM practices. Our findings also attest to the rapid change in the nature of HRM systems in domestic private firms, particularly large ones. Domestic private firms are less embedded in the traditional institutional environment and are more likely to adopt performance-enhancing HRM systems. Given their relative difficulty in accessing financial resources, domestic private firms may well resort to HRM practices as a source of performance. In keeping with the resource-based view, our study suggests that commitment-focused HRM enhances firm performance. With increased market competition, domestic private firms perhaps have learned how to manage human resources to their competitive advantage. The performance effect of advanced HRM practices was not significantly weaker in domestic private firms. A possible reason for this is that the domestic private firms in our sample are relatively large ones with good social standing, and can therefore offer competitive inducements to their employees.

This study makes several contributions to the strategic HRM literature. Previous studies have focused predominantly on the relationship between HRM and firm performance, but have ignored the differential utilization of HRM across different types of firms. In this study, we identified and provided support for ownership type as a variable that affects the use of commitment-focused HRM practices. Methodologically, we used two independent sets of respondents to rate the commitment-focused HRM system practices. Our factor analysis of commitment-focused HRM was based on both sets of responses.

Finally, our study provides additional support for the positive impact of commitment-focused HRM on firm performance in a transitional economy such as China's. It is interesting to note that certain practices in the commitment-focused HRM system traditionally have not been regarded as being compatible with Chinese culture. For example, China has been regarded as a society with egalitarian and high-power-distance values. Our results suggest that pay contingent on individual performance and decentralized decision making were important elements of the performance-enhancing HRM system, despite China's egalitarian and authority-centered traditions. Conversely, certain practices in the commitment-focused HRM system, such as pay contingent on organizational performance, are quite consistent with traditional Chinese values of collectivism.

Our study has several limitations. First, our sample size was relatively small, which may have limited the statistical power in detecting significant relationships. Second, our study was cross-sectional. This design limited our ability to make causal interpretations regarding the relationship between commitment-focused HRM and firm performance; future studies should use a longitudinal design to better examine this relationship. Third, we used only subjective performance measures in the study, though the additional use of objective performance measures would have been preferable. However, objective performance information is difficult to obtain in China and often inaccurate. Many scholars have found that subjective measures of performance are appropriate and have good reliability and validity in both joint-venture and non-joint-venture settings (e.g., Chandler and Hanks 1993, Geringer and Hebert 1991, Gong et al. 2005, Wall et al. 2004). For example, Wall et al. (2004) provided a wide range of evidence for validity (e.g., construct validity, convergent validity, and discriminant validity) for subjective performance measures.

Fourth, we employed institutional theory regarding the use of commitment-focused HRM practices. Institutional theory views firms as passive legitimacy seekers and conformers. However, firms may actively adopt commitment-focused HRM practices as a strategic choice in order to gain competitive advantage. This may be especially true for domestic private firms because they are subject to market pressures to a greater extent than are other types of firms, and they often have access to fewer financial resources. Thus, for domestic private firms, managing human resources may become a strategic choice that is not constrained by the institutional environment these firms face. Given that state-owned firms are somewhat insulated from competitive market pressures, the strategic choice argument (Child 1972) would give a similar prediction as the institutional theory (Scott 2001) regarding the relative utilization of commitment-focused HRM practices by state-owned firms and wholly foreign-owned firms. Future studies should explicitly test these two different explanations in settings where there is variance on managerial discretion to adopt new or different management practices or innovations.

ACKNOWLEDGMENT

We would like to acknowledge the financial support (grant # HKUST6249/03H) of the Research Grants Council of Hong Kong.

REFERENCES

Arthur, J. B. (1992). The link between business strategy and industrial relations systems in American steel minimills. *Industrial and Labor Relations Review,* 45, 488–506.
———. (1994). Effects of human resources systems on manufacturing performance and turnover. *Academy of Management Journal,* 37, 670–87.
Barney, J. B. (1991). Firm resources and sustained competitive advantage. *Journal of Management,* 17, 99–120.
Barney, J. B., and P. M. Wright. (1998). On becoming a strategic partner: The role of human resources in gaining competitive advantage. *Human Resource Management,* 37, 31–46.
Becker, E. B., and M. A. Huselid. (1998). High performance work system and firm performance: A synthesis of research and managerial implications. *Research in Personnel and Human Resource Management,* 16, 53–101.
Chandler, G. N., and S. H. Hanks. (1993). Measuring the performance of emerging business: A validation study. *Journal of Business Venturing,* 8, 391–408.
Chen, C. (1995). New trends in rewards allocation preferences: A Sino–U.S. comparison. *Academy of Management Journal,* 38, 408–28.
Child, J. (1972). Organizational structure, environment and performance: The role of strategic choice. *Sociology,* 6, 1–22.
China Private Economy Yearbook. (2002). (In Chinese). Beijing: Zhonghua gong shang lian he chu ban she.
Chow, I. H. S., and P. P. Fu. (2000). Change and development in pluralistic settings: An exploration of HR practices in Chinese township and village enterprises. *International Journal of Human Resource Management,* 11, 822–36.
Chow, I. H. S., and O. Shenkar. (1989). HR practices in the People's Republic of China. *Personnel,* December, 41–47.
Delery, J., and D. H. Dotty. (1996). Modes of theorizing in strategic human resource management: Tests of universal, contingency, and configurational performance predictions. *Academy of Management Journal,* 39, 802–35.
DiMaggio, P. J., and W. W. Powell. (1983). The iron cage revisited: Institutionalisomorphism and collective rationality in organizational fields. *American Sociological Review,* 48, 147–60.
Ding, D. Z.; G. Lan; and M. Warner. (2001). A new form of Chinese human resource management? Personnel and labor-management relations in Chinese township and village enterprises: A case study approach. *Industrial Relations Journal,* 32, 328–43.

Fan, D., and D. D. Li. (2001). *A survey of the economics literature of China's non-state enterprises.* Internal discussion at Hong Kong University of Science and Technology, Hong Kong.

Finkelstein, S., and D. Hambrick. (1996). *Strategic leadership: Top executives and their effects on organizations.* Minneapolis, MN: West Pub. Co.

Gerhart, B.; B. Wright, B.; P. M. McMahan; and S. A. Snell. (2000). Measurement error in research on human resources and firm performance: How much error is there and how does it influence effect estimates? *Personnel Psychology,* 53, 803–34.

Geringer, J. M., and L. Hebert. (1991). Measuring performance of international joint ventures. *Journal of International Business Studies,* 22, 249–64.

Gong, Y.; O. Shenkar; Y. Luo; and M. K. Nyaw. (2001). Role conflict and ambiguity of CEOs in international joint ventures: A transaction cost perspective. *Journal of Applied Psychology,* 86, 764–73.

———. (2005). Human resources and international joint venture performance: A system perspective. *Journal of International Business Studies*, 36, 505–18.

Goodall, K., and M. Warner. (1999). Enterprise reform, labor-management relations, and human resource management in a multinational context: Empirical evidence from Sino-foreign joint ventures. *International Studies of Management and Organization,* 29, 21–36.

Greenwood, R., and C. R. Hinings. (1996). Understanding radical organizational change: Bringing together the old and the new institutionalism. *Academy of Management Review,* 4, 1022–54.

Holton, R. H. (1990). Human resource management in People's Republic of China. *Management International Review,* 30, 121–36.

Huselid, M. A. (1995). The impact of human resource management practices on turnover, productivity, and corporate financial performance. *Academy of Management Journal,* 38, 635–72.

Huselid, M. A.; S. E. Jackson; and R. S. Schuler. (1997). Technical and strategic human resource management effectiveness as determinants of firm performance. *Academy of Management Journal,* 40, 171–88.

Ichniowski, C.; K. Shaw; and G. Prennushi. (1997). The effects of human resource management practices on productivity: A study of steel finishing lines. *American Economic Review,* 87, 291–313.

Ilgen, D. R., and J. R. Hollenbeck. (1991). The structure of work: Job design and roles. In M. D. Dunnette and L. M. Hough (Eds.), *Handbook of industrial and organizational psychology*, volume 2, pp. 165–207. Palo Alto, CA: Consulting Psychologists Press.

James, L. R.: R. G. Demaree; and G. Wolf. (1984). Estimating within-group interrater reliability with and without response bias. *Journal of Applied Psychology,* 68, 85–98.

———. (1993). r_{wg}: An assessment of within-group interrater agreement. *Journal of Applied Psychology,* 78, 306–9.

Lounsbury, M. (2001). Institutional sources of practice variation: Staffing college and university recycling programs. *Administrative Science Quarterly,* 46, 29–56.

Meindl, J. R.; Y. R. Cheng; and L. Jun. (1990). Distributive justice in the workplace: Preliminary data on managerial preferences in the PRC. In B. B. Shaw, J. E. Beck, G. R. Ferris, and K. M. Rowland (Eds.), *Research in personnel and human resources management, supplement 2*, pp. 221–36. Greenwich, CT: JAI Press.

Organ, D. W. (1988). *Organizational citizenship behavior: The good soldier syndrome.* Lexington, MA: Lexington Books.

Pfeffer, J. (1994). *Competitive advantage through people: Unleashing the power of the workforce.* Boston: Harvard Business School Press.

———. (1998). Seven practices of successful organizations. *California Management Review,* 40, 96–124.

Sabin, L. (1994). New bosses in the workers' state: The growth of nonstate sector employment in China. *China Quarterly,* 140, 944–64.

Scott, W. R. (2001). *Institutions and organizations* (2nd ed.). New York: de Gruyter.

Tsui, A. S.; D. Wang; and Y. Zhang. (2002). Employment relationships with Chinese middle managers: Exploring differences between state-owned and nonstate-owned firms. In A. S. Tsui and C. M. Lau (Eds.), *The management of enterprises in the People's Republic of China*, pp. 347–74. Boston: Kluwer Academic Publishers.

Von Glinow, M. A., and M. B. Teagarden. (1988). The transfer of human resource management technology in Sino-U.S. cooperative ventures: Problems and solutions. *Human Resource Management,* 27, 201–29.

Wall, T. D.; J. Michie; M. Patterson; S. J. Wood; M. Sheehan; C. W. Clegg; and M. West. (2004). On the validity of subjective measures of company performance. *Personnel Psychology,* 57, 95–118.

Wang, D.; A. S. Tsui; Y. Zhang; and L. Ma. (2003). Employment relationships and firm performance: Evidence from an emerging economy. *Journal of Organizational Behavior,* 24, 511–35.
Warner, M. (1995). *The management of human resources in Chinese industry.* New York: St. Martin's Press.
———. (1997). Management–labour relations in the new Chinese economy. *Human Resource Management Journal,* 7, 30–43.
Wright, P. M.; B. B. Dunford; and S. A. Snell. (2001). Human resources and the resource-based view of the firm. *Journal of Management,* 27, 701–21.
Youndt, M. A.; J. W. Dean; and D. P. Lepak. (1996). Human resource management, manufacturing strategy, and firm performance. *Academy of Management Journal,* 39, 836–66.
Zucker, L. G. (1987). Institutional theories of organization. *American Review of Sociology,* 13, 443–64.

15

LENOVO'S PURSUIT OF DYNAMIC STRATEGIC FIT

Steven White and Wei Xie

The purpose of this chapter is to elucidate the process by which new Chinese firms forming the "private" and "nonstate" sectors have achieved dynamic strategic fit and, as a group, come to represent the most dynamic and growing sector of the Chinese economy. These private and collective enterprises, the offspring of a series of economic reforms that began in the late 1970s, now account for a significant and increasing portion of China's GDP, as well as new employment. They not only generate a majority of China's export income, but have come to dominate global markets in many product categories, especially consumer goods and components (Zeng and Williamson 2003).

The birth and development of these enterprises, as well as their achieving fit between their generally hostile and changing environments on the one hand and their internal resources and capabilities on the other, have not been easy processes. For much of China's transition era, political ideology of state ownership and the institutional legacy of central planning and control by the Chinese Communist Party (CCP) have meant that private firms were only semilegitimate in the eyes of conservative hard-liners in the CCP bureaucracy. Conservatives resisted the first wave of economic and administrative reforms introduced in the early 1980s that signaled the beginning of China's transition period. The primary goal of these reforms was to make China's agriculture and state-owned manufacturing sectors more productive. The conservatives saw such developments as diluting the CCP's (and the government's) control and, therefore, power. They were even more suspicious of other reforms that created the institutional space for new types of firms—township-and-village enterprises (TVEs), collectives, institutional spin-offs, private firms, Sino-foreign joint ventures—to emerge.

As a result, for much of the more than two decades of China's transition to a more market-based economy, private firms were at best tolerated. They were at a significant disadvantage because they, unlike the state-owned enterprises (SOEs), did not have the important personal ties *(guanxi)* or administrative "parents" that could protect and channel scarce resources to them (Guthrie 1998, Peng and Heath 1996, Peng and Luo 2000, Steinfeld 1998, Xin and Pearce 1996). Only in 2004 were entrepreneurs allowed to join the Communist Party and have their property rights affirmed by a declaration of the National People's Congress. Even now, while private firms are being lauded for their advanced management systems and contributions to the economy (and, in particular, their tax remittances that support the government), the government continues its coddling of SOEs, especially the largest ones, through preferential loan access and protection from outright bankruptcy (Nolan 2001, Story 2003).

In addition to challenges from a generally hostile and evolving external environment, China's private firms have faced the same organizational challenges that all new firms face. Starting with whatever initial complement of resources and capabilities they had at their foundings, they have had to acquire the additional resources and capabilities that enabled them to compete and survive, through a combination of make, buy, and ally strategies. The challenge for these new Chinese firms, however, has been even greater than for firms in developed market economies, because the new firms have fewer managers with the experience and skills to make and implement strategic decisions in a competitive market environment. Managers from the state-owned sector—with its soft budget constraints and production rather than profit orientation—did not have the technical expertise or mind-set to lead these new firms (Walder 1995). Moreover, it was difficult to attract the few capable managers to the new firms because they could not offer the job security and welfare benefits (housing, education, medical care, etc.) that the state-owned firms and government bureaucracies could.

Of the new firms emerging in the non-state-owned sector, spin-offs of research organizations (institutes and universities) constitute a large proportion of the technology-based new firms and include many of the most successful new Chinese firms in high-tech industries. They were founded by the research organizations in response to the central government's two-pronged strategy of commercializing more R&D results (Gu 1999, Liu and White 2001). First, the central government began to reduce funding to these organizations, forcing them to generate their own revenues. This was accompanied by policy changes in the mid 1980s that allowed them to pursue financial objectives (alternative funding, from the central government's point of view) and granted the institutes more discretion over their budget allocations, human resources, wages, and other areas. Two policies, issued in 1986 and 1987, not only permitted, but even encouraged R&D professionals to establish commercial enterprises or spin-offs, first under the auspices of their home organizations, and later on their own.

The result of these policy changes has been a flood of spin-off foundings, with managerial incentives and degrees of strategic choice largely identical to those of private firms that did not emerge from established research organizations. Although these spin-off firms began with more legitimacy because of their links to state-supported institutes and universities, their internal management and incentives are similar to those found in other types of private firms; namely, they are under pressure to generate revenues, and they have wide discretion regarding how to accomplish that.

In this chapter, we use the case of Lenovo Group, a research institute spin-off that has grown into one of the world's largest producers of personal computers, to explore the process by which managers outside the state-owned sector—with harder budget constraints, pressure to generate revenues, and broader strategic choice not burdened by organizational legacies of central planning—have maintained dynamic strategic fit. Over the years since its founding, Lenovo has been able to broaden and deepen its set of resources and capabilities to respond to the changing opportunities and constraints inherent in its environment. Thus, the case should be able to provide insights into the interactions among environmental changes, managerial decisions, and an organization's internal features that result in alignment and, thereby, firm performance.

EXPLORATION, EXPLOITATION, AND DYNAMIC STRATEGIC FIT

China's private firms face hard budget constraints and must perform well financially in order to survive. The fundamental challenge facing them is how to achieve that performance given their disadvantages vis-à-vis state-owned or (in some industries) multinational competitors, major changes in their environment, and their limited initial complements of organizational resources and capabilities. Their challenge represents the central question motivating strategic fit research: namely, whether a firm that aligns its strategic resources (e.g., Barney 1991, Peteraf 1993) with the specific requirements in its environment performs significantly better than a firm that does not achieve such a match (Venkatraman 1989, Venkatraman and Prescott 1990).

The researchers who have investigated the strategy-structure-performance paradigm in the Chinese context generally conclude that performance is enhanced by the alignment between a firm's strategy and its environment. In one of the earliest studies that looked specifically at this relationship, Tan and Litschert (1994) found that appropriate coalignment was strongly related to performance, although the specific environment-strategy configuration in China at that time (1990) was quite different from that found in developed market economies. Lukas, Tan, and Hult (2001) also found coalignment between strategies and the environment, but the relationship with performance held only in particular types of environments. Similarly, Davies and Walters (2004) found that some, but not all, coalignments had a significant impact on performance, particularly in more "marketized" and munificent environments.

One criticism of the traditional approach to strategic fit research has been that it is generally static rather than dynamic. Zajac and his coauthors (2000) argued that a dynamic perspective should be explicitly incorporated into the study of fit, especially in changing environments. According to this perspective, strategy drives performance, and strategy must evolve to the extent that environmental or organizational contingencies change.

In the Chinese context, Tan and Tan (2004) showed empirically that the strategy-structure-performance relationship holds, as it did in a study in the same setting twelve years earlier (Tan and Litschert 1994), but that the specific content of the strategy had coevolved with changes in the industry and the overall Chinese business environment. The clear implication is that performance is a matter of fit, but the optimal choice of firm strategy—structure and resource deployment, as well as choice among developing alternative resources and capabilities—has changed. Firms in such a changing environment must be able to adapt dynamically, and that requires some degree of organizational change. More specifically, Zajac, Kraatz, and Bresser (2000) suggested that managers must decide whether to change and what type of change to undertake in order to realize what Davies and Walters (2004, 349) called "beneficial strategic change."

Prior research has examined this question of how Chinese firms respond to such imperatives from two different perspectives. One body of research has focused on the impact of the external environment in the form of institutions (e.g., Liu and White 2001, Peng 2003, Peng and Heath 1996, White and Linden 2002) and competition (e.g., White 2000). Managers have made strategic choices in response to these pressures in their environment (e.g., Child 1994). Others have focused on the learning process as organizations acquire new resources and capabilities in response to external pressures and changing opportunities (e.g., White and Liu 1998, Xie and White 2005, Xie and Wu 2003), following the earlier work of scholars who have focused on this process in South Korea (e.g., Amsden 1989, Kim 1997) and other newly industrializing economies (Bell and Pavitt 1993, Hobday 1995, Kim and Nelson 2000).

March's Exploration/Exploitation Distinction

The choices these managers are making—whether in response to institutional pressure or as part of a deliberate learning process—are qualitatively different, and here March's (1991) distinction between exploration and exploitation provides a useful way of framing their choices. Specifically, managers contemplating "beneficial organizational change" must allocate resources to two different types of activities: those that exploit a firm's existing set of resources and capabilities (conceptually defined as an alternative for which the probability distribution of returns is known), and those that explore new domains, with the intention of acquiring new resources and capabilities (but for which the probability distribution is not known). March argued that most adaptive processes within an organization tend to favor exploitation over exploration, with the perverse result that firms often become stuck in suboptimal positions.

Applied to the question of beneficial change and dynamic strategic fit, exploitation may be appropriate when environments are stable and a firm's initial set of resources and capabilities is adapted to that environment. Change should be limited to deepening those resources and capabilities, making them more efficient, or replicating them. On the other hand, when the environment undergoes major changes—and this is certainly the case in transition-era China—the firm must be able to continually explore new resources, capabilities, and structures that better match the new environment.

March also highlighted the importance of targets and goals as determinants of managers' choices between exploitation and exploration. Referring to both prospect theory (Kahneman and Tversky 1979) and Simon's (1955) concept of "satisficing" behavior, he proposed that exploitation will be preferred if the likely result of the activity approximately meets the desired target. When that expected result falls significantly short of the target, then managers are more likely to choose exploration.

A New Framework for Dynamic Strategic Fit

We integrate the central constructs of March's exploitation-exploration framework with those from the strategy-structure-performance paradigm to propose a framework for analyzing the process by which new firms in a transition environment achieve dynamic strategic fit (Figure 15.1). The key elements of this framework are seen in Figure 15.1.

Internal Conditions

New firms have internal structures and a particular set of resources and capabilities upon their founding, and these, as well as the firm's strategy will evolve, over time, in response to changes in strategic goals and the environment. Examples of resources and capabilities include core technology, fixed assets such as plants and equipment, or people with particular skills. They may be within a single functional domain or include multiple domains.

Environment

Because of its dependence on resources from its environment, a firm is also subject to pressures for change originating from the institutional structure of that environment. Two major sources of institutional pressures are government policy and competition.

Goals

Managers set and change their strategic goals in response to internal and external stimuli. Achievement of these goals is determined in part by the degree of fit between the firm's existing set of resources and capabilities and its environment.

Figure 15.1   **Recursive Model of Dynamic Strategic Fit**

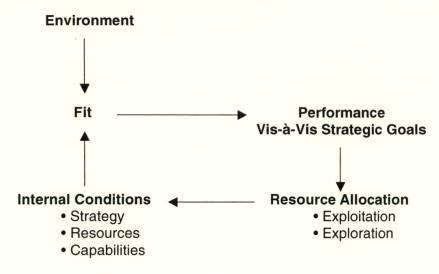

Resource Allocation Decisions

Managers must make resource allocation decisions that fundamentally represent a choice between exploiting and investing further in existing resources and capabilities, or attempting to acquire new ones.

Change

Significant changes in the environment or strategic goals will likely require organizational changes—different or new resources and capabilities—in order to realign the organization with its environment. We propose that these elements are related in a series of cause-effect interactions that start with the firm's initial set of resources and capabilities (internal conditions) and environmental pressures (external environment). Managers assess their ability to achieve their goals, which we will assume (in line with the strategy-structure-performance paradigm) is strongly affected by the match or mismatch between the firm's internal and environmental conditions. Managers make strategic choices about whether or not to introduce any changes in their firm's internal conditions (choosing action or inertia) and, if there are to be changes, to what types of activities (exploitation or exploration) they should allocate resources. We expect them to continue to make changes until they realize their desired level of performance vis-à-vis their goals. Changes in any of these elements (environment, internal conditions, goals) can create a new misfit and start the cycle of assessment and choices over again.

We use this integrated framework to study Lenovo's development in terms of the coevolution of Lenovo's strategic goals, its internal conditions, and its environment. Lenovo is an institutional spin-off, one of the major forms of new firms that have emerged during the transition period and that have been particularly successful in technology-based industries (Lu 2000). These firms have been formed from the spin-off of an entire institute, one of its subunits, or a group of individuals, and by 1993 were estimated to represent approximately half of the new ventures operating in China's many technology zones (Gu 1999, 83). Like the managers of the private, collective, and Sino-foreign joint ventures that were established outside the state-owned sector, Lenovo's managers had greater autonomy over strategic decisions but also faced a more hostile environment than SOEs. The analysis of Lenovo provides insights into the way in which these new firms have been able to maintain dynamic strategic fit by making beneficial strategic changes in response to the shifting opportunities and constraints of the Chinese business environment.

METHODOLOGY

Data on Lenovo and its environment were gathered from both archival sources and interviews. Initial data collection focused on archival sources, with work in English by Kraemer and Derick (1994a, b; 2001; 2002) and Lu (2000), and in Chinese by Chen (1997); Ling (2005); and Zhang, Chen, and Wu (2000), providing both industry environment and firm-level data. Following prior qualitative studies of longitudinal processes (Eisenhardt 1989; Van de Ven, Angle, and Poole 1989), we organized these data chronologically and used key events as anchors in semistructured interviews. In total, eighteen interviews were conducted over a three-year period, 2001–04, and interviewees included managers and engineers in Lenovo, as well as managers in other firms and industry analysts. We met with seven of the interviewees two or three times to clarify and elaborate on points that emerged in other interviews or from archival sources. Interview and archival data were used to triangulate on the temporal order of key developments and the causal links among these developments. Constructs and relationships emerging from our data were compared to a preliminary version of our process framework. The constructs and framework were subsequently modified to align them with the process uncovered in Lenovo. We present the sequential order of the constructs constituting our framework, and identify the linkages among them in order to track Lenovo's development process. We then discuss the implications of this process for the development of new firms in dramatically changing environments such as that of China, and explore the broader implications of our findings for practice and research.

THE SETTING: LENOVO GROUP LIMITED

The Lenovo Group Limited (formerly the Legend Computer Group) is currently the leading PC manufacturer in China by market share, and the largest manufacturer in Asia outside Japan. It consistently ranks as the top firm in after-sales service, above IBM and Hewlett Packard (HP) (*AsiaInfo Daily China News* 1999), and each year since 2000 has received the Intel PC Innovation Award for its innovative and home-oriented PC product designs. Lenovo began as a spin-off of the Institute of Computing Technology (ICT), a research institute under the Chinese Academy of Sciences (CAS), in 1984 (see Table 15.1 for a chronology of key corporate developments). Its first business was distributing and installing PCs produced by foreign manufacturers, before expanding into manufacturing and launching its own PC brand in 1991. Since 1994, it has been a public company, listed on the Hong Kong Stock Exchange. In 1997 it overtook both IBM and Compaq as the leading PC supplier in China (Table 15.2), and since then has remained in first place and expanded its share to almost 30 percent of the Chinese market. It has diversified its product lines beyond PCs and components (motherboards, add-on cards) to include servers, digital cameras, printers, telephone handsets, set-top boxes, and network facilities. The PC division, however, remains Lenovo's most important division and is the focus of the analysis presented in this chapter.

Table 15.1

Milestones in Lenovo's Development

Year	Events
1984	Established in 1984 as ICT Co., a spin-off of the Institute for Computer Technology, a government-funded R&D institute under the Chinese Academy of Sciences.
1987	Became a distributor for AST, and later for HP and other foreign-brand PCs.
1988	In October, ICT Co. was reorganized and renamed Legend Computer Group Co.
1988	Establishes Hong Kong Computer Group, a joint venture with a Hong Kong partner, to produce PC motherboards and add-on cards and operate a trading business.
1989	Renamed as Legend Group Co.
1991	Began to manufacture PCs and sell them under its own brand name in mainland China.
1993	Became the largest local PC manufacturer in China, behind only AST and Compaq.
1997	Overtook Compaq in terms of share of China's PC market.
1999	Became the first Chinese PC manufacturer to be the top seller (by units) in the Asia-Pacific region (excluding Japan).
2002	Changed its English name from Legend Holdings Limited to Legend Group Limited.
2003	Changed its logo from Legend to Lenovo.
2004	Changed its English name from Legend to Lenovo. Bought IBM's PC business.

SEQUENTIAL DEVELOPMENT AT LENOVO

In the following sections we present the findings from our investigation into the sequence and cause-effect interactions among Lenovo's external environment, strategy, and choices regarding resources and capabilities. Periods in Lenovo's development can be demarcated by the timing of its entry into major new functional activities: namely, 1984–90 (trade and distribution), 1991–2000 (manufacturing), and 2001–present (technological development).

1984–90: Trade and Distribution

Environment

In the 1980s, the Chinese government saw the development of China's PC industry as a national strategic priority and part of its broader, long-term goal of achieving self-reliance vis-à-vis foreign sources of technology and goods. To achieve this, the government selected and nurtured a few large firms that would eventually, it hoped, be able to compete with foreign firms. In the name of infant industry protection, the government also levied high tariffs on imports of foreign-made PCs. This regime did succeed in generating locally produced PCs, and the appointed manufacturers were able to assemble PCs from locally produced components. Furthermore, in spite of the poor quality and low reliability of these PCs, and the manufacturers' high production costs (by industry standards), the domestic firms were able to sell an increasing number of PCs to Chinese customers and earn high profits.

During most of the 1980s, however, total PC sales in China were negligible, and China was not a priority market for the leading multinationals such as IBM and HP. In contrast, second-tier foreign producers saw the disinterest of the leading multinationals as an opportunity, and firms

Table 15.2

Lenovo's Share of the Market (percent)

Rank	1992	1996	1997	1998	2002	2004
1	AST (27)	Compaq (9)	Lenovo (11)	Lenovo (22)	Lenovo (27)	Lenovo (25)
2	Compaq (19)	IBM (7)	IBM (8)	IBM (6)	IBM (9)	Founder (10)
3	Great Wall (11)	Lenovo (7)	Compaq (7)	Founder (6)	Founder (5)	Tsinghua Tongfang (8)
4	IBM (5)	Hewlett-Packard (7)	Hewlett-Packard (7)	Hewlett-Packard (6)	Dell (5)	Dell (7)

Sources: Lu (2000), Kraemer and Derick (2001), IDC, and Gartner reports.

such as California-based AST Research were the first foreign firms to enter China and quickly gained leading market shares.

Strategy

Lenovo, founded in 1984, was not one of the firms designated by the government to spearhead China's PC manufacturing industry; indeed, it did not receive a license to produce PCs until 1991. The eleven founding employees, however, were under pressure from their parent (ICT, under CAS) to take advantage of the new freedom to establish companies and engage in business activities granted to research institutes as part of an institutional experiment by the government (Lu 2000). Neither the parent organization nor these founders, however, had any business experience. Nor did the parent organization have extensive financial resources to invest in capital-intensive manufacturing.

Lenovo did receive some resources from its parent. First, ICT's leaders supported Lenovo in tangible ways, such as allowing Lenovo to use ICT's facilities free of charge. Lenovo could also do business under ICT's name, leveraging ICT's recognition among potential clients as a leader in IT research and major projects (satellites, rockets, large-scale computing), as well as the legitimacy conferred by its links to the Chinese government. Some interviewees saw these connections and conferred legitimacy as ICT's main contribution to Lenovo's development, rather than its technological resources and support.

The founders eventually decided to create a business around selling their services to other organizations—primarily installing computers, testing imported PCs, and training new users. Their first major client was Lenovo's grandparent, the Chinese Academy of Sciences, which awarded them a contract for RMB 700,000 (about $US300,000 at that time) to install and test imported computers for CAS.

Allocation of Resources

Starting in 1987, Lenovo expanded its activities to trade and distribution, becoming a distributor first for AST (the leading foreign brand in China at that time), and later adding HP and other foreign brands as they made inroads into the Chinese market. These activities soon became the primary source of revenue for Lenovo, and also generated capital, which Lenovo invested in a joint venture in Hong Kong to trade and later manufacture motherboards and add-on cards.

By distributing foreign-made PCs, Lenovo not only accumulated needed capital, but also learned how to organize sales channels and market PCs. Liu, the former CEO, even said, "Our earliest and best teacher was Hewlett-Packard" (Gold, Leibowitz, and Perkins 2001). Through these activities, Lenovo also began to build up its understanding of its Chinese customers and their PC purchasing habits.

By the end of this period, Lenovo had made significant progress in creating its own national distribution network, which was a scarce and competitively valuable resource, especially at this early stage of China's market transition. The only other organizations that had such networks at this time were the state-owned distribution organizations found in most industries—legacies of the central planning system responsible for fulfilling the allocation directives of the State Planning Commission and its relevant industrial bureau for manufacturing inputs, intermediary products, and final goods. Unlike such state-run distribution activities, however, Lenovo's distribution activities were customer focused by necessity; it could only survive by matching supply with customer demand.

Toward the end of this period, beginning with its joint venture in Hong Kong, Lenovo made its first foray into manufacturing, primarily add-on cards. One of its most successful add-on cards, for Chinese word processing, originated in the laboratories of its parent, ICT. Lenovo subcontracted developmental and engineering R&D to ICT, and ICT in turn transferred personnel to help with implementation at the production stage. These cards became an important source of revenue, in addition to that from the distribution of foreign PCs.

1991–2000: Manufacturing

Environment

From the beginning of the 1990s, China's Ministry of Electronics Industry (MEI) changed its policy for developing China's PC industry from "nationalism to pragmatism" (Kraemer and Derick 1994a). First, the government stopped insisting on self-reliance and encouraged local firms to acquire foreign technologies and become part of the international production network for PCs. Second, the government significantly reduced import tariffs on foreign-made PCs.

Reducing tariffs on imported PCs in 1992 had two significant effects on the multinationals and the competitive environment in China. First, the multinationals faced few domestic competitors because the government had allowed only a few firms—its picks to be China's champions—to produce PCs. Second, those domestic "champions" (such as Great Wall) had enjoyed relatively high profits from their protected local market, and they had not invested in learning and capability development to move them closer to international standards. As a result, multinationals quickly came to dominate the Chinese PC market in the first half of the 1990s. Later, once the government allowed new and aggressive domestic entrants (such as Lenovo and Founder) to manufacture PCs, the multinationals lost their absolute dominance.

Strategy

During the previous trade and distribution stage, Lenovo had begun to build up its market knowledge through its direct interaction with customers and extensive distribution network. It had also undertaken limited production and assembly of two major components: motherboards and add-on cards. Furthermore, these activities—trade, service, and component manufacturing—generated profits that Lenovo could reinvest. Unlike other firms that embarked on unrelated diversification financed by a core activity, Lenovo's managers remained focused on the PC industry. They decided they would capture more of the value-added activities in this industry by producing their own branded PC. Lenovo acquired a PC manufacturing license in 1991.

Lenovo's managers made several strategic choices related to their fundamental decision to remain focused on the PC industry and produce their own branded PCs. First, they would offer Chinese customers PCs with the latest processors, unlike the multinationals, which did not place a priority on supplying their latest models to the Chinese market. For example, the multinationals were selling their newest 486-based PCs in the United States but only their older and slower 386-based PCs in China, and these older models were also selling at prices higher in China than the newer ones in other markets. Lenovo, in contrast, quickly introduced PCs to the Chinese market that incorporated the latest Intel chips. This strategy simultaneously boosted Lenovo's image as a fast and technology-intensive producer and also reduced the stigma of lagging technology attached to local brands by Chinese consumers (*BusinessWeek* 1999).

Lenovo's second strategic choice, complementing its decision to incorporate leading technology in its PCs, was to design its PCs to appeal specifically to Chinese customers (Gold, Leibowitz, and Perkins 2001). The PCs being sold by multinationals were not differentiated to match local customers in markets such as China, considered minor at that time. Lenovo, in contrast, would design products for different market segments within China, from banks and other large organizations to small- and medium-sized enterprises in the corporate market, and similarly diverse individual customer groups.

Finally, Lenovo's managers decided that they would compete with multinationals on price. For comparable products, Lenovo's prices would be set at about two-thirds those of foreign-made PCs (*Wall Street Journal* 1997). For example, in August 1996, Lenovo was selling its 75 MHz Pentium-based PC for $US1,520, compared to similar models by AST and IBM selling for $US2,000 or more. Lenovo could do this because it had a lower cost structure than the multinationals. First, Lenovo's management costs were lower, especially compared to those of foreign firms with expatriate managers in China. Second, more foreign component manufacturers were setting up manufacturing operations in China, such as Seagate Technology for hard drives in Shenzhen. These manufacturers passed on some of their cost savings from their Chinese operations to Lenovo. At the same time, as a wave of Taiwanese firms entered China from the mid 1990s (Kraemer and Derick 2001), Lenovo also gained access to supplies of components and peripherals of the same quality as those used by leading multinationals. Finally, Lenovo's sales and service network reduced its distribution costs and further reduced Lenovo's cost structure.

Allocation of Resources

Lenovo continued to develop its distribution network, and this conferred competitive benefits beyond an improved cost structure. First, it gave Lenovo increasingly greater geographic coverage as compared to either multinationals or other domestic producers. By the end of the 1990s, Lenovo had approximately fifty authorized distributors in each of the seven regions into which it divided the Chinese market, and each distributor had its own reseller network. Altogether, there were approximately 2,000 resellers in Lenovo's distribution system, in addition to its 130 "1+1" PC specialty shops in major cities. IBM, in contrast, had about ten tier-one distributors, and primarily in large cities. Although there was competition among distributors, Lenovo was able to maintain a positive relationship with its distributors, many of which had grown with Lenovo over the years. In the mid 1990s, for example, Lenovo established the rule that its own regional sub-units would not sell PCs, but would only provide information and material flow service to distributors and resellers. Such policies and practices engendered greater loyalty among its distributors than those of other manufacturers, foreign or domestic. Even as Lenovo increased the depth and breadth of its distribution channels, it never had equity interests in its distributors, including its 1+1 specialty shops.

Lenovo's further expansion and elaboration of its distribution network and sales and service activities also supported marketing activities that informed its product design decisions. Lenovo incorporated feedback and experience in user needs from its distribution channels and marketing department into product design and innovation efforts in its business-level R&D centers. In addition to observing customer buying habits and choices, the company also actively sought customer input to help guide its product development activities. In 1998, for example, a Lenovo survey revealed that 80 percent of its customers bought PCs for Internet access. Even six months after purchase, however, fewer than 10 percent had actually used their PCs for that purpose. Lenovo found that for average users, configuring PCs to connect to an Internet service provider (ISP) was too complicated and time-consuming. Lenovo responded soon after with its Internet-ready PC, which incorporated six "hot keys" into the keyboard that automated such activities as Internet access, receiving e-mail, purchasing online, and accessing news. Within a year of its highly successful launch, this model had sold 900,000 units (*AsiaWeek* 2001).

Multinationals were another source of learning for Lenovo. Even while producing its own brand, Lenovo continued to distribute foreign-made PCs for HP, Toshiba, and IBM. In addition to solidifying Lenovo's position as the dominant PC distributor in China, it also provided the company with the opportunity to closely scrutinize foreign product designs and customer responses.

Lenovo also invested in new manufacturing capabilities, establishing three large-scale manufacturing bases in Beijing, Shanghai, and Huiyang (Guangdong Province) during this same period. These high-volume facilities gave Lenovo a more competitive cost structure because of the economies of scale they conferred. They also enabled the company to benefit rapidly and dramatically from learning-by-doing, which drove productivity gains. To undertake this manufacturing, Lenovo acquired leading production technology from its extensive imports of manufacturing equipment, along with extensive training by its suppliers. Its shop-floor engineers learned and successfully implemented leading manufacturing management processes without having the burden of legacy operations; that is, the poorly trained and unmotivated workers and substandard practices that plagued many of Lenovo's state-owned competitors.

Finally, Lenovo significantly broadened and deepened its internal R&D activities in order to support its cost-based and customer-focused strategy. Although Lenovo had a general understanding of the need for such activities to support its strategy, and had embarked on establishing an internal R&D capability in the late 1980s, its managers had no clear idea of how to structure or manage such activities. Its first attempt to establish a corporate-level R&D center with 200 personnel in 1990 was unsuccessful. The scientists and engineers they had recruited were not interested and too slow in reacting to what they considered mundane needs from production sites and marketing. They were more interested in developing cutting-edge technologies, such as large-scale integrated circuits and digital switches. Top management quickly realized this mismatch existed between Lenovo's strategic business needs and the interests of its corporate R&D center. They disbanded the center and assigned the R&D personnel to several new business-unit-level R&D centers that answered to business-unit managers. Lenovo's managers believe that this structure fostered closer interaction and alignment among R&D, manufacturing, and marketing functions and enabled Lenovo to implement its two-pronged strategy of low-cost manufacturing and innovative products closely matching the Chinese market.

2001–Present: Technological Development

Environment

Consistent with its industrial policy for the Chinese PC industry, the Chinese government has continued on the trajectory of market liberalization that began in the early 1990s. After several reductions in import tariffs during the 1990s, the government agreed to further tariff reductions—from 13 percent in 2001 to zero by 2005—as part of its WTO commitments. The government would also no longer restrict the local production of foreign firms in China to a percentage of their exports.

Multinationals have fully recognized the scale and potential of the Chinese PC market, and have finally accorded it high strategic priority. The PC penetration rate is still only approximately 1.5 percent, but already the Chinese market is the third largest in terms of unit shipments after the United States and Japan. To serve this market, all of the major multinationals are establishing more of their operations in China, either through joint ventures, or, more recently, wholly owned subsidiaries.

Strategy

So far, Lenovo has managed not only to defend, but to extend its lead in the domestic PC market. It has achieved world-class manufacturing capabilities, according to Andy Grove, founder and former CEO of Intel (SCMP 1998). Lenovo's managers, however, recognize several competitive threats they must address in order for Lenovo to continue to dominate its even more determined and focused rivals for an increasingly diverse domestic market. First, compared to leading multinationals such as Dell, HP, and IBM, which are more aggressively targeting the Chinese market, Lenovo lags behind in technological capabilities. At the same time, its domestic rivals are catching up, closing the formerly wide technological gap between themselves and Lenovo. Second, as more multinationals establish significant manufacturing bases in China, they will also have the same opportunities to reduce their cost structure and benefit from local sources of cost advantages, such as labor and component costs. Third, competition based on product innovativeness is gaining importance even as firms are less and less able to compete on price and costs.

To respond to these developments in the competitive landscape, and in view of a joint analysis by McKinsey & Company in 2000, Lenovo's management identified technology and innovation as the focus of its new strategic development. Their objective was to complement Lenovo's existing strategy of offering differentiated products incorporating leading technology to more finely delineated customer segments.

Allocation of Resources

To implement its strategy of more differentiated products for more specific customer segments, Lenovo is continuing to draw on its internal R&D capabilities. The company is developing more customized hardware configurations and software bundles for its Chinese customers. For example, within its notebook product category, it offers five series, each targeted to the needs of specific customer groups. In the home PC category, Lenovo offers four series, including one for children that helps them learn computer skills through games and entertainment, another for middle-aged and older users that incorporates touch-screen technology as an alternative to using a mouse or keyboard, another for high school students that offers more fashionable designs and learning software, and a fourth for adults that includes Lenovo's proprietary software.

Complementing its more differentiated product lines, Lenovo continues to elaborate its distribution system to more finely address geographic variation in customer purchasing power, attitudes, lifestyles, and consumption patterns (Cui and Lui 2000). In 2004 Lenovo increased the number of primary market regions to eighteen from seven. Managers of these regions report directly to the headquarters in Beijing, while the four regional platforms (north, south, east, and west) have only a logistics coordination function. Lenovo is also significantly expanding its 1+1 PC specialty shops to 600 by the end of 2004 (from 130 in 1999) in order to strengthen its linkage with end users. Finally, during this same period, and as a result of Dell's direct-sales success in China, Lenovo recognized a new segment of customers and added a telephone-based and direct-sales unit to serve them.

Although Lenovo continues to gather customer and market data via its distribution, marketing, and manufacturing activities, the nature of innovation implied by its current strategy places an even greater emphasis on R&D at both the applied and more fundamental levels. After several restructurings of its R&D activities, Lenovo's management has finally settled on a two-tier structure, corresponding to what it terms "technology for today" and "technology for tomorrow and the day after tomorrow."

The first tier, charged with developing technology for "today's" PCs, is located within the IT Business Cluster, which includes the server, notebook, consumer IT, commercial desktop, and several other business units. These are served by more specific labs; for example, the Desktop PC Development Center includes five supporting labs that are responsible for parts and components, commercial systems, consumer systems, architecture and standards, and application software, respectively. These labs are responsible for engineering systems and components based on needs identified in current operations, although in some cases they may subcontract research work to second-level R&D centers. These labs are supposed to collaborate with the production engineering departments within Lenovo's three manufacturing plants to ensure that their solutions are easy and cost-effective to implement in manufacturing.

Second-tier R&D is at the corporate level, under a single vice director, and includes four centers. The Lenovo Research Institute is at the heart of Lenovo's development of future key technologies. The current focus is on coordinating applications to develop the technologies and protocols that will make it possible to exploit opportunities for coordinating different information devices, including home appliances, telecommunications, and computers. The other three centers are charged with developing technology and platforms for all business units within Lenovo. The Software Design Center develops application software, the Industrial Design Center innovates in product appearance and attractiveness, and the Add-on Card Design Center develops motherboards and other parts and components to optimize the performance of Lenovo's products. These centers are intended to support the first-level research units, and relationships between the first- and second-level centers are governed by internal contracting agreements.

To fund this effort, Lenovo announced in 2000 that it would invest an additional RMB 1.8 billion ($US218 million) in the development of new technology. Already the effort seems to be bearing fruit, with Lenovo's invention, utility, and industrial design patents increasing dramatically since 1999 (Table 15.3). To further signal this change in emphasis as well as establish a

Table 15.3

Lenovo's Patents

Patent classification	1997	1998	1999	2000	2001	2002	2003
Invention patent	1	0	2	2	3	10	101
Utility model	0	0	6	18	15	90	102
Industrial design patents	4	11	28	31	53	125	104
Total	5	11	36	51	71	225	307

Source: Based on the patent database of China's Intellectual Property Bureau.

brand name that could be extended overseas, in 2003 Lenovo changed its name from Legend to Lenovo, meaning "leading innovation."

Because of the breadth of technologies and capabilities relevant to PCs, however, Lenovo's managers have recognized that they must supplement internal R&D activities, especially those targeting the future, with cooperative activities with other firms. To this end, it has formed alliances with China Telecom, IBM, National Semiconductor, and D-Link, among others. In August 2003, for example, it cofounded with Intel the Lenovo-Intel Future Technology Advancement Center. This center is charged with building reliable computation environments and key technologies for the next-generation Internet and designing leading-edge products that fuse computers and telecommunications.

DYNAMIC STRATEGIC FIT AS PROCESS

Our analysis of Lenovo's development from its founding through three major stages of its development reveal an iterative process among the firm's external environment, internal conditions (strategy, resources, and capabilities), and resource allocation decisions (Table 15.4). It shows the dynamic process by which the firm's managers attempted to align their strategy and internal resources and capabilities with the constraints and opportunities in their environment. In Lenovo's case, achieving alignment involved a series of resource allocations that resulted in its vertical integration into the PC business. Close inspection of these allocations further reveals that Lenovo's managers were simultaneously exploiting and exploring. Once they developed a new functional capability or resource—for example, their distribution network—in subsequent periods they deepened that capability or resource by "exploiting" it, in March's (1991) sense. The managers learned by doing, refined their capabilities, and expanded those capabilities within familiar domains. They also engaged in exploration when they allocated the firm's resources to new functional domains (manufacturing, R&D) or to qualitatively different domains with the same function (i.e., mass-production manufacturing into built-to-order manufacturing, product-development R&D into fundamental-technology R&D).

The exploitation element of March's framework is closely related to Nelson and Winter's (1982) conceptualization of routines (or resources and capabilities) as path dependent. It can also be related to Cohen and Levinthal's (1990) concept of absorptive capacity. This elicits the question of whether these evolutionary theories emphasizing path-dependent trajectories are incompatible with the notion of exploration and developing significantly different resources and capabilities. Indeed, March himself (1991) discussed exploration and exploitation as a tension within organizations. Lenovo's case seems to suggest that these may be very different processes,

Table 15.4

Stages in Lenovo's Pursuit of Strategic Fit

Trade and distribution, 1984–90	Manufacturing, 1991–2000	Technological development, 2001–present
Environment		
Government has policy of self-reliance and infant industry protection for computer industry; picks SOEs to be national champions. Leading multinationals not focused on Chinese market; second-tier MNCs enter; sell via resellers; profit margins and tariffs lead to high prices for PCs in Chinese market.	Government encourages integration of Chinese firms into global PC production network; grants PC manufacturing licenses to more domestic firms (including Lenovo); reduces import tariffs. More multinationals enter market and dominate local producers.	Government further liberalizes market, with import tariffs reduced to zero by 2005; removes export requirements for foreign manufacturers. Multinationals aggressively target Chinese market and increase local operations.
Strategy		
Choose business model: Distribute and install imported PCs for Chinese organizations and train users.	Distribute PCs and introduce own branded PC; compete on price with locally adapted models technologically competitive with multinational brands.	Compete based on technological sophistication and price; introduce build-to-order manufacturing capability to more precisely meet customer demands (Dell's business model); expand internationally.
Allocation of resources		
Exploitation: Use employees' computer expertise to sell, install, and train. *Exploration:* Create distribution network.	*Exploitation:* Further expand distribution network. *Exploration:* Establish new manufacturing facilities and R&D center for product development.	*Exploitation:* Product development based on expanded R&D capabilities. *Exploration:* Leading edge research in PC-related technologies; strategic alliances for collaborative development of some leading technologies; build-to-order marketing, sales and manufacturing system; international brand building.

but not necessarily antagonistic. Lenovo's managers undertook both activities and were successful in the sense of achieving their strategic goals and performing well vis-à-vis competitors. They were only able to do so because they could judiciously allocate resources across exploitation and exploration activities in their pursuit of dynamic strategic fit.

The Lenovo case illustrates the different means by which firms "explore" and acquire new resources and capabilities. Initially, Lenovo competed in sales and distribution by relying on other firms' products or technology developed by its institutional parent. In order to grow and take advantage of changes in the environment, Lenovo internalized first manufacturing and then R&D capabilities through a combination of acquisitions and internal development. More recently, it is pursuing collaborative alliances to co-develop new technologies.

The Lenovo case also highlights the simultaneous impact of environmental determinism and strategic choice, represented by the two sources of misfit that can be identified from our analysis.

The first is the environment, and the case provides numerous examples of how changes in government policy and the competitive environment created misfits between external constraints and opportunities and Lenovo's internal conditions (strategy and/or resources and capabilities), to which its managers responded through their resource allocation decisions. The second source of misfit is changes in the strategic goals introduced by the managers themselves. Lenovo's managers changed their goals from simply surviving by whatever activities (sales, distribution) to growing into a fully integrated PC manufacturer, and from a provider of low-cost, technologically competitive products to one producing technologically leading products. More recently, they have introduced a new goal, from being the dominant supplier in China to being a significant competitor internationally. The purchase of IBM's PC division represents an attempt to bring Lenovo's internal conditions (resources and capabilities) in line with that goal.

AREAS FOR FURTHER RESEARCH

A single case does not allow us to test hypotheses, but it does allow us to develop a process model that incorporates variables and contextual features of interest. The Lenovo case illustrates the iterative process inherent in the pursuit of dynamic strategic fit as a firm's environment, the strategies and goals of its managers, and its complement of resources and capabilities change over time. Although we assume that a firm that is able to maintain fit among these elements will perform better than those that cannot, our study design does not let us test such hypotheses. Further research could explore the performance implications of maintaining fit through carefully chosen paired case studies that also compare the process by which fit is maintained or not, and the ways in which performance is increased or not. Traditionally, research in the area of strategic fit has relied on static, cross-sectional research designs (Venkatraman 1989, Zajac, Kraatz, and Bresser 2000), while the question is fundamentally longitudinal. Large-scale quantitative studies can contribute to our deeper understanding of this phenomenon only if they also incorporate a temporal dimension.

A related issue that deserves further study is the difference between reactive and proactive misfit. In what situations should managers wait until a misfit develops and then attempt to address it, and when should they actively introduce misfits, such as the Lenovo managers did when they introduced new strategic goals? Are there any interactions among proactive and reactive misfits, allocation of resources to exploitation and exploration, and performance? Prior work has shown that the strategy-structure-performance relationship varies significantly with environmental features (e.g., Davies and Walters 2004, Tan and Litschert 1994, Tan and Tan 2004). It is not unreasonable to assume that the motivation driving fit-enhancing strategic changes—environmental pressure versus managerial volition—could also be an important contingency in dynamic strategic fit–performance relationships.

MANAGERIAL IMPLICATIONS

The findings from the Lenovo case have several clear implications for management. First, this case describes a development process by which a firm can simultaneously deepen its existing set of resources and capabilities and develop new ones. Decisions about how to allocate resources between exploitation and exploration must be made in reference to the firm's strategic goals and the opportunities and constraints in its environment. Lenovo's managers, over almost fifteen years, created a firm with an integrated set of functional capabilities, from R&D to manufacturing to sales and service.

The sequence in which they integrated is particularly significant, and we argue that it is a major factor in Lenovo's current competitiveness. As the case describes, Lenovo began as a distributor and sequentially added manufacturing and then R&D. Furthermore, each step in the process was informed by the knowledge and experience the firm had acquired further downstream. As a result, customer needs were embedded first in decisions about what types of products and designs to offer, and later in what types of technologies would have value in the market.

The case also shows how each stage in a firm's development of new capabilities requires different strategies and structures for maintaining fit. The firm will acquire different capabilities through different means; for example, through acting as a subcontractor to leading firms, collaborating with a partner, acquisitions, or licensing. Furthermore, as the firm develops capabilities in new functional areas, or broadens the range of capabilities in a particular function, the organization must be restructured to support effective and efficient coordination of increasingly diverse activities.

Lenovo's case also provides an alternative development model for new firms that do not have proprietary technology on which to build a company, or for spin-offs in which the parent's key contributions may not be technology. The parent's critical contribution was not proprietary technology or significant start-up funding, but seconded technical personnel, the freedom for them to undertake commercial activities, and their first commercial contract, which became their revenue stream. An additional critical contribution was legitimacy via connections to a government organization. Lenovo established itself on the basis of these factors and then grew through judicious decisions that eventually resulted in a fully integrated firm.

It is not yet clear, however, whether Lenovo's ability so far to maintain dynamic strategic fit in the Chinese environment will be transferable or beneficial as it attempts to expand into international markets. Although Lenovo is financially and competitively quite successful in the Chinese market, only 10 percent of its revenues now come from outside China. Such dominance of domestic over international sales may be simply a matter of managerial focus, but it may also represent an inherent limitation in the competitiveness of Lenovo's products in other markets. Although the Chinese market alone promises to be a major, growing PC market for the foreseeable future, the possibility that Lenovo's products may not match other markets' will have to be addressed as the firm sets international expansion as a major strategic goal. While the purchase of IBM's PC division gives Lenovo quick access to leading technology as well as a valuable brand, the value of those resources and capabilities will diminish as the industry develops further. In other words, Lenovo must now successfully manage exploration and exploitation, but with the objective of achieving a fit with global—not just Chinese—markets.

The Lenovo case has lessons that are relevant for latecomer firms, especially, but not only, those in developing countries like China. Investments in R&D may be considered vital for a firm to compete at the leading edge of an industry, and governments may even reward investments in R&D; yet it is necessary for a firm with limited resources, as compared to large multinationals, to realistically assess the opportunity costs and probable outcomes of such investments. A firm with limited resources should allocate them to activities and learning efforts that will enable it to compete successfully with its rivals. Developing resources and capabilities that set it apart from otherwise much better-funded and -endowed rivals represents a better strategic option than attempting to compete on the same basis with such firms. Lenovo's investments in distribution and product development attuned to Chinese customers, for example, have so far more than offset its investments in R&D that are, in absolute terms, hardly significant when compared to the R&D expenditures of its multinational rivals.

CONCLUSIONS

In this chapter, we have used the case of Lenovo to identify the process by which a new private firm has been able to maintain dynamic strategic fit vis-à-vis a dramatically changing policy and competitive environment. Lenovo has done so by implementing a series of beneficial strategic changes, simultaneously exploiting its existing resources and capabilities and exploring new ones. This process has important implications for other private and latecomer firms that also face hostile environments and must make decisions about which resources and capabilities to develop—as well as how to develop them—in order to match the opportunities and constraints of their environments.

ACKNOWLEDGMENTS

The research on which this chapter is based was financially supported by the NSF of China (NSF Research Project Reference: 70173008 and 70373005) and the Basic Research Fund of Tsinghua University (Project Number: JC2002049). The authors would like to thank three anonymous referees for their thoughtful and extensive comments on the draft, and the interviewees for their time and patience in answering our questions.

REFERENCES

Amsden, A. H. (1989). *Asia's next giant: South Korea and late industrialization.* Oxford: Oxford University Press.
Asiainfo Daily China News. (1999). June 16. www.asiaweek.com.
Asiaweek. (2001). The stuff of Lenovo. May 25. www.asiaweek.com/asiaweek/magazine/nations/0,8782,110144,00.html.
Barney, J. (1991). Firm resources and sustained competitive advantage. *Journal of Management,* 17, 99–120.
Bell, M., and K. Pavitt. (1993). Technological accumulation and industrial growth: Contrasts between developed and developing countries. *Industrial and Corporate Change,* 2, 157–210.
BusinessWeek. (1999). How Lenovo lives up to its name. February 5.
Chen, H. (1997). *Why Legend?* (in Chinese). Beijing: Beijing University Press.
Child, J. (1994). *Management in China in the age of reform.* Cambridge, UK: Cambridge University Press.
Cohen, W., and D. Levinthal. (1990). Absorptive capacity: A new perspective on learning and innovation. *Administrative Science Quarterly,* 35, 128–52.
Cui, G., and Q. Liu. (2000). Regional market segments of China: Opportunities and barriers in a big emerging market. *Journal of Consumer Marketing,* 17, 55–70.
Davies, H., and P. Walters. (2004). Emergent patterns of strategy, environment and performance in a transition economy. *Strategic Management Journal,* 25, 347–64.
Eisenhardt, K. (1989). Building theories from case study research. *Academy of Management Review,* 14, 532–50.
Gold, A. R.; G. Leibowitz; and A. Perkins. (2001). A computer Lenovo in the making. *McKinsey Quarterly,* 3, 73–83.
Gu, S. (1999). *China's industrial technology: Market reform and organizational change.* London: Routledge.
Guthrie, D. (1998). The declining significance of *guanxi* in China's economic transition. *China Quarterly,* 154, 254–82.
Hobday, M. (1995). *Innovation in East Asia: The challenge to Japan.* Aldershot, UK: Edward Elgar.
Kahneman, D., and A. Tversky. (1979). Prospect theory: An analysis of decision under risk. *Econometrica,* 47, 263–91.
Kim, L. (1997). *Imitation to innovation: The dynamics of Korea's technological learning.* Boston: Harvard Business School Press.
Kim, L., and R. R. Nelson. (2000). *Technology, learning and innovation: Experiences of newly industrializing economies.* Cambridge, UK: Cambridge University Press.

Kraemer, K. L., and J. Derick. (1994a). *National computer policy and development in China.* Working paper PAC-060A. Center for Research on Information Technology and Organization, University of California, Irvine.

———. (1994b). *From nationalism to pragmatism: IT policy in China.* Working paper PAC-060B. Center for Research on Information Technology and Organization, University of California, Irvine.

———. (2001). *Creating a computer industry giant: China's industrial policies and outcomes in the 1990s.* Working paper. Center for Research on Information Technology and Organization, University of California, Irvine.

———. (2002). Enter the dragon: China's computer industry. *Computer,* February, 28–36.

Ling, Z. (2005). *Lenovo's wind and cloud* (in Chinese). Beijing: Zhongxin Publishing.

Liu, X., and S. White. (2001). Comparing innovation systems: A framework and application to China's transitional context. *Research Policy,* 30, 1091–1114.

Lu, Q. (2000). *China's leap into the information age: Innovation and organization in the computer industry.* Oxford, UK: Oxford University Press.

Lukas, B.; J. Tan; and G. Hult. (2001). Strategic fit in transitional economies: The case of China's electronics industry. *Journal of Management,* 27, 409–29.

March, J. (1991). Exploration and exploitation in organizational learning. *Organization Science,* 2, 71–87.

Nelson, R., and S. Winter. (1982). *An evolutionary theory of economic change.* Cambridge, MA: Belknap Press.

Nolan, P. (2001). *China and the global economy: National champions, industrial policy and the big business revolution.* New York: Palgrave.

Peng, M. (2003). Institutional transitions and strategic choices. *Academy of Management Review,* 28, 275–96.

Peng, M., and P. Heath. (1996). The growth of the firm in planned economies in transition: Institutions, organizations and strategic choice. *Academy of Management Review,* 21, 492–528.

Peng, M., and Y. Luo. (2000). Managerial ties and firm performance in a transition economy: The nature of a micro-macro link. *Academy of Management Journal,* 43, 486–501.

Peteraf, M. (1993). The cornerstones of competitive advantage: A resource-based view. *Strategic Management Journal,* 14, 179–91.

SCMP. (1998). Legend gives Intel chief millionth PC. *South China Morning Post,* May 7.

Simon, H. (1955). A behavioral model of rational choice. *Quarterly Journal of Economics,* 69, 99–118.

Steinfeld, E. (1998). *Forging reform in China: The fate of state-owned industry.* Cambridge, UK: Cambridge University Press.

Story, J. (2003). *China: The race to market.* London: FT Prentice Hall.

Tan, J., and R. Litschert. (1994). Environment–strategy relationship and its performance implications: An empirical study of Chinese electronics industry. *Strategic Management Journal,* 15, 1–20.

Tan, J., and D. Tan. (2004). Environment–strategy co-evolution and co-alignment: A staged model of Chinese SOEs under transition. *Strategic Management Journal,* 26, 141–57.

Van de Ven, A.; H. Angle; and M. Poole. (1989). *Research on the management of innovation: The Minnesota studies.* New York: Ballinger.

Venkatraman, N. (1989). The concept of fit in strategy research: Toward verbal and statistical correspondence. *Academy of Management Review,* 14, 423–44.

Venkatraman, N., and J. Prescott. (1990). Environment-strategy coalignment: An empirical test of its performance implications. *Strategic Management Journal,* 11, 1–23.

Walder, A. (1995). Local government as industrial firms: An organizational analysis of China's transition economy. *American Journal of Sociology,* 101, 263–301.

Wall Street Journal. (1997). China's personal-computer industry is starting to beat out U.S. companies. November 19.

White, S. (2000). Competition, capabilities, and the make, buy, or ally decisions of Chinese state-owned firms. *Academy of Management Journal,* 43, 324–41.

White, S., and G. Linden. (2002). Organizational and industrial response to market liberalization: The interaction of pace, incentive and capacity to change. *Organization Studies,* 23, 917–48.

White, S., and X. Liu. (1998). Organizational processes to meet new performance criteria: Chinese pharmaceutical firms in transition. *Research Policy,* 27, 369–83.

Xie, W., and S. White. (2005). Windows of opportunity, learning strategies, and the rise of China's handset makers. *International Journal of Technology Management,* forthcoming.

Xie, W., and G. Wu. (2003). Differences between learning processes in small tigers and large dragons. *Research Policy,* 32, 1463–79.

Xin, K., and J. Pearce. (1996). *Guanxi:* Connections as substitutes for formal institutional support. *Academy of Management Journal,* 39, 1641–58.

Zajac, E.; M. Kraatz; and R. Bresser. (2000). Modeling the dynamics of strategic fit: A normative approach to strategic change. *Strategic Management Journal,* 21, 429–53.

Zeng, M., and P. Williamson. (2003). The hidden dragons. *Harvard Business Review,* 81, October, 92–99.

Zhang, F.; Z. Chen; and K. Wu. (2000). Reflections on the history of China's computer industry (in Chinese). *Diannao Shijie [Computer World].* January 10.

16

THE EMERGENCE OF CHINA'S PRIVATE-SECTOR FIRMS

THEORY DEVELOPMENT IN THE MIDST OF EVOLVING INSTITUTIONAL AND INDUSTRIAL CONDITIONS

CLAUDIA BIRD SCHOONHOVEN

The collected articles in this volume represent the most contemporary rendering of the status of scholarly research on private-sector firms in China today. In this chapter I focus specifically on management perspectives on Chinese private-sector firms, suggest a conceptual simplification of the multisyllabic, multiterm phrases used to describe Chinese business organizations, and outline some of the theoretical and empirical challenges facing scholars seeking to better understand private-sector firms in China. First, what are "management" perspectives? In these days of cross-disciplinary research in which scholars read widely across management, sociology, psychology, and economics, a management perspective (on anything) must be defined in the broadest terms possible. By management perspectives I mean research and theory on organizations, writ large, which ideally have implications for the behavior of managers and their organizations. Regardless of the theoretical focus of a specific empirical study, features of organizations will play a prominent role in research from a management perspective.

A management perspective encompasses a number of subgroups within the field of management itself, and it includes organizational behavior, meso (or middle-level) theory and research, macro organization and management theory, strategy and business policy, as well as scholars based in disciplines addressing any of these. For example, sociologists like Michael T. Hannan, who takes an organizational ecology perspective, and Richard Hackman, whose work is based on social psychology, frequently publish in Academy of Management and strategic management journals. Collectively an array of theoretical perspectives emerges from these various approaches to management phenomena, and good overviews can be found in Barney and Hesterley (2005), Pfeffer (1997), and Scott (2003). In any case, it is the theoretical phenomenon to be explained that will drive the range of theories that might be applied to understanding private-sector firms and their attendant managerial challenges in the Peoples Republic of China (PRC).

NECESSARY CONDITIONS FOR DERIVING ACTION IMPLICATIONS

I argue below that to derive sensible action implications for managers in China, several conditions need to be present. First, well-argued theory and well-executed empirical research are prerequisites before implications can be drawn and managerial prescriptions issued. Too often, managers worldwide read management how-to books—books often based upon scant empirical research and even less theory. Such books are strong on prescriptions for managers, but have little beyond the personal experience and observations of the authors to support their recommendations. Shelves of the popular business section of any contemporary bookstore reveal the current stock.

Second, the theoretical perspective taken in a given empirical study needs to be well informed about the Chinese context. Child (2000) has argued that both economic theory and the theory of technological change are low-context perspectives because they minimize the impact of national distinctiveness. I will argue that most of our theories of organizations are low context, as the bulk of existing empirical research and theory published in English has been developed by United States–based scholars, most of whom take the U.S. context for granted and assume no variation in institutional conditions. For example, in a review of the organizational mortality literature, Schoonhoven and Woolley (2005) found that prevailing theories and research about the death and survival of new firms are essentially context-free, and the current implicit mortality model does not accommodate key features of the Chinese context. The theoretical problem to be explained will also reveal inadequacies in our current theories, as several have observed that organization theories writ large are parochial dinosaurs (e.g., Boyacigiller and Adler 1991), heavily biased by their North American scholarly origins.

Third, China is presently in the midst of a set of institutional transformations that constitute experimental conditions to which Chinese managers as well as entrepreneurs starting private firms must continuously adapt. Managerial prescriptions derived from careful research must be cognizant of the evolving economic, legal, and ownership conditions in China. For example, while private business owners (mostly family-based) have existed in China in fairly large numbers since the 1980s (Gold 1990), the existence of China's market economy was not formally recognized until after the nation had joined the World Trade Organization (WTO) in 2002, and the Third Plenary of the 16th Chinese Communist Party (CCP) had convened in 2003.

Often research on organizations will date the beginning of a study from a major legal or regulatory change like this one, to acknowledge that institutional conditions were formally altered at that point. The practical implication is simply that scholars must not assume fixed institutional conditions in China, but rather must be alert for the likelihood that major assumptions about the context may not be valid. While institutions themselves are "taken-for-granted" entities, nonetheless institutional change in China is hardly complete as of 2006. This implies that both longitudinal and dynamic research designs will be necessary in the Chinese context, and they will need to include careful specification of the timing of significant events like China's 1988 formal recognition of private firms and its 2001 decision to admit entrepreneurs to the Communist Party.

Similarly, as recently as 2003 the venture capital investors in China were still operating without legal protection as China has yet to create a legal framework to support venture capital investments (Xiao, 2002). As of this writing, the only China-based venture capital association that could be identified, the Hong Kong Venture Capital Association, is located in Hong Kong, and its objective is to promote the VC industry in Hong Kong itself rather than China-wide (www.ChinaSite.com/Business/VentureCapital). As venture-capital investors become more organized and influential within China, one can predict that their legal status will likely change. However, until then, the organized investment capital in China today must be termed "nascent." In the United States, this same industry is referred to as "institutional venture capital," a phrase that conveys the industry's legitimacy, its legal status, and that the conditions under which venture capital investors may operate are well understood and codified in U.S. tax and investment laws; this has yet to be accomplished in China.

Evidence continues to accumulate that Chinese managers and entrepreneurs urgently need more substantive managerial knowledge than is currently available. This need can be observed empirically in the high death rates of new technology-based firms in China. Chen (1998) reported that 5,000 new ventures were founded between 1988 and 1998 in the Zhong Guan Cun technology development zone in Beijing. However, only 9 percent of these survived for five years, and only 3 percent survived eight years or more. Comparing these rates to those published in other studies, Schoonhoven and Woolley (2005) reported that a twenty times greater proportion of new U.S. and German firms survived their first eight to ten years of life than did the Beijing firms.[1] That most new technology-based firms do not survive very long is not news. However, the exceptionally high death rates for *China's new firms* suggests that the development of China's technology industries will take much longer than expected, will continue to be an inefficient process from both the entrepreneurs' and the government's perspectives, and will cost substantially more on a national basis than expected as the years and numbers of failed firms accumulate.

The requisite knowledge base needed to inform China's managers is still in its early stages of development. The few exemplars of the current state of scholarship can be listed readily: a special issue of *Organization Science,* Transformation of organizations in the PRC (Tsui et al. 2002); Tsui and Lau's (2002) the *Management of enterprises in the People's Republic of China;* Tsui and coeditors' first book, *Management and organizations in the Chinese context: Current issues and future research directions* (Li, Tsui, and Weldon 2000); and the current volume. All bear publication dates of 2000 or later. Similarly, the International Chinese Academy of Management Research (ICAMR), organized as the first formal association of scholars focused on creating managerial knowledge in China, held its first meeting in 2004, when it also launched the journal *Management and Organization Review (MOR),* dedicated to publishing Chinese management studies. Nonetheless, these publications and events have occurred in the past five years, and certainly not sufficiently fast to develop useful knowledge for the tens of millions of new Chinese private-sector firms founded over the past decade and the varying contexts within which they operate.

WHO AND WHAT ARE THE PRIVATE-SECTOR CHINESE FIRMS?

Increasingly, scholars have come to recognize that China's private-sector organizations cannot be characterized as a monolithic entity—as if few differences existed within the private sector. In their simplest definition, private-sector firms in China are simply business organizations that are not owned by the government, as Li (chapter 8 in this volume) and Wang (chapter 11 in this volume) imply when they refer to "nonstate enterprises."[2] Gregory et al. (2000) and Zhang (1999) defined China's domestic private sector as nonagricultural (1) individual and household businesses employing seven or fewer individuals and (2) private enterprises employing eight or more individuals. This latter category grew after 1988 when the constitution was amended to allow private firms to hire more than seven employees.[3] At the end of 2002, it was reported that there were 23.775 million individual and household businesses, and 24.35 million private enterprises in China (Zheng 2003, 148–49). Unfortunately, these data are not reported longitudinally, although at the individual level, the number employed in private enterprises had increased from 21.2 million in 1989 to 81.5 million in 2002 (Zheng 2003, 146). This 3.8-fold jump in the number of persons employed in the private sector over thirteen years suggests that the number of private enterprises themselves has also grown, but at an unknown rate.

Private-sector firms may or may not have evolved from the privatization of state assets. Indeed, Walder (chapter 17 in this volume) asserts that China's private sector has evolved not from the privatization of state assets, but rather from the establishment of new firms. If true, we can assume that, on average, most of China's private-sector firms were not previously state-owned, but were founded de novo and are therefore relatively young. This is not to understate the significance of the transformation of some state-owned enterprises (SOEs) (or some part thereof) into shareholding companies, and this phenomenon is well described in Bian and Zhang's (chapter 2 in this volume) description of the emergence of China's private economy.

Still, the term "private"-sector firms may be somewhat misleading. In common parlance in the West, private firms are owned by private individuals or corporations and, in the United States at least, they have minimal legislated financial disclosure requirements. Private firms are distinguished in the West from "publicly traded" firms, which have had an initial public offering, have stock openly traded on a stock exchange, and have substantial government-mandated financial disclosure requirements. In China, however, some proportion of private firms—those that Nee (1992) labeled "hybrids" (after Borys and Jemison 1989)—have taken new organizational forms; these use resources and governance structures from more than one existing organization. An example is township-and-village enterprises (TVEs), which share ownership with the local government in exchange for political protection and resources (Li, chapter 8 in this volume). However, according to Nee (1992) and the introductory chapter of this book (Tsui, Cheng, and Bian), their ownership structure is "in flux."

Theoretically, it would be helpful to place China's multiple organizational forms into a more abstract set of concepts, as a plethora of terms is used to describe China's business organizations. "Marketized" and nonmarketized firms, local corporatism, township-and-village enterprises (TVEs), state-owned enterprises (SOEs), domestic private firms, marketized redistributive organizations, informal privatization, partially public firms, and so on are among the confusing array of labels placed on China's business organizations. In 1992, Nee helpfully described the diversity of organizational forms in China as a continuum, based on the distribution of property rights, and these range from formal, hierarchical SOEs to small family-owned firms run by entrepreneurs. Nee (1992) explained that the variety of organizational forms (based on ownership variations) is a practical solution to problems spawned by a weak market structure, a plurality of property rights, and an incomplete transition to a market economy.

In my view, it is essential for scholars to obtain reliable ownership data in order to distinguish the degree to which organizations are privately owned. Rather than "typing" organizations, it is conceptually cleaner to describe the evolution of the actual ownership distribution as well as the year of founding (the age) of an organization. With these data we can specify founding conditions, both external and internal; founding conditions tend to be imprinted on organizations and are well understood to exert long-term effects on their future development (Boeker 1989, Stinchcombe 1965). Chapter 4 in the current volume (Vanhonacker, Zweig, and Chung), comparing Chinese private entrepreneurs who emigrated and then returned to China with those who remained steadfastly in China, illustrates the kinds of data that should be collected. The authors collected data over time on the number of shareholders, proportion of equity held by various ownership categories, relationship of shareholders to firm principals, and source of initial financial investment funds. Interestingly, local government investments accounted for 14 percent of the money raised by returned, former immigrant entrepreneurs. Should we label these firms state- or government-owned enterprises then? Of course not. However, we can speak of the *extent to which* an organization is government owned. The authors know the proportion of equity (a continuous variable) raised across a set of nine categories of investors, information that can be entered in analyses attempting to account for the relative performance of the focal business organizations.

Beyond labeling them "private," scholars also need to understand the lay of the land of China's private firms. It is essential to know the overall distribution of private firms over time, by industry (size, number of firms, employment, and industry-level performance statistics), and individual firms within industry (age as date of founding, size, ownership distribution, and various financial indicators of performance). By a "firm," I mean an organization that sells a product or service and seeks profits in excess of its costs. The National Bureau of Statistics of China and its publishing arm, the China Statistics Press, tend to provide more information on China's traditional industries (mining, leather, textiles, plastics, furniture, etc.) than on new technology-intensive sectors like electronics and telecommunications, which are grouped together in their tables of data (Zheng 2003). The publishers need to further differentiate China's technology-based industries, especially by identifying primary and emerging technology-intensive industries like computers, semiconductors, biotechnology, nanotechnology, and the like. Some industry-specific yearbooks are available, such as the *Pharmaceutical Industry Yearbook* created by the Ministry of Public Health; however, the biotechnology sector is minimally described therein (White and Liu 2002). Similarly, some market research companies (e.g., the China Daily Information Company) are now publishing directories; yet these are highly selective and include companies primarily on the basis of their size and market presence.

The agency responsible for gathering China's national industrial statistics and the market research companies typically sample on the dependent variable of firm performance, as only firms that exceed a certain sales volume (such as 5 million RMB, or about US$625,000) are reported (Zheng 2003, 461). Using the 5 million RMB criterion clearly misses most young firms and those with fewer than 100 employees, which are by far the greatest number of firms in the West. The same is likely to be true in China as well. In organizational research, overall population (industry) size and distribution by firm size within industry are data needed to construct a statistically meaningful sample. Clearly, knowledge of all firms is needed for population (industry) studies.

In studies of organizations, scholars typically control for industry and technology in order to specify the conditions under which findings obtain. In the West, most industry associations provide member directories, which are invaluable in creating population and sample data. The development of industry associations may well be in the future for China. In the West, new associations are typically founded with the financial support and coalescing of large, successful firms that perceive collective action within an industry to be beneficial. At this writing, only a small number of government-backed industry associations exist in China. One can only speculate about whether and when industry associations in China might become more autonomous, perhaps modeling practices of industry associations in the West.

As more information about private firms becomes publicly available, we will be able to design sensible studies, about whose validity and reliability we can become more confident. At present, most organizational research in China is based upon samples of unknown population size and they may be based on a convenience sample, where entree to the organization for research is obtained through personal relationships. With greater confidence in our population and sample statistics, meaningful managerial implications can be drawn from future organizational research in China.

MANAGERIAL STUDIES IN THIS VOLUME

The three empirical papers in this section are examples of the wide range of topics and levels of analysis that research on management perspectives addresses. Each research project was carefully crafted and well executed. In this section I will discuss each chapter with respect to the industries, ownership, size, and age of the organizations studied, the unit and level of analysis applied, and analyze the likely managerial implications in the paper.

In the first of these chapters, by Fahr, Cheng, Chou, and Chu, the industries studied were electronics, communication, steel, textiles, restaurants, and manufacturing. Within these, fifty-two private firms that were either family owned or joint ventures were the organizational contexts. Firms were midsize, with a mean of 207 employees and a range of from 20 to 735 employees. These were relatively young companies, whose average age was about seven years, although the youngest was a brand-new start-up and the oldest a mature sixteen years. The units of analysis were employees ($n = 292$), and their perceptions of their managers' leadership behavior, the employees' psychological responses, and their satisfaction with and dependence upon the managers were studied.

Among the primary findings of this cross-sectional study were that the authoritarian dimension of paternalistic leadership reduces employee satisfaction and commitment to the firm, whereas the benevolence and morality dimensions of paternalistic leadership increase employee satisfaction and commitment. For managerial implications to be derived, we would need to know whether the three dimensions could be independently manipulated—perhaps through managerial training or selective hiring and retention—in such a way that the beneficial aspects of paternalistic leadership could be retained for a firm's benefit. We would also require longitudinal research data before managerial implications are derived as the study's cross-sectional research design obscures the causal order of effects.

While the researchers wisely controlled for individual employee attributes (age, education, traditionality, and dependence on a manager for resources), nothing about the organizations themselves was taken into account in the analysis as a control, independent, or dependent variable. For example, is employee turnover, a significant hiring and training cost for firms, related to leader behavior? For which of these organizational contexts might authoritarianism be more or less problematic? Often employees of Chinese factories are very young—barely adults—and are housed in company living facilities. Could it be that authoritarian behavior that evokes fear and compliance has beneficial outcomes in such a setting, and is at least relatively efficient for socializing young workers, somewhat like military basic training? While training costs for (replacement) restaurant workers might be minimal, employees in electronics and communication factories are skilled workers; their loss (turnover) would be expensive, and their low commitment to the organization could impair work quality.

Although this study helpfully describes the organizational contexts of the research, these data are not used in the analysis. The study could have made a greater contribution to managerial knowledge in the Chinese context by analyzing organization-relevant variables and by collecting longitudinal data. We could then specify the conditions under which various managerial behaviors might be appropriate, given the presence of longitudinal data from which causality could be inferred.

The second empirical study presented in this volume, by Gong, Law, and Xin, focused on a mix of 117 firms in manufacturing, high-technology, and service industries. This is a firm-level analysis about the relationships between commitment-focused human resource management (HRM) systems and organizational performance. Cross-sectional data about the organizations were collected from human resource and middle managers. Ownership patterns varied across state ownership, domestic private firms, Chinese-foreign joint ventures, and wholly foreign-owned firms. The authors expected that firms practicing commitment-focused human resource management would be perceived as performing better with respect to return on assets and sales, labor productivity, and asset growth; with industry, ownership, and firm size (which averaged around 1,000 employees) controlled.

They found, as predicted, that utilization of commitment-focused HRM systems was positively related to overall firm performance; however, the cross-sectional nature of the data precluded drawing causal inferences. The firms more likely to utilize HRM systems were the domestic private, wholly foreign-owned, and international joint venture firms, whereas the state-owned firms were the least likely to use the systems. Although the authors do not report the ages of the firms, it is likely that the SOEs were older than the other three types of firms, and as such less likely to utilize the more contemporary HRM practices. It would be helpful to know at what point in time various features of the HRM systems had been adopted; these data would have allowed the researchers to take years of experience with the systems into account as a predictor of future (contemporary) firm performance. It is an open question as to whether these firms had purposively adopted the commitment-focused HRM practices as a strategic choice to gain competitive advantage, as the study provides no data about when and under what conditions the HRM systems were adopted. However, an alternative explanation presents itself: mimetic isomorphism (DiMaggio and Powell 1983) might have driven the adoption of these practices, as firms frequently mimic prevailing practices to demonstrate legitimacy to their external environment. So, while the practices are used in some firms in China, it would be helpful to understand the conditions under which they are adopted, and to understand the historical sequence of their adoption so that causality might be inferred from the data, and managerial prescriptions derived.

The third empirical study, by White and Xie, is a single case study conducted at the firm level of analysis: it is an historical description of the evolution of Lenovo, a producer of personal computers (PCs) and one of China's most successful technology-based firms. The industries in which Lenovo has competed include computer system services, the distribution of others' PCs, sales of add-in PC components, and the manufacture and sale of PCs, most recently utilizing leading-edge technology.

The company's success is notable for several reasons. Although the Chinese government targeted the PC industry as a national priority in the 1980s, Lenovo was not among those companies selected by the government to be nurtured as the foundation of China's future PC industry. Rather, Lenovo was a spin-off of the Institute of Computing Technology (ICT), itself a research institute of the Chinese Academy of Sciences (CAS), and neither the eleven founders nor the sponsors from ICT and CAS had prior commercial technology development, sales, or entrepreneurial experience. In all cases, Lenovo was *not* a SOE at founding, did not have state support, and had relatively "hard" profit requirements from its founding. White and Xie describe how, with few alternatives and little capital, Lenovo offered technical services in its early years—in much the same way that U.S. start-ups exploit their in-house technical knowledge to generate early income. When multinational computer firms began selling in China, Lenovo became a distributor for AST Computer and eventually for Hewlett Packard (HP), initiating the first of its strategic exploration activities, according to the authors. By alternating exploitation with exploration strategies, the authors describe how Lenovo took strategic advantage of changes in China's environment to eventually become the largest manufacturer of PCs in China, while simultaneously creating patented intellectual capital in its R&D labs to continue its exploration activities.

The Lenovo story is an interesting one for several reasons. First, Lenovo's founders were among the very first technology entrepreneurs in China at a time when SOEs still dominated China's market; private firms were legal, but the spirit of the law and government functioning did not allocate legitimacy to the new form. Nonetheless, the company did derive legitimacy from its parent ICT, because ICT was a leader in IT research and because of its links to the government through the CAS. As all new firms must develop legitimacy in the external environment, the ICT sponsorship undoubtedly facilitated Lenovo's early survival.

Its first major client, CAS, created substantial income for Lenovo. As it successfully delivered on its contracted services, Lenovo benefited from CAS's high visibility and respected status, further expanding the venture's legitimacy in the external environment. Early revenue growth was obtained at a fairly low cost by its arrangement with AST Computers to distribute their product; basically this arrangement functioned as an early strategic alliance that allowed Lenovo to learn the Chinese PC market. Although the authors refer to this as Lenovo's first strategic exploration, it was one obtained at relatively low risk to the venture—low-cost learning through an experienced industry participant that was highly motivated to penetrate the lucrative Chinese market. Even more learning was apparently obtained through a similar arrangement with HP.

Effectively relying on its parent ICT's labs for the R&D it used, Lenovo's successful PC add-on card was developed at ICT, and ICT facilitated Lenovo's first production experience by loaning their personnel during the process. New activities for Lenovo, certainly, but at relatively low out-of-pocket expense for R&D, experimental production runs, and shared manufacturing expenses with a joint venture partner in Hong Kong.

I would argue that Lenovo's early survival and growth were due to its success in creating strategic partnerships from which it learned a great deal while minimizing personnel, materials, and production costs during its early transition from a service firm to the development of its R&D, manufacturing, sales, and distribution capabilities. So, while one usually associates relatively high risks with exploration activities, Lenovo's genius was in minimizing risk while learning new skills and acquiring new capabilities as an interorganizational partner. It acquired early social capital via the established legitimacy of its parent ICT and its first major customer, the highly esteemed CAS. Its first R&D was without cost via ICT, and its first manufacturing was based upon shared costs with its Hong Kong joint venture partner. Lenovo added these capabilities to those learned from AST and HP in distribution and marketing. Thus, the Lenovo story is one of social learning through organizational partners, rather than simply through "smart" strategic decisions to alternatively exploit and explore. This interpretation is consistent with Li and Yang's report (chapter 12 in this volume) that much of the literature on China's private firms emphasizes different strategies to manage institutional constraints—like forming interorganizational relationships, for example. They observed that this emphasis differs from that of the conventional strategic management literature in Western contexts, which emphasizes achieving competitive advantage through building core competencies.

PRIVATE-SECTOR FIRMS AND ENTREPRENEURSHIP

Several chapters in this book note the growing size of China's private-sector firms; however, the *China Statistical Yearbook* data mentioned earlier seem to suggest that a preponderance of China's private firms are relatively young, having been founded since the mid 1980s. Evidence exists that the new firm formation rate in China has been quite high since approximately 1986. The 1999 *Yearbook* reported that 16,097 new technology-intensive firms existed in China in 1998. These statistics bode well for China's economy, given what we know about the contributions of entrepreneurship to national economies. In a large-scale study of twenty-nine countries on five continents, Reynolds et al. (2001) found that the rate of entrepreneurial activity in a country is positively associated with national economic growth.

Therefore, beyond paying close attention to the changing institutional context in China, students of Chinese management also need to recognize the relatively young age distribution of its private-sector firms. For example, in the Fahr, Cheng, Chou, and Chu study (chapter 13 in this volume) of private firms in six industries, their mean age is seven years. Similarly, among the 200

THE EMERGENCE OF CHINA'S PRIVATE-SECTOR FIRMS   305

sampled firms studied by Vanhonacker, Zweig, and Chung (chapter 4 in this volume), only 4 percent of the firms were founded before 1990. Of the remaining 96 percent, approximately half were founded in the 1990s, and the other half, very recently, after the year 2000. Why is the relatively young age of China's private-sector firms important?

It is well understood that organizations face different risks depending on their age. Young organizations are at a higher risk of death than older organizations (Carroll and Hannan 2000, Stinchcombe 1965). Referred to as Stinchcombe's "liability of newness" theory and described by Schoonhoven (2005), the riveting problem facing new, young organizations is survival. This factor should shift the theoretical perspectives brought to bear on a large proportion of China's private-sector firms, the younger ones. Despite this need, Li and Yang's review (chapter 12 in this volume) of the management and organization literature from 1986 through 2003 documents that, of the firm-level studies conducted on Chinese organizations, 75 percent focus on fairly standard strategic management topics like firm strategy/performance, corporate governance, and strategic human resources and employment relationships. Only 25 percent of these focus on questions related to venture creation and entrepreneurship in new entrepreneurial firms.

This is a theoretical problem to be faced squarely, as standard Western strategic management arguments are derived from the study of very large U.S. industrial firms (i.e., the Fortune 500) and their global counterparts, the Fortune 1000. To the last company, these firms are publicly traded, relatively old, highly successful, and sustaining competitive advantage along with growth in revenues and profits are the primary challenges they face. These hardly constitute a random sample of firms. Their selection on the dependent variable of successful performance ignores the hundreds of thousands of firms that did not survive or are mediocre performers. Strategic management theories—for example, the resource-based view of the firm, whose central question is how firms develop valuable, rare, inimitable, and nonsubstitutable resources—emphasize the creation of sustainable comparative advantage. In contrast, new, small, and young firms face the issue of stark survival. And in China, according to the scant available data (Chen 1998), new firms have died at an unprecedented rate, compared to their counterparts in Western nations (Schoonhoven and Woolley 2005).

Rather than imposing standard Western management perspectives on China's new firms, we need to discover through firsthand field research the conditions new private firms are facing, from founding through subsequent evolution. What actions are their founders and managers taking while attempting to cope with the environmental conditions they face? Without original field research to guide our theorizing about China's private firms, we will simply continue to apply tried-and-true Western managerial perspectives, without learning what is actually happening inside China's new firms. While the China context provides an opportunity for fresh theorizing (Tsui et al. 2004), fresh perspectives are more likely to be revealed when we enter the field to directly study China's new firms' founders' and managers' challenges and behaviors. Of the nine empirical studies reported in this volume, a third focus on either young or smaller family-based firms (Vanhonacker et al., Lin, White and Xie). It is essential, however, that the macro industrial and ownership data mentioned earlier be made available for understanding the distribution of China's private-sector firms. Without these statistics, scholars will be blindly studying discrete parts of the proverbial elephant's body without any systematic idea of how the entire beast is constructed.

Most existing (Western) theories of management and organization assume that managers intend to be rational, but behave so imperfectly (March and Simon 1958), and that organizations can adapt to changing external circumstances through choices their managers make (Boisot and Child 1999, Child 1972). For example, see the resource-based view described above (Penrose

1959). Similarly, resource-dependence theory (Pfeffer and Salancik 1978) assumes that organizations and their managers can proactively shape responses to external resource dependence, even going so far as to reduce dependencies through mergers, acquisitions, and governmental lobbying. Neoinstitutional theory (DiMaggio and Powell 1983, Meyer and Rowan 1977) argues that organizations adopt common solutions to institutional problems, and thereby exhibit mimetic isomorphism. Agency theory (Jensen and Meckling 1976) and transaction-cost economics (Williamson 1981) both assume economically rational actors who strive for efficiency. Are the underlying assumptions of these pillars of Western management theory valid in the Chinese context?

Rather than simply applying existing (Western) management theories, conducting more comparative studies of managers across country contexts would be helpful to determine whether the underlying assumptions are valid. The studies of Eastern values and differences in managerial values across three contexts by Ralston and colleagues (Ralston 1992, Ralston et al. 1993) come to mind as exemplars of the kinds of comparative research that are needed. So too does the comparative research of Frenkel and Kuruvilla (2002) on the logics of action in China, India, Malaysia, and the Philippines.

TECHNOLOGY-BASED FIRMS AND ENTREPRENEURSHIP IN CHINA

Last, a full discussion of managerial perspectives on China's private sector will not be complete unless we discuss China's strategic emphasis on the development of new technology-based industries. With its March 1986 program, China announced it had targeted ten new technology industries for development (Li, Schoonhoven, and Zhang 2005). To implement its strategy for developing China's technological and innovative capabilities, the nation created national technology development zones within which entrepreneurs were encouraged to found new firms focused on the ten targeted industries. The creation of technology development zones (or science parks) reveals a layer of social context that must be taken into account when technology-based entrepreneurship is addressed in China.

China's government maintains significant control over the nation's strategic resources—including tax policy, land use, and export and import rights. These resources are used selectively to attract new firms to the technology development zones, where entrepreneurs enjoy several advantages. First, entrepreneurs' income taxes are waived for the first three years of a firm's existence, and in years four through six, entrepreneurs pay only half of the new ventures' owed taxes, a considerable cash savings. Second, the technology development zones were implemented with fanfare, and new firms selected to be located within the technology zones enjoyed enhanced social status and the valuable external legitimacy afforded by the government's sponsorship of the zones. Last, access to government-mediated resources beyond taxes is more likely when a zone's initial and ongoing support is from the national government, its agencies, and departments. While China also contains technology development zones founded by provincial and local governments, Li, Schoonhoven, and Zhang (2005) found that growth in revenues and industrial productivity are significantly greater in the zones sponsored by the national government than in the others.

The flip side of these "advantages" is the unheralded high death rate of young firms, a phenomenon Chen (1998) observed in one development zone. The high start-up rate, combined with the high death rate, demonstrates that the development of China's targeted technology industries has proceeded very inefficiently to date. Schoonhoven and Woolley (2005) argued that part of the reason for the high death rate is that the ten targeted industries are essentially nascent industries brand new to China, and as such, a pool of experienced and knowledgeable high-technology industry executives and entrepreneurs has not existed until very recently. Research has consistently shown that the prior, prefounding experience of entrepreneurs reduces the mortality rate of new firms (e.g., Agarwal, Sarkar, and Echambadi 2002; Carroll et al. 1996).

China also has fewer years of experience commercializing technology-based products. Despite this limited experience, in a study of the Beijing experimental zone's technology ventures, Li and Atuahene-Gima (2001) found that a greater emphasis on a product innovation strategy was related to stronger new venture performance. This was contingent, however, upon the government and its agencies providing concurrent institutional support for the firms, including financing and facilitating the attainment of licenses to import needed technology. Thus, the institutional context continues to play a significant role in the performance of China's young technology-based ventures. These in turn comprise a significant component of China's future industrial base as well as its growing private-sector base.

CONCLUSIONS AND THE RESEARCH ROAD BEFORE US

In this chapter, I have argued that a significant segment of China's private-sector firms are relatively young, and as such they face the omnipresent challenge of surviving their first perilous years. The needs of new and young firms are qualitatively different from those faced by older, established, and, by virtue of their advanced age, relatively successful firms. The problem, however, is that most organization theory developed in the West—especially strategic management theory—is based upon observations of a very small number of elite, publicly traded, highly successful industrial firms. This means that the prevailing management theories are based upon sampling on the dependent variables of high-performance and wildly successful firms. What is not sufficiently understood is how new organizations survive their early years when their liabilities of failing are greatest. This situation is exacerbated in China because of the high level of generalized uncertainty faced by business organizations owing to China's emerging market economy and the ongoing evolution of property rights from collectivist to private ownership.

A further theoretical complication is that research on new-firm mortality in the West is based on the assumption of institutional stability and little change. In fact, 80 percent of the extant population mortality studies have been conducted in the United States, with the remainder located exclusively in Western Europe, Israel, and Argentina. No empirical research reported in the mainstream management journals between 1995 and 2005 has focused on mortality rates of populations or industries in Asia-Pacific countries. It should not be surprising, then, that the total inventory of constructs used to predict organizational mortality completely ignores the broader sociocultural, legal, political, and economic contexts within which new firms are embedded (Schoonhoven and Woolley 2005). In contrast, a prominent feature of organizational life in the PRC is that changes underway on multiple institutional fronts have created a precarious and uncertain environment for new young firms in China.

One survival strategy of new firms has been the evolution of hybrid organizational forms that use resources and governance structures from more than one existing organization. Nee (1992) observed that the multiple organizational forms that have evolved in China over the past twenty-five years are the various adaptations private (and private ownership–desiring) organizations have made to an institutional environment that still conveys mixed signals about the legitimacy and desirability of privately owning a business organization.

The evolution of hybrid organizational forms in China has resulted in a plethora of confusing terms describing organizational "types" that exist in China's private sector today. I have modestly proposed that in the future organizational scholars gather ownership data on focal business firms, and henceforth describe them as to the varying proportions of ownership different investing groups have in the organizations. In this way, ownership can be quantified and controlled, as necessary, in larger-scale studies conducted in China.

Beyond the fact that many private-sector firms in China are relatively young is the observation that China has bet its industrial future on the development of ten targeted technologies, and that substantial incentives exist to induce entrepreneurs to found companies within these emerging technology industries. While this chapter is a call to institutionally contextualize the study of new firms, in China the situation is more complex, as most of the nation's new technology firms have been induced to locate in technology development zones sponsored by various levels of government. Many new technology firms may thus be embedded in a social context (Granovetter 1985) at once more complicated and at the same time perhaps more sterile than the social contexts of firms founded outside of the technology development zones. In all cases, Granovetter's work helps us recognize that variation exists in the extent of the institutional embeddedness of economic action in China.

Although I have highlighted new and technology-based firms within China's private sector, I do not intend that we ignore the significance of existing large industrial firms (mostly state- and partially privately owned) or the significance of new stars in the private economy like Lenovo. Just as new firms and new industries modify the fabric of existing industries and competition (Schoonhoven and Romanelli 2001), so too do the prevailing giants of industry help create the conditions under which new firms must survive.

In China a key omnipresent power is the national government, which continues to control social and political stability as it simultaneously guides the evolution of China's market economy. Walder (chapter 17 in this volume) has argued that, in the future, relationships between corporations (private sector), state and national government agencies, and elite families will become a new preoccupation of scholars. Certainly, the newly emerging elite families and leaders of major corporations will be a natural focus for the business press in Asia as well as the United States. The public fascination with power and individual success appears to be insatiable. Nonetheless, I will close this chapter with an urging for scholars of management and organization to attend especially to the emergence and evolution of China's *new young firms* in the private sector, and within this the substantial activity transpiring within its emerging technology-based private firms.

NOTES

1. Chen's paper is descriptive and it reports raw data without detailed methodological information. English-language management journals that publish mortality studies define "deaths" carefully. However, what Chen regards as a "death" may not equate perfectly to definitions in other studies cited by Schoonhoven and Woolley (2005) in their paper about comparative mortality rates. Until more China research is conducted in the same Beijing zone, over the same period, including comparable conceptual definitions and statistical controls, it will not be possible to determine whether Chen's reported findings under-, over-, or accurately report death statistics for the period.

2. Walder (1995, 270) defined "government ownership" thus: "the government holds all rights to control, income flows, and sale or liquidation for those rights it chooses to transfer to agents who are either hired to manage those assets or who obtain these rights in lease contracts. Furthermore, state-owned industrial enterprises are owned and administered by multiple levels of government jurisdiction, ranging from ministries of the central government down to rural townships and villages" (Walder 1995, 272). The term "state ownership" is reserved for larger public (government-owned) firms that were formerly at the center of the input-output government planning of the earlier post–World War II years in China.

3. See Gold's (chapter 7 in this volume) cogent description of the evolution of the legal status of pri-

vately managed enterprises in China. For example, Gold describes how and why in 1988 the constitution was amended to permit private companies to hire more than seven employees.

REFERENCES

Agarwal, R.; M. Sarkar; and R. Echambadi. (2002). The conditioning effect of time on firm survival: an industry life cycle approach. *Academy of Management Journal,* 45(5), 971–94.

Barney, J., and W. Hesterly. (2005). *Strategic management and competitive advantage concepts.* Upper Saddle River, NJ: Prentice Hall.

Boeker, W. (1989). Strategic change: The effects of founding and history. *Academy of Management Journal,* 32(3), 489–515.

Borys, B. and Jemison, D. B. (1989). Hybrid arrangements as strategic alliances: Theoretical issues in organizational combinations. *Academy of Management Review,* 14, 2, 234–49.

Boyacigiller, N. A., and N. J. Adler. (1991). The parochial dinosaur—Organizational science in a global context. *Academy of Management Review,* 16(2), 262–90.

Carroll, G. C., and M. T. Hannan. (2000). *The demography of corporations and industries.* Princeton, NJ: Princeton University Press.

Carroll, G. R.; L. S. Bigelow; M.D.L. Seidel; and L. B. Tsai. (1996). The fates of de novo and de alio producers in the American automobile industry, 1885–1981. *Strategic Management Journal,* 17, 117–37.

Chen, J. J. (1998). The mystery of the short life of entrepreneurs. *Coastal Economics,* 6, 42–43.

Child, J. (1972) Organizational structure, environments, and performance: The role of strategic choice. *Sociology,* 6, 1–22.

———. (2000). 'Theorizing about organizations cross-nationally.' *Advances in International Comparative Management,* 13, 27–75.

DiMaggio, P., and W. Powell. (1983). The iron cage revisited: Institutional isomorphism and collective rationality in organizational fields. *American Sociological Review,* 48(2), 147–60.

Frenkel, S., and S. Kuruvilla. (2002). Logics of action, globalization, and changing employment relations in China, India, Malaysia, and the Philippines. *Industrial and Labor Relations Review,* 55, 387–412.

Gold, T. B. (1990). Urban private business and social change. In Davis and Vogel (Eds.), *Chinese society on the eve of Tiananmen,* pp. 157–78. Cambridge, MA: Harvard University Press.

Granovetter, M. (1985). Economic action and social structure: The problem of embeddedness. *American Journal of Sociology,* 91(3), 481–510.

Gregory, N.; S. Nenev; and D. Wagle. (2000). *China's emerging private enterprises.* Washington, DC: International Finance Corporation.

Jensen, M. C., and W. H. Meckling. (1976). Theory of the firm: Managerial behavior, agency costs and ownership structure. *Journal of Financial Economics,* 3(4), 305–60.

Li, H., and K. Atuahene-Gima. (2001). Product innovation strategy and the performance of new technology ventures in China. *Academy of Management Journal,* 44(6), 1123–34.

Li, H.; C. B. Schoonhoven; and A. Zhang. (2005). The evolution of technology development communities in China 1991–2000: A community analysis of technology zone growth. Working Paper. Merage School of Business, University of California, Irvine.

Li, J. T.; A. S. Tsui; and E. Weldon. (Eds.) (2000). *Management and organizations in the Chinese context: Current issues and future research directions.* London, UK: Macmillan Press.

March, J. G., and H. Simon. (1958). *Organizations.* New York: John Wiley and Sons, Inc.

Meyer, J. W., and B. Rowan. (1977). Institutionalized organizations: Formal structure as myth and ceremony. *American Journal of Sociology,* 83, 340–63.

National Bureau of Statistics. (2003) *China statistical yearbook.* Beijing: China Statistics Press.

Nee, V. (1992). Organizational dynamics of market transition: Hybrid forms, property rights, and mixed economy in China. *Administrative Science Quarterly,* 37(1), 1–27.

Penrose, E. (1959). *The theory of the growth of the firm.* Oxford: Oxford University Press.

Pfeffer, J. (1997). *New directions for organization theory: Problems and prospects.* New York: Oxford University Press.

Pfeffer, J., and G. Salancik. (1978) . *The external control of organizations: A resource dependence perspective.* New York: Harper & Row.

Ralston, D. A. (1992). Eastern values: A comparison of managers in the US, Hong Kong, and the People's Republic of China. *Journal of Applied Psychology,* 77, 664–71.

Ralston, D. A.; D. J. Gustafson; F.M. Cheung; and R.H. Terpstra. (1993). Differences in managerial values: A study of US, Hong Kong and PRC managers. *Journal of International Business Studies,* 24, 249–75.

Reynolds, P. D.; S. M. Camp; W. D. Bygrave; E. Autio; and M. Hay. (2001). *Global entrepreneurship monitor, global 2001 summary report.* Wellesley, MA: Babson College.

Schoonhoven, C. B. (2005). The liability of newness. In M. A. Hitt (Ed.), *Entrepreneurship*, pp. 171–75. Oxford, England: Blackwell Publishing.

Schoonhoven, C. B., and E. Romanelli. (2001). *The entrepreneurship dynamic: Origins of entrepreneurship and the evolution of industries.* Palo Alto, CA: Stanford University Press.

Schoonhoven, C. B., and J. L. Woolley. (2005). New firm mortality rates in China: Contextualizing new venture survival models. Working Paper. Merage School of Business, University of California, Irvine.

Scott, W. R. (2003). *Organizations: Rational, natural and open systems.* Fifth Edition. Upper Saddle River, NJ: Prentice Hall.

Stinchcombe, A. L. (1965). Social structure and organizations. In J. G. March (Ed.), *Handbook of Organizations.*, pp. 142–93. Chicago: Rand McNally.

Tsui A., and C. M. Lau. (2002). *The management of enterprises in the People's Republic of China.* Boston, MA: Kluwer Academic Publishers.

Tsui, A.; C. B. Schoonhoven; M. Meyer; L. Lau; and G. Milkovich. (2004). Organizations and management in the midst of societal transformation: The People's Republic of China. *Organization Science,* 15(2), 1–25.

Walder, A. G. (1995). Local governments as industrial firms: An organizational analysis of China's transitional economy. *American Journal of Sociology,* 101(2): 263–301.

White, S., and X. Liu. (2002). Networks and incentives in transition: A multilevel analysis of the pharmaceutical industry. In A. Tsui and C. M. Lau (Eds.), *The management of enterprises in the People's Republic of China.* Boston, MA: Kluwer Academic Publishers.

Williamson, O. E. (1981). The economics of organization: The transaction cost approach. *American Journal of Sociology,* 87, 548–77.

Xiao, W. (2002). *The new economy and venture capital in China. Perspectives,* 3(6), September 30. The Overseas Young Chinese Forum (www.oycf.org).

Zhang, H. (1999). The rise of another bloc—The restoration and growth of the private economy. In Zhang and Ming (Eds.), *Report on the development of Chinese private enterprises.* Beijing: Shehui kexue wenxian chubanshe.

17

CHINA'S PRIVATE SECTOR

A GLOBAL PERSPECTIVE

Andrew G. Walder

China's path toward a private economy has been distinctive. Of all the world's transitional economies, only Vietnam's has taken a similar trajectory: rapid economic growth and a slow and gradual approach to the privatization of the state sector. Most observers identify these two features as the ones that make China's path distinctive, and discussions of the growth of China's private sector invariably focus on the specifics of economic policy, or the characteristics of emerging markets and firms. China's political system, to the extent that it is mentioned in these analyses, is usually viewed as a barrier, an inconvenient anachronism that delays and retards the workings of the market. From a comparative perspective, however, there can be clear advantages to a gradual evolution of political institutions—advantages that have helped to spare China many of the economic woes of the other transitional economies. For the purposes of this volume, however, China's political institutions also shape the private sector that emerges, the way that it emerges, and the questions asked about its present and its future.

The puzzle presented by China (and Vietnam) first became apparent to me a few years ago at a large meeting of economists who convened to identify the distinctive features of China's reform path. One of the keynote speakers, an analyst from the World Bank, presented a slide portraying growth trends in more than a dozen transitional economies in the decade after 1990. The trend line for almost all of these economies was sharply downward for the first five to six years, after which gross domestic product began to increase once again. However, in the vast majority of these nations, annual GDP had yet to return to 1990 levels by the year 2000. The star performer of Eastern Europe and the former Soviet republics was Poland: its trend line turned upward earlier, and by 2000 real GDP was some 40 percent above 1990 levels. The trend line for China, however, was literally off the charts (see Figure 17.1), and that for Vietnam was not far behind. China's economy moved sharply upward from 1990, and a decade later, its real economy had almost tripled in size.

These data touched off a long and detailed discussion of the institutional and policy differences that could have accounted for such sharply divergent economic trends. Some thought that the differences were attributable to the varied economic structures of the countries at the onset of reform. Others thought it was the different rates of privatization, the extent to which a nation's leaders listened to ill-informed Western economists, the sequencing of reform, labor costs, opportunities for international trade, openness to international capital, monetary policy, and so forth.

Figure 17.1   **Growth of Real GDP in Transitional Economies, 1990–2001**

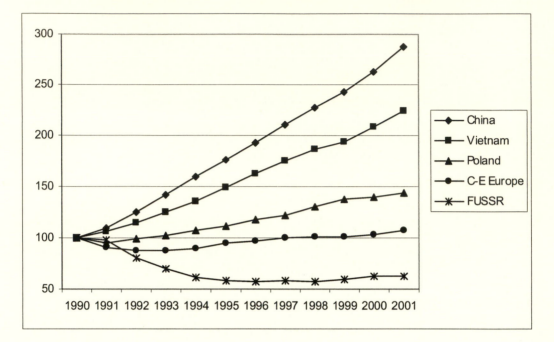

Sources: State Statistical Bureau (1999); World Bank (2002a).
Notes: C-E Europe is Central and Eastern Europe combined; FUSSR is the former Soviet republics combined.

Proponents of different arguments often made coherent cases, but there was no clear winner—in every case, the feature that seemed to distinguish China was shared by at least a handful of relatively unsuccessful economies.

My own contribution to the discussion was, at first, only half-serious. I observed that there was one characteristic that clearly distinguished China and Vietnam from all the other transitional economies under discussion, and that this characteristic should be taken seriously as an explanation for the divergent trends—China and Vietnam were the only two countries still ruled by Communist parties. The half of the observation that was not serious—intended as irony—was that Communism was good for the growth of a private market economy. The half of the observation that was very serious was that stable political institutions have advantages over political collapse and large-scale institution building. The unstated implication was that the presumed theoretical disadvantages of having a Communist Party preside over gradual reform while maintaining the state sector intact were obviously outweighed by the advantages of political and institutional continuity. My observation did not stimulate much discussion; the proposition was filled with irony but had no clear policy implications. However, I was determined to examine further the different political trajectories of the world's transitional economies and to consider how macropolitical factors shape a country's course of economic transformation and growth.

What features of China's path to a private economy make it so distinctive and might account for its remarkably rapid expansion? In this chapter, I will outline two broad features that make China's path distinctive. The first is macropolitical, and its impact can be appreciated only in comparative perspective. China's political institutions have exhibited strong continuity,while maintaining strong barriers to the rapid privatization of state assets. This combination is a distinctive one, and it has avoided some of the worst problems often associated with rapid privatization in the midst of disruptive political change. The second factor is institutional, at the firm level. Property rights have evolved gradually but steadily through the massive entry of small firms and the "creeping privatization" of public assets in a highly competitive market environment. This path has created a domestic private sector with some distinctive characteristics, and it also presents challenges. The chapter concludes by identifying research questions about the current private sector, and its future expansion, through growth or through the continuing transformation of the remaining state sector.

THE ROLE OF MACROPOLITICS

Political change—or the relative lack thereof—may not explain divergent patterns of economic growth. But a nation's pattern of political change has a decisive impact on the way in which a private sector emerges in a transitional economy. Political factors largely determine the pace and extent of privatization, the policy and regulatory environments within which the private sector operates, and the way in which a private sector emerges. In all of these respects, China has differed from almost all other transitional economies, and these political factors have quietly shaped the private sector that has emerged, and the questions that we ask about it.

Regime Change versus Political Continuity

The private sectors of the world's transitional economies have grown up under startlingly varied political circumstances, and the differences are not limited to the distinction commonly drawn between post-Communist and Communist regimes. There are enormous political differences in the post-Communist regimes as well, and in many cases one can reasonably question whether some post-Communist regimes have changed much more than China. Transitional economies vary widely in the extensiveness of regime change—defined as the degree to which, prior to or simultaneous with the onset of market reform, Communist Party hierarchies lose their political monopoly and must compete with other organized entities for political power. Extensive regime change alters political institutions in two decisive ways. First, the old party hierarchy loses its ability to appoint officials in all government agencies, public institutions, and publicly owned enterprises. Second, the party hierarchy itself disintegrates, leading to the disappearance of a national system of party posts that paralleled the governmental and enterprise hierarchies within which careers were organized and which itself controlled large concentrations of property in the form of real estate, vehicles, and bank accounts. In this situation, if the former ruling party survives at all, it does so as a much smaller electoral party that offers few career opportunities and controls only meager assets. The most rapid and decisive cases of such regime change have occurred in Central Europe and the former Soviet Baltic republics.

In China (and Vietnam) the party hierarchy and its control over appointments and public assets have changed very slowly, and in some respects not at all. However, many of the newly independent post-Communist states that emerged from the collapse of the Soviet Union and Yugoslavia initially exhibited little more regime change than China. Party hierarchies in these new states survived largely intact. In the most extreme of these cases, former Communist parties were reborn with a nationalist orientation, and many continued to rule as dictatorships (Collins 2002, Luong 2002, Roeder 1994). The Communist hierarchies in Belarus, Kazakhstan, Kyrgyzstan, Turkmenistan, and Uzbekistan withdrew from the Soviet Union as it collapsed in Moscow and established nationalist dictatorships that survived a number of years. In such regimes, planned economies are dismantled and market reforms are implemented by single-party dictatorships that initially preserve much of their former organizational structures, appointment powers, and assets.

At the other end of the spectrum of regime change is the former East Germany, where the party and governmental structures of the German Democratic Republic were rapidly dismantled as it was absorbed into the Federal Republic of Germany. Similar, but less drastic, are the extensive regime changes introduced following challenges by strong oppositional movements that resulted in the disintegration of ruling parties and early elections that defeated their remnants. This process led rapidly to procedural democracies in which challengers of the old regimes held the balance of political power. According to McFaul (2002), this scenario occurred in the Czech Republic, Estonia, Hungary, Latvia, Lithuania, Poland, Slovakia, Slovenia and, after some delay, Croatia. Some of these new governments adopted an explicitly anti-Communist stance, rapidly dismantled former administrative structures, and passed laws designed to systematically bar those with ties to the former regime from elite positions (Eyal, Szelényi, and Townsley 1998; 108–11, 128–31). In the middle of this spectrum are regimes—most notably Russia—in which neither challengers nor Communist-era elites clearly dominated post-Communist governments. This category includes one current dictatorship (Tajikistan), two democracies (Bulgaria and Mongolia), and the "partial democracies" of Moldova, Russia, Ukraine, Albania, Azerbaijan, and Macedonia (McFaul 2002).

Policy and Regulatory Environments

The second set of circumstances under which a private economy emerges is found in policy and regulatory environments that either create opportunities for, or barriers to, asset appropriation by political officials or their relatives and friends. Asset appropriation occurs when incumbent elites keep managerial control of public assets as they are privatized, or convert them into personal ownership. Whether they can do so depends, in part, on whether they are able to hold onto political power, but it also depends on the policy and regulatory environment created by the government.

Rates of Privatization

The first noteworthy feature of a policy environment is the pace of the privatization, which has varied sharply across countries. Many transitional economies resisted the rapid conversion of state assets to some form of private ownership, while others privatized early and rapidly. By the end of the 1990s, the private sector's estimated share of gross national product in transitional economies ranged from 20 percent to 80 percent. Not all transitional economies began reform at the same time, however. Therefore average *rates* of privatization vary even more. China's private sector (excluding the collective sector) is now fairly large, but its reforms began much earlier, and the average annual rate of increase in the proportion of the economy in the private sector has been only 3 percent. The annual increase in countries like Russia, which began much later, but privatized much more rapidly, is close to 8 percent (see Table 17.1). This percentage is not a direct expression of the pace of privatization, but is instead the product of two separate processes: the conversion of state assets to private ownership, and the entry of new firms (through

Table 17.1

Growth of the Private Sector in Transitional Economies

Country	Private-sector share, 2000 (%)	Onset of transition	Average annual increase in private-sector share (%)
Belarus	20	1991	2.2
Turkmenistan	25	1991	2.8
Tajikistan	30	1991	3.3
Uzbekistan	45	1991	5.0
Vietnam	50	1986	3.6
China	55	1982	3.1
Ukraine	55	1991	6.1
Kazakhstan	55	1991	6.1
Kyrgyzstan	60	1991	6.7
Poland	65	1989	5.9
Russia	70	1991	7.8
Lithuania	70	1991	7.8
Estonia	75	1991	8.3
Hungary	80	1989	7.3
Czech Republic	80	1989	7.3

Sources: European Bank for Reconstruction and Development (1999, 23–24), except Vietnam (World Bank 2002b, 11) and China (refers to 1998 gross output value, calculated from State Statistical Bureau 1999).

foreign investment, private investment, or small household effort). If we recognize that some of the economies in the middle range of this distribution—particularly China and Vietnam—have achieved these levels primarily through encouraging foreign investment and small-scale private firms, it is even more evident that the pace of converting state assets to new ownership forms is highly variable.

State policies that delay privatization create barriers to asset appropriation by elites. If privatization proceeds at a rapid pace, however, asset appropriation will be constrained only by the presence of effective regulatory prohibitions against the practice, something that varied widely across those transitional economies that moved quickly to privatize state assets. These constraints do not vary directly with the extensiveness of regime change.

Regulatory Constraints

While asset appropriation occurs in all transitional economies, it is relatively constrained under two very different kinds of policy/regulatory environments. The first such environment occurs in the reform Communist regimes and the post-Communist dictatorships that resist privatization of public assets and that retain strong prohibitions against the theft of state property. The relatively small degree of asset appropriation under these circumstances is not due to the strength of legal and regulatory structures, which are notoriously weak, but to the delayed onset and slow pace of privatization. Under these circumstances, state agencies and public firms may engage in a form of asset *conversion* in which they transfer public assets to private entities that are under their own organizational control. These strategies permit state firms to evade state regulation and taxes by earning larger incomes off the books (Lin 2001). The proceeds may be used for a variety of purposes, including larger executive compensation (in salaries and fringe benefits) and potentially also the (corrupt) diversion of funds into private hands. In these cases, incumbent officials may extract larger incomes from such arrangements, but they do not assume ownership of these still-public assets. Asset conversion differs from asset appropriation in that it does not transfer ownership or effective control of private corporate assets to individuals or other private entities. The privatized assets are owned by a public organization and the heads of that organization benefit only as long as they continue to hold public office. Asset appropriation does occur in these settings, but it proceeds at a relatively slow pace and involves a relatively small percentage of national assets, primarily in circumstances where the transfers can be hidden or where the perpetrators are able to move abroad permanently (Ding 2000a, b, c).

The second setting in which asset appropriation is relatively constrained is paradoxically very different from the first: extensive regime change coupled with orderly privatization that transfers assets under transparent rules. Under these circumstances, incumbent elites either lose their positions of influence too quickly to appropriate state assets, or the process of privatization is too well-regulated and monitored. The most extreme case in this regard is the former East Germany, but Poland, the Czech Republic, and Hungary also exhibit these characteristics (Eyal et al. 1998, chap. 4; King 2001a, b). In countries that have sold large proportions of state enterprises directly to foreign corporations, incumbent elites have been unable to maintain control over public assets, and elite strategies to perpetuate managerial control have been defeated (Hanley, King, and Janos 2003).

Constraints on asset appropriation are weak, on the other hand, under two different kinds of circumstances. The first is when a ruling Communist Party survives largely intact but rules under a new name after abandoning its commitment to public property and central planning. These circumstances prevail in many of the newly independent republics that abruptly withdrew from the Soviet Union with little internal opposition or regime change. This situation permits the widespread transfer of state assets into the hands of officials, their kin, and their associates, or the extraction of large incomes from the discretionary powers of office. Elites may continue in political posts or depart from them at their discretion. In these settings, the primary question is how fully the opportunities for asset appropriation are monopolized by those at the top of the hierarchy.

The second kind of circumstance that permits extensive asset appropriation occurs when a nation in the midst of extensive regime change rapidly privatizes state assets without establishing barriers to prevent insiders from seizing control. This process typically permits incumbent managers of public enterprises and industrial bureaus to retain their posts as they privatize public assets. They emerge as modern corporate executives, freed of the restraints of the command economy, who may now allocate to themselves vastly increased pay and benefits, including stock shares, paralleling typical managerial practices in corporate capitalism. The process may also permit selected managers and economic bureaucrats to directly assume personal ownership of large concentrations of new privatized public assets. Those who are able to complete such maneuvers move into a new private business oligarchy with origins in the Communist-era elite. Such outcomes were relatively common in Russia, where by 1993 regime insiders had acquired majority shares in two-thirds of privatized and privatizing firms (McFaul 1995, 210) and a small number of wealthy oligarchs had assumed control of certain key sectors of the economy (Goldman 2003, 98–122; Hoffman 2002). "In the initial battles between the Russian government's blueprint for privatization and the interests of these directors' interest groups, societal forces from the ancien régime prevailed" (McFaul 1995, 211). One economically damaging side effect of this

Figure 17.2 **Four Paths to a Private Economy**

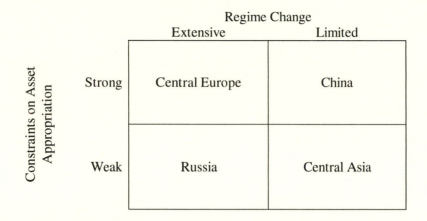

process is that the business oligarchy initially tends to move its assets abroad out of fear that subsequent leaders will seek to recover them (Tikhomirov 1997).

FOUR PATHS TO A PRIVATE ECONOMY

I have drawn two simple distinctions among the world's transitional economies, distinguishing countries that experienced rapid and extensive regime change from those that did not, and countries where constraints on asset appropriation were strong from those where they were weak. These two distinctions create four combinations of circumstances, each of which defines a distinctive trajectory of private-sector growth. These four paths correspond to experiences observed in Central Europe, Russia, Central Asia, and China. They are summarized in Figure 17.2.

The Central European Path

These were countries in which Communist hierarchies collapsed at the outset of reform and former ruling parties were defeated in early elections. These economies have systematically privatized state assets but regulated and monitored the process in a way that placed limits on asset appropriation by Communist-era elites. The former German Democratic Republic appears to most closely approximate this pure type of transitional economy. Despite significant variations across cases, the Central European regimes of the Czech Republic, Estonia, Hungary, and Poland appear to approximate this type. These regimes all produced between 65 and 80 percent of GDP in the private sector by the end of the 1990s, as is shown in Table 17.1.

Of the four paths, this one has been the least favorable for Communist-era elites. They lost their positions at high rates and encountered strong barriers to appropriating assets. Unless elites had managerial or technical skills that were directly transferable to skilled labor markets in a corporate economy, they were likely to lose their posts, and they had relatively few opportunities to appropriate business assets. In the Czech Republic, Hungary, and Poland, only 39 percent of those who were in the political elite in 1988 were still in positions of authority in 1993, and another 21 percent had retired early. Over 70 percent of those in elite managerial-technical positions in 1988, however, were still in similar positions in 1993, suggesting the importance of relevant occupational experience in elite survival (Böröcz and Róna-Tas 1995; Eyal et al. 1998, chap. 4). In the same three Central European countries, fewer members of the 1988 political elite reported owning businesses in 1993 (18.4%) than reported retiring early (20.9%), and the vast majority of such ownership was limited shares in very small enterprises. The much larger group of managerial-technical personnel who kept their positions were no more likely to emerge with ownership shares (Eyal et al. 1998, 120–23, 138–42; also see Hanley 2000; Szelényi, Szelényi, and Kovách 1995). The same combination of circumstances appears to hold for Lithuania, Latvia, Estonia, and Slovenia and, in extreme form, for East Germany.

Because these democratic regimes are small and highly dependent on international credit and foreign investment, and because they have been eager to join NATO and the European Union, they have also been far more amenable to the adoption of Western legal and regulatory standards than other transitional economies.

The Russian Path

There are other countries that have experienced rapid and extensive regime change but in which, despite extensive change in political institutions, constraints on asset appropriation were weak. This setting provided incumbent officials with greater opportunities to maintain control of large concentrations of state assets as they were privatized (or to privatize them themselves) and to enter the emerging market economy with large business advantages. Russia is perhaps the clearest example of this type. In Russia, 70 percent of GDP was produced in the private sector by 1999.

In Russia and other regimes of this type (for example, Ukraine), many Communist-era officials have been compelled to leave their government posts as a result of regime change (in part because many agencies, especially party organizations, have been abolished). Constraints on asset appropriation, however, have been relatively weak owing to periods of regime instability or to privatization programs that occurred rapidly or in an unregulated manner. Such instability provided incumbent officials with greater opportunities to maintain control of public assets as they were privatized or to obtain personal ownership of assets and enter the emerging market economy with large business advantages. Elite turnover in Russia was less pronounced than in Central Europe, in part because regime change began two years later. But 36 percent of those in the political elite in 1988 had already moved out of these positions by 1993. The ability of Soviet-era managers and planners to retain elite positions, however, was much higher than in Central Europe—only 18 percent of those in elite positions in the economic bureaucracy in 1988 were no longer in the 1993 economic elite, reflecting the Russian elite's ability to maintain control over assets (McFaul 1995). Moreover, almost two-thirds of the private business elite in 1993 were former members of the Communist Party (Hanley, Yershova, and Anderson 1995, 654–62).

The Central Asian Path

These nations experienced limited regime change. Their Communist hierarchies did not collapse, but instead they withdrew from multinational federations like the former USSR and continued to rule initially as dictatorships while they abandoned their commitment to state ownership and the command economy. The initial periods of reform in these countries proceeded with the entire Communist-era elites still largely in place, and constrained neither by continuing state commitment to public property nor by effective regulations to restrict asset appropriation. These circumstances have been approximated in the regimes that initially moved toward markets and privatization while political power was still in the hands of holdover old regime dictatorships: for example, Kazakhstan, Kyrgyzstan, and Uzbekistan.

In these countries the Communist hierarchies initially survived intact but abandoned their commitment to public ownership. Officials have had the option of remaining in their posts and extracting incomes from their regulatory or other discretionary powers as a market economy expands, or of entering private business through ownership or control of public assets. They also have had the option of leaving office after appropriating public assets to engage in full-time business pursuits. Which option individual members of the elite have chosen, and their relative economic success, depended in large part on the kinds of positions they occupied and the kinds of influence and connections they have accumulated in the past. These countries experienced little elite turnover, and their new business elite has strong roots in the Communist-era elite. Corruption is endemic, as officials who have remained in their posts extract incomes from their offices.

The Chinese Path

There are, interestingly, two radically different types of regimes under which the privatization process places relatively strong constraints on asset appropriation. Central Europe represents the first type, and China and Vietnam, paradoxically, represent the second. High constraints on asset appropriation in these economies exist for radically different reasons. China and Vietnam have experienced a measure of political liberalization, but virtually no regime change. These Communist hierarchies have survived almost intact for the first two decades of reform and privatization, leaving incumbent elites in place, seemingly well poised to seize state assets. The only thing that has restricted asset appropriation in these countries has been that privatization of the largest concentrations of state assets was delayed for more than a decade and proceeded very slowly thereafter. In these regimes, private-sector expansion occurred first largely outside the state economy, in agriculture and small-scale enterprise. Because the old elite remained in place and economic regulation was weak, asset appropriation occurred, but it was limited in scope relative to Russia and Central Asia because the pace of privatization was so much slower.

In China and Vietnam incumbent elites have not been compelled to leave their posts, but the delayed onset and gradual subsequent pace of privatization provided fewer opportunities for asset appropriation. Here officials had two options. The first was to remain in their posts and attempt to extract higher incomes from them. This strategy could take several forms: (1) the use of influence to obtain better jobs or business opportunities for family members; (2) the extraction of incomes from the discretionary powers of an office (including methods defined as corruption), and (3) the use of influence to assist one's own family's private business undertakings. The second option for elite members was to leave their posts for salaried positions in the private sector or to open private businesses of their own. Because of the slow pace of privatization and the limited ability of officials to appropriate public assets, the first option has been the dominant one.

DISTINCTIVE FEATURES OF THE CHINESE PATH

China's rapid economic advance has probably occurred partly because of, rather than in spite of, the distinctive macropolitical features of its path. China's political institutions did not collapse, and the country was not forced to fundamentally remake its economic institutions in a rapid fashion. The decision to protect the state sector and privatize these assets slowly, and only after a long delay, was often criticized as excessive and counterproductive caution, but it prevented the large-scale appropriation of state assets observed in Russia, Central Asia, and similar regimes. Only the Central European regimes appear to have rapidly privatized the bulk of state assets without their widespread theft. But these were relatively stable democracies with small economies tightly linked into, and dependent upon, the international system. Had the Chinese government collapsed in the Russian manner, or had it chosen to rapidly privatize state assets in the manner of Poland, its private sector today would look vastly different and would more closely resemble the private sectors in Russia or perhaps Central Asia—and perhaps China's overall economic prospects would mirror these countries' as well. These speculations aside, it is clear that China's path of macropolitical change has decisively shaped its now-thriving private sector.

Start-Ups versus Ownership Change

Macropolitical factors shape emerging private economies. Economies like that of the Soviet Union—those that rapidly privatize large concentrations of public assets—create large-scale private sectors dominated by oligarchs, many of whom are former political officials or their associates. Regimes like China's, those that resist privatization of large state assets, force private sectors to grow up gradually from below, through thousands of initially small-scale start-ups or spin-offs from state firms. These private firms grow up in sectors that do not compete directly with state enterprise. Instead, they fill in the gaps in the public sector, meeting demand initially in agricultural sidelines, consumer goods, and service sectors ill served by the former state sector. Rapid growth in the nonstate sector occurs through fierce product competition among thousands of small firms, none of which are able to dominate a sector or use national political influence to manipulate the rules of the game.

As a result, China's private sector resembles a swarm of bees; the number of firms in the private sector vastly outstrips that in the remaining state sector and, although employment per firm is very small, overall employment in the private sector, and overall output, is now several times that in the state sector. A direct corollary of this pattern of growth is that the vast majority of entrepreneurs did not come out of the party or government bureaucracy. This is, in part, due to sheer numbers—the number of new enterprises vastly outstrips the number of officials. It is also due, however, to the relatively small size of the undertakings and their relative unattractiveness to officials who are not being forced out of office by political change and whose salaries and benefits have risen steadily with economic growth, through both legal and illegal means.

China's economy therefore exhibits a pronounced dualism that is absent from most other transitional economies, especially those in Central Europe and Russia. In Central Europe, the process was managed politically in such a way that the former state sectors now no longer exist, and new political leaders and new owners inhabit a private sector highly influenced by the European Union and with business practices increasingly resembling those of Europe. In Russia, the politics of rapid privatization resulted in a private sector dominated by large private corporations and a politically powerful business oligarchy. We have come to take for granted the fact that China's private sector has so far grown up primarily not from the privatization of state assets but from the establishment of new firms that permit the economy as a whole to "grow out of the plan" (Naughton 1995). However, the prior experiences of Central Europe and Russia should make us acutely conscious that China's state sector, still comprising the vast majority of large firms and still representing an enormous concentration of capital investment, has yet to make the transition already traversed—in highly different ways—at the other end of the Eurasian continent.

The Collective Sector Detour

One distinctive Chinese path toward a private economy has been through a new and vibrant sector of collectively owned firms. Analysts have often been unsure how to categorize the publicly owned township-and-village enterprises (TVEs) that are not tied to government plans and that compete fiercely on local, regional, and national product markets. While sharing few of the characteristics of the state sector, they are by no means privately owned. We usually classify them in the "nonstate" sector and refer to them as a "hybrid" or "mixed" property form. However we classify them, these enterprises represent one of the most important and distinctive components of China's rapid economic growth over the past two decades and, in recent years, the accelerating expansion of the private sector.

In the early 1980s market liberalization created an enormous opportunity in the consumer goods, services, and small-scale construction sectors—gaps in the urban-oriented planned economy that were always ill-served by the state sector. Village and township officials responded rapidly to these opportunities and mobilized capital to invest in new small-scale firms that produced goods and services to meet this historic overhang of demand. This rural collective sector was the fastest-growing component of the economy in the 1980s and outstripped the state sector in employment and output by the early 1990s.

This sector had no counterpart in other transitional economies, and it was anomalous in terms of economic theories that identified the incentive advantages of private ownership and saw public ownership as the problem, not the solution (Walder 1995). This sector, however, was a direct expression of China's path of political change and its initial hesitancy about private ownership. Rural government was intact, and party officials remained powerful. They used their control over revenues and credit and engaged in a massive effort at capital formation and investment that boosted the Chinese economy for a decade. Initially they suppressed private enterprises that competed directly with publicly owned firms.

The massive entry of new firms naturally led to increased competition and its counterpart—falling profit margins—by the late 1980s. By the mid 1990s most of these publicly owned firms were operating in the red and government officials were looking for ways to divest themselves of these liabilities (Kung 1999). The response was a wave of privatization in which the firms were sold off to private owners in large numbers. By the end of the 1990s the rural public sector had shrunk to less than half its size at its height. The strongest of these firms survived as private firms, and for the first time, privatization of public assets, rather than new start-ups, become the primary source of private-sector growth in rural regions. The owners of the vast majority of these new private firms were their former managers. Analysis of pre- and postprivatization performance has suggested that this privatization represents a salvaging of a restructured rural public sector, and not a corrupt appropriation and liquidation of public assets (Li and Rozelle 2000, 2003).

During the heyday of China's rural public sector, some critics of privatization suggested that these firms represented an alternative to private ownership in a market economy. The subsequent decline and privatization of this sector has lent greater confidence to those who argued all along that privatization was the way to go, and that efforts to perpetuate public ownership were detrimental to economic reform. But we have learned something completely new and unanticipated by China's collective sector detour: it propelled rural China toward a market-oriented and increasingly private nonagricultural economy. The early debates about privatization were largely irrelevant; there was little rural enterprise to privatize in the late 1970s. These new public-sector start-ups mobilized capital and provided training and experience that launched hundreds of thousands of small- and medium-sized firms into a market economy. This could not have happened if the Chinese regime collapsed like many post-Communist regimes, and it would not have been attempted under a new democracy with a commitment to private ownership and Western business practices. The survival of the Chinese regime and its caution about private enterprise had an unanticipated outcome—publicly sponsored start-ups as a roundabout path toward a thriving private sector.

Creeping Privatization via Reallocation of Property Rights

There is a fundamental difference between the concepts of privatization and changes in property rights. As an economic policy, privatization implies the sale of assets to new owners who exercise the entire bundle of property rights over an asset: the rights of control, income, and sale. When one says that privatization of public assets in China has been limited and delayed, it does not mean that there has been little change in the allocation of property rights. In fact, China's path of reform has been noteworthy for the extensive gradual changes in the allocation of property rights— short of outright privatization—that have occurred in both formal and informal ways. This extensive property rights reallocation is another reason why many firms that are under nominal public ownership are nonetheless included in the nonstate category. The process has been underway for two decades, and it continues today.

Considerable evidence exists that widespread changes in property rights—short of outright privatization—have had a significant impact on economic performance in China. Throughout the economy, property rights have evolved away from the standard allocations under classic state socialism, in which key managerial decisions are made above the level of the enterprise and all residual income flows to supervising agencies. Throughout the Chinese economy, increasing levels of control and income rights have been allocated to managers within firms, primarily through various forms of management contracts. The evolution has been well documented in surveys of rural TVEs, but the principles have been widely applied in other sectors of the Chinese economy, including, to some extent, the urban state sector.

Property rights allocations can be described as a continuum ranging from traditional state-sector property arrangements to full-scale privatization. The following first step was typical of early managerial reforms: salaried managers were granted greater control over production and marketing decisions and given incentive contracts for meeting performance criteria, and firms were permitted to keep profits above targeted levels. A second step allocated greater control and income rights to managers: salaried managers "contracted out" public enterprises, agreed with public agencies about basic business plans, and agreed to split enterprise profits on a percentage basis. A third step granted further control and income rights to the managers: managers bid to lease public enterprises for a fixed period and agreed to pay lump sums to owning agencies in return for assuming responsibility over all operations, rights to all residual income, and responsibility for debts incurred. A final step, finally, is what we usually think of as "privatization": the enterprise is sold outright to a bidder—although sometimes with contractual stipulations that require them to continue to employ local individuals for a certain number of years. The new owner has most of the rights normally connected with private ownership, including the right to sell the assets (Walder and Oi 1999).

This standard evolutionary progression captures the essence of Chinese property rights reforms over the past twenty years. The full evolution through all four stages has been observed most completely in the rural industrial sector, but the basic principles have been applied in a wide variety of urban and rural circumstances—although the large-scale state sector remains largely stuck in the early phases. It has been apparent, however, that property rights can be reallocated in ways that have a major impact on incentives and economic behavior. Few will disagree that the intermediate stages of property rights reform have incentive properties that still are not as desirable as those of full private property rights. However, to a considerable extent this is entirely beside the point, both theoretically and practically. In terms of economic theory, the real issue is not what allocation of property rights is theoretically optimal, but whether the intermediate stages can lead to a significant improvement in incentives and economic performance. How much better is good enough? In terms of practical policy, this gradual evolution has permitted a stable Communist regime to create market-oriented firms with considerably improved incentive structures that gradually come to mimic private property and, in many cases, result finally in actual privatization. This phenomenon of creeping privatization is one of the major lessons to be learned from the Chinese pattern of reform.

QUESTIONS FOR THE FUTURE

Today's private sector is the result of a historically distinctive process: the rapid expansion of a sector of small-scale private start-ups, the creeping privatization of many small- and medium-sized public firms, and the increasingly outright privatization of collective and smaller state enterprises. The questions that we ask about this sector are therefore distinctive as well. In considering the performance and future evolution and growth of today's private sector, two relationships loom as crucial: the relationship between a private firm and government agencies, and between the firm and the remaining state-sector firms.

The relationship between the firm and government entities is crucial, because government decisions still weigh heavy on the ability of a firm to expand and grow. An illustration of the centrality of this relationship is in the financing of firms. Commercial credit and capital funds from the Chinese banking system heavily favor state-owned entities. Loans are more readily obtained, and on softer terms, for favored state firms. For a private firm to obtain comparable funding (or to expand into lines of production that may compete with state entities), support must be gained at the relevant level of government. This support may come in a variety of ways: by appointing government officials (or their relatives) to boards of directors or key management positions, or by offering a state entity an ownership stake. Such support may also be the product of a firm's path toward the private sector: private firms that are *former* state or collective enterprises may continue to enjoy ties with government agencies or specific officials that are a product of their prior incarnations. These ties may facilitate favorable treatment in government decisions, but they may also entail vestigial obligations that date from the firm's privatization (for example, to maintain employment at a given level). Therefore, knowing the history of a firm and its web of network ties—which are often of a political nature—will be a crucial factor in understanding the firm's prospects.

Relationships with state-sector firms are also crucial. Private companies that are spin-offs or "attached units" of public entities are a common example. The ties that these firms have with state organizations vary in strength and scope, and they may confer competitive advantages or liabilities. To the extent that a state entity continues to interfere informally in the appointment of top management or in major business decisions, or to the extent that it continues to make harmful resource demands on private firms, it will hamper their progress. On the other hand, the management of the state entity may in fact use a private firm as a means to siphon off state assets in ways beneficial either to the business or to the top managers. In either case, the observed performance of the firm will depend heavily on a network of political and economic ties—both formal and informal—that are characteristic of substantial private firms in China today.

Careful attention to a firm's relationships with the government and with the state sector highlights a central research problem: the proper unit of analysis. Just as the ownership structure of Chinese firms has evolved gradually, their boundaries remain, in many ways, blurred. This does not mean that the staples of generic management research—personnel, accounting, technology, innovation, leadership—are unimportant in the Chinese context. They are in fact vital and fundamental issues. But in order for effective technologies and organizational techniques to be implemented and have their desired impact, it is essential to understand a firm's network ties to state entities, and the ways these ties can facilitate or hamper the firm's performance and growth.

A final question for the future is—superficially at least—not about China's private sector at all. Instead, it is about the once-dominant large-scale state sector, which now produces only a minority of total output and employs an even smaller proportion of the national labor force. However, it is still an economically key sector: it comprises the majority of China's fixed capital investment in heavy industry, and its firms still hold monopoly or oligopoly positions in many domestic product areas. Few of these firms are ready to compete in the international arena, and the sector is undergoing a process of restructuring that will shrink or eliminate firms that operate in obsolete or technologically backward product areas.

It seems inevitable that the further expansion of China's private sector into large-scale, capital-intensive activities will involve the transformation of the remaining bastion of large-scale state corporations, by degrees, in ways earlier observed in the rural collective sector. Research on China's state sector is therefore, to a considerable extent, research on China's future private sector. From a global perspective, the trajectory of China's reforms leaves the country in a unique position. It now has a large and thriving private sector, but the bulk of large-scale state assets remains in public hands. A comparative perspective suggests pointed questions about the future of these firms. Will these assets be appropriated by members of the political elite and their associates in the fashion observed in Russia, creating a private business oligarchy with a monopoly position in some sectors and enormous political influence? Or will this outcome be avoided by a privatization process similar to that observed in Central Europe, in which foreign multinationals and international capital and financial institutions play a major role? Or will this corporate sector be transformed via a mixture of these two modes, or in ways qualitatively different from what has been observed elsewhere?

The early Russian pattern was associated with political instability and collapse, while the Central European examples reflect the small size and economically dependent position of the many new democracies in the region. China has so far been too stable and its economy too large for it to travel the same path. The key remaining questions are therefore about corporate governance and ownership reform in the state sector. We should expect an evolution of property rights within the state sector analogous to that earlier observed in rural industry—and it is already underway. However, the task is much larger and much more complicated. These firms represent enormous concentrations of capital assets, and ownership change will require significant downsizing and reorganization. The gradual evolution of these firms through the creation of private spin-offs, debt-for-equity swaps with domestic or foreign banks, listing on domestic and foreign stock markets, and partnerships and foreign joint ventures will transform the ownership structure and international competitiveness of large Chinese firms. This represents the last phase of a historically unprecedented transformation of what was, only three decades ago, one of the world's most orthodox (and backward) socialist economies.

Research on this sector will put new topics on the agenda and will differ from the type of research conducted in the past. The household survey, surveys of small firms, and interviews with entrepreneurs and local officials will be less effective. Researchers increasingly must understand the field of corporate governance and master elements of corporate finance, corporate law, and the workings of domestic and international equity markets. The ownership, income, and asset holdings of China's emerging corporate elite are infinitely more complicated and obscure than the activities of the household and small private firms that we have studied in the past.

The final stages of this process will have ramifications far beyond the fields of management, sociology, and economics. They will determine whether large Chinese corporations—when they emerge as private or quasi-private entities—will become a significant force in the international economy. These final stages will determine who owns these assets and what a new propertied elite will look like, and thereby they will remake the upper reaches of the Chinese social structure. It is hard to imagine a process that will be more decisive in determining China's economic and political future, and its future role in the world.

REFERENCES

Böröcz, J., and Á. Róna-Tas. (1995). Small leap forward: Emergence of new economic elites. *Theory and Society,* 24, 751–81.
Collins, K. (2002). Clans, pacts, and politics in Central Asia. *Journal of Democracy,* 13, 137–52.
Ding, X. (2000a). Systemic irregularity and spontaneous property transformation in the Chinese financial system. *China Quarterly,* 163, 655–76.
———. (2000b). Informal privatization through internationalization: The rise of nomenklatura capitalism in China's offshore business. *British Journal of Political Science,* 30, 121–46.
———. (2000c). The illicit asset stripping of Chinese state firms. *China Journal,* 43, 1–28.
European Bank for Reconstruction and Development. (1999). *Transition report 1999: Ten years of transition.* London: Stationery Office.
Eyal, G.; I. Szelényi; and E. R. Townsley. (1998). *Making capitalism without capitalists: Class formation and elite struggles in post-Communist Central Europe.* New York: Verso.
Goldman, M. I. (2003). *The piratization of Russia: Russian reform goes awry.* New York: Routledge.
Hanley, E. (2000). Cadre capitalism in Hungary and Poland: Property accumulation among communist-era elites. *East European Politics and Societies,* 14, 143–78.
Hanley, E.; L. King; and I. T. Janos. (2003). The state, international agencies, and property transformation in post-Communist Hungary. *American Journal of Sociology,* 108, 129–67.
Hanley, E.; N. Yershova; and R. Anderson. (1995). Russia: Old wine in a new bottle? The circulation and reproduction of Russian elites, 1983–1993. *Theory and Society,* 24, 639–68.
Hoffman, D. E. (2002). *The oligarchs: Wealth and power in the new Russia.* New York: Public Affairs.
King, L. P. (2001a). Making markets: A comparative study of postcommunist managerial strategies in Central Europe. *Theory and Society,* 30, 493–538.
———. (2001b). *The basic features of postcommunist capitalism in Eastern Europe: Firms in Hungary, the Czech Republic, and Slovakia.* Westport, CT: Praeger.
Kung, J. K-S. (1999). The evolution of property rights in village enterprises: The case of Wuxi County. In J. C. Oi and A. G. Walder (Eds.), *Property rights and economic reform in China,* pp. 95–120. Stanford, CA: Stanford University Press.
Li, H., and S. Rozelle. (2000). Saving or stripping rural industry: An analysis of privatization and efficiency in China. *Agricultural Economics,* 23, 241–52.
———. (2003). Privatizing rural China: Insider privatization, innovative contracts, and the performance of township enterprises. *China Quarterly,* 176, 981–1005.
Lin, Y. (2001). *Between politics and markets: Firms, competition, and institutional change in post-Mao China.* Cambridge, UK: Cambridge University Press.
Luong, P. J. (2002). *Institutional change and political continuity in post-Soviet Central Asia.* New York: Cambridge University Press.
McFaul, M. (1995). State power, institutional change, and the politics of privatization in Russia. *World Politics,* 47, 210–43.
———. (2002). The fourth wave of democracy *and* dictatorship: Noncooperative transitions in the postcommunist world. *World Politics,* 54, 212–44.

Naughton, B. (1995). *Growing out of the plan: Chinese economic reform, 1978–1993.* New York: Cambridge University Press.

Roeder, P. G. (1994). Varieties of post-Soviet authoritarian regimes. *Post-Soviet Affairs,* 10, 61–101.

State Statistical Bureau, People's Republic of China. (1999). *China statistical yearbook 1999.* Beijing: State Statistical Bureau.

Szelényi, S.; I. Szelényi; and I. Kovách. (1995). The making of the Hungarian post-Communist elite: Circulation in politics, reproduction in the economy. *Theory and Society,* 24, 697–722.

Tikhomirov, V. (1997). Capital flight from post-Soviet Russia. *Europe-Asia Studies,* 49, 591–615.

Walder, A. G. (1995). Local governments as industrial firms: An organizational analysis of China's transitional economy. *American Journal of Sociology,* 101, 263–301.

Walder, A. G., and J. C. Oi. (1999). Property rights in the Chinese economy: Contours of the process of change. In J. C. Oi and A. G. Walder (Eds.), *Property rights and economic reform in China,* pp. 1–24. Stanford, CA: Stanford University Press.

World Bank. (2002a). *Transition: The first ten years. Analysis and lessons for Eastern Europe and the former Soviet Union.* Washington, DC: The World Bank.

———. (2002b). *Vietnam: Delivering on its promise. Development report 2003.* Poverty Reduction and Economic Management Unit, East Asia and Pacific Region, Report No. 25050-VN. Washington, DC: The World Bank.

ABOUT THE EDITORS AND CONTRIBUTORS

Yanjie Bian (sobian@ust.hk) is professor and head of the Division of Social Science and director of the Survey Research Center at Hong Kong University of Science and Technology. He earned his PhD in sociology from the State University of New York at Albany. His research interests include social networks and social capital, social stratification and mobility, economic sociology, and contemporary Chinese societies. He is currently leading a team to conduct the long-term project of China's General Social Survey.

He Cai (lpsch@zsu.edu.cn) is Professor of Sociology in Zhongshan University in Guangzhou. His research is in the area of organizations and economic sociology. His recent publications examined changes in employment relationships and in workers' attitudes in organizations in China's reform era. He is conducting extensive case studies of interfirm relationships in China.

Dong-Hua Chen (sufechen@263.net) is professor at Nanjing University and research fellow at Shanghai University of Finance and Economics. He earned his PhD in accounting from Shanghai University of Finance and Economics. His research interests include corporate governance in the Chinese context, contracting roles of accounting information, and regulation in transition economies.

Bor-Shiuan Cheng (chengbor@ntu.edu.tw) is professor at the National Taiwan University where he also earned his PhD in industrial and social psychology. His research interests include leadership and *guanxi* networks in Chinese context, supervisory and organizational commitment, and organizational culture and organizational change.

Leonard Cheng (leonard@ust.hk) is Chair Professor of Economics at the Hong Kong University of Science and Technology. He earned his PhD in economics from the University of California at Berkeley. His research interests include international trade and investment, currency crisis, FDI in China, applied game theory, market structure, technological innovation and imitation, and high tech companies in Hong Kong/Shenzhen.

Li-Fang Chou (crhonda@seed.net.tw) is a PhD candidate in the Department of Psychology, National Taiwan University. She received a Master's degree in social science at the Institute of Agricultural Extension, NTU. Her research interests include leadership, *guanxi* in Chinese context, social networks, and team dynamics.

Xiao-Ping Chu (chucp@lingnan.net) is professor at Lingnan College of Zhongshan (Sun Yat-Sen) University. His research interest include human resource management, enterprise organization, Chinese organizational behavior, management comparison. He earned his PhD at Xian Jiaotong University.

Siu Fung Chung (cmcsf@graduate.hku.hk) received an MA in public policy and management from City University of Hong Kong and an M.Phil (community medicine) and PhD from The University of Hong Kong. She is currently a director of the John Cathedral HIV Education Centre in Hong Kong. She was a teaching assistant in Division of Social Science, The Hong Kong University of Science and Technology.

Joseph P. H. Fan (pjfan@cuhk.edu.hk) is professor at the School of Accountancy and the Department of Finance of the Chinese University of Hong Kong (CUHK). He is also deputy director of the Center for Institutions and Governance at CUHK. He received his PhD degree in finance from the University of Pittsburgh. His research interest includes corporate governance, corporate finance, and organizational economics. His current research focuses on how institutional factors interact with accounting, finance, governance and organization of firms in East Asia and China.

Jiing-Lih Farh (mnlfarh@ust.hk) is chair professor in the Department of Management of Organizations at Hong Kong University of Science and Technology. He received his PhD degree in organizational behavior from Indiana University at Bloomington. His current research interests focus on culture, leadership, and organizational behavior in Chinese contexts. He has authored over forty articles in the international journals of management.

Thomas B. Gold (tbgold@berkeley.edu) is Associate Dean of the Institutes of International and Area Studies and Associate Professor of Sociology at the University of California, Berkeley. He is also executive director of the Inter-University Program for Chinese Language Studies, whose teaching program is at Tsinghua University in Beijing. He earned his PhD in sociology from Harvard University. His research interests include private business in China; social and political change in Taiwan; laid-off workers in China; and *guanxi*.

Yaping Gong (mnygong@ust.hk) is an assistant professor at Hong Kong University of Science and Technology. He earned his PhD in human resources management/organizational behavior from the Ohio State University. His research interests include HRM in multinational firms and cross-border alliances, strategic (international) HRM, cross-cultural adjustment, goal orientations, multinational teams, and organizational demography. Her articles have been published in the *Academy of Management Journal, Journal of Applied Psychology, Journal of Management, Journal of International Business Studies, Management International Review, International Journal of Human Resource Management,* and *International Journal of Intercultural Relations.*

Kenneth Law (mnlaw@ust.hk) is professor at the Department of Management of the Hong Kong University of Science and Technology. He earned his PhD in human resources management from the University of Iowa in 1991. His research interests include strategic human resources management, selection, compensation, management in Chinese context, emotional intelligence and research methodology in OB/HRM.

David Daokui Li (davidli@ust.hk) is Associate Professor of Economics at the Hong Kong University of Science and Technology and Professor of Economics at Tsinghua University. His research areas include economics of transition, corporate finance, international economics and China's economy.

Jiatao Li (mnjtli@ust.hk) is head of the department of Management of Organizations at the Hong

Kong University of Science and Technology. He earned his PhD in strategy and international management from University of Texas at Dallas. His current research interests are in the areas of global strategy, organization theory, international corporate governance, alliances and joint ventures, and management and organizations in China.

Qiang Li (qlee@mail.tsinghua.edu.cn) is chair and professor in the Department of Sociology, Tsinghua University, Beijing. His research areas include social stratification and mobility, labor markets, and urban sociology. His recent research projects have focused on changing boundaries of social stratification and social groups in China's economic transformation.

Yi-min Lin (y.lin@ust.hk) is Associate Professor of Social Science, Hong Kong University of Science and Technology. His research focuses on organizations and institutions in China. He is the author of *Between Politics and Markets: Firms, Competition, and Institutional Change in Post-Mao China* (2001 and 2004).

Claudia Bird Schoonhoven (kschoonh@uci.edu) is Professor of Organization and Strategy at the Paul Merage School of Business, University of California, Irvine and a visiting professor of management at Xian Jiaotong University. She earned her PhD in organization theory and behavior at Stanford University. Her research interests include the creation and application of organization theory to problems related to technology-based firm evolution, innovation, the creation of new firms and new industries, and entrepreneurship.

Anne S. Tsui (anne.tsui@asu.edu) is Motorola Professor of International Management at the W.P. Carey School of Business, Arizona State University, Professor of Management at the Hong Kong University of Science and Technology and Distinguished Visiting Professor at the Peking University. She was the fourteenth editor of the *Academy of Management Journal* and is a fellow of the Academy of Management. Her research has received a number of awards including the Administrative Science Quarterly Scholarly Contribution Award, the Best Paper in the Academy of Management Journal Award, and the Scholarly Achievement Award from the Human Resource Division of the Academy of Management. Her book *Demographic Differences in Organizations: Current Research and Future Direction* (1999) with Barbara Gutek was a finalist for the 2000 Terry Book Award, Academy of Management. Dr. Tsui is 87th (among 778) most cited researcher in business and economics (January 1993 to January 2003) and 21st of the top 100 most cited scholars in management (1981–2001).

Wilfried R. Vanhonacker (mkwvan@ust.hk) is chair professor, department head, executive director of the Center for Marketing and Distribution (CMD) at Hong Kong University of Science and Technology. He gained a PhD in management from Purdue University (Indiana) in 1979. Having been involved extensively with foreign corporations operating in and doing business with China since 1985, Professor Vanhonacker has developed extensive experience and expertise in setting up and operating businesses in the PRC.

Andrew G. Walder (walder@stanford.edu) is Professor of Sociology at Stanford University, and Senior Fellow in the Stanford Institute for International Studies. He earned his PhD at the University of Michigan, and has previously taught at Columbia University, Harvard University, and the Hong Kong University of Science and Technology. He continues to do research on politics and society in contemporary China.

Yijiang Wang (ywang@csom.umn.edu) is professor at the University of Minnesota, special-term professor at Tsinghua University (Beijing, China) and visiting professor at Cheung Kong Graduate School of Business (Beijing, China). He earned his PhD in economics from Harvard University. His research interests include human capital theory, incentive theory, organizational design, human resource management, and other organization-related topics. He also has a strong interest in and has published widely on topics in economics of transition.

Steven White (steven.white@insead.edu) is Professor of Asian Business at INSEAD. He received his PhD in Management from the Sloan School of Management, M.I.T., and has held positions at the Hong Kong University of Science and Technology and the Chinese University of Hong Kong. His current research projects investigate collaborative networks, cross-cultural alliances, and the internationalization of Chinese firms.

T. J. Wong (tjwong@cuhk.edu.hk) is Professor of Accountancy and Associate Dean (Research) at the Faculty of Business Administration of the Chinese University of Hong Kong (CUHK). He is also Director of the Center for Institutions and Governance at Chinese University. He received his BBA (summa cum laude) from Dickinson College (Carlisle, PA) and MBA and PhD degrees from UCLA. His research interests focus on how institutions affect corporate governance and accounting in China and other emerging markets.

Changqi Wu (topdog@gsm.pku.edu.cn) is professor and head of Department of Strategic Management at Guanghua School of Management, Peking University. He earned his doctorate in applied economic sciences from the Catholic University of Louvain. His research interests include industrial organization, competitive strategy, international business and business regulation.

Xiaogang Wu (sowu@ust.hk) is Assistant Professor of Social Science at the Hong Kong University of Science and Technology and Research Affiliate of the Population Studies Center at the University of Michigan, Ann Abor. He received his PhD in Sociology from University of California, Los Angeles. His research interests include social stratification and mobility, education, labor markets and economic sociology, and quantitative methodology.

Wei Xie (xiew@em.tsinghua.edu.cn) is associate professor at School of Economics and Management of Tsinghua University. He earned his PhD in management science from Tsinghua University. His research interests include management of technology, competitive strategies of Chinese local firms in IT industry.

Katherine Xin (katherinexin@ceibs.edu) is Professor of Management and Michelin Chair in Leadership and HRM at the China Europe International Business School in Shanghai, China. She earned her PhD in management from University of California, Irvine. Her research interests include leadership, organizational culture, *guanxi* networks in the Chinese context, and strategic human resource management.

Jing Yu Yang (g.yang@econ.usyd.edu.au) is a lecturer in the Discipline of International Business at the University of Sydney. Her research interests include international business management, corporate strategy, and organizations and management in China.

Zhanxin Zhang (zhangzx@cass.org.cn) is an associate professor at Chinese Academy of Social Sciences. He earned his PhD in social science from Hong Kong University of Science and Technology. His research interests include social stratification, human capital, and labor market segmentation in transitional China.

Xueguang Zhou (xzhou@ust.hk) is Professor of Management in the Department of Management of Organizations at Hong Kong University of Science and Technology. His current research examines interfirm contractual relationships and changing employment relations in China's transitional economy. In addition, he works on a research project to study the institutional logic of reputation building in the marketplace.

David Zweig (sozweig@ust.hk) is Chair Professor, Division of Social Science, and Director of the Center on China's Transnational Relations, The Hong Kong University of Science and Technology. He taught at Queen's University, Kingston, Ontario, and The Fletcher School of Law and Diplomacy and was a post-doctoral fellow at Harvard University. His most recent book is *Internationalizing China: Domestic Interests and Global Linkages* (2002). His current research includes Chinese who have studied overseas, the impact of WTO on the pharmaceutical sector in China, and China's resource-based foreign policy. He is also co-editor of *Globalization and China's Reforms: An IPE Perspective* (Routledge, forthcoming). He has a PhD in political science from the University of Michigan (1983).

INDEX